VOLUME
1

RUSSIAN STAGE ONE

Live from RUSSIA!

Second Edition

The Russian-American Collaborative Series

RUSSIAN IN STAGES

RUSSIAN STAGE ONE

Live from RUSSIA!

Second Edition

Authors

Maria D. Lekić, University of Maryland, College Park

Dan E. Davidson, ACTR and Bryn Mawr College

Kira S. Gor, University of Maryland, College Park

In cooperation with

Irina Dubinina, Brandeis University

Thomas J. Garza, Jr., University of Texas, Austin

Natalia Vanyushkina, Susquehanna University

Series Editor

Dan E. Davidson

KENDALL/HUNT PUBLISHING COMPANY
4050 Westmark Drive   Dubuque, Iowa 52002

American Council of Teachers of Russian
1776 Massachusetts Ave., NW Washington, DC 20036

Русский язык: Этап 1
Репортажи из России

М. Лекич

Д. Дэвидсон

К. Гор

В сотрудничестве с
И. Дубининой, Т. Гарза и Н. Ванюшкиной

Учебник
2-ое издание

Под редакцией
Д. Дэвидсона

KENDALL/HUNT PUBLISHING COMPANY
4050 Westmark Drive   Dubuque, Iowa 52002

actr American Council of Teachers of Russian
1776 Massachusetts Ave., NW Washington, DC 20036

To access the online supplement to this book, please go to:
http://www.livefromrussia.org
LOGIN: student
PASSWORD: student

The 2008 edition of *Russian Stage One: Live from Russia!* reflects the continuing rapid changes that have occurred in day-to-day Russian life and culture over the past decade. The authors' primary goal in producing *Live from Russia!* was to ensure that language and cultural information presented in the book are completely up to date, not only post-Soviet, but clearly reflective of the norms of the Putin/Medvedev era. This led the authors and ACTR to the decision to undertake a complete remake of the familiar soap opera story, which serves as the thematic base of the text. The time of the new version of the story is 2008, and much in the lives of the characters, as well as in the city of Moscow and around Russia, has changed in comparison to the initial shooting of *Live* in 1996. Cell phones and text-messaging are a regular part of Russian life in 2008; the tempo of Russian business life has evolved considerably.

The depiction of the regions and cultural diversity of Russia represents another significant change in the new version of *Live from Russia!*, including the change in title. Olya now travels to several different regions of Russia, sending back her "video-otkrytki" to her friends as well as to the studio where she works. The "otkrytki" are referenced in the video, but if students want to see them, they will go to the new dedicated website, www.LivefromRussia.org to view and discuss them in Russian. The "otkrytki" feature various cities and regions of Russia, such as Kazan', St. Petersburg, Vladivostok, Yaroslavl', and Sochi, site of the 2014 Winter Olympics. Over time many other "otkrytki" will be added to her collection.

An established major world language, Russian is one of the five official languages of the United Nations and is spoken as a mother tongue, second language, or foreign language by over 320 million persons around the world. Russian is an important language of scientific discourse, of international trade, and trans-national and trans-regional communication, serving as a *lingua franca* within and across the regions and huge geographical territories of Eastern Europe and Eurasia. Russian is the state language of the Russian Federation and primary language of inter-ethnic communication for Russia's richly diverse population, of whom ethnic Russians make up just under 80% of the current 141 million total. Russian is also spoken beyond the borders of Russia: approximately 24 million ethnic Russians reside in the nations immediately bordering Russia. In recent decades, Russian citizens and Russian-speaking citizens of other Eurasian nations have also taken up residence in many countries of the world, including Australia, Canada, the European Union, Israel, and the U.S., where, according to the most recent data, approximately 3 million Russian speaking persons now live.

Thanks to its natural and intellectual resources, Russia has emerged again as a major player on the geo-political scene, an energy "super power." For that reason, American student motivations for learning Russian today are remarkably wide-ranging, as job opportunities in international business, finance, science, information technology, media, education, health care, international development, and government have now all but eclipsed academia as a principal employer of speakers of Russian. High levels of competency in speaking, listening, and reading are increasingly the goals of today's learners and many students now plan for a substantial period of advanced language training in Russia as a necessary complement to study begun in school or college in the U.S. Moreover, the proficiency, standards, and Language Flagship movements of recent years have now provided students, teachers, and employers with a set of benchmarks that help set realistic expectations for the measurement of student progress in mastering Russian language and culture. During the same period, the field has developed a large body of research in Russian second-language acquisition that has yielded important practical information for students on how to get the most out of formal study of the language, at what stage study abroad is most beneficial, and how to take fullest advantage of one's own personal foreign-language learning style.

Live from Russia! constitutes a comprehensive program for elementary Russian at the university level. These materials are intended for students with no prior knowledge of Russian to achieve the ACTFL "novice-high" proficiency level in speaking, listening, and reading in most cases, and, in some cases, to see them over the "intermediate" threshold. *Live from Russia!* also provides a strong basis for sequencing to the intermediate and upper intermediate courses *(Russian Stage Two: Welcome Back!)* and to the content-based series which may be undertaken at higher levels of study: *Political Russian, Scientific Russian, Business Russian, Years of Change, Reading for Close Analysis*, and others. In short, the ACTR "Stages" series can provide a solid underpinning for the student who needs to acquire competency in Russian for use in a wide range of professions.

The new *Live from Russia!* consists of a 100-minute video series, comprising a total of fourteen episodes, one for each unit in the text. The course itself is divided into two volumes consisting of seven units in Volume I and eight units in Volume II; each unit, in turn, is designed for approximately ten days (two weeks) of instruction. The program is *learner-centered* in several important ways: it emphasizes the acquisition of individualized communicative skills, it provides students with running commentaries and unit-by-unit analyses and vocabularies, and it supports instructor efforts to accommodate different learning styles within the same classroom.

A 50-minute video story (contained on the DVD included with each volume), based on the daily experiences of a young American in Moscow who interacts with Russian contemporaries, is the core of *Live from Russia!*. Using Russian language in authentic, "real-life" social interactions, the video program provides the necessary support for the university-level two-semester or intensive introductory course. All the episodes are connected by an engaging plot line, a Russian "soap opera." The American, Kevin, finds himself in a wide range of inherently interesting personal, cultural, and social situations, as he joins his Russian friends for social events, birthdays, eating out, travel and routine shopping. Through him and his friends (Tanya, Misha, and Olya), one encounters some of the realities of living in Russia, university exams, law enforcement authorities, university officials, romantic attachments, jealousy, and occasional misunderstandings.

Situation- and culture-based throughout, the new *Live from Russia!* offers pre-communicative and fully communicative language activities that place a premium on tailoring communication to specific personal, life-like situations. Each speech situation provides a model that is then used by students to express their own opinions, meanings, or experiences on the topic in question. Topics and situations recur naturally within the overall story line to provide the spiraling patterns necessary for building control of the lexical and content areas essential for speaking, listening, and reading proficiency in Russian, while preserving a level of control over dosage and requirements for active mastery of grammar.

The course also provides a one-week introductory lesson designed to familiarize the beginning student with the sounds of Russian, basic phonetic rules, the Cyrillic alphabet, the basics of reading authentic Russian, and some very elementary grammar (noun gender, pronouns, and agreement). The minimal lexicon of the introductory lesson provides a basis for the vocabulary encountered in the first video lesson.

The Instructor's Manual contains suggestions and annotations to aid the teacher in using the program, including a full script of the video adventure, a sample test for each of the fourteen units, answer keys, and a learning strategies component, designed to assist the teacher in addressing the needs of a wide range of individual learning styles in using the materials contained in *Live from Russia!* For scheduling purposes, instructors will note that each Unit of the new textbook contains the same number of "Days" as was the case in the 1996 edition. Each "Day" corresponds to a standard 50-minute class hour.

The grammar commentaries in *Live from Russia!* are located at the end of each lesson and are cross-referenced for the convenience of the learner and teacher throughout the two texts. Examples are updated and explanations have been made more "user friendly" throughout. Basic sound analysis and phonetic transcriptions have been united in a single Cyrillic-base notational system, which is useful for analysis and learning, but less confusing for the beginning-level learner of Russian.

The *Stage One: Live from Russia!* program consists of:

DVD I (Introductory Unit and Units I - VI)
Textbook – Vol. I (Introductory Unit and Units I - VI)
Workbook – Vol. I (Homework Exercises to Accompany Textbook I)
Audio CD I (Interactive audio and drills)

DVD II (Units VII – XIV)
Textbook – Vol. II (Units VII - XIV)
Workbook – Vol. II (Homework Exercises to Accompany Textbook II)
Audio CD II (Interactive audio and drills)

Instructor's Manual (Introductory Unit, Units I - XIV, Learning Strategies Commentary)

On-line Activities and Support (including Video "Postcards" and Support Activities)

The dedicated website for *Stage One/Live* provides a rich array of supplementary and reference materials for users of the new text. Most importantly, the new site is intended as a central location of cooperation and resource-sharing for all teachers (faculty and graduate students) using the textbook, a design that allows easy access to available materials, as well as user-friendly authorware to permit teachers to create new activities or to customize existing materials for local needs.

The authors of *Russian Stage One: Live from Russia!* gratefully acknowledge the contributions to the 2008 edition of this text of many of our colleagues in the Russian and modern foreign language field, and in particular, students in our courses at the University of Maryland and Bryn Mawr College, as well as at Brandeis University, Susquehanna University, and the University of Texas at Austin.

As noted in earlier editions, the authors have benefitted from the established practice within American and international Slavic studies of subjecting major textbooks to a regular process of public review and discussion, through both major journals and newsletters, dedicated sections at national conferences of AATSEEL, and international symposia organized by ACTR, and the International Association of Teachers of Russian Language and Literature (MAPRIAL).

As was the case with the first version of the video-based course, the author team has been extremely fortunate that a number of the members of the original video production crew agreed to work on the 2008 version of the textbook as well, among them Svetlana Prudovskaya (Voice of America), Tatyana Kirsh (professor emerita, Moscow Linguistics University), Irina van Dusen (Voice of America), and an ORT-based professional production team. Suffice it to say that without their strong commitment to the goals of the *Live from Russia!* text, their concern for cultural appropriateness, and technical expertise, the 2008 edition of *Live from Russia!* would not have become a reality.

Young Russianists entering the field today bring a fresh perspective to the teaching of Russian and a keen understanding of why and how Americans undertake the study of the language in a rapidly globalizing world. The authors are pleased to acknowledge in this space the suggestions and contributions of young specialists who, as recent undergraduates or graduate students, offered their time, critical thinking, and suggestions to the authors at various stages in the development and testing of this manuscript: Tony Brown, Kim Fedchak, Ewa Golonka, Camelot Marshall, William Rivers, Maria Shardakova, Andrew Tomlinson. A number of senior American scholars have contributed generally to the field of foreign languages and to Russian-language study and have influenced the authors' understanding of the ways in which adults learn foreign languages: Richard Brecht, Anne Chamot, Sibelan Forrester, Betty Leaver, Cindy Martin, Mary Nichols, Benjamin Rifkin, Cynthia Ruder, and the late Wilga Rivers, to name only the most obvious. While there is no intent here to impute endorsement by these individuals of this or any other textbook, the authors are pleased to acknowledge their professional contributions to the improvement of Russian and foreign-language teaching more generally in the U.S. over the past two decades.

The 2008 edition of *Live from Russia!* has received important material assistance through the competitive grants competition conducted by the Russkiy Mir Foundation in Moscow; the authors and ACTR are pleased and honored to express particular gratitude to the Chairman of the Board of Russkiy Mir, Academician Ljudmila Verbitskaya, and to the Foundation's Executive Director, Dr. Vyacheslav Nikonov, and his staff for their critical support of these materials. Institutional debts are more difficult to calculate and harder still to convey in a personalized way. The present project has a number of such debts to acknowledge: first, to the more than 100 American colleges and universities which have used the *Stages* in their Russian-language courses and which have, in general, supported the study of Russian language and culture; second, to Bryn Mawr College and the University of Maryland at College Park for their continuing support of the authors of these materials and of the important new direction in their research and teaching that this project reflects; and third, and perhaps most importantly, to the Washington and Russia-based staff of ACTR for their commitment to collaboration and curriculum development and the myriad forms of both technical assistance and strategic support this has ensured. The authors take special pleasure in acknowledging the valuable assistance at various stages in this project provided by Lisa Choate, David Patton, Sofia Kasmeridi, Daria Firsova, Maria Whittle, Samantha Keyser, and to the ACTR multi-media group, Ken Petersen, William Morse, and Evan Villemez, for their on-going technical support and creative contributions to the *Live from Russia!* website. Finally, the authors want to take special note of the work of Carrie Van Den Broeke, who served for the past 14 months as principal technical editor at ACTR of *Live from Russia!*, and contributed in more ways than the authors can enumerate here to the timely, accurate, and expert preparation of the present publication at each successive stage of its development.

When any major text undergoes revision, it is inevitable that some of the materials included or decisions taken by the authors may appear unclear or in need of refinement. Much that has changed in the conception and implementation of this series over the years is the direct result of suggestions shared by teachers and users of these materials. The authors and publishers welcome further suggestions for the improvement and continuing modification of this text in the future.

The Authors
ACTR, Washington, D.C.
2008

Maria D. Lekić

Maria D. Lekić, associate professor of Russian at the University of Maryland, is lead author of *Live from Russia!* and director of curriculum and test development for the American Council of Teachers of Russian (ACTR). She is author or co-author of four college and pre-college level textbooks of Russian as well as more than 20 scholarly articles in the field of Russian language, literature, and second language acquisition. She also serves as editor of *Russian Language Journal*. Since 2004, Dr. Lekić has directed Curriculum and Examination Development of the Prototype AP Russian Program and ACTR on-line proficiency testing in Russian for university-level students. She is the principal architect and academic director of the overseas National Russian Flagship Program at St. Petersburg University. Dr. Lekić received the Ph.D. in Slavic languages and literatures from the University of Pennsylvania and her undergraduate degree from Moscow State Pedagogical University.

Dan E. Davidson

Dan E. Davidson is President and co-founder of American Councils for International Education: ACTR/ACCELS and Professor of Russian and Second Language Acquisition at Bryn Mawr College, where he has held the rank of full professor since 1983. Davidson received the M.A. and Ph.D. degrees in Slavic Languages and Literatures from Harvard University. His teaching and research focus primarily on adult second language acquisition, immersion learning, curriculum and assessment development, and intercultural pragmatics. He is the author, co-author or editor of 26 books and more than 40 scholarly articles, including the "Russian in Stages" collaborative textbook series, which he helped launch in the 1970's, and a twenty-year longitudinal, empirical study of adult second language acquisition during study abroad. To date, Davidson has directed or co-directed 28 Ph.D. dissertations at Bryn Mawr in the field of Russian and second-language acquisition. Through his work at American Councils, Davidson has contributed to the design, implementation, and evaluation of a wide range of US government and privately funded international education programs for US and foreign students, scholars, and professionals with special emphasis on teacher professional development and training.

Kira Gor

Kira Gor is Associate Professor at the University of Maryland, College Park where she teaches Russian linguistics, language, and culture in the Russian Program and second language acquisition and processing in the Ph.D. Program in Second Language Acquisition. She holds a Ph.D. in experimental phonetics from St. Petersburg State University and a Ph.D. in Russian and second language acquisition from Bryn Mawr College. She has authored and coauthored over 30 journal articles and book chapters on cross-linguistic processing and second language acquisition of phonology and morphology, and a book *Interlanguage Phonology and Second Language Orthography* (St. Petersburg University Press, 1997). Since 2005, she is in charge of the Russian component of the project Linguistic Correlates of Proficiency funded by the Center for Advanced Study of Language (CASL).

Irina Dubinina

Irina Dubinina is the Director of the Russian Language Program at Brandeis University (Waltham, MA). She is completing her dissertation on pragmatics of requests by Russian heritage speakers at Bryn Mawr College. Her research interests include bilingualism, heritage languages, bilingual code-switching, and Russian language pedagogy.

Thomas Garza

Thomas Garza is Distinguished Teaching Associate Professor and Chair of Slavic and Eurasian Studies and the Director of the Center for Russian, East European and Eurasian Studies at the University of Texas at Austin. He teaches courses in Russian language and literature, foreign language pedagogy, and contemporary Russian culture. His current research interests include the attitudes of Russian youth toward the Chechen war and conscription, and the place of the vampire myth in Slavic literature and culture.

Natalia Vanyushkina

Natalia Vanyushkina taught Russian as a second language at Yaroslavl State University in Russia and currently teaches Russian language at Susquehanna University and the Russian Language Institute at Bryn Mawr College. She received her Ph.D. in Russian from Bryn Mawr College and has done extensive research on Russian contemporary proverbial language and its role in acquiring a second language and culture. Her statistical analysis of proverbial usage in written and oral communication of native Russians and self-reported knowledge of the most common proverbs among American learners of Russian was published in Vol. 57 of *Russian Language Journal*.

GREETINGS

— Здра́вствуйте!
— Здра́вствуйте!

— Здра́вствуй!
— Здра́вствуй!

— Здра́вствуй!
— Здра́вствуйте!

— Здра́вствуйте!
— Здра́вствуйте!

1. A. As you can see, there are two different ways of greeting people in Russian. The level of formality in the relationship determines which greeting to use.

Analyze the different situations pictured above. Which word is the formal form of greeting? Which is the informal one?

B. Now greet each other in class. Greet each other as if you were:

a. two high school students

b. two university professors

c. an adult and a child
d. two college students
e. siblings
f. a parent and child

The Russian Alphabet▲			
Cyrillic Letter	**Name of Letter**	**Cyrillic Letter**	**Name of Letter**
А а *Аа*	a	П п *Пп*	pe
Б б *Бб*	be	Р р *Рр*	er
В в *Вв*	ve	С с *Сс*	es
Г г *Гг*	ge	Т т *Тт*	te
Д д *Дд*	de	У у *Уу*	u
Е е *Ее*	ye	Ф ф *Фф*	ef
Ё ё *Ёё*	yo	Х х *Хх*	kha
Ж ж *Жж*	zhe	Ц ц *Цц*	tse
З з *Зз*	ze	Ч ч *Чч*	che
И и *Ии*	i	Ш ш *Шш*	sha
Й й *Йй*	i kratkoye (short i)	Щ щ *Щщ*	scha
К к *Кк*	ka	Ъ ъ	tvyordi znak (hard sign)
Л л *Лл*	el	Ы ы	yeri
М м *Мм*	em	Ь ь	myagkiy znak (soft sign)
Н н *Нн*	en	Э э *Ээ*	e oborotnoye (reversed e)
О о *Оо*	o	Ю ю *Юю*	yu
		Я я *Яя*	ya

▲ The Russian alphabet, Cyrillic, is named in honor of the Byzantine scholar and monk, Cyril (826–69), who, together with his brother Methodius (820–85), elaborated the first Slavic writing system in the second half of the ninth century.

2. A. Many American chain restaurants have opened franchises in Moscow, St. Petersburg, and other Russian cities. Read the following restaurant names in Russian and match the Russian restaurant names with their English counterparts.

Макдо́налдс   Baskin-Robbins®

Пи́цца Хат   McDonald's®

Ба́скин-Ро́ббинс   Pizza Hut®

B. Look at the menus on the following page from a McDonald's restaurant in Moscow.

Can you read any of the words in Russian? Find the Russian equivalents for:

Big Mac®   га́мбургер

hamburger   чи́збургер

cheeseburger   десе́рты

desserts   Биг-Мак

Filet-o-fish®   филе́-о-фиш

C. What beverages does McDonald's serve? Find the Russian equivalents for:

Sprite®   ко́ка-ко́ла

Diet Coke®   спрайт

Fanta®   ко́ка-ко́ла лайт

Coke®   фа́нта

D. Look once again at the matching Russian and English names and try to identify the sounds represented by the individual Russian letters.

ОБЕДЫ КОМБИНИРОВАННЫЕ

ХЭППИ МИЛ

  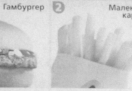 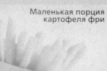

3. A. Write the cursive letters in the chart below (refer to the alphabet table).

Note that sometimes there is a discrepancy between how the capital and lowercase form of a letter is written, for example, $\mathscr{D}$, $\mathscr{g}$.

What other instances of this can you find?

B. Practice reading the letters in the chart.

Print			Cursive	
Capital	Small	Name of Letter	Capital	Small
А	а	a		
Б	б	be		
Г	г	ge		
Д	д	de		
З	з	ze		
К	к	ka		
Л	л	el		
М	м	em		
Н	н	en		
О	о	o		
П	п	pe		
Р	р	er		
С	с	es		
Т	т	te		
У	у	u		

4. A. Read the captions beneath each of the pictures out loud.

B. Show your partner these pictures. Say what is in the picture. Make "mistakes" and see if the listener detects them.

тут = here (is)

Тут дом.

торт
торт

сок
сок

суп
суп

стол
стол

стул
стул

рот
рот

нос
нос

мост
мост

дом
дом

кот
кот

5. Animals living in different countries speak different languages, or at least humans tend to think so! For example, an American rooster says "**Cock-a-doodle-do**", while a Russian rooster says:

ку-ка-ре-ку́!

A. Let's find out what Russian animals say. Guess which animal says what, then check your answers with the answer key at the bottom of the page.*

1. га-га-га!   a) cow
2. ко-ко-ко!   b) goose
3. му-му!   c) hen
4. ку-ку!   d) cuckoo
5. кар-кар-кар!   e) crow

B. Now practice the pronunciation of the animal sounds. Try to memorize what one of the animals says.

6. Imagine that you have just arrived in Moscow. As soon as you step off the plane, you find yourself surrounded by signs in Russian. While you are driving in Moscow, you see more places and signs.

1. аэропо́рт   garage
2. такси́   park
3. авто́бус   cafe
4. метро́   stadium
5. рестора́н   telephone
6. кафе́   university
7. бар   bank
8. теа́тр   taxi
9. музе́й   metro
10. институ́т   theater
11. университе́т   bar
12. банк   bus
13. парк   institute
14. телефо́н   museum
15. стадио́н   restaurant
16. гара́ж   airport

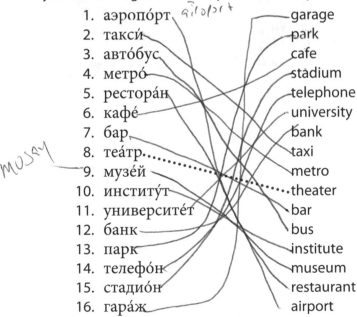

Many Russian words may seem very familiar to you. This is because Russian uses many **borrowed words** from English, French, Italian and other languages.

*1 (b), 2 (c), 3 (a), 4 (d), 5 (e)

INTRODUCTION

1. You already know half of the letters in the Russian alphabet. Do they look like the English ones? Do they have similar sounds? Most of the new letters you will learn today will look unusual.

   Read the captions for the pictures below.

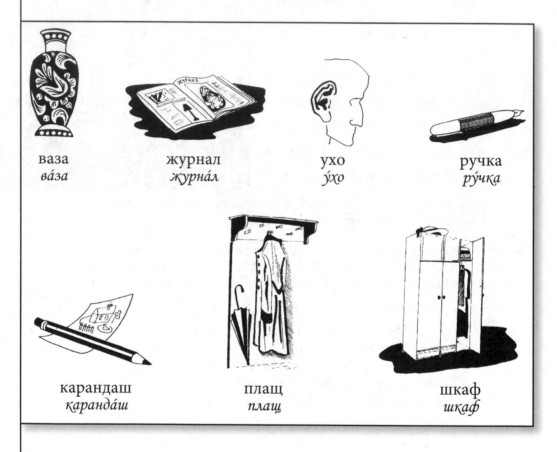

ваза
ваза

журнал
журнал

ухо
ухо

ручка
ручка

карандаш
карандаш

плащ
плащ

шкаф
шкаф

2. **А.** Write the new letters in cursive in the chart below. Which sounds have counterparts in English? Which ones are completely new sounds?

Print			Cursive	
Capital	Small	Name of Letter	Capital	Small
В	в	ve		
Ж	ж	zhe		
Ф	ф	ef		
Х	х	kha		
Ч	ч	che		
Ш	ш	sha		
Щ	щ	scha		

B. Now read the letters in the chart out loud.

Stress and Vowel Reduction

The place of the accent (stress) in English and Russian words affects the rhythm and quality of individual syllables. Compare the sound of the first syllable in the English words "phóto" and "photógraphy". Notice how the length and force of the **o** is weaker in "photography" where it is not in the stressed syllable.

The vowels **o** and **a** in Russian reduce to /a/ when not stressed. These changes are only reflected in the pronunciation of the word. The phonetic transcriptions, shown in Cyrillic between backslashes / /, are intended to help remind you about vowel reduction and other aspects of Russian pronunciation which are not immediately obvious from the spelling.

The place of the stress in a Russian word is marked by a "stress mark" (´).

3. Practicing pronunciation. Unstressed **a** = /a/

A. мáма   кóшка "cat"   кáрта "map"
лáмпа   сýмка "purse"   кóмната "room"
вáза   рýчка "pen"   пáпа "dad"
банáн   сáхар "sugar"   салáт "lettuce", "salad"

B. парадóкс   авангáрд   катастрóфа
каравáн   аппарáт

Definitions of words similar to English are not included.

4. Practicing pronunciation. Unstressed **o** = /a/

/a/	/a//a/	
А. окно́ "window"	**голова́** "head"	
доска́ "board"	**молоко́** "milk"	**соба́ка** "dog"
В. у́хо "ear"	**хорошо́** "good"	**сло́во** "word"
пло́хо "bad"	**ко́смос** "outer space"	

Gender

	/a/	/a/
он – he	**она́** – she	**оно́** – it
стол – он	соба́ка – она	окно́ – оно́

All nouns in Russian have gender: they are either masculine, feminine, or neuter.

5. Read the following words to your partner. The partner should provide the pronoun that corresponds to the gender of the nouns you read.

> — Соба́ка.
> — Она́.

Look at the ending of each word to determine the gender. A consonant ending (marked as a "zero ending" -Ø) is masculine, -a is feminine, -o is neuter.

1. соба́ка	5. сло́во	9. сло́во
2. стол	6. ла́мпа	10. журна́л
3. окно́	7. ко́шка	11. ру́чка
4. каранда́ш	8. у́хо	12. бана́н

6. Show your partner the pictures in exercise 4 (page 6) and exercise 1 (page 8), and tell him or her what you see. One of you should then replace the noun with the appropriate pronoun: **он, она́,** or **оно́.**

вот = here (is)

> —Вот ко́шка.
> —Вот она́.
>
> —Вот торт.
> —Вот он.

7. Read the following ads from Russian magazines and newspapers.

Working in groups of 3, pretend that one of you is interested in foods, the other in electronics, and the third in automobiles. Make lists of things of interest to each of you. (You may write them in English.) Read your lists to the class.

FOODS	ELECTRONICS	AUTOMOBILES
_____	_____	_____
_____	_____	_____
_____	_____	_____
_____	_____	_____
_____	_____	_____
_____	_____	_____
_____	_____	_____
_____	_____	_____

Hard and Soft Consonants

For almost every consonantal sound we have in English, Russian has two sounds: a hard consonant and a soft consonant. The pairs of words below differ only by virtue of the hard and soft "л"s, but see what a difference in meaning the hard/soft distinction can make!

Hard	**Soft**
у́гол /у́гал/ "corner"	у́голь /у́галʲ/ "coal"
по́лка /по́лка/ "shelf"	по́лька /по́лʲка/ "polka"

The -ь indicates that the preceding consonant is soft when there is no vowel after the consonant. It does not have a sound of its own and cannot be pronounced in isolation. When a vowel appears after a consonant, the vowel indicates whether the preceding consonant is soft or not.

лук /hard л+ук/   "onion"
люк /soft лʲ+ук)/   "manhole"

In other words, the five Russian vowel sounds are spelled with one set of letters after hard consonants, and with an <u>alternative</u> set of letters after soft consonants. You will need to learn both sets of letters at this time in order to read and pronounce Russian correctly.

Hard consonants +	а	о	у	э	ы
Soft consonants +	я	ё	ю	е	и

1. Read the following words containing both hard and soft consonants. Then compare the pronunciation of the hard and soft consonants.

A. Hard consonants

э́то "this"	мэр "mayor"	э́ра "era"
сыр "cheese"	сын "son"	ры́ба "fish"

The letter **ё**
occurs only
when it is
stressed,
otherwise it is
spelled **e**.

B. Soft consonants

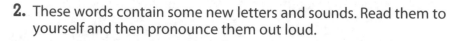

/т^ьо́т^ьa/	/каст^ьу́м/
тётя "aunt"	**костю́м** "suit"
день "day"	**институ́т** "institute"
здесь "here"	**магази́н** "store"
биле́т "ticket"	**кварти́ра** "apartment"

2. These words contain some new letters and sounds. Read them to yourself and then pronounce them out loud.

чай "tea"   **музе́й** "museum"   **пи́цца** "pizza"

3. Write these new letters in cursive in the chart below.

The letters **ь,**
ъ and **ы** never
occur word-
initially as the
first letter in the
word; therefore
they are never
capitalized.

Print			Cursive	
Capital	Small	Name of Letter	Capital	Small
Е	е	ye		
Ё	ё	yo		
И	и	i		
Й	й	i kratkoye (short i)		
Ц	ц	tse		
	ъ	tvyordiy znak (hard sign)		
	ы	yeri		
	ь	myagkiy znak (soft sign)		
Э	э	e oborotnoye (reversed e)		
Ю	ю	yu		
Я	я	ya		

Personal Pronouns

я	I	мы	we
ты	you (singular informal)	вы	you (plural, singular formal)
он она́ оно́	he she it	они́	they

The personal pronoun **я** is only capitalized when it is the first word in a sentence.

Use **ты** only when you are addressing a family member, a close friend, or a child. Use **вы** when you addressing an adult, a person of authority, a stranger, or any group of two or more people.

4. Getting acquainted

   A. With your instructor's help, write your name in Cyrillic letters.

       Во̄ Вова

   B. Introduce yourselves to each other in class using the following model.

> — Здра́вствуй, я И́ра!
> — Здра́вствуй, я Ви́ктор.

5. Identifying objects

Name as many objects as you can in this drawing of a city street. When you tell your partner what you have identified, s/he should respond with a statement that either affirms or corrects your observation.

это =this (is)
да = yes
нет = no

— Э́то магази́н.
— Да, э́то магази́н. / Нет, э́то рестора́н.

такси́, авто́бус, музе́й, банк, парк, стадио́н, институ́т, кафе́

6. Which of the following sports have you played? Sound out each word – you'll be surprised how many you know. Match each of the sports with its corresponding picture by writing the name of the sport under the appropriate illustration.

спорт:	альпини́зм	бадминто́н	баскетбо́л
	бейсбо́л	бокс	волейбо́л
	гимна́стика	гольф	сёрфинг
	ре́гби	те́ннис	тури́зм
	футбо́л	ша́хматы	хокке́й

Футбол

теннис _____ _____

_____ _____

Intonation

1. Read through the first two questions and answers and fill in the answer to the last question.

— Это ко́шка?   — Это ко́шка?   — Это ко́шка?
— Да. Это ко́шка.   — Нет. Это соба́ка.   — *Нет это собака*

As you can see, a yes-no question is worded exactly the same as a statement in Russian; the only difference is the intonation. It is very important to understand Russian intonation so you can understand whether someone is asking you a question or making an observation. This section will help you hear the difference between the two.

Intonational Construction 1 (IC-1): Statements

The intonational center (stressed syllable) of a statement is pronounced with a sharply falling tone.

Э́то ко́шка.

Э́то к
          о́
             ш
             ка.

Intonational Construction 3 (IC-3): Yes-No Questions

The intonational center of a yes-no question is pronounced with a very sharp rise, a "jump up".

Э́то ко́шка?

                    к о́ ш
Э́то
                              ка?

2. Read the following questions and answers out loud with a partner. Exaggerate your intonation.

1. — Э́то собака?   — Да. Э́то собака.

2. — Э́то автобус?   — Да. Э́то автобус.

3. — Э́то ресторан?   — Да. Э́то ресторан.

4. — Э́то магазин?   — Да. Э́то магазин.

5. — Э́то банк?   — Нет. Э́то гостиница.

6. — Э́то музей?   — Нет. Э́то институт.

магази́н = store

гости́ница = hotel

— Э́то слон?   — Э́то слон?
— Да. Э́то слон.   — Нет. Э́то лев.

слон = elephant

лев /лʲеф/ = lion

3. Look at the following surrealist drawings and discuss them with your partner. Can you come to an agreement about what the drawings represent?

4. Check to see if you remember the names of your classmates.

               3
— Ты Максим?
   1   1   1   1
— Да, я Максим./ Нет, я Олег.

THE ALL-IMPORTANT /Й/ ("Y" SOUND)

Compare the sound represented by "y" in the English words "yellow", "young", and "boy." This is similar to the Russian "y" sound (called "yot"), which is represented by the letter **й** when it is the *last* letter in the word or is *followed* by a consonant. For example, **мой** "my", **май** "May" (the month), and **спрайт** "Sprite".

As we learned before, the main function of the double set of vowels in Russian is to spell hard and soft consonants. Vowels from the second row in the chart[1] indicate the presence of the soft consonant /**й**/ ("yot"), when the sound occurs at the *beginning* of a word or *after* another vowel: я, ю́мор, Я́лта, ноя́брь.

In essence these letters represent "yot" plus the basic vowel sound, as demonstrated in the examples below.

---

[1] See the vowel chart on page 13 of this introduction.

5. Practicing pronunciation

/йа/ /йу́мар/ /ийу́нʲ/

я "I" **ю́мор** "humor" **ию́нь** "June"

Росси́я "Russia"

ноя́брь "November"

ию́ль "July"

фотогра́фия "photograph"

Plural of Nouns			
Pronoun	**Singular**	**Pronoun**	**Plural**
он	магази́н	они́	магази́**ны**
она́	ка́рта		ка́рт**ы**
оно́	окно́		о́кн**а**

6. Provide the plural of the following nouns.

Singular	Plural
магази́н	магази́ны
окно́	о́кна
ла́мпа	Лампы
костю́м	Костюмы
авто́бус	автобусы
ва́за	ва́зы
гости́ница	гостиницы
кварти́ра	кварти́ры
ка́рта	карты

7. You are organizing a vacation for a group of American tourists who plan to travel through Russia.

A. Using the map on the insert for reference, put together an itinerary for them. The itinerary should follow this basic plan: start in the far east of Russia; move west through Siberia; when you reach the region near Ukraine in the western part of Russia, move north. Include as many cities in your itinerary as you can.

Новосиби́рск	Кострома́
Арха́нгельск	Москва́
Магада́н	Владивосто́к
А́страхань	Орёл
Ту́ла	Ряза́нь
Яросла́вль	Му́рманск

B. Read your list out loud and compare it with your classmates' lists.

C. Which cities would you visit if you had a choice of 2? Guess what your partner would choose.

```
        3                        3
— Магада́н?                — Магада́н?
   1         1               1              1      1
— Да. Магада́н.            — Нет, не Магада́н. Ту́ла.
```

Vowel Reduction after Soft Consonants

We learned earlier that the Russian vowels **o** and **a** reduce to /a/ when they are not in the stressed syllable of a given word. This rule only pertains to **o** and **a** after **hard** consonants. After **soft** consonants, the vowels **a** (spelled as **я**), and **e**, reduce to /и/.

1. Practicing pronunciation: vowel reduction

A. Unstressed **e** = /и/

/тʲиа́тр/	/мʲитро́/
теа́тр	**метро́**
кинотеа́тр "movie theater"	**чемода́н** "suitcase"
рестора́н	**телефо́н**
университе́т	**а́дрес**

B. Unstressed **я** = /и/

/мʲе́сʲиц/
ме́сяц "month"
де́вять "nine"
де́сять "ten"

Devoicing of Final Consonants

Some consonant sounds in Russian and in English are produced with the vibration of the vocal cords, while other sounds are not. If you touch your neck in the area of the throat while making a buzzing sound, "z-z-z-z-z …", you can feel your vocal cords vibrating. If you do the same thing while producing a hissing sound, "s-s-s-s-s …", you can tell that your vocal cords are not vibrating. We say that the "z" sound is a voiced consonant, while the "s" sound is a voiceless consonant. Except for voicing, "z" and "s" have essentially identical articulation.

The voiced/voiceless distinction is important for proper pronunciation in Russian. **A voiced consonant in the final position in a word is pronounced like its voiceless counterpart.**

Paired Voiceless and Voiced Consonants	
Voiceless	**Voiced**
п	б
п^ь	б^ь
ф	в
ф^ь	в^ь
с	з
с^ь	з^ь
т	д
т^ь	д^ь
ш	ж
к	г
к^ь	г^ь

2. Practicing pronunciation: devoicing final consonants

Study and practice pronouncing the words below. Work with a partner as you read the list out loud; help each other devoice the final consonants.

/ш/
1. гара́**ж**

/п/
4. хле**б** "bread"

/ш/
2. бага́**ж** "luggage"

/с/
5. гла**з** "eye"

/к/
3. дру**г** "friend"

/т/
6. го́ро**д** "city, town"

The negative particle **не** is unstressed and is pronounced as /н^ьи/ together with the next word.

3. Over the summer you took pictures of some places you visited. You labeled them, but all the labels got mixed up. Correct the mistakes.

>   1   1
> Э́то не музе́й. Э́то магази́н.

гара́ж

музе́й

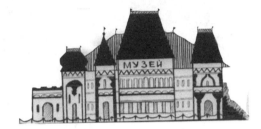

гости́ница

университе́т

парк

Intonation: Question Words

— Что э́то?
— Э́то кинотеа́тр.

— Что э́то?
— Э́то гости́ница.

The word **что** is pronounced as /што/.

Intonational Construction 2 (IC – 2): Questions with a question word

Both questions that contain a question word (who, what, etc.) and statements have a falling tone. In questions with a question word the center is pronounced with strong emphasis.

^{2}
Что э́то?

$$\overline{}$$
Ч
  т
    о
      э́то?
$$\underline{}$$

4. Practice your intonation as you and your partner read these questions and answers out loud to each other.

рюкза́к =
  backpack

^{2}	^{2}	^{2}
— Что э́то?	— Что э́то?	— Что э́то?
^{1}	^{1}	^{1}
— Э́то су́мка.	— Э́то чемода́н.	— Э́то рюкза́к.

5. A security officer at the airport in Russia asks you questions about your luggage. Tell him what you have.

^{2}
— Что э́то?

^{1}
— Э́то чемода́н.

сумка, каранда́ш, ка́рта, рюкза́к, чемода́н, журна́л, ру́чка, чай, плащ

6. A. Guess which animal says what. Check your answers at the bottom of the page.*

1. ква-ква!
2. гав-гав!
3. и-а!
4. ку-ка-ре-ку́!
5. и-го-го!
6. ме-е-е!
7. мя́у-мя́у!
8. бе-е-е!
9. чик-чири́к!
10. кря-кря!
11. хрю-хрю!

a) rooster
b) bird (sparrow)
c) sheep
d) frog
e) donkey
f) pig
g) dog
h) goat
i) horse
j) cat
k) duck

B. Practice the pronunciation of the animal sounds. Try to memorize what one of the animals says.

7. On the following page is the website of a Russian travel agency that offers organized tours to all parts of the world.

*1 (d), 2 (g), 3 (e), 4 (a), 5 (i), 6 (h), 7 (j), 8 (c), 9 (b), 10 (k), 11 (f)

ВХОД
ДЛЯ
АГЕНТСТВ

ПРОМО

Остров Джерба
Последние места
на заезды 12 и 13 мая!
14967 руб.

PDA / english version

(495) 7-999-444
(812) 33-555-33

быстрый поиск по турам

новости / контакты

| Москва ▼ | Египет ▼ | все даты ▼ | искать |

| | по сайту |

путевки сервис путеводитель вопросы и ответы о фирме

08.05.2008

туры: горящие | поиск | по России и СНГ | майские | экскурсионные | на поезде | круизы | авиатуры | автобусные | под бюджет | по неделям | индивидуальные | специальные проекты | расписание авиарейсов | **авиабилеты** | скидки | где купить

⌂ ⁜ путевки ⁜ горящие туры

Список горящих туров

	из Москвы	из Санкт-Петербурга	из Екатеринбурга	из Калининграда
Болгария	8,590 руб.	13,091 руб.	7,465 руб.	
Греция	6,715 руб.	18,718 руб.	12,341 руб.	
Испания	15,717 руб.		12,341 руб.	
Италия	26,970 руб.			
Марокко	20,218 руб.			
Португалия		28,846 руб.		
Таиланд	22,844 руб.	32,222 руб.		
Тунис	12,716 руб.			
Турция	5,965 руб.	16,467 руб.	10,841 руб.	7,465 руб.
Франция	34,472 руб.			
Хорватия	13,467 руб.	19,843 руб.		
Черногория	14,967 руб.	20,593 руб.		
Чехия	11,216 руб.	13,467 руб.		

ТУРЫ В ЕГИПЕТ

Туры в Египет из Москвы и
Санкт-Петербурга ⁜⁜⁜

ЧАРТЕРНЫЕ РЕЙСЫ В ЧЕХИЮ

Еженедельные чартерные рейсы
в Чехию из Санкт-Петербурга.
⁜⁜⁜

ЛОНДОН - ПАРИЖ из СПб

Тур Лондон - Париж на майские
праздники из Санкт-Петербурга.
Бульвар Пикадилли,
Трафальгарская площадь,
поездка под Ла-Маншем и другие
достопримечательности двух
столиц - за 9 дней/8 ночей! ⁜⁜⁜

Москва ⁜. **(495)** 7-999-444

Санкт-Петербург ⁜. **(812)** 33-555-33

Екатеринбург   Новосибирск
Казань   Нижний Новгород

все агентства "Невы" ⁜⁜⁜

Сайты компании: www.nevatravel.ru | agent.nevatravel.ru
ski.nevatravel.ru | promo.nevatravel.ru
www.turmail.ru | www.nevavoiage.ru

член Ассоциации
Туроператоров России
(АТОР)

лауреат премии "Лидеры
Российского Турбизнеса"
(2001 г.)

ЛАТА

член Международной
Ассоциации Воздушного
Транспорта (IATA)

Звезда Travel.ru за 2007 год

версия для печати / карта сайта / наверх ⁜

путевки сервис путеводитель вопросы и ответы о фирме Copyright © 2007 ЗАО "Фирма Нева"
Реклама на сайте

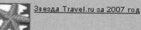
Участник
Rambler's

A. List a few of the tours (country or city) by continent.

<u>Евро́па</u>	<u>А́зия</u>	<u>А́фрика</u>
Испа́ния	Ту́рция	Туни́с
_____	_____	_____
_____	_____	_____

B. List 3 tours that sound like a bargain to you.

_____   _____   _____

C. If you won the lottery, which 3 places would you visit first? Write your choices below, then compare them to your classmates' choices.

_____   _____   _____

А

авангáрд avant garde
Австрáлия Australia
автóбус bus
áдрес address
Áзия Asia
альпинúзм mountain climbing
Амéрика America
аппарáт apparatus
Архáнгельск Arkhangelsk
Áстрахань Astrakhan
Áфрика Africa
аэропóрт airport

Б

багáж luggage
бадминтóн badminton
банáн banana
банк bank
бар bar
баскетбóл basketball
Бáскин-Рóббинс Baskin-Robbins
бейсбóл baseball
Биг-Мак Big Mac
билéт ticket
бокс boxing

В

вáза vase
Владивостóк Vladivostok
воллейбóл volleyball
вот here (is)
вы you (formal)

Г

гáмбургер hamburger
гарáж garage
гимнáстика gymnastics
глаз eye
головá head
гольф golf
гóрод city, town
гостúница hotel

Д

да yes
дéвять nine
десéрт dessert
дéсять ten
день day
дом house
доскá blackboard
друг friend

Е

Еврóпа Europe

Ж

журнáл magazine

З

здесь here
здрáвствуй(те) hellow

И

инститýт institute
Испáния Spain
июль July
июнь June

К

каравáн caravan
карандáш pencil
кáрта map
катастрóфа catastrophe
кафé cafe
квартúра apartment
кинотеáтр movie theater
кóка-кóла Coke
кóка-кóла лайт Diet Coke
кóмната room
кóсмос outer space
Костромá Kostroma
костю́м suit
кот cat (male)
кóшка cat (female)

Л

лáмпа lamp
лев lion
лук onion
люк manhole

М

Магадáн Magadan
магазúн store
май May
Макдóналдс McDonald's
мáма mother
мéсяц month
метрó subway
мой my
молокó milk
Москвá Moscow
мост bridge
музéй museum
Мýрманск Murmansk
мы we
мэр mayor

Н

не not
нет no
Новосибúрск Novosibirsk
нос nose
ноя́брь November
Нью-Йóрк New York

О

окнó window
он he, it
онá she, it
онú they
онó it
Орёл Oryol

П

пáпа father
парадóкс paradox
парк park
пúцца pizza
Пúцца Хат Pizza Hut

плащ raincoat
плохо bad
полка shelf
полька polka

Р

регби rugby
ресторан restaurant
Россия Russia
рот mouth
ручка pen
рыба fish
рюкзак backpack
Рязань Ryazan

С

салат salad, lettuce
сахар sugar
сёрфинг surfing
Сидней Sidney
слово word
слон elephant
собака dog
сок juice
спорт sport
спрайт Sprite
стадион stadium
стол table
стул chair
сумка purse, bag

суп soup
сын son
сыр cheese

Т

такси taxi
театр theater
телефон telephone
теннис tennis
тётя aunt
торт cake
Тула Tula
Тунис Tunis
туризм tourism
Турция Turkey
тут here
ты you (informal)

У

угол corner
уголь coal
университет university
ухо ear

Ф

фанта Fanta
филе-о-фиш Filet-o-fish
фотография photograph
футбол football

Х

хлеб bread
хоккей hockey
хорошо good

Ч

чай tea
чемодан suitcase
чизбургер cheeseburger
что what

Ш

шахматы chess
шкаф closet

Э

эра era
это this (is), these (are)

Ю

юмор humor

Я

Ялта Yalta
Ярославль Yaroslavl

UNIT

1

*A*fter his arrival at the airport in Moscow and first trip through the city, Kevin learns his Moscow address and makes his first new friends in Moscow.

Здра́вствуйте, э́то я!

You will learn how to:

- SAY HELLO AND GOODBYE
- INTRODUCE YOURSELF AND OTHERS
- IDENTIFY LOCATION
- IDENTIFY PEOPLE AND THINGS
- IDENTIFY OWNERSHIP
- MAKE A PHONE CALL
- APOLOGIZE AND ACCEPT AN APOLOGY
- NEGATE A STATEMENT
- COUNT FROM 1 TO 10
- MAKE INQUIRIES OVER THE PHONE
- EXPRESS GRATITUDE
- DISCUSS PROFESSIONS AND OCCUPATIONS
- ASK FOR PERMISSION
- ASK FOR DIRECTIONS
- DESCRIBE YOUR FAMILY AND YOURSELF
- HAVE A CONVERSATION IN AN INFORMAL SETTING

▶ Take a guess.

1. "Здра́вствуйте, э́то я!" is the title of the first film.

Since «*Здра́вствуйте*» is a form of

☐ farewell   ☐ insult   ☐ greeting

it's safe to assume that this video clip is about

☐ meeting people

☐ the importance of being polite

☐ the departure

2. A. Judging by the pictures above, the city where the action takes place is

☐ Петербу́рг, Росси́я

☐ Москва́, Росси́я

☐ Голливу́д, США (USA)

B. The two characters are about to meet at a

☐ рестора́н   ☐ гости́ница   ☐ аэропо́рт

гости́ница = hotel

▶ First watch the video with SOUND OFF and see if your predictions were correct.

3. A. At the airport.

What signs do you see at the airport?

☐ телефóн   ☐ кинотеáтр

☐ кафé   ☐ магазúн

☐ банк   ☐ пóчта

☐ бар   ☐ газéты

☐ ресторáн   ☐ туалéт

☐ Макдóналдс   ☐ журнáлы

B. Identify the different things which Кéвин has.

☐ чемодáн   ☐ фотоаппарáт

☐ видеокáмера   ☐ гитáра

☐ рюкзáк   ☐ сýмка

C. What kind of transportation did they use to leave the airport?

☐ лимузúн   ☐ автóбус

☐ таксú   ☐ метрó

☐ машúна   ☐ троллéйбус

4. Along the way Кéвин sees many different places. Do you recognize any of them? (банк, Кремль, кинотеáтр, музéй, теáтр, Макдóналдс)

магазúн = store

пóчта = post office

чемодáн = suitcase

рюкзáк = backpack

сýмка = bag, purse

машúна = car

кинотеáтр _____ _____

_____

▶ Now watch the video with the SOUND ON.

SOUND ON

5. A. What is the name of the first young woman?

☐ Áня ☐ Táня ☐ Hácтя

B. What is the name of the first young man?

☐ Кéвин ☐ Давúд ☐ Даниúл

C. Táня introduces Кéвин to her friend at the airport. What is his name?

☐ Олéг ☐ Максúм ☐ Сергéй

▶ Let's review the video.

POSTviewing

6. The first two dialogs in the film are between people who have never met, but know each other's names.

A. Now that you know the names of the main characters, you can reconstruct their first conversation.

— Вы _____?

— _____.

—Здра́вствуйте! Я _____ ².

—Óчень прия́тно. ²

—Óчень прия́тно. ²

B. You now know how Russians introduce themselves. Now try to reconstruct the second introduction.

—Здра́вствуйте! _____ — Ма́ша?

—Да. А _____ Ви́ктор?

—_____. Óчень прия́тно.

—Óчень прия́тно.

C. Can you guess what *óчень прия́тно* means?

☐ Excuse me.

☐ Nice to meet you.

☐ Goodbye.

7. Practicing pronunciation

óчень прия́тно   здра́вствуйте   до свида́ния

8. Practicing introductions

A. When you don't know the name of the person you are meeting, introduce yourself this way:

—Здра́вствуйте! Я ¹ Том. ²

—А я Ни́на. ¹

—Óчень прия́тно. ²

—Óчень прия́тно. ²

—Здра́вствуй! Я Ли́за. ² ¹

—А я Оле́г. ¹

—Óчень прия́тно. ²

—Óчень прия́тно. ²

The conjunction **a** signals the introduction of a new contrasting topic in the conversation.

Compare:
"Aren't you Viktor?"
«А вы Ви́ктор?»

Exclamations, including greetings, are pronounced using IC-2.

When you are talking to someone your own age (or to a child), use the informal **Здра́вствуй!** rather than the formal **Здра́вствуйте!**

Now you and your partner introduce yourselves.

_____. Я — _____.

—А я _____.

—Óчень прия́тно.

—Óчень прия́тно.

B. How did Ке́вин and Серге́й say goodbye to each other in the video?

☐ óчень прия́тно   ☐ до свида́ния

☐ извини́те   ☐ пожа́луйста

Now say goodbye to each other!

1. Imagine that you find yourself in Moscow with a friend who made the mistake of dropping out of Russian class. All your friend can do is ask, «Что э́то?» Help him identify these signs by reading the signs displayed.

> 2
> — Что э́то?
>
> 1
> — Э́то **стадио́н**.

2. When you arrive in Moscow the customs official at the airport wants to know what you have in your suitcase. He keeps asking, «Что э́то?»

Which of the following things did he find in your suitcase? Act out your encounter with the customs official.

> 2
> — Что э́то?
>
> 1
> — Э́то **чемода́н**.

книга = book

куртка = short
jacket

письмо = letter

словарь =
dictionary

B. Now you are showing a child pictures of your friends. S/he asks
who these people are.

```
         2
  — Кто это?
        1
  — Это Лена.
```

кто = who

C. The child is exploring your room and finds your poster collection.
Answer the child's questions about what is pictured in the
posters.

```
         2
  — Кто это?
         1
  — Это собака.
         2
  — Что это?
         1
  — Это карта.
```

In Russian **кто**
(who) refers
to people and
animals, while
что is used
with things.

Барт Си́мпсон, тигр, бана́н, Бэ́тмен, Москва́, ко́шка, маши́на, пингви́н, Супермéн, гори́лла

Singular and Plural Forms of Nouns					
Singular			**Plural**		
он	авто́бус	слова́рь	они́	авто́бусы	словари́
она́	шко́ла	тётя		шко́лы	тёти
оно́	сло́во	мо́ре	они́	слова́	моря́

Notice that in a small number of nouns the stress may shift: **слова́рь – словари́, окно́ – о́кна**. Stress shifts will be discussed later. For now, you can refer to the vocabulary at the end of the unit to find out whether a noun has shifting stress.

3. Practicing pronunciation

> **маши́ны   гаражи́   ножи́   карандаши́**

4. Divide the class into two groups. One group will argue that the nouns listed are singular, and the second group will argue that they are plural.

Spelling Rule

к and г are
followed by и,
never by ы

соба́ка →
   соба́ки

кни́га → кни́ги

> **Group 1:** Э́то **бана́н**.
>
> **Group 2:** Э́то **бана́ны**.

музе́й (*sing.*) –
музе́и (*pl.*)

журна́л, рюкза́к, музе́й, ка́рта, слова́рь, ку́ртка, ко́шка, парк, кни́га, университéт, банк, газéта, чемода́н, ру́чка, теа́тр, соба́ка

5. Name as many groups of objects as you can.

> 1
> Э́то **бана́ны**.

1. Getting and giving information

On his way from the airport, Кéвин snapped some pictures. Later on, he couldn't remember what the places in the pictures were. Help absent-minded Кéвин figure out what these pictures are.

> 3
> — Э́то **гостиница**?
> 1
> — Нет, э́то не **гостиница**.
> 2
> — А что э́то?
> 1
> — Э́то **школа**.

Э́то Макдóналдс?

Э́то школа?

шкóла = grade school

Э́то гостúница?

Э́то автóбус?

троллéйбус = trolley bus

Э́то библиоте́ка?   Э́то по́чта?

библиоте́ка =
library

2. Using the map below, identify different places in town.

> ²
> — Что э́то?
> ¹
> — Э́то библиотека.

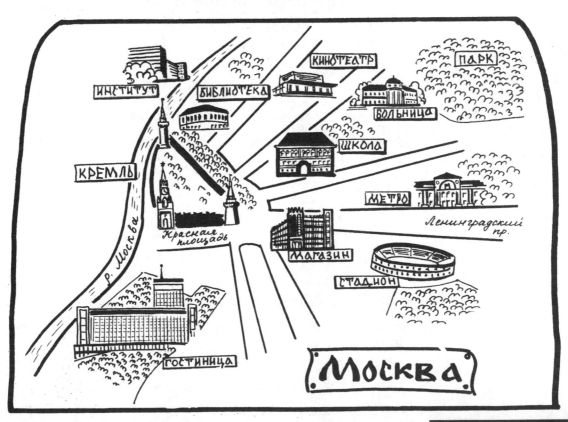

Possessive Pronouns				
	masculine журна́л	**feminine** су́мка	**neuter** окно́	**plural** ве́щи
я	мой	моя́	моё	мои́
ты	твой	твоя́	твоё	твои́
мы	наш	на́ша	на́ше	на́ши
вы	ваш	ва́ша	ва́ше	ва́ши

ве́щи = things

багаж = luggage

кварти́ра = apartment

рюкза́к /рʲугза́к/: For pronunciation, see Analysis 1, 15

→ NB: the gender of the pronoun depends on the gender of the noun it describes, NOT the person to whom it refers

3. Practicing pronunciation

мой дом   моя́ ма́ма   моё окно́   мои́ ве́щи

твой а́дрес твоя́ соба́ка твоё письмо́ твои́ словари́

наш бага́ж   на́ша кварти́ра на́ше письмо́ на́ши кни́ги

ваш рюкза́к ва́ша су́мка   ва́ше окно́   ва́ши джи́нсы

4. Expressing possession

A. Say that the following things belong to you.

1. Э́то **мой** журна́л.
2. Э́то _____ каранда́ш.
3. Э́то _____ чемода́ны.
4. Э́то _____ су́мка.
5. Э́то _____ костю́м.
6. Э́то _____ ко́шка.
7. Э́то _____ окно́.
8. Э́то _____ ру́чка.

B. Ask your friend who the following things belong to.

1. Э́то **твой** фотоаппара́т?
2. Э́то _____ су́мки?
3. Э́то _____ бага́ж?
4. Э́то _____ письмо́?
5. Э́то _____ чемода́ны?
6. Э́то _____ соба́ка?

C. Say that the following things belong to you and your family.

1. Э́то **наш** а́дрес.
2. Э́то _____ кварти́ра.
3. Э́то _____ дом.
4. Э́то _____ ве́щи.
5. Э́то _____ шко́ла.
6. Э́то _____ магази́ны.
7. Э́то _____ окно́.
8. Э́то _____ парк.

D. How would you ask if the following things belong to your teacher and/or your classmates?

1. Э́то **ваш** журна́л?
2. Э́то _____ маши́на?
3. Э́то _____ газе́ты?
4. Э́то _____ ру́чка?
5. Э́то _____ сви́тер?
6. Э́то _____ ка́рты?

5. Provide the right response.

A. 1. Э́то **ваш** бага́ж?   Нет, не **моя**.

2. Э́то **ваши** ве́щи?   Да, **наши**.

3. Э́то **ваша** су́мка?   Нет, не **мой**.

4. Э́то **твоё** письмо́?   Да, **моё**.

B. 1. Э́то **ваш** рюкза́к?   Да, **наше**.

2. Э́то **ваши** кни́ги?   Нет, не **моя**.

3. Э́то **твоя** маши́на?   Да, **наши**.

4. Э́то **наше** метро́?   Да, **мой**.

C. 1. Э́то **ваша** ка́рта?   Да, **мой**.

2. Э́то **ваши** чемода́ны?   Нет, не **наш**.

3. Э́то **ваш** слова́рь?   Да, **наша**.

4. Э́то **твой** телефо́н?   Нет, не **мои**.

Numbers

6. Listen to the pronunciation of the numbers 0-10, then practice counting.

0. ноль
1. оди́н
2. два
3. три
4. четы́ре
5. пять
6. шесть
7. семь
8. во́семь
9. де́вять
10. де́сять

> Unstressed **я** is pronounced as /**и**/.

7. Making a call

Before Та́ня leaves to pick up Ке́вин from the airport, she calls to find out whether his flight is on time. Unfortunately, she gets a wrong number.

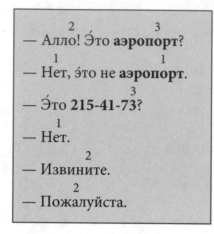

— Алло! Э́то **аэропо́рт**?
— Нет, э́то не **аэропо́рт**.
— Э́то **215-41-73**?
— Нет.
— Извини́те.
— Пожа́луйста.

извини́те =
I'm sorry,
excuse me.

пожа́луйста =
(here) That's
OK.

Call the following places and have your partner say that you have reached the wrong number.

университе́т (972-05-33)
библиоте́ка (388-86-65)
музе́й (341-90-70)
магази́н (464-12-54)▲

▲ Note that Russians, unlike Americans, use an extra dash to separate the last two digits.

1. We return to our story now…

Before you watch the video, do you remember the names of the characters?

The young woman's name is _____ , the young man

whom she meets at the airport is _____, and

the driver's name is _____ .▲

2. Кéвин brought 4 pieces of luggage with him to Moscow. Can you list these pieces in Russian?

a. _____   c. _____

b. _____   d. _____

Check if your answers are correct as you watch the video.

▲ Cars are a luxury for the average Russian. If a family is lucky enough to own a car, they would have just one. In general, even though cars are very expensive, there are many more cars on the streets of Russian cities in comparison with the Soviet times. Many large cities struggle with the same issues as their western counterparts: traffic jams, accidents, pollution. The number of women drivers has grown exponentially since the early 1990s, but most drivers are still men.

▶ Read the following two exercises before you watch the video with the SOUND ON.

3. Táня asks Кéвин to identify his luggage. Fill in the missing possessive pronouns.

Táня: — Кéвин, э́то ваш чемода́н?

Кéвин: — Да, _____ .

Táня: — Э́то _____ сýмка?

Кéвин: — Сýмка? Нет, не моя́.

4. Can you put the following lines from the video in order? Write the number (1-4) for the order in which each line appears.

_____ — А кафé там?

_____ — Туалéт? Вон там.

_____ — Кафé? Да, вон там.

_____ — Извини́те, где тут туалéт?

Expressing Possession in Russian

5. At the airport

A. You are meeting a Russian friend at the airport. Help identify your friend's luggage.

> 3
> — Э́то ваш **чемода́н**?
> 1   1   1   1
> — Да, мой./Нет, не мой.

The intonational center of yes-no questions with IC-3 falls on the word you want to emphasize (in this case, whether the things are *yours*).

бага́ж, чемода́н, сýмка, рюкза́к, фотоаппара́т, ве́щи

B. Ке́вин was very fortunate – he recovered all of his luggage intact. Unfortunately, others are not always so lucky. Imagine yourself at the airport as a poor traveler who has lost everything. Go to the airline representative and try to recover the missing luggage.

Вы:	— Извини́те пожа́луйста, где мой **бага́ж**?
Official:	— Ваш **бага́ж**? Вот он!
Вы:	— Спаси́бо!

Извини́те, пожа́луйста.
= Excuse me please.

> су́мка, па́спорт, рюкза́к, ве́щи, компью́тер, чемода́н

6. At the university

A. You have just finished changing in the locker room at your university's swimming pool and are getting ready to go home. You notice that your things, which are sitting on the bench, have gotten mixed up with another student's. Ask the student which things belong to him/her.

> 3
> — Э́то твои **ве́щи**?
> 1   1   1   1
> — Да, мои./Нет, не мои.

учéбник = textbook

> су́мка, кни́ги, рюкза́к, журна́лы, слова́рь,
> учéбники

B. Imagine that you are in a university classroom after Russian class and someone has accidentally taken off with one of your things. Get the person's attention and explain that the object belongs to you.

> 2   1
> — Извините, э́то моя **ру́чка**.
> 2   2
> — Ой, извините, пожа́луйста.

Извини́те is used very much like "Excuse me!"

1. To apologize: "Excuse me if I said something wrong."
2. To get someone's attention: "Excuse me, you dropped your pen."

> су́мка, кни́ги, рюкза́к, га́мбургер, ко́ка-ко́ла,
> слова́рь, стул, газе́ты, карандаши́, шокола́д,
> бана́н

7. On a bus tour

A. Two groups go on a bus tour in Russia and their belongings get mixed up. Sort them out.

> **Group 1:** — Э́то наши **фотоаппара́ты**?
>   3
>
> **Group 2:** — Нет, э́то наши **фотоаппара́ты**.
>   1   1

> кни́ги, журна́лы, су́мки, газе́ты, га́мбургеры,
> ви́зы, соба́ка, ру́чки, бана́ны, ко́шка, чемода́ны

B. Ask whether an item is yours; your partner answers that the item is his/hers. Apologize for your mistake. Switch roles.

> 3
> — Э́то мой **рюкза́к**?
> 1   1
> — Нет, это мой **рюкза́к**.
>   2
> — Извини́те, пожа́луйста.
>   2
> — Пожалуйста.

Пожа́луйста may be used as an equivalent for three different expressions in English:
1. Please. (polite request)
2. It's okay. (reassurance)
3. You're welcome. (acceptance of gratitude)

ка́рта, су́мка, ру́чка, слова́рь, газе́ты, шокола́д

C. Suppose you want to find out where your dictionary is. Act out conversations with your partner, using this model.

> 3
> — Э́то **мой** слова́рь?
> 1   1
> — Нет, э́то **мой** слова́рь.
>   2
> — А где **мой**?
>   1
> — Вот **он**.
>   2
> — Спаси́бо.
>   2
> — Пожалуйста.

ру́чка, каранда́ш, рюкза́к, су́мка, сок, кни́ги, ка́рта

Professions/Occupations

▶ Кéвин has pictures of his family in his wallet. Тáня asks him to describe who is in the pictures.

Тáня:　　Кто э́то?

Кéвин:　　Э́то моя́ мáма.　　Онá **ветеринáр**.
　　　　　Э́то мой брат.　　Он **студéнт**.
　　　　　Э́то моя́ сестрá.　　Онá **бизнесмéн**.
　　　　　Э́то мой пáпа.　　Он **ветеринáр**.

брат = brother
сестрá = sister

Some other professions:

антропóлог	матемáтик
архитéктор	мéнеджер
бизнесмéн	программи́ст
биóлог	психóлог
бухгáлтер	фи́зик
врач▲	фотóграф
геóлог	хи́мик
инженéр	экономи́ст
истóрик	юри́ст
домохозя́йка	

программи́ст = programmer

бухгáлтер = accountant

домохозя́йка = homemaker

врач = doctor/ physician

юри́ст = lawyer

▶ Did you notice that the names of professions listed above are all masculine except homemaker? Some, but not all, professions also have feminine forms:

он	онá	
актёр	актри́са	actor/actress
журнали́ст	журнали́стка	journalist

▲ The majority of doctors and teachers in Russia are women.

он	она́	
официа́нт	официа́нтка	waiter/waitress
певе́ц	певи́ца	singer
писа́тель	писа́тельница	writer
преподава́тель	преподава́тельница	university instructor
продаве́ц	продавщи́ца	salesperson
студе́нт	студе́нтка	student
учи́тель	учи́тельница	grade-school teacher
шко́льник	шко́льница	grade-school student

1. Practicing pronunciation

экономи́ст	био́лог
ме́неджер	психо́лог
бухга́лтер	антропо́лог
бизнесме́н	гео́лог

Remember that the final **г** is pronounced as /к/.

2. Talking about professions/occupations

   A. Do you know how to write the occupations of your family members in Russian?

Э́то я и моя́ семья́.[1]

Я **студе́нт**.[1]

Э́то моя́ ма́ма. Она́ _____.[1]

Мой па́па _____.

Мой брат _____.

Моя́ сестра́ _____.

семья́ = family
For pronunciation, see Analysis I, 15.

Па́па is a masculine noun, so all modifiers are masculine: **мой** па́па, **твой** па́па.

B. Now talk about yourself.

> — Я студе́нт.
>
> — **И** я студе́нт.
>
> — Моя́ ма́ма **врач**.
>
> — А моя́ ма́ма **исто́рик**.

Requesting, Granting, and Acknowledging Permission

There are many ways of requesting, granting, and acknowledging permission in Russian.

Мо́жно is used to ask permission to do something. In English this translates as "may I," or "is it all right/OK to do this?" For example, "May I come in?", "May I use your phone?"

> — Мо́жно?
> — Да, пожа́луйста.
> — Спаси́бо.

You can use this word when you want to borrow something. What you are asking permission for is implied by the given context. Take a look at what happens when the answer is negative:

> — Мо́жно?
> — Нет.
> — Извини́те.

The negative answer is followed by an apology, **извини́те**. Is this the way you would say it in English?

3. Basic conversation skills and courtesy requirements

Provide a Russian equivalent for the following:

— Nice to meet you. _____

— Thank you. _____

— You're welcome. _____

— Is this the bank? _____

— No, this isn't the bank. _____

— This is a store. _____

— I'm sorry. _____

— That's OK./No problem. _____

— Excuse me. _____

— Where is the telephone? _____

— Over there. _____

— May I? _____

— Go ahead. _____

4. Requesting and granting permission

Ask if you may borrow different things on another person's desk
(you can point to what you want). One person is kind, answering yes,
while the other refuses to lend anything.

— Э́то твой **каранда́ш**? ³	— Э́то твой **журна́л**? ³
— Да, **мой**. ¹ ¹	— Да, **мой**. ¹ ¹
— Мо́жно? ³	— Мо́жно? ³
— Да, пожалуйста. ¹ ¹	— Нет. ¹
— Спаси́бо. ²	— Извини́. ²

Извини́ is the familiar form of **извини́те**.

5. Getting information

A. You are an exchange student waiting for a friend on a busy street corner in Moscow. Your friend is running late, and during your long wait you are approached by various people asking directions. You know this part of the city well, so help them find where they need to go.

> — Извините, где тут **телефон**? [²...²]
>
> — **Телефон?** Вот тут./Вон там. [³ ¹ ¹]
>
> — Спасибо. [²]
>
> — Пожалуйста. [²]

[
cafe, metro, stadium, park, bank, hotel, garage, store, movie theater, museum, library, post office
]

B. You just moved to Moscow and have decided to go on a walk to familiarize yourself with the neighborhood.

Unfortunately, you forgot your glasses and can't see any of the signs on the buildings. Ask people on the street for information about the different sights.

> — Извините, э́то **университет**? [² ³]
>
> — Нет. Э́то не **университет**. Э́то **институт**. [¹ ¹ ¹]
>
> — А где **университет**? [²]
>
> — **Университе́т** вон там. Вон **он**. [¹ ¹]
>
> — Спасибо. [²]
>
> — Пожалуйста. [²]

[
café, restaurant, metro, museum, park, bank, institute, store, movie theater, school, library, post office, hotel
]

1. On the way from the airport Та́ня and Ке́вин see different places in Moscow. Can you remember any of them?

List any three in Russian.

a. _____

b. _____

c. _____

2. Here is a list of different places in Moscow. While watching the video, check the ones they pass on the way home.

☐ больни́ца   ☐ ба́нки   ☐ шко́ла

☐ парк   ☐ гости́ница   ☐ магази́ны

☐ институ́т   ☐ теа́тр   ☐ кафе́

☐ метро́   ☐ ба́ры   ☐ рестора́ны

☐ университе́т   ☐ музе́й   ☐ гара́ж

☐ стадио́н   ☐ кинотеа́тр   ☐ Кремль

3. Ке́вин saw monuments to which two Russian writers?▲

Пу́шкин	Го́голь
Толсто́й	Достое́вский
Че́хов	Солжени́цын

POSTviewing ▷

4. Identifying occupations

A. Do you remember when Та́ня tells Ке́вин about Че́хов?▲▲

Ке́вин:	— Э́то кто?
Та́ня:	— Э́то Че́хов.
Ке́вин:	— Э́то ваш писа́тель?
Та́ня:	— Да, э́то наш писа́тель.

B. Now reconstruct the conversation about Пу́шкин.▲▲▲

Ке́вин:	— Кто э́то?
Та́ня:	— Э́то Пу́шкин.
Ке́вин:	— А, _____! Он поэ́т, да?
Та́ня:	— Да, он _____ и писа́тель.

> The questions «Кто он?» «Кто она́?» refer to people's professions or occupations.

5. Describing professions and family relationships

A. Серге́й tells Ке́вин about himself and his family. He shows Ке́вин a 20-year-old sketch of his family.

Я **шко́льник**.

Моя́ ма́ма **бухга́лтер**.

Мой па́па **программи́ст**.

Моя́ сестра́ Ната́ша **студе́нтка**.

▲ Russians take great pride in their authors and poets. This explains the abundance of monuments to Russian writers on Moscow streets.

▲▲ **Anton Pavlovich Chekhov (1860–1904)** is a prominent Russian short-story writer and playwright. His most famous plays are *The Seagull, Uncle Vanya, Three Sisters,* and *The Cherry Orchard*.

▲▲▲ **Alexander Sergeevich Pushkin (1799–1837)** is known as the father of Russian literature. A poet, dramatist, and prose writer, he is the most beloved and well known writer in Russia.

Андре́й —
программист

Мари́на —
бухга́лтер

муж = husband
жена́ = wife
сын = son
до́чка = daughter

Ната́ша —
студе́нтка

БЕЛКИНЫ

Серге́й –
шко́льник

B. How would you describe this family if you were:

1. Андре́й Бе́лкин   2. Ната́ша Бе́лкина

3. Мари́на Бе́лкина

Серге́й: — Э́то мой **па́па**.
          — Он **программи́ст**.

The center of IC-3 here
is on the noun because
that is the word in
question.

6. Talking about your family

Split up in pairs and "show" each other pictures from your
wallets. Your friend tries to guess the identity of the people
in your pictures. You correct your friend's mistakes. Practice
using both the long and short answers.

— Оле́г, э́то твой **па́па**?
— Нет, э́то мой **брат**.
  (Нет, **брат**.)

Addressing a person
by name is normal in
Russian conversations.
Use IC-2 when
addressing a person in
this manner.

Forms of address at the
beginning of a sentence
are pronounced with
IC-2.

папа, брат, подруга, сестра, мама, друг

 7. Acting out typical situations in Russian: meeting people

You and your family are visiting a Russian friend, who introduces you to his/her friends at the sports club. First read the conversations, and then introduce Та́ня to your own brother and Серге́й to your sister using the same vocabulary.

Ю́ля: — Здра́вствуйте!

сестра́: — Здра́вствуйте!

Ни́на: — Сестра, э́то моя́
   — подру́га Юля.
   — А э́то моя́ мама.

Ю́ля: — О́чень прия́тно.

сестра́: — О́чень прия́тно.

   — Юля, вы студе́нтка?

Ю́ля: — Да.

сестра́: — А я врач.

Бори́с: — Здра́вствуйте!

брат: — Здра́вствуйте!

Макси́м: — Борис, э́то мой папа.
   — А э́то мой друг Борис.

брат: — О́чень прия́тно.

Бори́с: — О́чень прия́тно.

брат: — Борис, вы студе́нт?

Бори́с: — Да.

брат: — А я программи́ст.

8. How do you picture your future? Ask your partner which picture s/he would choose to describe himself/herself in 10 years.

3
— Это твой **дом**?
   1 1   1   1
— Да, это. /Нет, не это.

city, house, wife, husband, cat

1

DAY 7

Below is a letter Та́ня received from a friend. Although some of the words will be unfamiliar to you, you should be able to understand the basic sense of the letter. The exercises on the next page will help you direct your reading.

Ко́лледж Парк

1 декабря́

Здра́вствуй, Та́ня!

in

live

dormitory

Сего́дня 1 декабря́, а зна́чит, я уже́ 3 ме́сяца в◊ Аме́рике. Я живу́◊ в Ко́лледж Па́рке и учу́сь в Мэриле́ндском университе́те. Я живу́ в общежи́тии◊ на ка́мпусе. Университе́т—ря́дом. У меня́ уже́ есть друг, Стив Дже́ксон. Он студе́нт Джорджта́унского университе́та. Мы с ним познако́мились в библиоте́ке Конгре́сса.

I think | difficult

Стив—бу́дущий экономи́ст. У него́ в програ́мме 4 ку́рса: матема́тика, стати́стика, эконо́мика и компью́тер. По-мо́ему◊, э́то так тру́дно◊ и неинтере́сно!

parents

Да, я забы́ла тебе́ сказа́ть, что я тут де́лаю. Я записа́лась на 5 ку́рсов: америка́нская исто́рия (э́то интере́сно), поли́тика (э́то о́чень тру́дно), англи́йский, литерату́ра и социоло́гия.▲ В воскресе́нье мы (Стив и я) бы́ли в Нью-Йо́рке, там живу́т роди́тели◊ Сти́ва. Они́ о́чень симпати́чные. И па́па, и ма́ма – ветерина́ры. У них до́ма 3 соба́ки и 2 ко́шки.

▲ This statement might be confusing to a Russian university student. Russian students' university curricula are pre-set, depending on the department they have been accepted to. Students do not select and sign up for each individual course.

Слу́шай, у меня́ к тебе́ больша́я про́сьба◊. У Сти́ва
есть брат Ке́вин и сестра́ Мэ́ри. Она́—бизнесме́н. Ке́вин—
профессиона́льный фото́граф. Его́ фотогра́фии да́же
печа́тают◊ в журна́лах «Тайм», «Ньюс Уик» и «Пипл».
Ке́вин непло́хо говори́т по-ру́сски. Он учи́л ру́сский язы́к в
Мэриле́ндском университе́те. Он живёт в Вашингто́не.

Ке́вин хо́чет пое́хать в Москву́. Он плани́рует де́лать
фотоальбо́м о Росси́и. Он бу́дет в Росси́и май, ию́нь, ию́ль и
а́вгуст. Он хо́чет жить, в основно́м, в Москве́, но пое́хать в
Звени́город, Псков и Но́вгород. В Москве́ он хо́чет жить не
в гости́нице, а в кварти́ре, э́то не так до́рого. Е́сли мо́жно,
помоги́◊ Ке́вину найти́◊ кварти́ру и вообще́ помоги́ ему́.

Обнима́ю◊,

Да́ша.

request

are published

help | find

Love (in this context)

1. Scan the letter for the following information.

   Who wrote the letter? _____ Dawa _____.

   Where did the letter come from? ___ Maryland ___.

   When was it written? ___ December ___.

   What university does Та́ня's friend go to? ___ ~~Mary~~ UMaryland ___.

2. Now read through the first paragraph.

   A. Determine:

      the university where Да́ша's friend studies: _____

      what her friend's first name is: _____

      what her friend's last name is: _____

B. The person mentioned in the second paragraph is studying to be an economist. Who is it?

☐ Да́ша   ☐ Стив   ☐ Ке́вин

C. In order to become an economist he has to take many different courses. Can you name some of them?

_____

3. Now read through the third paragraph.

What did you find out about Стив's parents?

_____

How many pets do they have at home? _____

Do you think it has anything to do with the Jacksons' professions? _____

How many courses is Да́ша taking? _____

Can you name the course she likes? _____

4. Now read through the fourth paragraph.

Try to answer the following questions:

What is Стив's sister's occupation? _____.

Who is Ке́вин? _____.

What is his occupation? _____.

Which university did Ке́вин attend? _____.

Where does he live? _____.

5. Now read through the fifth paragraph.

Write down when Ке́вин is planning to be in Russia.

_____

Name the cities Кéвин would like to visit in Russia.

_____

_____

6. A. You also found out that Кéвин is going to Russia because:

    ☐ He loves Russian music.

    ☐ He wants to create a photo album of Russia.

    ☐ He is unemployed and looking for a job.

    ☐ He wants to master the Russian language.

B. How long is Кéвин planning to stay in Russia?

    ☐ four months

    ☐ indefinitely

    ☐ a year

    ☐ two weeks

Video Review

1. Imagine that you are the director of this video. Divide the video into two parts and give each part a title. First write it in English and then in Russian.

a. _____

b. _____

2. Do you remember what luggage Ке́вин brought with him to Moscow? Name each item in Russian.

a. _____   c. _____

b. _____   d. _____

3. Do you remember what places they saw on their way home from the airport? List them below.

_____

_____

4. Practicing pronunciation

чемода́н фотоаппара́т

рестора́н гости́ница

кинотеа́тр словарь

PART I. Аэропо́рт

VIEWING

5. Put the mini-episode titles from Part 1 of the video in order.

Ма́ша meets Ната́ша _____9_____

Helping a stranger _____3_____

Ке́вин meets Серге́й _____6_____

Identifying luggage _____2_____

Ке́вин meets Та́ня _____1_____

6. A. Here is a transcription of the first conversation between Ке́вин and Та́ня, only the lines are mixed up. Put them in order. When you finish, act out the conversation with your partner.

— О́чень прия́тно. _____

— Да. _____

— Здра́вствуйте, я Ке́вин. _____

— Вы Та́ня? _____

— О́чень прия́тно. _____

B. Try the same thing with the dialog between Ната́ша and Ма́ша.

— Да. О́чень прия́тно. _____

— Да. А вы Ма́ша? _____

— О́чень прия́тно. _____

— Здра́вствуйте. Вы – Ната́ша? _____

7. Below you see the script of the episode in which Кéвин identifies his luggage. Fill in the blanks as you are listening to the video.

Тáня: — Кéвин, где _____ багáж?

Кéвин: — Вот он.

Тáня: — Так, чемодáн тут, _____ тут…

Кéвин: — Но э́то не _____ сýмка!

Тáня: — Не _____?! Извинúте, э́то не вáша сýмка?

Натáша: — Да, моя́. Спасúбо!

Тáня: Кéвин, а чемодáн _____?

Кéвин: Чемодáн мой. И рюкзáк тóже мой.

Тáня: Э́то всё?

Кéвин: А где _____ фотоаппарáт?

Тáня: Фотоаппарáт? Где же фотоаппарáт?! А, вот _____!

Кéвин: Спасúбо, Тáня!

Тáня: Пожáлуйста!

8. You have been to the airport so many times now that you must be an expert on finding things there! Answer the following questions from the next mini-episode yourself. Then read the dialog you have written together with a partner.

— Извинúте, где тут туалéт?

— _____.

— А кафé там?

— _____.

PART II. МОСКВА

9. Once again, we are going to go for a spin around Moscow
with Ке́вин, Та́ня, and Серге́й. Fill in the missing words in
the dialog while you are watching Part II of the video.

Та́ня: — Это на́ша Москва́.

Ке́вин: — Это стадио́н?

Та́ня: — Да, это стадио́н.

Ке́вин: — А это парк?

Та́ня: — Да, ___Это___ парк.

Ке́вин: — Как краси́во!

Та́ня: — Ке́вин, а это ___что___?

Ке́вин: — Это Кремль.▲

Ке́вин: — Та́ня, что это?

Та́ня: — Это музе́й.

Ке́вин: — И это ___музей___?

Та́ня: — Нет. Это библиоте́ка.

Ке́вин: — А это метро́?

Та́ня: — Да, метро́.
    ___Метро___ Пу́шкинская.

Ке́вин: — А что это?

Та́ня: — Это кинотеа́тр.

Ке́вин: — Ой, Макдо́налдс!

Серге́й: — Да, это ___ВАШ___ Макдо́налдс.

Ке́вин: — Кто это?

Та́ня: — Это Пу́шкин.

Ке́вин: — А, Пу́шкин! Он поэ́т, да?

▲ The word Kremlin literally means fortress. Many old Russian cities have their own Kremlins as their centers;
behind the Kremlin walls, you will find an ensemble of churches, palaces, and government buildings.

Та́ня:	— Да, ~~поэт~~ _поэт_ и писа́тель. А э́то у́лица Тверска́я. Тут то́лько магази́ны.
Серге́й:	— А вот банк, и э́то банк, ба́нки, _ба́нки_, ба́нки…
Та́ня:	— Э́то телегра́ф.
Ке́вин:	— А э́то теа́тр?
Та́ня:	— Да, э́то _теа́тр_.
Ке́вин:	— А что э́то?
Та́ня:	— Э́то гости́ница.
Ке́вин:	— Э́то кто?
Та́ня:	— Э́то Че́хов.
Ке́вин:	— Э́то ваш писа́тель?
Та́ня:	— Да, э́то _наш_ писа́тель.

10. Asking for directions

You are in St. Petersburg and need to find out how to get to different places. Ask passers-by for directions.

> — Извини́те, где тут **стадио́н**?
> — **Стадио́н**? Вон там.
> — Спаси́бо.
> — Пожа́луйста.

[
hotel, theater, hospital, movie theater, restaurant "Cosmos", metro
]

11. Talking about family members and their professions

You are looking at pictures of your family with a friend. Read the following dialogs aloud with your partner, then act out similar dialogs about your own parents.

— Э́то твоя́ сестра́?
— Нет, э́то моя́ ма́ма.
— Ма́ма? А кто она́?
— Она́ **врач**.
— И па́па **врач**?
— Нет, он **учи́тель**.

— Э́то твой брат?
— Нет, э́то мой па́па.
— Па́па? А кто он?
— Он **инжепер**.
— И ма́ма **инжене́р**?
— Нет, она́ **учи́тельница**.

1

1. Using the telephone

   A. Dictate your phone numbers to each other. Write them down. And then dictate them back. Check to see if you got them right.

   B. Sometimes it's hard to distinguish voices over the phone, especially in Russia, where the phone lines can be a little tricky. Divide into pairs and call each other on the phone. Substitute your own names for the ones in the model. Exaggerate your intonation a little so that the person on the other end of the line can understand you.

   > Сергéй: — Алло, Таня? Это ты?
   >
   > Тáня: — Да, я.
   >
   > Сергéй: — Здравствуй, это Сергей.
   >
   > Тáня: — Кто?
   >
   > Сергéй: — Сергей.
   >
   > Тáня: — Здравствуй, Сергéй.

   C. Read this conversation through with two other people, then act it out. Switch roles so that each person gets to play every part.

   > Борúс: — Алло, извините, это **Таня**?
   >
   > Óля: — Нет, это Óля. Таня!
   >
   > Тáня: — Алло.
   >
   > Борúс: — Таня, здравствуй, это Борис!

	3
Та́ня:	— Кто?
	2
Бори́с:	— Бори́с.
	2
Та́ня:	— Здра́вствуй, Бори́с!

D. Before leaving the house to meet Ке́вин, Серге́й called the airport in order to find out whether the plane was on time but got the wrong number. Act out similar phone conversations.

	2 3
Серге́й:	— Алло́! Э́то аэропо́рт?
	1 1 1 1
	— Нет, э́то не аэропо́рт. Э́то кварти́ра.
	2
Серге́й:	— Извини́те, пожа́луйста.
	2
	— Пожа́луйста.

university, theater, hotel, restaurant, movie theater, stadium, hospital, museum, library, institute, post office, store, school

2. Starting a conversation: introducing yourself

You are at a party at your Russian friend's house, and you meet a guest. Fill in the blanks in the following dialogs and act them out with your partner.

A. — _____!

    (say hello)

— Здра́вствуй!

— _____.

    (your name is …)

— А я Ната́ша/Оле́г.

— _____.

    (you are glad to meet her/him)

— Óчень прия́тно.

— _____.

(ask if s/he is a student)

— Нет, я ме́неджер.

— _____.

(say that you are a student)

Don't forget to begin the sentence with «А»

В. — _____.

(say hello)

— Здра́вствуй! Я Андре́й/Мари́на.

— _____.

(your name is …)

— _____.

(you are glad to meet her/him)

— Óчень прия́тно.

— _____.

(ask if s/he is a student)

— Да.

— _____.

(say that you too are a student)

Don't forget to begin the sentence with «И»

3. Expressing possession

Fill in the blanks and act out the conversations.

А. At the Lost and Found

— Э́то ва́ши ве́щи?

— Нет, не _____.

— Э́то _____ су́мка?

— Нет, не моя́.

— А где _____ су́мка?

— Вон _____. Вон там.

— Вот, пожа́луйста.

— Спаси́бо.

B. Looking at a family album

Олéг: — Вот _____ семья́.

Ната́ша: — Интере́сно! Э́то твоя́ ма́ма?

Олéг: — Нет, сестра́. Она́ журнали́стка.

Ната́ша: — Кто э́то?

Олéг: — Э́то _____ па́па.

Ната́ша: — А кто он?

Олéг: — Он программи́ст.

Ната́ша: — Э́то _____ брат?

Олéг: — Нет, друг. Он студéнт.

Ната́ша: — Спаси́бо.

Олéг: — Пожа́луйста.

4. Your room is a mess. Work with your partner to determine where your things are.

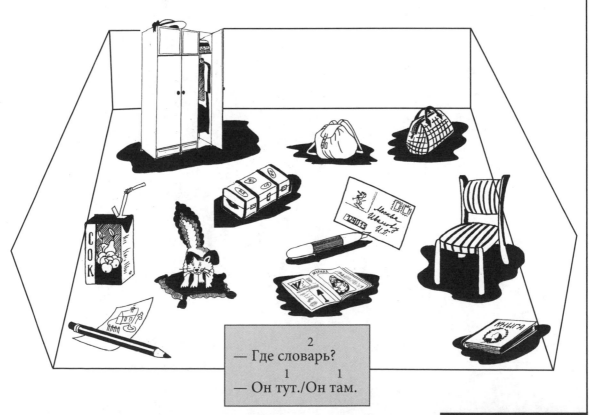

2
— Где словарь?
1   1
— Он тут./Он там.

5. Acting out typical situations in Russian

   A. You are trying to call a store (437-90-61) but get a wrong number. Apologize for your mistake. Make the conversation as long as possible, repeating information as it is often hard to hear the voice on the other end of the phone in Russia.

   B. You are at the airport with your brother or sister. Your luggage is all mixed up in a pile. Find out whose things are whose.

things, suitcase, backpack, bag

   C. While you are at your friend's house, you need to use the telephone. Find out where it is and ask if you may use it.

   D. Your Russian friend invites you over to her/his family's house for dinner. Act out a dialog in which you get acquainted with the family. Ask about the family members' occupations.

1. The Russian Sentence

The basic components of the Russian sentence are *subject* and *predicate*. The subject of a sentence is usually a noun, noun phrase (i.e. a noun with modifiers or other subordinate words), pronoun, or the indeclinable introductory demonstrative это ("this/that is," "these/those are"). The predicate of a sentence may be a verb, a noun, a noun phrase, an adjective, or an adverb.

Sentence		
Subject	**Predicate**	**Translation**
Это	Кéвин.	This is Kevin.
Тáня	дóма. (adv.)	Tanya is at home.
Это	моя́ сýмка.	This/That is my bag.
Наш дом	там. (adv.)	Our house is over there.
Моя́ сестрá	студéнтка.	My sister is a college student.

Note that Russian has no articles.

2. "To Be" in Russian

In Russian sentences like those above, the link verb (the Russian equivalent of "to be") is absent in the present tense. Any sentence missing an overt verb may be translated using the simple "am", "are", or "is" form of the verb "to be". This form in Russian is sometimes referred to as the "zero-form", as it stands in contrast to the past and future tenses of "to be", which are never omitted:

Тáня дóма.	Tanya *is* at home.
Тáня **былá** дóма.[1]	Tanya *was* at home.
Тáня **бýдет** дóма.[1]	Tanya *will be* at home.

3. Word Structure

Russian is an inflected language; therefore, within each word we can distinguish the unchangeable part of the word (*stem*) from the changeable part (ending). Compare these two forms of the word Москвá ("Moscow").

---

[1] See Analyses IV and VI, respectively.

Э́то Москва́.   Москв + а
"This is Moscow."   (stem) + (ending)

В Москву́!   Москв + у
"To Moscow!"   (stem) + (ending)

Note the division of the following words into stems and endings.

окно́ "window"   окн + о
ма́ма "mama"   мам + а

Within the stem of a word one may further distinguish a *root*, which contains the basic meaning of a word. The root may or may not be accompanied by prefixes or suffixes. Since the kernel of every Russian word is the root, and one root may produce as many as dozens of related words, the recognition of roots is extremely helpful for word analysis and practical word-building.

4. Gender of Nouns in the Nominative Case

All Russian nouns belong to one of three grammatical classes called *genders*: masculine, neuter, or feminine. In the *nominative case* (i.e. the usual form of the sentence subject and the form in which nouns are given in all dictionaries), gender is indicated by one of three possible endings. Masculine nouns end in "zero" -ø[2] (spelled –ь after a soft consonant), neuter nouns end in –о (spelled -е after a soft consonant), and feminine nouns end in -а (spelled –я after a soft consonant). Study the gender endings of each of the following nouns:

Sentence				
Gender	**Ending**	**Examples**		
m.	-ø (-ь)	hard stem[3]	+ ø	магази́н
		soft stem	+ ь	слова́рь
n.	-о (-е[4])	hard stem	+ о	окно́
		soft stem	+ е	мо́ре
f.	-а (-я)	hard stem	+ а	ка́рта
		soft stem	+ я	тётя

---

[2] Nominative Singular of Nouns: ø stands for "zero"; the absence of an overt ending is a signal of the same order as the presence of such endings as –о and –а.

[3] A hard stem ends in a hard consonant, a soft stem ends in a soft consonant. A soft consonant followed by ø or another consonant is marked in Cyrillic by the soft sign «ь»: слова́рь /слава́рʲ/

[4] The two dots over the letter ё (е dieresis), which spells о after a soft consonant, is only written when it is stressed. Otherwise, the two dots are omitted and the letter is spelled as е.

5. Nominative Plural of Nouns

		Sentence		
Gender	Ending	Singular	Ending	Plural
m. f.	-ø (-ь) -a (-я)	магази́н, слова́рь ка́рта, тётя	-ы (-и) -ы (-и)	магази́ны, словари́ ка́рты, тёти
n.	-o (-е)	окно́, мо́ре	-a (-я)	о́кна, моря́

To form the nominative plural of all nouns ending in **-a** (-**я**) and of most nouns in **-ø** (-**ь**), the nominative singular ending is replaced by **-ы** (-**и**). The nominative plural of neuter nouns is formed by replacing the nominative singular ending with **-a** (-**я**).

6. Special Spelling Rules in Russian

While the choice of vowel letters (**ы** vs. **и**, **a** vs. **я**, etc.) In the spelling of most Russian words is determined exclusively by the hardness or softness of the preceding consonant, there are three situations in Russian when there is no choice. Two of the three situations requiring special rules have already arisen in the course of Unit I and need to be reviewed and learned immediately.

RULE One: AFTER **к** and **г**, as well as **ш** and **ж**[5], only **и** is spelled (never **ы**).

RULE Two: AFTER **ш**, **ж**, **ч**, **щ**, and **ц** in the endings of nouns and modifiers, the letter **o** may be written only if it is stressed; otherwise the letter **e** is used.

Examples: Since the pair **ы/и** pluralizes masculine and feminine nouns, you should be aware of the operation of Rule One in cases such as the plural of feminine nouns ending in –**ка**, of which there are thousands of examples in Russian.

Sing.	Plural
ру́чка	ру́чки
кни́га	кни́ги
парк	па́рки
каранда́ш	карандаши́[6]
нож	ножи́

You have already encountered examples of the stressed **o** rule after **ш**. The word **хорошо́** is spelled the way it is because of the stress on the final syllable. The neuter form of **на́ше**, on the other hand, is stem-stressed, hence the final **o** is spelled **e** (Rule Two). Note the operation of Rule One in the spelling of the plural form **на́ши** as well.

хорошо́   but: наш, на́ша, на́ше, на́ши

---

[5] **ч**, **щ** as well as **x** will be added to the rule later in the semester.

[6] The spelling convention does not affect the pronunciation of the vowel after the two unpaired hard consonants **ж** and **ш**: ножи́ /нажы́/, карандаши́ /карандашы́/, на́ши /на́шы/

7. Use of the Pronouns: он, она́, оно́, они́

Nouns of any gender may be replaced by the corresponding personal pronouns.

Nominative Case of Pronouns			
Gender	Noun	Pronoun	Examples
m. n. f.	дом окно́ су́мка	он оно́ она́	Э́то дом. **Он** тут. Э́то окно́. **Оно́** тут. Э́то су́мка. **Она́** тут.
pl.	газе́ты о́кна	они́ они́	Э́то газе́ты. **Они́** тут. Э́то о́кна. **Они́** тут.

Note that pronouns in the singular reflect the grammatical gender of their antecedent (i.e. the noun to which they refer), whether referring to animate beings or to inanimate objects. In the plural (**они́**) gender is not reflected. Compare the following examples in Russian and in English:

Э́то университе́т. **Он** там.	This is a university. *It* is over there.
Э́то студе́нт. **Он** тут.	This is a student. *He* is here.
Э́то ма́ма. **Она́** тут.	This is mom. *She* is here.
Э́то окно́. **Оно́** тут.	This is a window. *It* is here.
Э́то газе́ты. **Они́** тут.	These are newspapers. *They* are here.
Э́то о́кна. **Они́** тут.	These are windows. *They* are here.

8. Second Person Pronouns

The second person singular pronoun **ты** is used by Russians when addressing relatives, children, intimate friends, and animals. The second person plural form **вы** is the normal, polite way of addressing one person, and is the only way of addressing two or more persons.

9. Possessive Pronouns in the Nominative Case: мой, твой, наш, ваш

The forms of the possessive pronouns are as follows:

> **мой** "my", **твой** "your", **наш** "our", **ваш** "your".

Adjectives and most pronouns change their form in accordance with the gender of the noun which they accompany or replace. This adaptation of one word to reflect grammatically the form of another is called *agreement*. The word which dictates the form is called the *head word* and the word which agrees with it is a *modifier*.

Note how each of the following possessive pronouns changes form according to the gender of the head word.

Agreement of Possessive Pronouns			
Gender	Endings	Examples	
		"my"	"our"
m.	**-ø** (-ь)	мой дом	наш дом
n.	**-о** (-е)	моё окно́	на́ше окно́
f.	**-а** (-я)	моя́ кни́га	на́ша кни́га
pl.	**-ы** (-и)	мои́ газе́ты	на́ши газе́ты
		мои́ о́кна	на́ши о́кна

Твой follows the same pattern as **мой**; **ваш** is similar to **наш**.

10. The Interrogative Pronoun кто

Unlike in English, the interrogative pronoun **кто** "who" is used not only with respect to people but all members of the animal kingdom.

— Кто э́то?   What is that?
— Э́то ко́шка.   That is a cat.

11. Word Order

On the communicative level, the simple Russian sentence may be divided into two parts: old information (the *theme*) and new information (the *rheme*). The general rule for normal (non-emphatic) word order in statements is *theme* + *rheme*. In other words, the new information is normally placed at the end.

Now examine the word order in the replies to the following questions and compare it with the English word order. Note that the old information (in parentheses) may be omitted in the answer.

— Где Та́ня?   Where is Tanya?
— (Та́ня) тут.   Tanya is here.
A: *theme*   *rheme*

— Кто Ми́ша?   What does Misha do?
— (Ми́ша) — ветерина́р.   Misha is a veterinarian.
A: *theme*   *rheme*

The intonational center coincides with the new information. Compare:

            3
— Э́то <u>ва́ша</u> су́мка?
        rheme
    1   1   1   1
— Да, э́то <u>моя́</u> су́мка. (Да, моя́.)
        rheme

            3
— Э́то ва́ша су́мка?
        rheme
        1 1   1 1
— Да, <u>э́то</u> моя́ су́мка. (Да, э́то.)
        rheme

12. Adverbs of Place

Locations may be expressed with the help of such adverbs of place as **тут** "here", **там** "there", **дома** "at home", and **где** "where".

— Где Кéвин?	Where is Kevin?
— Кéвин тут.	Kevin is here.
— Где Тáня?	Where is Tanya?
— Тáня дóма.	Tanya is at home.

13. Masculine Nouns Ending in –a

A few nouns denoting male persons end in **–a** (**-я**). This group includes the nouns **пáпа** "daddy", **дéдушка** "grandfather", **дя́дя** "uncle", and also a large number of diminutives of masculine first names, such as **Вáня** from **Ивáн**, **Ди́ма** from **Дми́трий**, and **Волóдя** from **Влади́мир**.

These nouns require masculine modifiers.

мой дя́дя	"my uncle"
наш дéдушка	"our grandfather"

14. Profession

Some masculine nouns denoting a person's profession, trade, occupation, etc., may refer to female as well as male members of that profession, trade, etc.

Ми́ша ветеринáр, и Натáша ветеринáр.	Misha is a veterinarian, and Natasha is a veterinarian.

15. Russian Phonetics: Pronunciation Rules

A. THE RUSSIAN WRITING SYSTEM

The Russian Cyrillic alphabet consists of 33 letters representing a total of 41 basic sounds: 36 consonantal sounds and five vowel sounds. As you have now seen, the five vowels are represented by two separate sets of vowel letters, one following a hard consonant, the other following a soft consonant:

"Hard"	а	о	у	э	ы
"Soft"	я	ё	ю	е	и

There are fifteen pairs of consonants in Russian, one hard and one soft in each pair:

п—п^{b}	б—б^{b}	м—м^{b}
т—т^{b}	д—д^{b}	н—н^{b}
ф—ф^{b}	в—в^{b}	л—л^{b}
с—с^{b}	з—з^{b}	р—р^{b}
к—к^{b}	г—г^{b}	
х—х^{b}		

Analyze the following sets of words to make sure that the spelling and pronunciation of hard and soft consonants is clear in every case:

Hard consonants			Soft consonants		
ток	/ток /	"current"	тёк	/т^ьок/	"was flowing"
тук	/тук/	"knocking sound"	тюк	/т^ьук/	"sack"
лук	/лук/	"onion"	люк	/л^ьук/	"manhole"

When a soft consonant is not followed by a vowel sound, softness is indicated by the purely graphic symbol "**ь**", which has no other phonetic value:

словáрь	/славáр^ь/	"dictionary"
письмó	/п^ьис^ьмó/	"letter"

There are six consonantal sounds in Russian which are not paired; three are always hard and three are always soft:

ш, ж, ц are hard;
and ч, щ, й are soft[7].

Note that the Russian alphabet has just one letter for both the hard and the soft consonant.

The spelling of the soft consonant /й/ (often called yot) takes several forms, depending on the environment in which the sound occurs. At the end of a word or before a consonant it is spelled **й** (called "i kratkoe" in Russian, or short i). When followed by a vowel, yot is spelled as a single letter together with the vowel, using the second row of the two-row vowel chart shown above. Hence, the Cyrillic form **я** when standing alone represents **й**+**a** and means "I". Study the examples analyzed below.

Я ем.	/й+а/ /й+е+м/	"I am eating."
май	/м+а+й/	"May" (month)
юрист	/йур^ьист/	"lawyer"
каюта	/кайута/	"cabin"

Note that **и** does not spell yot in the beginning of a word:

институт   /инст^ьитут/

A soft consonant followed by a yot is not an uncommon occurrence in Russian words. For example, in the end of the word семья "family", **м^ь+й+a** are each pronounced as distinctive sounds. This cluster is worth mastering early on in your study of Russian. Here are a few further examples of the pattern:

статья	/стат^ь+й+á/	"article"
пьéса	/п^ь+й+éса/	"play"

---

[7] Since **ч**, **щ**, and **й** are <u>always</u> soft, this softness is not marked in phonetic transcriptions: **я** /й+а/.

B. PHONETIC RULES

The Russian alphabet does not exactly conform to the principle of one symbol for one sound. As you will learn, however, it is possible to pronounce almost any Russian word you read correctly by applying a small set of phonetic rules, most of which we have already encountered. To assist you in learning the phonetic rules, this text makes use of standard Russian phonetic transcription, Cyrillic symbols set off between slashmarks /.. /, to prompt you concerning the phonetic rules which cause the pronunciation of a word to differ from the written form of the word.

There are two basic types of phonetic rules; one affects the pronunciation of vowels, the other the pronunciation of consonants.

Vowel Reduction. When a Russian vowel is not stressed, it undergoes both qualitative and quantitative changes. These rules are very simple to summarize and relatively easy to make automatic in your own pronunciation of Russian

After a hard consonant, the vowels /a/ and /o/ change to /а/.

она́ /ана́/	газе́та /газ^ье́та/
окно́ /акно́/	молоко́ /малако́/

After a soft consonant, the vowels /e/ and /a/ (spelled as я) change to /и/.

а́дрес /а́др^ьис/	теа́тр /т^ьиа́тр/
де́вять /д^ье́в^ьит^ь/	де́сять /д^ье́с^ьит^ь/

Devoicing/Voicing Consonants. There are 11 pairs of voiced and voiceless consonant sounds in Russian:

Voiceless	Voiced
п	б
п^ь	б^ь
ф	в
ф^ь	в^ь
с	з
с^ь	з^ь
т	д
т^ь	д^ь
ш	ж
к	г
к^ь	г^ь

The most important consonant rule in Russian phonetics states that any voiced consonant will be pronounced voiceless when it is at the end of a word. This phonetic change is not reflected in the spelling of the word.

друг	/друк/
го́род	/го́рат/
муж	/муш/

The Consonant Cluster Rule. When a cluster of consonants (two or more) occurs in a Russian word, the voicing of the final voiced or voiceless element in the cluster determines the voicing of the whole cluster.

во́дка	/во́тка/	д → т before к
ло́жка	/ло́шка/	ж → ш before к
рюкза́к	/рʲугза́к/	к → г before з

There is only one exception to this rule: the voiced consonant pair /в - вʲ/, which devoices to /ф - фʲ/, but does not itself condition voicing of a preceding unvoiced consonant.

авто́бус	/афто́бус/
до свида́ния	/дасвʲида́нʲийа/

These two rules do not apply to the voiced consonants which lack voiceless counterparts: /м, мʲ, л, лʲ, н, нʲ, р, рʲ, й/.

NOUNS

авто́бус bus
а́дрес address
актёр actor
актри́са actress
антропо́лог anthropologist
аэропо́рт airport
бага́ж (sg. only) luggage
бана́н banana
банк bank
бар bar
библиоте́ка library
бизнесме́н businessperson
био́лог biologist
больни́ца hospital
брат brother
бухга́лтер bookkeeper,
    accountant
ветерина́р veterinarian
ве́щи (pl.) things
видеока́мера video camera
ви́за visa
врач (pl. врачи́) doctor
газе́та newspaper
га́мбургер hamburger
гара́ж (pl. гаражи́) garage
гео́лог geologist
гита́ра guitar
голова́ head
гори́лла gorilla
го́род city
гости́ница hotel
день day
джи́нсы jeans
дом house, building
доска́ board
друг male friend
дя́дя uncle
жена́ wife
журна́л magazine
журнали́ст journalist (male)
журнали́стка journalist
    (female)
инжене́р engineer
институ́т institute
исто́рик historian
каранда́ш (pl. карандаши́)
    pencil

ка́рта map
кафе́ (indecl.) cafe
кварти́ра apartment
кинотеа́тр movie theater
кни́га book
ко́ка-ко́ла Coca-cola
ко́мната room
компью́тер computer
ко́рпус building
костю́м suit
ко́шка cat
ку́ртка jacket
ла́мпа lamp
лимузи́н limousine
магази́н store
ма́ма mom
матема́тик mathematician
маши́на car
ме́неджер manager
метро́ (indecl.) metro, subway
молоко́ milk
мо́ре sea
муж husband
музе́й museum
нож (pl. ножи́) knife
но́мер number
нос (pl. носы́) nose
о́вощ vegetable
окно́ (pl. о́кна) window
официа́нт waiter
официа́нтка waitress
паке́т here: plastic bag
па́па dad
парк park
па́спорт passport
певе́ц (pl. певцы́) singer
    (male)
певи́ца singer (female)
пингви́н penguin
писа́тель writer
писа́тельница writer (female)
письмо́ (pl. пи́сьма) letter
пи́цца pizza
подру́га female friend
по́чта post office
поэ́т poet
преподава́тель university
    instructor (male)

преподава́тельница
    university instructor
    (female)
программи́ст programmer
продаве́ц (pl. продавцы́)
    salesperson (male)
продавщи́ца salesperson
    (female)
психо́лог psychologist
restoráн restaurant
ру́чка pen
рюкза́к (pl. рюкзаки́)
    backpack
са́хар sugar
сви́тер sweater
семья́ family
сестра́ (pl. сёстры) sister
слова́рь (pl. словари́)
    dictionary
сло́во word
слон (pl. слоны́) elephant
соба́ка dog
сок juice
спорт (sg. only) sport
стадио́н stadium
стол (pl. столы́) table
студе́нт university student
    (male)
студе́нтка university student
    (female)
стул chair
су́мка bag, purse
суп soup
сын son
сыр cheese
такси́ (indecl., neut.) taxi
теа́тр theater
телефо́н telephone
тётя aunt
тигр tiger
тролле́йбус trolley bus
туале́т restroom
у́лица street
университе́т university
у́хо ear
уче́бник textbook
учи́тель grade school teacher
    (male)

учи́тельница grade school teacher (female)
фи́зик physicist
фотоаппара́т camera
фото́граф photographer
фрукт fruit
хи́мик chemist
хлеб bread
центр downtown
чай tea
чемода́н suitcase
шко́ла grade school
шко́льник grade school student (male)
шко́льница grade school student (female)
шокола́д chocolate
экономи́ст economist
юри́ст lawyer

PROPER NOUNS

Арха́нгельск Arkhangelsk
Байка́л Lake Baikal
Во́лга the Volga river
Волгогра́д Volgograd (city in Russia)
Воро́неж Voronezh (city in Russia)
Голливу́д Hollywood
Джорджта́ун Georgetown
Ко́лледж парк College Park
Кострома́ Kostroma (city in Russia)
Кремль Kremlin
Макдо́налдс McDonald's
Москва́ Moscow (capital of Russia)
Но́вгород Novgorod (city in Russia)
Новосиби́рск Novosibirsk (city in Russia)
Нью-Йо́рк New York

Псков Pskov (city in Russia)
Росси́я Russia
Росто́в (city in Russia)
Санкт-Петербу́рг St. Petersburg
Сахали́н Sakhalin (island)
Ура́л the Ural mountains

PRONOUNS

ваш, ва́ша, ва́ше, ва́ши your (s)
всё everything
вы you
кто who
мой, моя́, моё, мои́ my, mine
мы we
наш, на́ша, на́ше, на́ши our (s)
он he, it
она́ she
оно́ it
они́ they
твой, твоя́, твоё, твои́ your (s)
ты you
что what
э́то this/these (is/are)
я I

ADVERBS

где where
здесь here
краси́во beautiful
отли́чно excellent
о́чень very
там there
тут here

NUMERALS

ноль zero
оди́н one

два two
три three
четы́ре four
пять five
шесть six
семь seven
во́семь eight
де́вять nine
де́сять ten
раз one (when counting)

CONJUNCTIONS

а and, but
и and

PARTICLES

вон (over) there
вот here (is/are)
не not

EXPRESSIONS

алло́ hello (on the telephone)
да yes
до свида́ния goodbye
здра́вствуйте, здра́вствуй hello
извини́те (извини́) I'm sorry, excuse (me)
Как интере́сно! How interesting!
Мо́жно … ? May I … ?
Нет no
Ой! Oh! Ouch!
О́чень прия́тно. Very nice (to meet you).
пожа́луйста please; go ahead; that's OK; you're welcome
пра́вда (in this case) really
спаси́бо thank you
так so

Кто здесь
живёт?

*K*evin and Tanya make their way to his new apartment
in Moscow. Tanya helps him get settled in by showing him
around the apartment.

You will learn how to:

- Describe a typical Russian apartment
- Identify things in the kitchen
- Address someone with the formal as well as informal "you"
- Express location
- Describe your daily schedule
- Talk about where people live
- Discuss jobs and vacations
- Express negation using verbs
- Ask "whose is this"
- Ask for information politely
- Talk about eating meals
- Talk about different languages and nationalities
- Express curiosity
- Disagree with someone
- Ask alternative questions
- Describe your apartment or house

▶ In just a minute, you are going to watch the second part of the adventures of Táня and Кévин.

PREviewing

1. As you remember from the first episode, this is the building where Кévин is staying. Next to it is a picture of Кévин's apartment. Using the pictures above, write down Кévин's address.▲

▲ Russians write addresses the reverse of how Americans write addresses. For example: RUSSIA, Moscow 345678 (zip code), street name, building number, apartment number, name of addressee.

2. Take a closer look at the sign above the entrance to Ке́вин's building.

подъе́зд /падйе́ст/ = entrance

The number of the **подъе́зд** is very important since Russian buildings with the same address have many entrances, each leading to a different set of apartments.

Where do you think apartment 200 would be located in this building? _____

▶ Watch the video with the SOUND OFF.

SOUND OFF

Like Ке́вин, you will find some surprises inside the apartment. Keep your eyes open and see if you can spot some differences in the following areas: apartment size, layout, interior, furniture, electronics, and food.

3. A. At the beginning of the episode Та́ня is looking for:

☒ apartment keys
☐ her address book
☐ her wallet

B. Ке́вин's new apartment▲ can be classified as a:

☐ studio apartment
☐ two-room apartment
☒ three-room apartment

▲ When describing an apartment, Russians refer to the total number of rooms (kitchen and bathroom are not counted as separate rooms), not to the number of bedrooms like Americans do.

C. Identify the rooms you see in the apartment.

☐ family room ☐ dining room

☒ living room ☒ bathroom

☐ study ☐ bedroom

☐ half bath ☒ kitchen

☐ master bedroom

D. It seems the apartment is already furnished. What are some things that you see there?

☐ стол ☐ дива́н ☐ кре́сло

☐ ла́мпа ☐ телеви́зор ☐ сту́л

☐ телефо́н ☐ компью́тер ☐ ра́дио

> дива́н = couch
>
> кре́сло = armchair

E. What is Та́ня doing in the kitchen?

☐ cleaning up

☒ fixing food

☐ dancing

4. A. At the end of the episode, some visitors arrive at the apartment. Can you guess who these people are?

☐ the neighbors

☒ the owners of the apartment

☐ Та́ня's friends

B. How do Ке́вин and the visitors react to each other? They are:

☒ puzzled

☐ happy

☐ indifferent

▶ Watch the video with the SOUND ON.

SOUND ON

Read through the following questions and answer as much as you can before you watch the video with the sound on. Finish answering the questions while you watch.

5. Та́ня has problems with the lock. What does Ке́вин say when he offers to help her?

_____ ?

6. A. Mark off the rooms as you hear them named.

- ☐ ку́хня
- ☐ туале́т
- ☐ ва́нная
- ☐ гости́ная
- ☐ спа́льня
- ☐ столо́вая

B. When they are looking around in the apartment, Ке́вин asks Та́ня:

- ☐ where the nearest grocery store is located
- ☐ when the rent is due
- ☐ who lives in this apartment

C. Та́ня picks up a picture of the family that lives in the apartment. Check off the family members as she identifies them.

- ☐ па́па
- ☐ сын
- ☐ ма́ма
- ☐ до́чка

D. Ке́вин and Та́ня look into one of the bedrooms. How does Та́ня know that this room is a boy's room?

- ☐ It's messy.
- ☐ There are only toys that a boy would play with.
- ☐ His picture is hanging on the wall.

E. Та́ня has lost something again! What is she looking for?

- ☐ фотоаппара́т
- ☐ паке́т
- ☐ рюкза́к

паке́т = plastic bag

7. A. Та́ня names the food items that she brought as she pulls them out of the bag; match them with their English definitions.

хлеб	butter
ма́сло	tomatoes
помидо́ры	salami/sausage
колбаса́	bread

B. What does Ке́вин think of the sandwiches?

- ☐ He likes them.
- ☐ He doesn't even try them.
- ☐ He throws them in the trash.

C. Since **чай** means tea, what does **ча́йник** mean?

☐ tea bag

☑ teakettle

☐ tea store

D. Looking out of the window, Ке́вин tries to identify different sights. Which ones does Ке́вин discuss with Та́ня?

☐ Кремль

☐ институ́т

☐ стадио́н

E. Before Та́ня leaves, what does she write down and hand to Ке́вин?

☑ her phone number and address

☐ Ке́вин's security code

☐ the landlord's phone number

Did you notice that when Та́ня and Ке́вин first meet at the airport, they use the polite form of address, **«вы»**? However, once they become more comfortable with each other, Та́ня suggests that they use the friendly form of address, **«ты»**. She says:

Ке́вин, дава́йте на «ты». = Ке́вин, let's use **«ты»**.

8. Video wrap-up: mini-episode titles

Now you have seen the entire second episode. We have divided the episode into two parts and given them names in English. Can you translate these names into Russian?

Here is your apartment! _____

This is your kitchen. _____

9. Practicing pronunciation: IC-2

$$\overset{2}{\text{Где сыр?}} \quad \overset{2}{\text{Где кухня?}} \quad \overset{2}{\text{Где сумка?}}$$

$$\overset{2}{\text{Где хлеб?}} \quad \overset{2}{\text{Где нож?}}$$

$$\overset{2}{\text{Где бутерброд?}} \quad \overset{2}{\text{Где чайник?}}$$

Questions with a
question word are
pronounced with IC-2

сыр = cheese
нож = knife

10. Finding things in the kitchen

Imagine that you are at a friend's place and want to make sandwiches. You need to find the right ingredients. Match your questions with your friend's responses.

Где колбаса́?   Вот они́.

Где помидо́ры?   Вот она́.

Где хлеб?   Вот оно́.

Где ма́сло?   Вот он.

11. English equivalents

A. What does Ке́вин say when he offers to help Та́ня in the kitchen? _____ ?

B. How do Russians ask, "Who's there?" when someone is at the door? _____ ?

C. When Та́ня leaves, she says, «**До за́втра!**» which is another way of saying

_____

До свида́ния! До за́втра!

How to Express Location: The Prepositional Case

Та́ня в университе́т**е**. Та́ня is **at** the university.	Кни́га в су́мк**е**. The book is **in** the purse.

Location is expressed in Russian using the preposition **в** "in/at," plus a noun with the prepositional case ending, **-е**.

в + _____ **-е** (for all genders)

университе́т	**в** университе́т**е**
кварти́ра	**в** кварти́р**е**
письмо́	**в** письм**е́**

There is a very small group of nouns that take the preposition **на** instead of **в** to express location. There is no way to predict which nouns take **в** and which nouns take **на**: you must simply memorize them.

да́ча	**на** да́ч**е** = at the dacha
рабо́та	**на** рабо́т**е** = at work
ку́хня	**на** ку́хн**е** = in the kitchen
стадио́н	**на** стадио́н**е** = at the stadium
по́чта	**на** по́чт**е** = at the post office

да́ча = cottage

1. Practicing pronunciation: prepositional phrases

Remember to read the prepositional phrase as a single word.

рестора́н	**в рестора́не**
магази́н	**в магази́не**
университе́т	**в университе́те**
су́мка	**в су́мке**
кни́га	**в кни́ге**
письмо́	**в письме́**
больни́ца	**в больни́це**
гости́ница	**в гости́нице**
институ́т	**в институ́те**
рабо́та	**на рабо́те**

2. Где Та́ня?

Below are pictures of photos where Та́ня has been. Match each picture with the appropriate caption.

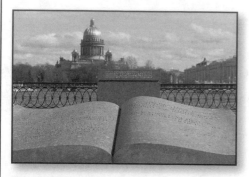

Э́то я в Петербу́рге.

Э́то я в Ташке́нте.▲

Э́то я в Пу́шкине. ▲

Э́то я на да́че.

Э́то я в Ки́еве.▲

Э́то я в Па́вловске. ▲

▲ Пу́шкин and Па́вловск are suburban towns near St. Petersburg. They are famous for their beautiful parks and magnificent palaces, which served as summer residences for the czars. Пу́шкин bears the name of the great Russian poet and writer; Па́вловск is named after the czar Paul (Па́вел) the First (1754–1801). Ки́ев is the capital of Ukraine. Ташке́нт is the capital of Uzbekistan.

3. Где Стив?

Your brother Стив is home, but he doesn't want to talk to anyone! When his friends call, cover for him by saying that he is somewhere else.

> — Стив дома?³
> — Нет¹
> — А где он?²
> — **В магазине.**¹

в библиотеке, в университете, в парке, на работе, в кафе, в театре, на стадионе, в институте

4. Профессор в холодильнике?

Everything is in the wrong place! Fix the sentences on the left by providing a more appropriate location for the subject.

Соль **в чае**.	Соль _в супе_ .
Сахар **в супе**.	Сахар _в чае_ .
Собаки **на работе**.	Собаки _на кухне_ .
Профессор **в холодильнике**.	Профессор _в библиотеке_ .
Машина **на кухне**.	Машина _____ .
Мама **в сумке**.	Мама _____ .
Кошка **в рюкзаке**.	Кошка _____ .
Молоко **в туалете**.	Молоко _____ .
Кремль **в Лос-Анжелесе**.	Кремль _____ .
Помидоры **в библиотеке**.	Помидоры _____ .

5. Finding your belongings

It seems that your mother is always moving your things around! Ask her where your things are.

> книга (рюкзак) → — Где моя **книга?**²
> — Она **в рюкзаке.**¹

$$\left[\begin{array}{l}\text{карандаши́ (рюкза́к), газе́та (паке́т), письмо́ (чемода́н),}\\\text{журна́л (су́мка), фотогра́фия (кни́га), уче́бники}\\\text{(маши́на), ру́чка (су́мка)}\end{array}\right.$$

6. Describing your schedule

Where do you usually spend your time in the mornings, afternoons, and evenings?

Weekdays:

Ýтром я _____ . Днём я _____ . Ве́чером я _____ .

Weekends:

_____

у́тром = in the
  morning
днём = in the
  afternoon
ве́чером = in
  the evening

$$\left[\begin{array}{l}\text{до́ма, в университе́те, на рабо́те, в библиоте́ке, в}\\\text{магази́не, на стадио́не, в па́рке, в ба́ре, в кафе́, в}\\\text{рестора́не, в кинотеа́тре, в музе́е}\end{array}\right.$$

| Та́ня живёт в Москве́. | Да́ша живёт в Ко́лледж Па́рке. |

In the present tense, Russian verbs agree with the subject in <u>person</u> (я, ты, он, etc.) and <u>number</u> (singular or plural).

The verb жить (жйв-) "live"

Present Tense

я живу́	мы живём
ты живёшь	вы живёте
он/она́ живёт	они́ живу́т

7. Pronunciation practice: the verb **жить**

А. я живу́, ты живёшь, он живёт,
мы живём, вы живёте, они́ живу́т

B. 1. Я живу́ здесь.

2. — Где ты живёшь?
   — Я живу́ в Детро́йте.

3. Да́ша живёт в Ко́лледж Па́рке.

4. Мы живём на да́че.

5. —Та́ня, где вы живёте?
   —Я живу́ в Москве́.

6. Мои́ роди́тели живу́т в Бо́стоне.

роди́тели = parents

8. Talking about where people live

A. Discuss where you, your family and your friends live.

> 1
> Та́ня живёт **в Москве**.

1. Я живу́ _____ .

2. Мой па́па живёт _____ .

3. Моя́ ма́ма живёт _____ .

4. Моя́ сестра́ _____ живёт _____ .
   (her name)

5. Мой брат _____ живёт _____ .
   (his name)

6. Моя́ подру́га _____ живёт _____ .
   (her name)

7. Мой друг _____ живёт _____ .
   (his name)

B. Discuss where you, your family and your friends live.

1. — Где живёт твоя́ подру́га?   — Она́ _____ .

2. — Где _____ твои́ роди́тели? — Они́ _____ .

3. — Где _____ твоя́ сестра́?   — Она́ _____ .

4. — Где _____ твой брат?   — Он _____ .

5. — Где _____ твой друг?   — Он _____ .

When the subject is a personal pronoun in questions with question words like **где**, it precedes the verb. When the subject is a noun, it follows the verb.

6. — Где ты _____ ?   — Я _____ .

7. — Где _____ твоя́ семья́?   — Мы _____ .

9. А где вы живёте?

This conversation might have taken place between Та́ня, Серге́й, and Ке́вин.

Notice the different intonation patterns when the response begins with **и** and **а**.

Та́ня: — Я живу́ в Москве́.^{1}

Се́ргей: — **И** я живу́^{1} в Москве́. (I live in Moscow, **too**.)

Ке́вин: — **А** я живу́ в Вашингтоне.^{1}

Где ты живёшь? Ask your partner.

> — Где ты живёшь?^{2}
>
> — Я живу́ **в Бо́стоне**.^{1}
>
> — **И** я живу́^{1} **в Бо́стоне**. /**А** я живу́ в Балтиморе.^{1}

Past Tense

In the past tense, Russian verbs agree with the subject in number (singular, plural) and gender (masculine, feminine, neuter). Note the stress shift pattern.

> он жил
> она́ жила́
> оно́ жи́ло
> они́ жи́ли

If there is a stress shift in the past tense form of the verb, it follows only this pattern.

10. А где он жил **ра́ньше?**

A. Let's talk about where people used to live. Fill in the correct form of the verb **жить** in the past tense and read the dialogs with a partner.

ра́ньше = previously, used to

> ¹
> — Ке́вин живёт в Москве́.
> ²
> — А где он **жил** ра́ньше?
> ¹
> — В Вашингто́не.

— Серге́й живёт в Москве́.   — Да́ша живёт в Аме́рике.

— А где он _____ ра́ньше?   — А где она́ _____ра́ньше?

— В Росто́ве.   — В Москве́.

— Я живу́ в Петербу́рге.   — Мы живём в Нью-Йо́рке.

— А где ты _____ ра́ньше?   — А где вы _____ ра́ньше?

— В Ки́еве.   — В Ло́ндоне.

B. Now talk about yourself. Where did you used to live?

> ²
> — Где ты жила́ ра́ньше?
> ¹
> — Ра́ньше я жила́ **в Балтимо́ре**.

▶ Today we will learn how to conjugate **-ай** stem verbs. This is the largest class of verbs in Russian. Once you learn this model, you will be able to conjugate thousands of Russian verbs.

рабо́тать (рабо́т**ай**-)
"to work"

отдыха́ть (отдых**а́й**-)
"to rest, vacation"

чита́ть (чит**а́й**-)
"to read"

гуля́ть (гул**я́й**-)
"to go for a walk"; "not to be working"

де́лать (де́л**ай**-)
"to do"

зна́ть (зн**а́й**-)
"to know"

The verb рабо́тать (рабо́тай-) "work"

Present Tense

я рабо́та**ю**	мы рабо́та**ем**
ты рабо́та**ешь**	вы рабо́та**ете**
он/а́ рабо́та**ет**	они́ рабо́та**ют**

Past Tense

> он рабо́тал
> она́ рабо́тал**а**
> они́ рабо́тал**и**

1. Translation warm-up

Read and translate the following sentences, paying attention to the grammatical agreement of the verb and the subject.

1. Та́ня студе́нтка. **Она́** не рабо́та**ет**. **Она́** мно́го чита́**ет**.

2. А́нна Бори́совна — учи́тельница. **Она́** рабо́та**ет** в шко́ле.

3. Ке́вин — фото́граф. **Он** жив**ёт** и рабо́та**ет** в Москве́.

4. — Ми́ша, где **ты** рабо́та**ешь**?
   — **Я** рабо́та**ю** в кли́нике.

5. **Мы** отдыха́**ем** на да́че.▲

6. **Ми́ша и Та́ня** мно́го гуля́**ют**. **Они́** гуля́**ют** в па́рке.

7. — Ке́вин, что **ты** де́лал вчера́?
   — **Я** отдыха́л. А ты?
   — А **я** чита́л.

8. — Та́ня, что **вы** де́лали ле́том?
   — **Я** рабо́тал**а**.
   — А где?
   — В библиоте́ке.

2. Practicing pronunciation: the verbs **отдыха́ть** and **гуля́ть**

> я отдыха́ю
> ты отдыха́ешь
> он/она́ отдыха́ет
> мы отдыха́ем
> вы отдыха́ете
> они́ отдыха́ют

> In order to negate a verb, place the negative particle **не** directly before the verb.

> вчера́ = yesterday

> ле́том = in the summer

> Unstressed **е** in the verb endings is pronounced as /и/.

▲ Russians take a one-month vacation each year. Those who can afford it go to resorts or travel with tourist groups. Some people will visit their relatives in the countryside or stay at the country house (**да́ча**).

я не гуля́ю
ты не гуля́ешь
он/она́ не гуля́ет
мы не гуля́ем
вы не гуля́ете
они́ не гуля́ют

3. Talking about lifestyles

мно́го = a lot

ма́ло = little

A. Check what best describes you.

	мно́го	**ма́ло**	
Я	_____	_____	гуля́ю.
Я	_____	_____	отдыха́ю.
Я	_____	_____	рабо́таю.
Я	_____	_____	чита́ю.

Now tell each other about yourselves.

> ¹
> Я **мно́го** гуля́ю. Я **ма́ло** отдыха́ю. ¹

B. Fill out the chart for your partner.

	мно́го	**ма́ло**	
Alek Name	___X___	_____	гуля́ет
	_____	___X___	отдыха́ет
	_____	___X___	рабо́тает
	___X___	_____	чита́ет

C. Share the information about your partner with the rest of the class.

> ¹
> Андре́й **ма́ло** гуля́ет.
> ¹
> Ли́за **мно́го** рабо́тает.

D. Form sentences using the words below. Make sure that the verb you choose agrees with the subject on the left.

> **1**
> **Та́ня** ма́ло гуля́**ет**.

Та́ня		чита́ю.
Я		гуля́ет.
Ты	мно́го	рабо́таешь.
Мои́ роди́тели	ма́ло	отдыха́ем.
Вы		рабо́тает.
Мой друг		гуля́ют.
Мы		чита́ете.

4. Talking about where people work

Find out where your partner works. If you do not know the Russian word for the place where you work, ask your instructor.

> **2**
> — Где ты рабо́таешь?
>
>   **1**   **4**   **2**
> — Я рабо́таю **в библиоте́ке**. А ты? Где ты рабо́таешь?

5. Учи́тель рабо́тает в ба́ре?!?

Correct the "mistakes" in the following sentences.

> **1**
> Учи́тель рабо́тает **в баре**.
> **1**   **1**
> Нет, учи́тель рабо́тает **в шко́ле**.

1. Официа́нтка рабо́тает в ~~газе́те~~. *pectopoli*
2. Фото́граф рабо́тает в ~~гараже́~~. *nopke*
3. Профе́ссор рабо́тает в магази́не.
4. Журнали́ст рабо́тает в университе́те.
5. Актёр рабо́тает в больни́це.
6. Врач рабо́тает в па́рке.
7. Фи́зик рабо́тает в рестора́не.
8. Ме́неджер рабо́тает на стадио́не.

6. Что дéлает Кéвин?

Can you come up with captions for the following pictures of Кéвин?

_____

_____

7. Talking about your plans for the evening

Ask your classmate what s/he is doing tonight. If you aren't sure what you are doing tonight, you can say **Я не знáю** = I don't know.

сегóдня
/сʲивóднʲа/
= today
In this word **г** is
pronounced /в/.

> 2
> — Что ты делаешь сегóдня вéчером?
> 1   4
> — **Я рабóтаю.** А ты?
> 1   1
> — **И я рабóтаю./А я отдыхáю.**

8. Что ты де́лал(а) вчера́?

Ask your classmate what s/he did last night.

> — Что ты де́лал(а) вчера?
>   ²
> — **Я гуля́ла в парке**. А ты?
>   ¹   ⁴

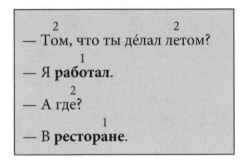

9. Describing how you spent your summer

Ask each other what you did during the summer.

> — Том, что ты де́лал летом?
>   ²   ²
> — Я **работал**.
>   ¹
> — А где?
>   ²
> — В **ресторане**.
>   ¹

ле́том = in the summer

10. Talking about where you have vacationed, lived, and worked

Above is the map of the U.S. with all of the state names in Russian. Talk about where you have vacationed, lived, and worked. In your answer, **only the word штат** should be in the prepositional case.

— Сара, где ты отдыха́ла?[2] Где ты рабо́тала?[2] Где ты жила?[2]

— Я отдыха́ла **в шта́те Калифорния**.[1] Я рабо́тала **в шта́те**

Висконсин.[1]

11. Getting acquainted

Familiarize yourself with the following dialog. Then act out similar dialogs by substituting words from the reference list below for those in bold.

Серге́й: — Здра́вствуйте![2]

Мари́на: — Здра́вствуйте![2]

Серге́й: — Я **Серге́й**[1] **Петро́в**. А вы?[4]

Мари́на: — А я **Мари́на Гаврилова**[1].

Серге́й: — О́чень прия́тно.[2]

Мари́на: — О́чень прия́тно.[2]

Серге́й: — **Марина**[2], а кто вы?[2]

Мари́на: — Я **преподаватель**[1]. А вы?[4]

Серге́й: — А я **врач**[1].

Мари́на: — Где вы рабо́таете?[2]

Серге́й: — **В больни́це**[1]. А вы?[4]

Мари́на: — А я **в университете**[1].

Серге́й: — А где вы живёте?[2]

Мари́на:	— **В Мэ́дисоне**[1]. **В шта́те Виско́нсин**[1]. [4] А вы?
Серге́й:	— А я живу́ **в Санкт-Петербу́рге**[1].

[
Person 1:   Áнна Па́влова, актри́са, теа́тр, Новосиби́рск
Person 2:   Том Мо́ррис, журнали́ст, газе́та, штат Небра́ска
]

[
Person 1:   Никола́й Гро́мов, официа́нт, рестора́н «Ко́смос», Но́вгород
Person 2:   Ири́на Смирно́ва, учи́тельница, шко́ла но́мер 5, Арха́нгельск
]

[
Person 1:   Ли́за Смит, ме́неджер, магази́н «Кей Март», Балтимо́р, штат Мэриле́нд
Person 2:   Влади́мир Го́лубев, программи́ст, университе́т, Псков
]

Кто здесь живёт?

Asking for Information

> You already know how to get someone's attention to ask for information:
>
> — **Извините**, где кварти́ра но́мер 10?
>
> A different way of saying it is:
>
> — **Скажите**, **пожа́луйста**, где кварти́ра но́мер 10?
>
> which literally means: "Tell (me) please, where is apartment number 10?"

1. A. What is a better English equivalent for this?

_____

B. If **скажи́те** is the formal form of address, how would you informally address a friend? (Think of **здра́вствуй<u>те</u>** and **здра́вствуй**.)

_____

Yet another way of asking for directions or information is:

3
— **Вы не знаете**, где университе́т?

This means, "*Do you happen to know* where the university is?"
Russians use the negative particle **не** in polite requests like this
one.

VIEWING

▶ Read through the following questions. Do as much
as you can before you watch the video with the
SOUND ON. Finish answering the questions while
you watch.

2. What objects in the apartment catch your attention? Check
them off as you see them.

☐ кре́сло   ☐ стол

☐ ко́шка   ☐ компью́тер

☐ телеви́зор   ☐ соба́ка

☐ ка́рта   ☐ ла́мпа

☐ дива́н   ☐ телефо́н

3. When Та́ня sees the inside of the apartment, she is:

☐ pleased

☐ unhappy

☐ angry

4. Asking for directions

POSTviewing

A. Muscovites are always ready to give directions – except,
of course, when they don't know! In this case, you may
get the polite reply: **Я здесь не живу́**.

Ask for directions to the places listed below.

3
— Вы не знаете, где тут банк?
1   1
— Я не знаю. Я здесь не живу.
2
— Извините.
2
— Пожалуйста.

subway, store, park, institute, restaurant, stadium, library, telephone, hospital, hotel, post office

B. Suppose you are looking for your new friend's apartment in Moscow. Ask a passerby for directions.

              2   2

— Скажи́те, пожа́луйста, где **кварти́ра но́мер 10**?

            3   1

— **Кварти́ра 10?** Вон там.

        2

— Спаси́бо.

        2

— Пожалуйста.

кварти́ра но́мер (1-10), дом но́мер (1-10)

5. Showing someone around your home

You have decided to host a Russian exchange student.▲ Show him/her around your apartment or house, listing the things which are in each room. Consult with your instructor if there is a word you would like to use but don't know.

            1   1

Э́то наш дом. Вот моя́ **ко́мната**.

              1   3   1

В ко́мнате **телефо́н**. По-моему, тут красиво.

по-мо́ему = I think

краси́во = (it's) nice, beautiful

спа́льня, ку́хня, ко́мната, компью́тер, кни́ги, кре́сло, дива́н, стол, стул, ла́мпа, шкаф, телефо́н, телеви́зор

▲ Russians always take off their shoes when they enter their apartments in attempt to keep their homes clean. They change into slippers and usually have extra slippers on hand for guests.

6. Скажи́те, пожа́луйста, где мои́ ве́щи?

You just had your apartment renovated, and it looks terrific! However, the workers have moved all of your furniture, and you can't seem to find anything. Ask the supervisor where everything is.

> ² ²
> — Скажите, пожа́луйста, где **мои́ вещи**?
> ³ ³ ¹
> — **Ва́ши вещи**? По-моему, они́ **в спа́льне**.

> шкаф, спа́льня; стол, ко́мната; журна́лы, туале́т; кни́ги, спа́льня; ла́мпа, ку́хня; стул, ку́хня

7. Finding out where someone is

Find out where the following people are.

> ³
> — Ты не знаешь, где **Ке́вин**?
> ³ ¹
> — **Кевин**? По-мо́ему, **он в музе́е**.

> Серге́й, стадио́н; Да́ша, библиоте́ка; Та́ня, институ́т; па́па, да́ча; ма́ма, рабо́та; Ке́вин, ку́хня

Interrogative Pronoun: Чей? (Whose?)

Interrogative pronouns agree in gender and number with the nouns they modify, just like the possessive pronouns **мой**, **твой**, **наш**, **ваш**.

дом **чей?**	кварти́ра **чья?**	окно́ **чьё?**	ве́щи **чьи?**
мой	моя́	моё	мои́
твой	твоя́	твоё	твои́
наш	на́ша	на́ше	на́ши
ваш	ва́ша	ва́ше	ва́ши

The possessive pronouns **его́** "his", **её** "her(s)" and **их** "their(s)" do not agree in case and number with the nouns they modify. They are "frozen" forms; they never change.

дом **чей?**	кварти́ра **чья?**	окно́ **чьё?**	ве́щи **чьи?**
его́	его́	его́	его́
её	её	её	её
их	их	их	их

8. Practicing pronunciation

Чей: Чей э́то дом? Чей э́то журна́л? Чей э́то каранда́ш? Чей э́то бана́н?

Чья: Чья э́то соба́ка? Чья э́то маши́на? Чья э́то ко́мната? Чья э́то кварти́ра?

Чьё: Чьё э́то молоко́? Чьё э́то письмо́? Чьё э́то ма́сло? Чьё э́то окно́?

Чьи: Чьи э́то помидо́ры? Чьи э́то ве́щи? Чьи э́то кни́ги? Чьи э́то бутербро́ды?

9. Now, making sure that your possessive pronouns agree in gender with the noun they modify, answer the questions from exercise 8 using any of the possessive pronouns in the tables above.

> — Чей э́то дом? ²
>
> — Э́то их дом. ¹

10. Asking someone to repeat information

Pretend that you don't hear what your partner says. Ask him/her to repeat what s/he has told you.

— Э́то мой дом.

— **Чей?**

— Мой.

1. Э́то его́ рюкза́к.	6. Э́то мои́ журна́лы.
2. Э́то на́ша кварти́ра.	7. Э́то их шкаф.
3. Э́то её письмо́.	8. Э́то мои́ ве́щи.
4. Э́то мои́ ключи́.	9. Э́то его́ соба́ка.
5. Э́то её па́па.	10. Э́то их ко́мната.

> When you ask someone to repeat what has just been said, use IC-3 as you would in a yes-no question.

11. Кто здесь живёт?

You are looking at some photographs of people's homes with a friend. Find out whose places they are.

— Кто здесь живёт? **Чья** э́то **ко́мната?**
— Здесь живёт **Кевин**. Э́то **его́** ко́мната.

> ко́мната, я, моя́   да́ча, они́, их
> кварти́ра, мы, на́ша   дом, Та́ня, её

Та́ня говори́т **по-ру́сски.**   Ке́вин говори́т **по-англи́йски.**

The verb говори́ть (говори́-) "speak"

Present Tense

я говорю́	мы говори́м
ты говори́шь	вы говори́те
он/а́ говори́т	они́ говоря́т

Past Tense

он говори́л
она́ говори́ла
оно́ говори́ло
они́ говори́ли

1. Practicing pronunciation: the verb **говори́ть**

по-англи́йски ▲

хорошо́ = well

Я говорю́ по-англи́йски. Я хорошо́ говорю́ по-англи́йски.

по-испа́нски

Ты говори́шь по-испа́нски? Ты хорошо́ говори́шь по-испа́нски?

по-ру́сски

пло́хо = badly

Ке́вин говори́т по-ру́сски. Кевин пло́хо говори́т по-ру́сски.

▲ British English is the most commonly taught foreign language in high schools, universities, and colleges in Russia. If your Russian friends speak English with you, they will most likely speak with a British accent and use words like "flat" (apartment).

по-францу́зски

Мы говори́м по-францу́зски.[1] Мы говори́м и чита́ем по-францу́зски.[1]

по-неме́цки

Вы говори́те по-неме́цки?[3] Вы хорошо́ говори́те по-неме́цки?[3]

по-япо́нски

Они́ не говоря́т по-япо́нски.[1]

In Russian, if **они́** does not refer to any particular group of people, it is dropped.

В Нью-Йо́рке говоря́т по-англи́йски.	English is spoken in New York. Literally: They speak English in New York.

---

2. Где говоря́т по-ру́сски?

Match the name of the city with the language spoken there.

— Где говоря́т **по-ру́сски**?[2]
— В Москве́.[1]

В Москве́.
В То́кио
В Мадри́де   говоря́т
В Пари́же
В Берли́не
В Ло́ндоне

по-англи́йски
по-францу́зски
по-неме́цки
по-испа́нски
по-япо́нски
по-ру́сски

3. Talking about what languages people speak

Ask each other what languages they speak. Include all languages you have ever studied even if you only know a few words. Find out what languages you and your partner both speak. Pay attention to the intonation in your response.

> — Я говорю́ **по-испа́нски**[1]. А ты?[4]
>
> — И я говорю́ по-испа́нски.[1]/ А я говорю́ **по-францу́зски**[1].

4. Describing how well people speak different languages

A. Speaking a language involves different skills. A good reader may be a fair listener, but a novice speaker. What can you say about yourself?

> Я хорошо́ чита́ю по-испа́нски[1].

Я	хорошо́	понима́ю	по-англи́йски
	пло́хо	говорю́	по-францу́зски
		чита́ю	по-неме́цки
			по-испа́нски
			по-япо́нски
			по-ру́сски

<table>
<tr><td>понима́ть</td></tr>
<tr><td>(понима́й-)</td></tr>
<tr><td>= understand</td></tr>
</table>

B. Now that you know which languages your partner speaks, find out how well s/he understands, reads, and speaks each one.

> — Ты **хорошо́**[3] говори́шь по-неме́цки?
>
> — Да, хорошо́.[1]/ Нет, пло́хо.[1][1][1]

5. International coffee hour

A. Imagine that you are attending an international coffee hour for new students at Moscow State University. Students approach you asking whether or not you speak their native language. Answer their questions.

```
         2                              1
— Здравствуйте!  Я Жан-Люк.
           1
— А я Сара.
                   2
— Очень приятно.
                   2
— Очень приятно.
         2              3
— Сара, вы говорите по-францу́зски?
   1      1      1            1
— Да, говорю./ Нет, не говорю.
```

Мо́ника, по-неме́цки; Аки́ра, по-япо́нски; Ломба́рдо,
по-испа́нски; Дже́йн, по-англи́йски

B. The conversation at the coffee hour soon turns to food! Here are
some words you will need to know in order to talk about this:

за́втракать (за́втракай-) have breakfast
обе́дать (обе́дай-) have lunch
у́жинать (у́жинай-) have dinner

You are interested in finding out where students usually have
lunch between classes. Ask your new friends where they eat lunch.

```
           2
— Где вы обедаете?
                       1           4
— Я обе́даю в университете.  А вы?
   1                                                    1
— И я обе́даю в университе́те./ А я обе́даю в кафе.
```

в университе́те, в кафе́, в рестора́не, до́ма

6. Где вы за́втракаете? Обе́даете? У́жинаете?

Let's talk about where you have your meals. Check the appropriate
answer. Add the right location to the list.

A. Где вы за́втракаете? ▲

Я за́втракаю

Всегда́	Ча́сто	Ре́дко	Иногда́	
✗				до́ма
_____	_____	_____	_____	в университе́те
_____	_____	_____	_____	на рабо́те
_____	_____	_____	_____	в колле́дже
_____	_____	_____	_____	в шко́ле
_____	_____	_____	_____	в рестора́не
_____	_____	_____	_____	в кафе́
_____	_____	_____	_____	в ба́ре
_____	_____	_____	_____	в гараже́

B. Now exchange this information with your new friends. Watch for word order: who + when + what + where.

> — Я всегда́ за́втракаю **до́ма**. А ты?
>   1   4
> — И я всегда́ за́втракаю **до́ма**./ А я нет.
>   1   1
>   Я всегда́ за́втракаю **на рабо́те**.
>   1

C. Где вы обе́даете?▲▲

Я обе́даю

Всегда́	Ча́сто	Ре́дко	Иногда́	
_____	_____	_____	_____	до́ма
_____	_____	_____	_____	в университе́те
_____	_____	_____	_____	на рабо́те
_____	_____	_____	_____	в колле́дже
_____	_____	_____	_____	в шко́ле
_____	_____	_____	_____	в рестора́не
_____	_____	_____	_____	в кафе́
_____	_____	_____	_____	в ба́ре
_____	_____	_____	_____	в гараже́

▲ The Russian breakfast is a big meal: oatmeal/cream of wheat (**ка́ша**), eggs, **бутербро́ды**, cheese. **Творо́г**, a product similar to farmer's cheese, with sour cream is also frequently served. Hot tea and instant coffee are common breakfast drinks. Juice traditionally is not a part of a typical Russian breakfast.

▲▲ Russians generally eat lunch (**обе́д**) between 1:00 and 2:00 in the afternoon in buffets or cafeterias at their places of work or study. **Бутербро́ды**, cakes, and hot tea (loaded with sugar!) are staple items.

> — Я всегда́ обе́даю **в университете**.[1]
> — И я всегда́ обе́даю **в университе́те**.[1]/ А я нет.
> Я всегда́ обе́даю **дома**.[1]

D. Где вы у́жинаете?▲

Я у́жинаю

Всегда́	Ча́сто	Ре́дко	Иногда́	
———	———	———	———	до́ма
———	———	———	———	в университе́те
———	———	———	———	на рабо́те
———	———	———	———	в колле́дже
———	———	———	———	в шко́ле
———	———	———	———	в рестора́не
———	———	———	———	в кафе́
———	———	———	———	в ба́ре
———	———	———	———	в гараже́

> — Я всегда́ у́жинаю **в ресторане**.[1]
> — И я всегда́ у́жинаю **в рестора́не**.[1]/А я нет.
> Я всегда́ у́жинаю **в кафе**.[1]

7. Ра́ньше и сейча́с

Describe the changes in your eating habits since you have become a college student.

> Ра́ньше я за́втракал(а) до́ма, а сейча́с
> я за́втракаю в институ́те.

▲ Russians eat dinner (у́жин) at home with the whole family at the end of the working day. Many women cook from scratch after having worked all day and shopped for fresh food. Pre-cooked frozen meals are rare.

Ча́шки на по́лке

Фру́кты на столе́

Saying where objects are located: "on"

PREviewing

на по́лке = **on** the shelf   **на** столе́   = **on** the table

на плите́ = **on** the stove   **на** дива́не = **on** the couch

на сту́ле = **on** the chair   **на** таре́лке = **on** the plate

The preposition **на** + prepositional case can indicate that something is on the surface of something else.

1. The director of the video arrived on the set (Ке́вин's new apartment) and found a gigantic mess!

Что э́то!? Ча́йник на дива́не, кни́га на плите́, помидо́ры на сту́ле, бутербро́ды на по́лке, ма́сло на столе́, телеви́зор на плите́, хлеб на сту́ле, ла́мпа на дива́не, Ке́вин на таре́лке!!!

Put these things back in their proper places. Work individually.

Ча́йник на _nolke_ , кни́га на _stole_ ,

помидо́ры на _plite_ , бутербро́ды на _tapelke_

ма́сло на _tapelke_ , телеви́зор на ~~stole~~

dibane

хлеб на _____*столе*_____, лáмпа на _____*полке*_____,
Кéвин на _____*диване*_____.

2. Here are a few more **-ай** stem verbs that you will need to do the next assignment:

Present Tense

я спрáшиваю	мы спрáшива**ем**
ты спрáшива**ешь**	вы спрáшива**ете**
он/á спрáшива**ет**	они́ спрáшива**ют**

Now you fill in the past tense forms: он _____

она́ _____

они́ _____

Now you can conjugate **отвечáть (отвечáй-)** "answer," which is another **–ай** verb and hence follows the same pattern.

The verb отвечáть (отвечáй-) "answer"

Present Tense

я_____   мы_____

ты_____   вы_____

он/онá_____   они́_____

Past Tense

он _____

онá _____

они́_____

Read through the following questions and answer as many as you can before you watch the video with the SOUND ON. Finish answering the questions while you watch.

SOUND ON

3. Match the following lines from Та́ня and Ке́вин's conversation to the appropriate speaker. Then read your answers aloud together with a partner.

> таре́лка = plate
> ви́лка = fork
> ча́шка = cup

Та́ня спра́шивает: «Что ты де́лаешь? Э́то обе́д?»

Ке́вин отвеча́ет: «Хорошо́, где таре́лки, ви́лки, ножи́, ча́шки»

Та́ня отвеча́ет: «Что-что? Не понима́ю. Я плохо́ говорю́ по-ру́сски.»

Ке́вин спра́шивает: «Нет, э́то не обе́д. Мы всегда́ обе́даем днём. А э́то про́сто бутербро́ды и фру́кты.»▲

> Repetition in **что-что** (IC-3), pronounced in this case as one word, is for emphasis.

4. Answer the following questions **да** or **нет**.   **да/нет**

Ке́вин пло́хо понима́ет по-ру́сски?   _____

Та́ня всегда́ обе́дает днём?   _____

Та́ня врач?   _____

5. What are some of the things that Та́ня points out to Ке́вин as they are looking out the window in the kitchen?

☐ гости́ница «Росси́я»   ☐ мой институ́т

☐ Кремль   ☐ аэропо́рт

☐ мой дом   ☐ моя́ рабо́та

Remember when Ке́вин complains to Та́ня that he can't understand what she is saying to him?

Ке́вин: — Не понима́ю. Я пло́хо говорю́ по-ру́сски.

Та́ня: — **Что ты**, Ке́вин! Ты о́чень хорошо́ говори́шь по-ру́сски!

Что вы! /Что ты! signal strong disagreement in response to the preceding statement.

▲ **Бутербро́д** is actually a German word that means, literally, bread and butter. The Russian **бутербро́д** can have different toppings like caviar, cheese, or cold cuts. Unlike Americans, most Russians prefer to use real butter, and not vegetable oil-based spreads on their **бутербро́д**.

6. Disagreeing

The following sentences are not true. Disagree with the statements as your partner makes them, and then correct each statement.

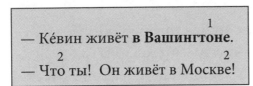

> 1
> — Кéвин живёт **в Вашингтоне**.
> 2   2
> — Что ты! Он живёт в Москве!

1. Тáня живёт **в Петербýрге**.
2. Кéвин **не говори́т** по-рýсски.
3. Сергéй живёт **в Нóвгороде**.
4. Кéвин живёт **на дáче**.
5. Аэропóрт Шеремéтьево **в Петербýрге**.
6. Тáня **не понимáет** по-рýсски.
7. Кéвин **не понимáет** по-англи́йски.
8. Тáня всегдá обéдает утром.
9. В Амéрике говоря́т **по-япóнски**.
10. Кремль **в Нью-Йóрке**.

Intensifying Adverbs

Here are some of the adverbs we have already seen:

краси́во, плóхо, хорошó, неплóхо, интерéсно, мнóго, мáло

If you want to intensify these words (quickly – very quickly), just add **óчень** before the adverb:

Он мнóго говори́т. – Он **óчень** мнóго говори́т.

7. Making a strong statement

Now answer the following questions intensifying your response. Work with a partner.

> 3
> — Вы **хорошо** читáете по-францýзски?
> 1
> — Я **óчень хорошó** читáю по-францýзски.

1. Кéвин **плóхо** говорúт по-рýсски?
2. Тáня **интерéсно** говорúт?
3. Кéвин **хорошó** понимáет по-рýсски?
4. Сергéй **мáло** отдыхáет?
5. Студéнты **мнóго** гуляют?
6. Вáши родúтели **мнóго** рабóтают?

8. Describing how well people know different languages

Make up sentences describing how the following subjects speak and understand different languages.

> 1
> — Мой пáпа хорошо понимáет по-францýзски.

моя кóшка		понимáть	по-рýсски
моя собáка	хорошó	говорúть	по-немéцки
моя подрýга	неплóхо		по-англúйски
мой друг	плóхо		по-францýзски
я			по-испáнски
мой родúтели			

9. Setting the table

Imagine you are having a housewarming party at your new place. Make an inventory of all the items you will need to set the table.

_____   _____

_____   _____

_____   _____

_____   _____

_____   _____

_____   _____

Now find a partner. One of you should offer the other items needed to set the table; your partner will accept or refuse them. Try to confuse your partner by offering some things that are not needed (**му́сор**, **ко́шка**, etc.)

му́сор = garbage

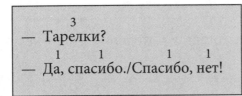

10. How often does this happen?

Respond to the statement and specify how often this happens. Use the adverbs **всегда́**, **ча́сто**, **ре́дко**, **иногда́** in your response.

1. Сестра́ рабо́тает.

2. В Москве́ интере́сно.

3. Та́ня обе́дает днём.

4. Брат отдыха́ет.

5. Мы за́втракаем у́тром.

6. Они́ у́жинают ве́чером.

7. Ма́ма говори́т по-францу́зски.

8. Я гуля́ю у́тром.

11. Интере́сно.... "I wonder …"

Do you remember what Та́ня says when she is looking for the tea kettle?

Та́ня: — Интере́сно, где здесь ча́йник?

Ке́вин: — Вот он!

A. How would you translate the first sentence into English?

_____

B. Help your forgetful partner find what s/he needs.

ключи́ = keys

> — Интере́сно, где **ключи́**?
> — Вот они́.
> — Спаси́бо.
> — Пожа́луйста.

[purse, book, address, newspaper, jacket, dictionary, passport]

C. You and your partner have just begun new jobs. One of you works at a terrible office where everything is broken, while the other works at a nice office where everything works perfectly. Show your partner around your office, answering questions about the equipment there.

— Э́то мой офис.
1

— Интере́сно, **факс** рабо́тает?
2   3

— Нет, не рабо́тает./Да, рабо́тает.
1   1   1   1

— Интере́сно, а **при́нтер** рабо́тает?
2   3

— Нет, не рабо́тает./Да, рабо́тает.
1   1   1   1

телефо́н, телеви́зор, холоди́льник, компью́тер, ксе́рокс, калькуля́тор, ска́нер, монито́р, ра́дио

Москва́

6 февраля́

Дорога́я Да́ша!

Спаси́бо за твоё письмо́. Я ду́мала, что ты живёшь в Вашингто́не, а ты живёшь в Колле́дж Па́рке. Там интере́сно? Когда́ экза́мены в Мэриле́ндском университе́те? Ты ча́сто гуля́ешь в Вашингто́не? Что ты там де́лаешь?

new place
now | in the past
was building
important

Мы живём хорошо́. Па́па рабо́тает на но́вом ме́сте◊. Он тепе́рь◊ рабо́тает в комме́рческом ба́нке. Ра́ньше◊ он стро́ил◊ социали́зм, а тепе́рь он стро́ит капитали́зм. Прогре́сс! Он говори́т, что бухга́лтер сейча́с са́мая ва́жная◊ профе́ссия. А по-мо́ему, бухга́лтер всегда́ бухга́лтер. Ма́ма по-пре́жнему рабо́тает в на́шей шко́ле. Рабо́тает о́чень

it's a pity

мно́го, ча́сто говори́т о пе́нсии. Жа́лко◊, она́ хоро́шая учи́тельница.

В институ́те всё по-пре́жнему: ле́кции, семина́ры,

term paper

рабо́та, рабо́та, рабо́та! Все студе́нты так живу́т. Курсова́я рабо́та◊ – э́то специа́льность, и э́то о́чень серьёзно.

Моя́ сестра́ О́льга тепе́рь журнали́ст на телеви́дении. В Москве́ она́ на рабо́те у́тром, днём и ве́чером. А ещё она́

business trips

ча́сто е́здит в командиро́вки◊. Она́ уже́ была́ на Байка́ле, на Ура́ле, на Камча́тке.

Да, ты говори́шь, что у тебя́ уже́ есть друг. Так вот, и у

I have

меня́ тепе́рь есть◊ друг. Его́ зову́т Ми́ша. Он уже́ рабо́тает. Он ветерина́р. Я не зна́ю, где он рабо́тает, по-мо́ему, в

about
about

ветерина́рной кли́нике. Он о́чень ма́ло говори́т об◊ э́том. Но зато́ он всё вре́мя говори́т о◊ би́знесе. Он хо́чет организова́ть ветерина́рный це́нтр. Ве́чером он почти́ всегда́ рабо́тает. По-мо́ему, он совсе́м не отдыха́ет. Ми́ша живёт в це́нтре, на Арба́те, и иногда́ мы там ве́чером гуля́ем.▲ Краси́во! Ла́дно, я не хочу́ тебе́ пока́ мно́го говори́ть о Ми́ше. Но я ду́маю, что э́то у нас серьёзно.

Тепе́рь о Ке́вине Дже́ксоне. О́ля говори́т, что есть◊   there is
хоро́шая кварти́ра. В э́той кварти́ре живёт её друг. А ле́том
он в командиро́вке, и Ке́вин мо́жет◊ жить в его́ кварти́ре.   can

Обнима́ю!

Та́ня

1. Number the paragraphs in Та́ня's letter. Scan the letter to determine who Та́ня talks about in each paragraph. Use those names to give each paragraph a title.

1. _____

2. _____

3. _____

4. _____

5. _____

6. _____

2. Та́ня writes a lot about work. Scan the text to find the professions of the following people:

па́па_____

О́льга_____

ма́ма_____

Ми́ша_____

3. Underline all of the geographical place names in the letter.

4. Fill in the missing place names using the words below for reference.

1. Да́ша lives in _____

▲ Arbat is one of the first urban developments located outside of the Kremlin walls in Moscow. It is an essential part of the old city. In the 1980's the Arbat became the first Moscow street open to pedestrian traffic only. It is famous for its shops, art galleries, restaurants, cafes, theaters, street vendors, and musicians.

2. Да́ша frequently visits _____

3. О́льга has taken business trips to _____,
_____ and _____.

4. Ми́ша lives in the center of Moscow, on the
_____.

Kamchatka, St. Petersburg, Baikal, College Park, Arbat, the Urals,
Washington, D.C.

 5. Asking for information: Скажи́, пожа́луйста …

If Та́ня were showing a new friend some photographs, she might
say the following:

Э́то я. Я живу́ в Москве́. Я студе́нтка. Э́то моя́ семья́. Э́то
мой па́па. Он бухга́лтер. Он рабо́тает в ба́нке в Москве́.
Э́то моя́ сестра́ О́льга. Она́ журнали́стка. Она́ живёт в
Москве́ и рабо́тает на телеви́дении. Э́то моя́ ма́ма. Она́
учи́тельница и рабо́тает в шко́ле. Э́то мой друг Ми́ша. Он
ветерина́р и рабо́тает в кли́нике. Э́то моя́ подру́га Да́ша.
Она́ студе́нтка и живёт в Аме́рике.

One partner will play Та́ня and the other partner will ask her about
her friends and family. Try to ask as many questions as possible.

>   ²   ²   ²
> — Та́ня, скажи́, пожа́луйста, где рабо́тает твой па́па?
>
>   ¹
> — Он рабо́тает в ба́нке.

[
твоя́ сестра́, твоя́ ма́ма, твой друг Ми́ша, твоя́ подру́га
Даша
]

и́ли = or

6. В Москве́ **и́ли** в Петербу́рге? Asking alternative questions and
answering them.

Now ask questions to check your partner's memory about Та́ня's
family and friends. Be polite and use the opening phrases provided.

>   3   2
> — Её пáпа рабóтает в Москве́ и́ли в Петербу́рге?
>
>   2   3   2
> — **Скажи́, пожáлуйста,** её пáпа рабóтает в Москве́ и́ли в Петербу́рге?
>
>   3   3   2
> — **Ты не знáешь,** её пáпа рабóтает в Москве́ и́ли в Петербу́рге?
>
>   1
> — Он рабóтает в Москве́.

1. Дáша живёт в Москве́ и́ли Коллéдж Пáрке?
2. Мáма рабóтает в институ́те и́ли в шкóле?
3. Мáма учи́тельница и́ли журнали́стка?
4. Ми́ша рабóтает в кли́нике и́ли в университéте?
5. Óльга живёт на Урáле и́ли в Москве́?
6. Óльга рабóтает в шкóле и́ли на телеви́дении?
7. Ми́ша живёт в Нью-Йóрке и́ли в Москве́?
8. Тáня фотóграф и́ли студéнтка?
9. Óльга и Тáня сёстры и́ли подру́ги?

> Questions with **и́ли** are pronounced with IC-3 plus IC-2.

7. List all the questions that Тáня asks Дáша in her letter in English.

_____

_____

_____

_____

8. A. It appears that Ми́ша, Тáня's new friend, plays an important role in her life. Scan the paragraph that deals with Ми́ша and answer the following questions in English.

    1. What does Ми́ша do for a living?

    _____

    2. Where does he work?

    _____

3. What can you say about his attitude towards work?

   _____

4. What is the favorite place for Та́ня and Ми́ша to meet?

   _____

B. Suppose you run into Та́ня's ex-boyfriend, who is dying to know the details about her latest love interest. Using your answers in part A, tell him everything you know about Ми́ша (in Russian).

9. Retelling a story

Now see if you can retell Та́ня's story in the third person. Fill in the blanks.

_____ Та́ня. Она́ _____ в Москве́.

_____ студе́нтка. Э́то её семья́. Э́то _____ па́па. Он

_____ в Москве́ в ба́нке. Э́то _____ сестра́ О́льга. Она́

живёт в Москв___ и рабо́тает на телеви́дении. Э́то _____

ма́ма. Она́ учи́тельница и рабо́тает в шко́л__. Э́то _____

друг Ми́ша. Он _____ и рабо́тает в кли́нике. Э́то

_____ подру́га Да́ша. Она́ студе́нтка и _____

в Аме́рик___.

10. See if you can guess the meaning of these words. (It helps if you read them aloud.) Compare your answers with your partner's answers.

комме́рческий банк _____

социали́зм _____

капитали́зм _____

ле́кция _____

семина́р _____

ветерина́рный центр _____

ветерина́рная кли́ника _____

Video Review

PREviewing

1. Today we are going to explore Кéвин's new apartment one last time!

   A. Can you translate the following mini-episode titles into Russian?

   It's nice here. _____

   Where is apartment number 10? _____

   Goodbye Тáня! _____

   Who lives here? _____

   In the kitchen. _____

   B. Put the mini-episode titles above in the correct order.

2. This is the first mini-episode in which Тáня helps Кéвин move into his apartment. Unfortunately, the person who transcribed this was not listening carefully and made a few mistakes. Correct the errors as you watch.

Та́ня:	— А вот и моя́ кварти́ра, Ке́вин.
Ке́вин:	— Но́мер де́сять.
Та́ня:	— А где же ключи́?
Ке́вин:	— А, вот они́.
Та́ня:	— Ой, кто тако́е?
Ке́вин:	— Мо́жно я?

3. Now we're finally inside the apartment! Fill in the blanks below with the missing room names.

Та́ня: — Так, где тут _____? Наве́рное, там.

Ке́вин: — Ой, извини́те. Э́то шкаф?▲

Та́ня: — Нет, э́то _____.

Ке́вин: — Ой, извини́те. А где шкаф?

Та́ня: — Не зна́ю. Я ду́маю, он там _____.

Ке́вин: — Э́то _____?

Та́ня: — Нет, э́то ва́нная.

4. Интере́сно, кто здесь живёт? Fill in the missing words.

Ке́вин: — Вы не зна́ете, чья э́то кварти́ра? Кто здесь живёт?

Та́ня: — Я ду́маю, здесь живёт _____:

_____, _____, и их,

_____. Вот его́ ко́мната.

Ке́вин: — _____, а не _____?

▲ Most Russian apartments do not have closets, so Russians store their clothes and valuables in cupboards and wardrobes.

Та́ня: — Вот его́ игру́шки, маши́ны. Вот его́ ве́щи.

Та́ня: — Тут живёт _____.

Вот _____. А вот его́ роди́тели.

Э́то его́ _____. А э́то его́

_____. А там их ко́мната.

Ке́вин: — Интере́сно, где они́ сейча́с?

Та́ня: — Я не зна́ю.

5. The following transcription is of conversation between Та́ня and Ке́вин as they are sizing up his new apartment. Try to unscramble the following lines from their conversation by placing a number next to each line to indicate the correct order.

_____ — А где мой паке́т? Ах, да, он на ку́хне, на столе́.

_____ — Телефо́н? Да, **рабо́тает**.

_____ — По-мо́ему тут непло́хо: дива́н, ла́мпа. Телеви́зор! Рабо́тает. DVD пле́ер то́же рабо́тает.

_____ — Отли́чно! И телефо́н рабо́тает?

6. The order of the food items in the following dialog has been scrambled. Place numbers over each item to indicate its order of appearance in the video.

Та́ня: — Так, апельси́ны, ма́сло, помидо́ры, хлеб, колбаса́.

Та́ня: — А где же бана́ны?
— Вот они́.

7. Now it's time to check out the kitchen.

Fill in the missing verb endings.

Ке́вин: — Тут хорошо́! Рабо́та_____?

Та́ня: — Что, холоди́льник?

Та́ня: — Рабо́та_____.

Ке́вин: — Что вы де́ла_____? Э́то обе́д?

Та́ня: — Зна́ете, Ке́вин, дава́йте на «ты».

Ке́вин: — На «ты»? Отли́чно. Что ты де́ла_____?

Э́то обе́д?

Та́ня: — Нет, э́то не обе́д. Мы всегда́

обе́да_____ днём. А э́то про́сто

бутербро́ды и фру́кты.

8. In this scene Та́ня and Ке́вин are looking out of the window trying to identify different sights in Moscow. Fill in the missing words. Hint: the missing information indicates a location.

Ке́вин: — Краси́во! А где Кремль?

Та́ня: — Ка́жется _____.

Ке́вин: — А где ты живёшь?

Та́ня: — Я живу́_____. А мой

институ́т_____.

9. Wrap-up: summary

Suppose that your friend, who doesn't speak any Russian, has come to sit in on your Russian class. Sum up the story.

10. Situations

A. Your hungry sister arrives just as you are leaving to spend the night at a friend's. Since you have just returned from the store, you tell her about what food is in the kitchen and where it is. She says, "very good", "thank you", and "good-bye".

B. Describe your own apartment or house. List the rooms in your home/apartment and describe what is in each room. Comment on the rooms (it's beautiful there, it's nice there.)

C. You are having a Russian guest over who is curious to see your place. Show him/her around.

2

DAY 9

1. Где Та́ня?

Remember the game "Where is Waldo?" Та́ня runs around so quickly, one moment she is here, the next she is gone. All of you have just seen her in a different place.

> ³
> — Ты не знаешь, где Та́ня?
> ¹
> — Она́ в гараже.
> ¹   ¹
> — Нет, она́ на стадионе.

[room, kitchen, theater, university, café, restaurant, summer house, institute, movie theater, work, library.]

2. Finding your belongings

Your 6-year-old Russian cousin, who is visiting from Moscow, has decided to re-arrange everything in your house. You can't find a thing! Ask your cousin where your things are.

> ²
> — Где моя́ **чашка**?
> ³   ¹
> — Твоя́ ча́шка? Она́ **в спальне**.
> ³   ²
> — В спальне? Где?
> ¹
> — На **полке**.

[
purse, sandwiches, pencil, cup, oranges, tomatoes, butter, telephone, forks, salami, plates, dictionary, keys, pen
]

[
bedroom, half bath, kitchen, room
]

[
couch, shelf, stove, refrigerator, table, chair, purse, backpack, armchair
]

3. Talking about yourselves

Find a partner. Ask each other questions using the phrase **скажи́, пожа́луйста.** Pay close attention to intonation.

> ```
>            2                           2
> — Скажи, пожа́луйста, где ты живёшь?
>            1          4
> — Я живу́ в Мэриленде. А ты?
>    1      1                  1
> — И я./А я нет. Я живу́ в Нью-Йорке.
> ```

1. Где ты живёшь?
2. Ты рабо́таешь?
3. Ты ча́сто гуля́ешь?
4. Где ты отдыха́ешь?
5. Твоя́ семья́ живёт в Москве́?
6. Твои́ роди́тели сейча́с отдыха́ют?
7. Где ты у́жинаешь?
8. Ты всегда́ за́втракаешь?
9. Где ты за́втракаешь?
10. Ты ча́сто обе́даешь до́ма?

4. Кто здесь рабо́тает?

You have a lot of friends who work at the same company in Moscow and one of them is giving you a tour of the office. Find out where each of your friends works.

> — Ты не знаешь, кто здесь рабо́тает? ³
>
> — Здесь рабо́тает Ольга. Э́то её ко́мната. ¹ ¹

Серге́й; Ве́ра и Ли́за; А́ня; Бори́с; Игорь и Андре́й

5. Reconstructing the conversation

Reconstruct the questions that prompted the answers below. Read your short dialogs to the class.

1. — _____?

   — Кошка? Она́ в спальне. ³ ¹

2. — _____?

   — Я рабо́таю в больнице. ¹

3. — _____?

   — Э́то её су́мка. ¹

4. — _____?

   — Ле́том? Я отдыха́л(а). ³ ¹

5. — _____?

   — Э́то мой университет. ¹

6. — _____?

     ³   ¹
   — Я думаю, тут живёт семья.

7. — _____?

                        ¹
   — Я обедаю в кафе.

8. — _____?

                  ¹
   — Это наши вещи.

9. — _____?

               ¹
   — Она учительница.

10. — _____?

           ¹   ¹   ¹
    — Нет, это не музей. Это институт.

11. — _____?

              ¹
    — Это моя собака.

6. Translation

Prepare yourself for a career in translation.

A. Translate the following statement of an American doctor interviewed on Moscow television. Work in pairs sentence by sentence.

My mother is a journalist. She used to work at the university. Now she works at a newspaper. I am a doctor. I work in a hospital. We live in Washington. My brother is an actor. He works in a theater in New York. My sister speaks and reads Russian very well. She works at a school in Moscow.

B. Translate Да́ша's conversation with an American student. Work in groups of three.

Студе́нт: — Dasha, where do you live?

Да́ша: — Now I live in College Park. How about you?

Студе́нт: — I live in College Park, too. And where did you used to live?

Да́ша: — I used to live in Moscow. I speak English poorly.

Студе́нт: — What are you talking about? You speak English very well.

7. Situations

   Act out the following situations.

1. You are looking for Apartment #8. Ask a passerby where it is. Unfortunately, the person doesn't know since s/he doesn't live there. Apologize for inconveniencing this person.

2. You and your friend Оле́г love to talk about eating. Ask each other when and where you have breakfast, lunch and dinner.

3. You are very studious and like to read as much as you can, but your good friend prefers to take walks outside — s/he is an outdoor person. Construct a conversation that might occur between the two of you as you describe to each other what you like to do. Include details about where and how often you walk, read and work.

1. The Russian Verb (CF. also Unit V)

Russian verbs express information about tense, gender/number, and person. In most of its forms, the ending of the verb, the part added to the *stem*[1], has two elements, rather than one, as with nouns.

2. The Present Tense Verb

The present tense forms of a verb consist of a present tense vowel followed by an ending denoting person (I, you, he/she/it, we, they, etc.).

Я рабо́та**ю** до́ма.	I work at home.
Ты рабо́та**ешь** там.	You work over there.
Он/она́/оно́ рабо́та**ет** тут.	He/she/it works here.
Мы рабо́та**ем** до́ма.	We work at home.
Вы рабо́та**ете** там.	You work over there.
Они́ рабо́та**ют** тут.	They work here.

The present tense of the Russian verb has six forms. The first element of the verb ending, an initial vowel or **ø** (in the 1st person, singular form), identifies the form as present tense. The two vowels **-ё** and **-и** function as tense markers and indicate *first (I)* and *second (II)* conjugations, respectively. The second element of the ending marks the person (first, second, or third) and number (singular or plural) of the verb. The verb must agree in person and number with the subject, which is normally a noun or pronoun.

Sections 3 and 4 below use common verbs to exemplify and explain the formation of first and second conjugation verbs.

3. Formation of the Present Tense: First Conjugation

The verb stem corresponding to "read" is чита́й-. To form the first person singular present tense "I read", add the present tense marker **-ø** and the 1st person singular marker **–у** to the stem:

$$\text{чита́й-} + \text{ø} + \text{у} = \text{чита́ю}$$

Recall that a vowel preceded by **й** is spelled with a single letter (here, **й + у = ю**)

The full present tense conjugation pattern of чита́ть (чита́й) is as follows:

---

[1] See also Analysis V.

First Conjugation					
		Stem + Ending Markers =			**Form**
			Conj.(I) +Person		
Sing.	я	чита́й- +	-ø +	-у	я чита́ю
	ты	чита́й- +	-ё +	-шь	ты чита́ешь
	он/она́/оно́	чита́й- +	-ё +	-т	он/она́/оно́ чита́ет
Pl.	мы	чита́й- +	-ё +	-м	мы чита́ем
	вы	чита́й- +	-ё +	-те	вы чита́ете
	они́	чита́й- +	-у +	-т	они́ чита́ют

Study also the present tense formation of the non-suffixed first conjugation verb жить (жи́в-)[2] "live":

		Stem + Ending Markers =			**Form**
			Conj.(I) +Person		
Sing.	я	жи́в ø- +	-ø +	-у	я живу́
	ты	жи́в ø- +	-ё +	-шь	ты живёшь
	он/она́/оно́	жи́в ø- +	-ё +	-т	он/она́/оно́ живёт
Pl.	мы	жи́в ø- +	-ё +	-м	мы живём
	вы	жи́в ø- +	-ё +	-те	вы живёте
	они́	жи́в ø- +	-у +	-т	они́ живу́т

[2] See Analysis II, 8 for a discussion of this notation.

4. Formation of the Present Tense: Second Conjugation

The verb говори́ть (говори́-) "say, speak" illustrates a second conjugation verb:

Second Conjugation[3]					
		Stem + Ending Markers =			Form
			Conj.(I) +Person		
Sing.	я	говори́ +	-ø +	-у	я говорю́[4]
	ты	говори́ +	-и +	-шь	ты говори́шь
	он/она́/оно́	говори́ +	-и +	-т	он/она́/оно́ говори́т
Pl.	мы	говори́ +	-и +	-м	мы говори́м
	вы	говори́ +	-и +	-те	вы говори́те
	они́	говори́ +	-а +	-т	они́ говоря́т

The large majority of Russian verbs are first conjugation. For that reason, we shall assume for now that all stems take first conjugation vowels unless specifically indicated as second conjugation. In Unit V we will observe how the verb stem enables us to predict the choice of conjugation.

5. The Infinitive

The infinitive is the normal citation form of the Russian verb in dictionaries, glossaries, and handbooks. (For other uses of the infinitive, see below.) The infinitive ending is -**ть**, in certain limited cases –**ти** or **чь**.

говори́- + **ть** = говори́ть "to speak"

6. The Past Tense

Ке́вин говори́л хорошо́.	Kevin spoke well.
Та́ня говори́ла хорошо́.	Tanya spoke well.
Мы говори́ли хорошо́.	We spoke well.

---

[3] When two vowels combine, the first one is dropped. See "Combination Rules" below, Analysis II, 7.

[4] Note that the stem consonant -**рь**- is soft, hence the **ю**, **ят** spelling.

The past tense marker is –л which is followed by the appropriate gender/number marker as to agree with the subject:

				Examples
говори́ +	л +	-ø	(masculine subject)	он говори́л
(verbal stem)		-a	(feminine subject)	она́ говори́ла
		-o	(neuter subject)	оно́ говори́ло
		-и	(plural subject)	они́ говори́ли

Note that *person* is not expressed in the past tense, only gender. Ке́вин would say, «я говори́л» whereas Та́ня would say, «я говори́ла». Also note that all genders share the same plural past tense form:

Де́вушки чита́ли. The girls were reading.
Ма́льчики чита́ли. The boys were reading.

7. The Combination Rules

These rules apply to the *junctures* where endings are combined with stems. You can see from the foregoing examples that some verb stems end in a consonant (e.g., жи̋в-, рабо́тай-), whereas others end in a vowel (e.g., говори́-). Moreover, some endings begin with a consonant (**-ть, -л, - ла**, etc.), while others begin with a vowel (**-у, -ёшь, -ёт**, etc.). Simple additions of endings to stems, will take place *whenever unlikes are combined*, i.e. whenever a stem that ends in a *vowel* (говори́- + ть) accent should be directly over и is combined with a consonantal ending, or whenever a stem ending in a *consonant* (жив + у), is combined with a vocalic ending.

However, when two consonants or two vowels come together at the juncture of stem and ending, the first one will "truncate", or be deleted. Note the form of the infinitive and past tense forms of the consonantal stem жи̋в-:

First consonant (в) + second consonant (ть) simplifies to second consonant (ть).

жи̋в + ть = жи**ть**
жи̋в + л = жил
   + ла = жила́
   + ло = жи́ло
   + ли = жи́ли

Stated briefly, *unlikes add, likes truncate*.

Thus, if C stands for "consonant" and V for "vowel",

$$C + V = CV \qquad\qquad V + C = VC$$

whereas,

$$C_1 + C_2 = C_2 \qquad\qquad V_1 + V_2 = V_2$$

Study the complete sample conjugation of the verb работать (рабóтай-) "work"

Present Tense			Process	Form
Sing.	1st pers.	я	рабóтай + ø + у	я рабóтаю
	2nd pers.	ты	рабóтай + ё + шь	ты рабóтаешь
	3rd pers.	он/онá/онó	рабóтай + ё + т	он/онá/онó рабóтает
Plural	1st pers.	мы	рабóтай + ё + м	мы рабóтаем
	2nd pers.	вы	рабóтай + ё + те	вы рабóтаете
	3rd pers.	онѝ	рабóтай + у + т	онѝ рабóтают

	Process	Form
Infinitive:	рабóтай + ть	рабóтать

[й + ть=ть] because $C^1 + C^2 = C^2$

Past	
Process	Form
он рабóтай + л	он рабóтал
онá рабóтай + ла	она рабóтала
онѝ рабóтай + ли	они рабóтали

[й + л = л]

8. Stress in Verbs

A stress mark (´) placed over a basic stem indicates that the stress falls on the marked syllable in *all* forms of the conjugation. The mark (ˣ) over a stem signals a *shifting* stress pattern, of which there are but two possible varieties: for basic stems containing suffixes, the stress shifts in the *present* tense[5]; for basic stems without suffixes, the stress shifts in the *past* tense.

In the past tense shift, stress moves from the ending to the stem in all forms except for the feminine singular (in present tense, stress remains fixed on the ending). The following conjugation of жѝв- "live" exemplifies the past-tense shifting pattern in Russian.

---

[5] For examples of present tense shift see Analysis V.

Present Tense		
	Sing.	**Plural**
1st pers.	я живу́	мы живём
2nd pers.	ты живёшь	вы живёте
3rd pers.	он/она́/оно́ живёт	они́ живу́т

Infinitive: **жи́ть**

он жил
она́ жила́
оно́ жи́ло
они́ жи́ли

9. Tense

Russian has only three tenses: past, present, and future. There are no Russian equivalents of the English indefinite, continuous, or perfect forms or of the forms of the future-in-the-past. Thus, a present tense form of the Russian verb corresponding to the English "work" may, depending on context, be translated in the following ways:

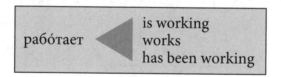

рабо́тает → is working / works / has been working

Сего́дня Ке́вин рабо́тает.   Kevin is working today.
Ке́вин мно́го рабо́тает.   Kevin works a lot.
Ке́вин давно́ рабо́тает.   Kevin has been working for a long time.

The past tense has the following possible English equivalents:

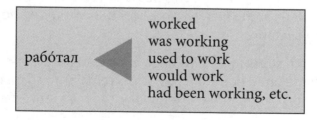

рабо́тал → worked / was working / used to work / would work / had been working, etc.

Ке́вин вчера́ до́лго <u>рабо́тал</u>.
Ке́вин <u>рабо́тал</u>, когда́ вы звони́ли.
Ра́ньше Ке́вин <u>рабо́тал</u> в рестора́не.
В университе́те Ке́вин <u>рабо́тал</u> в библиоте́ке.

Kevin <u>worked</u> for a long time yesterday.
Kevin was <u>working</u> when you called.
Kevin used to <u>work</u> at a restaurant.
In college Kevin <u>would work</u> at the library.

Context and your native intuition will help you select the appropriate English equivalents for Russian tense forms.

10. Third-Person Possessive Pronouns

The third-person possessive pronouns *never* change for agreement. Note the pronunciation of the masculine/neuter forms: **его́** /йиво́/ "his" or "its".

Э́то **его́** дом.
Э́то **его́** ко́мната.

This is his house.
This is his room.

Э́то **её** дом.
Э́то **её** ко́мната.

This is her house.
This is her room.

Э́то **их** дом.
Э́то **их** ко́мнаты.

This is their house.
These are their rooms.

11. Interrogative Possessive "whose"

The interrogative possessive agrees with its head word in number, gender, and case. The root of the word **чй-** is non-syllabic (does not contain a vowel). Study the spelling and pronunciation of the four forms we have seen so far.

Gender	Sing.	Forms
m.	ø	**чей** /чʲей + ø/
f.	a	**чья** /чʲй + a/
n.	o	**чьё** /чʲй + o/
pl.	и	**чьи** /чʲй + и/

— **Чей** э́то чемода́н?
— Э́то мой чемода́н.

Whose suitcase is this?
This is my suitcase.

— **Чья** э́то су́мка?
— Э́то его́ су́мка.

Whose bag is this?
This is his bag.

— **Чьи** э́то су́мки?
— Э́то на́ши су́мки.

Whose bags are these?
These are our bags.

12. The Prepositional Case

Place may be indicated in Russian by means of prepositional phrases consisting of the preposition **в** "in" or **на** "on the surface of" and the *prepositional case* of a noun.

Ке́вин живёт **в Москве́**.	Kevin lives *in Moscow.*
Ма́ма рабо́тает **в шко́ле**.	Mother works *at a school.*
Кни́га **на столе́**.	The book is *on the desk.*

but,

Кни́га **в столе́**.	The book is *in the desk.*

13. Formation of the Prepositional Case of Nouns

The prepositional case ending for most Russian nouns is **-e**.

Formation of the Prepositional Case of Nouns		
Case/Gen.	**Endings**	**Forms**
Nom. m.	**-ø/(-ь)**	стол, слова́рь
n.	**-o/(-e)**	окно́, мо́ре
f.	**-a/(-я)**	ка́рта, ку́хня
Prep. m.		в столе́, словаре́
n.	**-e**	в окне́, в море́
f.		на ка́рте, на ку́хне

14. Nouns Used with the Preposition на

A small group of Russian nouns occur in the prepositional case only with the preposition **на** when location is to be designated. For these nouns, the preposition **на** is the only means of expressing "in", "at", as well as "on". Here are some examples.

Он живёт **на да́че**.	He lives at the dacha.
Она́ рабо́тает **на по́чте**.	She works at the post office.
Они́ обе́дают **на ку́хне**.	They have lunch in the kitchen.

Keep in mind that whenever the preposition **на** is used with any other noun, the preposition retains its literal meaning "on the surface of" or "on top of".

15. Titles

Titles of newspapers, periodicals, books, articles, names of ships, trains, etc. are always set off in quotation marks; only the first letter of the first word is capitalized.

Э́то газе́та «Коммерса́нт».	This is the newspaper *Kommersant*.
Э́то журна́л «Москва́».	This is the magazine *Moscow*.
Влади́мир Петро́вич рабо́тает в газе́те «Аргуме́нты и фа́кты».	Vladimir Petrovich works at the newspaper *Arguments and Facts*.

NOUNS

- апельси́н orange
- бутербро́д sandwich
- ва́нная bathroom
- ви́лка fork
- гости́ная living room
- *гость guest*
- да́ча dacha (cottage)
- дива́н sofa
- до́чка daughter
- *игру́шка toy*
- *калькуля́тор calculator*
- кли́ника clinic
- ключ key
- колбаса́ salami, sausage
- колле́дж college
- кре́сло armchair
- *ксе́рокс photocopier*
- ку́хня kitchen
- ло́жка spoon
- ма́сло butter
- *монито́р monitor screen*
- *му́сор trash, garbage*
- нож knife
- обе́д lunch
- о́фис office
- паке́т plastic bag
- плита́ stove
- подъе́зд entrance
- по́лка shelf
- помидо́р tomato
- *при́нтер printer*
- *профе́ссор professor*
- рабо́та work
- ра́дио radio
- *ра́ковина sink*
- роди́тели (pl.) parents
- *са́хар sugar*
- *ска́нер scanner*
- *соль salt*
- сосе́дка neighbor (female)
- спа́льня bedroom
- столо́вая
- сын son
- сыр cheese
- таре́лка plate
- телеви́зор television set

- *факс fax*
- фотогра́фия photograph
- хлеб bread
- холоди́льник refrigerator
- ча́йник teakettle
- ча́шка cup
- шкаф closet, walk-in closet, wardrobe
- штат state

PROPER NOUNS

- *Арба́т Arbat (street in Moscow)*
- *Балтимо́р Baltimore*
- *Берли́н Berlin*
- *Бо́стон Boston*
- *Вашингто́н Washington*
- *Детро́йт Detroit*
- *Ки́ев Kiev (capital of Ukraine)*
- *Ло́ндон London*
- *Лос-А́нжелес Los Angeles*
- *Мадри́д Madrid*
- *Мэ́дисон Madison*
- *Оде́сса Odessa (city in Ukraine)*
- *Па́вловск Pavlovsk (city in Russia)*
- *Пу́шкин Pushkin (city in Russia)*
- *Пари́ж Paris*
- *Сара́тов Saratov (city in Russia)*
- *Ташке́нт Tashkent (capital of Uzbekistan)*
- *То́кио Tokyo*

PRONOUNS

- его́ his
- её her
- их their
- чей, чья, чьё, чьи whose

VERBS

- говори́ть (говори́-) speak
- гуля́ть (гуля́й-) walk
- де́лать (де́лай-) do
- ду́мать (ду́май-) think
- жить (жи̂в-) live

- за́втракать (за́втракай-) have breakfast
- знать (знай-) know
- обе́дать (обе́дай-) have lunch
- *опа́здывать (опа́здывай-) be late*
- отвеча́ть (отвеча́й-) answer
- отдыха́ть (отдыха́й-) rest
- понима́ть (понима́й-) understand
- рабо́тать (рабо́тай-) work
- спра́шивать (спра́шивай-) ask
- у́жинать (у́жинай-) have dinner
- чита́ть (чита́й-) read

ADVERBS

- бы́стро fast
- ве́чером in the evening
- *вку́сно tasty, delicious*
- всегда́ always
- вчера́ yesterday
- днём in the afternoon
- до́ма at home
- здесь here
- иногда́ sometimes
- интере́сно interesting
- ле́том in the summer
- ма́ло little, few
- мно́го much, many
- *наве́рное probably*
- непло́хо not bad
- *отли́чно excellent, great*
- о́чень very
- пло́хо bad
- по-англи́йски (in) English
- по-испа́нски (in) Spanish
- по-неме́цки (in) German
- по-ру́сски (in) Russian
- по-францу́зски (in) French
- по-япо́нски (in) Japanese
- *про́сто simply*
- ра́ньше previously, used to
- ре́дко seldom
- сего́дня today
- сейча́с now

ýтром in the morning
хорошó good
чáсто often

PREPOSITIONS

в in, at
на on, in/at

CONJUNCTIONS

úли or

EXPRESSIONS

ах oh
Вы не знáете … ? (Ты не
  знáешь …?) Do you
  happen to know … ?
Давáйте на «ты». Let's use ты.
До зáвтра. See you tomorrow.
  (goodbye)
интерéсно … I wonder …
Как же так? How come?

по-мóему in my opinion, I
  think
Скажúте, пожáлуйста …
  Please tell (me) …
Что ты! (Что вы!) What are
  you talking about? What
  do you mean?

*T*anya leaves Kevin to settle into his new apartment and heads home on the metro. Tanya then gets ready for her date with Misha after deliberating over what to wear.

Что де́лать?

You will learn how to:

- INFORMALLY GREET SOMEONE AND SAY GOODBYE
- ASK ABOUT AND DESCRIBE OBJECTS
- INQUIRE ABOUT THE ATTRIBUTES OF A GIVEN NOUN
- FORM ANTONYMS OF ADJECTIVES
- STATE YOUR OPINION
- EXPRESS UNCERTAINTY
- EXPRESS DISAGREEMENT
- REACT TO A NEGATIVE RESPONSE
- DISCUSS WHERE PEOPLE LIVE, WORK, ETC.
- INTRODUCE PEOPLE TO EACH OTHER
- CONDUCT A TELEPHONE CONVERSATION
- AGREE AND DISAGREE IN INFORMAL CONVERSATIONS
- TALK ABOUT LIFE IN COLLEGE
- DESCRIBE YOURSELF
- CONDUCT AN INFORMAL CONVERSATION
- TALK ABOUT FASHION
- EXPRESS YOUR PREFERENCES

▶ After saying goodbye to Кéвин, Тáня rushes home to change before her big date with her boyfriend Мúша later that evening. We're about to see how Тáня gets home.

1. The letter M you see above stands for:

☐ Макдóналдс

☐ метрó▲

☐ магазúн «Москвá»

▲ The Moscow metro (subway) system is one of the largest and most beautifully decorated metro systems in the world. The first several stations were built in 1935. Today the Moscow metro system has one hundred and seventy-six stations and nine lines that connect the downtown area with suburbs as far as 10–15 miles away. A "ring" line runs all around the center of the city and intersects with the rest of the lines.

2. A. In order to take the subway, Та́ня will need to buy a subway card (**биле́т**) from the **ка́сса**. The word **ка́сса** refers to the cash register where you pay for a theater ticket, groceries, a train ticket, or clothing. The person who works at a **ка́сса** is called a **касси́р**.

Can you come up with an English translation for the word **ка́сса**? If you can't come up with one word, can you think of a few equivalent expressions?

_____

_____

B. One can buy **биле́т** for a single ride or for multiple rides. The cost of a one-way trip anywhere on the subway line, regardless of the length of the trip is 19 rubles (the price for January 2008). How much would this ride cost in American dollars?

_____

_____

3. Take a look at the title of this episode «**Что де́лать?**» Who might say this? Someone who is:

☐ bored

☐ at a loss

☐ angry

4. Та́ня says «**Что де́лать?**» at the end of this episode. Can you speculate as to what might cause her to say this?

_____

_____

▶ Now watch the video with the SOUND OFF.

SOUND OFF

VIEWING

5. Here we get a chance to see what Та́ня's apartment looks like. Who is home when she first arrives? What are these people doing?

_____

6. Та́ня is rushing home to change for her big date with her boyfriend Ми́ша.

A. Circle the items of clothing Та́ня considers wearing.

Оде́жда

оде́жда = clothing

шарф   ту́фли   ю́бка   брю́ки   ма́йка

кроссо́вки   ко́фта   пла́тье   руба́шка

B. What does Та́ня's mom think about her daughter's taste in clothing? She:
- ☐ is critical
- ☐ approves
- ☐ is indifferent

C. Та́ня's dad
- ☐ remains neutral
- ☐ is supportive of his daughter
- ☐ disapproves of all the fuss

D. Judging by the outfits she is looking at, where do you think Та́ня is going on a date? To the:
- ☐ да́ча
- ☐ теа́тр
- ☐ стадио́н

7. A young man and woman come to visit Та́ня. Who do you think they are?

☐ relatives

☐ friends

☐ neighbors

8. How would you describe Та́ня's reaction to the phone call at the end of the episode?

☐ shocked

☐ overjoyed

☐ angry

▶ Now watch the video with the SOUND ON.

SOUND ON

9. Which topics does Та́ня discuss with her parents? Check all that apply.

☐ институ́т

☐ Ке́вин

☐ оде́жда

☐ рабо́та

☐ у́жин

у́жин = dinner

10. How do Та́ня's friends address her mother?

☐ ма́ма

☐ А́нна Бори́совна

☐ А́ня

11. Ле́на introduces her new friend to Та́ня's parents. What is his name?

☐ Па́ша

☐ Никола́й

☐ Са́ша

12. A. What topics do Та́ня and Ле́на discuss? Check all that apply.

☐ теа́тр

☐ институ́т

☐ друзья́

☐ рабо́та

☐ Са́ша

☐ де́ти

друг (sg.) = friend
друзья́ (pl.) = friends

ребёнок (sg.) = child
де́ти (pl.) = children

B. How does Та́ня say goodbye to Ле́на?

- ☐ До свида́ния!
- ☐ До за́втра!
- ☐ Пока́!

пока́ = bye

13. A. If you said that Та́ня was shocked by her phone conversation, you were right! Can you tell who is calling?

- ☐ Ми́ша
- ☐ Ке́вин
- ☐ Ле́на

B. Where is this person calling from?

- ☐ мили́ция
- ☐ больни́ца
- ☐ кварти́ра

мили́ция = police station, police

Using Polite and Informal Forms of Address

> POSTviewing

> Ле́на and Са́ша address Та́ня's mother using her first name and *patronymic*: **А́нна Бори́совна.** For both men and women, the patronymic is created from a person's father's first name by adding **–ович** (for men) and **–овна** (for women) and literally means, "the son/daughter of …." In Russian this is the most polite way to address an adult.

This chart lists various forms of address. The *diminutive* form is a shorter version of the first name and is used informally. It is similar to the English "Bob" instead of Robert or "Liz" instead of Elizabeth.

Diminutive	First Name	First name + Patronymic
А́ня	А́нна	А́нна Бори́совна
Ви́тя	Ви́ктор	Ви́ктор Степа́нович
Та́ня	Татья́на	Татья́на Ви́кторовна
О́ля	О́льга	О́льга Ви́кторовна
Да́ша	Да́рья	Да́рья Фёдоровна
Ле́на	Еле́на	Еле́на Алекса́ндровна
Ми́ша	Михаи́л	Михаи́л Ива́нович

14. A. Compare the patronymics of the men and women in the list above. How are the endings different?

_____

_____

B. Now find and underline the name of each person's father in the patronymics (ex. А́нна <u>Бори́с</u>овна.)

C. Suppose Та́ня introduces Ке́вин to her friends and family. What form of address would he use with the following people?

друг Ми́ша _____

ма́ма _____

па́па _____

сестра́ О́ля _____

подру́га Да́ша _____

15. Greetings and goodbyes

A. Did you notice that there were some new words and phrases for "hello" and "goodbye" in this episode? Place the words below in the appropriate column. Check the ones that are informal.

здра́вствуйте   до свида́ния

~~алло́~~ Allo!   до за́втра

приве́т   ~~пока́~~ noka

до́брый (ве́чер)   _____

[алло́, до́брый ве́чер, пока́, до за́втра, приве́т]

B. How would you say "hello" and "goodbye" to the characters in the video, assuming you were meeting them for the first time? Use the chart of Russian names from the opposite page as a reference.

> 2
> До́брый вечер, А́нна Бори́совна!

16. Тáня can never find anything, including her own clothes. Act out a conversation in which she asks her mom where her clothes are.

> 3
> — Ты не знаешь, где мои́ **джи́нсы**?
> 1   1
> — Вот они́, **на сту́ле**.

джи́нсы, ку́ртка, сви́тер, футбо́лка, ю́бка, ко́фта,
пла́тье, ту́фли, шарф, ма́йка, кроссо́вки, костю́м

стул, ку́хня, дива́н, кре́сло, по́лка, ко́мната

1. Let's colorize this picture! Name the color of each item shown.

Dictionaries always list adjectives in the masculine form.

бе́лый	white
голубо́й	(light) blue
жёлтый	yellow
зелёный	green
кори́чневый	brown
кра́сный	red
ора́нжевый	orange
се́рый	grey
чёрный	black

> 2
> — Какой это цвет?
> 1
> — Это **оранжевый** цвет.

Adjectives

	masculine Какой?	feminine Какая?	neuter Какое?	plural Какие?
unstressed ending	кра́сн**ый** *шарф*	кра́сн**ая** *ко́фта*	кра́сн**ое** *пла́тье*	кра́сн**ые** *ту́фли*
stressed ending	голубо́**й**	голуба́**я**	голубо́**е**	голубы́**е**

2. Practicing pronunciation: adjectives

бе́лый шарф, бе́лая ю́бка, бе́лое пла́тье, бе́лые ту́фли

ру́сский уче́бник, ру́сская кни́га, ру́сское сло́во, ру́сские газе́ты

хоро́ший костю́м, хоро́шая кварти́ра, хоро́шее письмо́, хоро́шие маши́ны

большо́й мост, больша́я библиоте́ка, большо́е общежи́тие, больши́е ко́мнаты

3. Describe the adjectives below in terms of how the endings are spelled. Underline all the endings which involve the spelling rules you have learned.

он	она́	оно́	они́
кра́сный	кра́сная	кра́сное	кра́сные
ру́сский	ру́сская	ру́сское	ру́сские
хоро́ший	хоро́шая	хоро́шее	хоро́шие
плохо́й	плоха́я	плохо́е	плохи́е
большо́й	больша́я	большо́е	больши́е

▲ Russian college students almost always live with their parents if their university is located in their hometown. If they are from a different city they usually live in the dormitory. Dormitories in Russia very often are located quite a distance away from the actual universities and colleges.

4. Assign colors to the following list of food items. Remember that the adjective you choose must agree with the noun it modifies.

> **бе́лый** хлеб
> **чёрный** хлеб

салат = lettuce

_____ сала́т   _____ молоко́

_____ бана́ны   _____ сыр

икра́ = caviar

_____ помидо́ры   _____ икра́

Antonyms

хоро́ший → плохо́й good bad	большо́й → ма́ленький large small	
но́вый → ста́рый new old	молодо́й → ста́рый young old	
	дли́нный → коро́ткий long short	

Sometimes antonyms can be formed simply by adding the prefix **не**-:

краси́вый → **не**краси́вый
beautiful   not beautiful

интере́сный → **не**интере́сный
interesting   not interesting

симпати́чный → **не**симпати́чный
nice   not nice

> 2
> — **Како́й** э́то го́род?
> 1
> — Э́то **большо́й** го́род.

> 2
> — **Кака́я** э́то маши́на?
> 1
> — Э́то **но́вая** маши́на.

5. Како́й э́то дом?

А.

но́вая - ста́рая

большо́й - ма́ленький   хоро́шее - плохо́е

— **Како́й** э́то дом?   — **Кака́я** э́то маши́на?   — **Како́е** э́то общежи́тие?
— Э́то ___ дом.   — Э́то ___ маши́на.   — Э́то ___ общежи́тие.

B. Now describe your own (or your family's) house, car, and your
dormitory using the words below.

>   1
> Наш дом **краси́вый**.
>   1
> Моя́ маши́на **красная**.
>   1
> Моё общежи́тие **большо́е**.

> большо́й - ма́ленький, но́вый – ста́рый, хоро́ший
> – плохо́й, краси́вый – некраси́вый; бе́лый, чёрный,
> кори́чневый, се́рый, кра́сный, ора́нжевый, зелёный,
> жёлтый, голубо́й

> **Како́й** can also be used for emphasis in exclamations:
>   2
> **Како́й** ста́рый дом!
> "What an old house!"

6. Below are some of Ке́вин's observations about things he has seen in Moscow. Fill in the appropriate form of како́й in Ке́вин's statements, making sure that it agrees in gender and number with the noun it modifies.

Exclamations are pronounced with IC-2.

> Како́й ста́рый дом! [2]

1. _Како́й_ дли́нный мост!
2. _Каки́е_ интере́сные лю́ди!
3. _Како́е_ краси́вое метро́!
4. _Кака́я_ ста́рая у́лица!
5. _Како́е_ ма́ленькое кафе́!
6. _~~Кака́я~~ Кака́я_ больша́я гости́ница!
7. _Каки́е_ краси́вые де́ти!
8. _Како́й_ хоро́ший парк!
9. _Како́й_ стра́нный челове́к!
10. _Како́й_ симпати́чный ребёнок!

стра́нный = strange

7. Describing places

A. Imagine that Та́ня is showing Ке́вин some pictures of her old neighborhood. Since they are blurry (Та́ня is a lousy photographer), Ке́вин is constantly asking questions about what is pictured. Provide Та́ня's responses using antonyms for the adjectives Ке́вин uses.

> Ке́вин: — Э́то **но́вый** дом? [3]
>
> Та́ня: — Нет, **ста́рый**. [1] [1]

1. Э́то хоро́шая гости́ница?

2. Э́то ста́рая больни́ца?

3. Э́то ма́ленькие магази́ны?

4. Э́то но́вый музе́й?

5. Э́то больша́я у́лица?

6. Э́то дли́нный мост?

B. A travel agent is showing you and your roommate pictures of different places in Russia. You can't seem to agree on where to go. Contradict your roommate using the adjectives provided.

> — Э́то **краси́вый** го́род.
>
> — Нет, э́то **некраси́вый** го́род.

1. Э́то _____ го́род.

2. Э́то _____ дом.

3. Э́то _____ у́лицы.

4. Э́то _____ кварти́ра.

5. Э́то _____ ко́мнаты.

6. Э́то _____ гости́ница.

7. Э́то _____ музе́й.

8. Э́то _____ теа́тр.

> но́вый – ста́рый, хоро́ший – плохо́й, большо́й –
> ма́ленький, краси́вый – некраси́вый, интере́сный –
> неинтере́сный, симпати́чный – несимпати́чный

8. A. In the following conversation, Кéвин learns that Сергéй used to live in Ростóв. Кéвин asks him about the city.

Кéвин:	Сергей, ты всегда жил **в Москве́**?
Сергéй:	Нет, ра́ньше я жил **в Ростове**.
Кéвин:	Это **краси́вый** гóрод?
Сергéй:	**Очень краси́вый**.
Кéвин:	Это **новый** гóрод?
Сергéй:	Нет, **старый**. **Очень ста́рый**.
Кéвин:	А **большой**?
Сергéй:	Да, **большой**.

B. Now ask your partner about places where s/he used to live, using Кéвин and Сергéй's dialog as a model.

большóй – ма́ленький, краси́вый – некраси́вый, нóвый – ста́рый

Э́тот дом большо́й, а **тот** дом ма́ленький.

Э́та соба́ка больша́я, а **та** соба́ка ма́ленькая.

Э́то окно́ большо́е, а **то** окно́ ма́ленькое.

Э́ти маши́ны больши́е, а **те** маши́ны ма́ленькие.

The Demonstrative Pronouns Э́тот/Тот (This/That)			
Singular			Plural
masculine	feminine	neuter	
э́тот	э́та	э́то	э́ти
тот	та	то	те

1. По-мо́ему….

Transform the following statements about fashion into opinions by adding **по-мо́ему** to the beginning of each statement.

> 1
> Э́та ко́фта краси́вая. →
> 3   1
> **По-моему**, э́та ко́фта краси́вая.

1. Э́ти ту́фли о́чень мо́дные.
2. Э́тот шарф краси́вый.
3. Э́то пла́тье коро́ткое.
4. Э́ти кроссо́вки немо́дные.
5. Э́та ма́йка хоро́шая.
6. Э́ти брю́ки плохи́е.
7. Э́ти джи́нсы мо́дные.
8. Э́та руба́шка некраси́вая.

2. Look at the picture of two houses on the previous page. Working with your partner, list as many adjectives as you can to describe each house. Then, construct sentences that describe both houses.

> 3   1
> Э́тот дом большо́й, а тот дом ма́ленький.

[
ма́ленький, большо́й, ста́рый, краси́вый, смешно́й, но́вый, некраси́вый, интере́сный, плохо́й
]

3. As you are looking for bargains in a thrift store, an eager salesperson tries to help you find just the right thing. Fill in the missing part of his/her sentences.

> 3   1
> Э́ти джи́нсы больши́е, а **те** — ма́ленькие.

1. _____ ко́фта интере́сная, а _____ — неинтере́сная.

2. _____ шарф дли́нный, а _____ — коро́ткий.

3. _____ кроссо́вки мо́дные, а _____ — немо́дные.

4. _____ ту́фли хоро́шие, а _____ — плохи́е.

5. _____ пла́тье но́вое, а _____ — ста́рое.

6. _____ ма́йка краси́вая, а _____ — некраси́вая.

4. Practicing pronunciation: adjectival phrases

жёлтый плащ, жёлтая ю́бка, жёлтое пла́тье, жёлтые кроссо́вки

ора́нжевый шарф, ора́нжевая руба́шка, ора́нжевое пла́тье, ора́нжевые брю́ки

Зелёный сви́тер, зелёная ма́йка, зелёное пла́тье, зелёные джи́нсы

5. You are at a store helping your friend, who is color-blind, pick out some new clothes. Tell your friend what color each item is.

> — Э́та ку́ртка кра́сная?
>
> — Нет, она́ зелёная.

э́тот	ко́фта	чёрный
	ю́бка	кра́сный
	пла́тье	жёлтый
э́та	брю́ки	голубо́й
	джи́нсы	бе́лый
э́то	руба́шка	зелёный
	ту́фли	ора́нжевый
э́ти	шарф	кори́чневый
	ку́ртка	се́рый
	кроссо́вки	
	ма́йка	
	сви́тер	
	плащ	
	костю́м	

Superlatives

большо́й го́род	**са́мый** большо́й го́род в ми́ре
больша́я ко́мната	**са́мая** больша́я ко́мната в кварти́ре
большо́е окно́	**са́мое** большо́е окно́ в до́ме.
больши́е магази́ны	**са́мые** больши́е магази́ны в го́роде

Placed before an adjective **са́мый** transforms the adjectival phrase into a superlative phrase: **са́мый большо́й дом** = the biggest house, **са́мый краси́вый дом** = the most beautiful house. **Са́мый** agrees with the noun exactly the way any other adjective does.

6. Како́й са́мый краси́вый цвет?

A volunteer conducts a poll of the class. Write the names of colors on the board and count up the number of votes for each color. Which color is the most popular?

— Како́й са́мый краси́вый цвет?

— По-моему, са́мый краси́вый цвет — **бе́лый**.

— Са́мый популя́рный цвет в на́шем кла́ссе — **кра́сный**.

7. Insert the appropriate form of **са́мый**.

Э́то **са́мый** интере́сный журна́л в библиоте́ке.

1. Э́то _____ весёл**ые** де́ти в шко́ле.

2. Э́то _____ интере́сн**ые** фи́льмы в го́роде.

3. Э́то _____ вку́сн**ый** сала́т на столе́.

4. Э́то _____ стра́нн**ое** пла́тье в магази́не.

5. Э́то _____ мо́дн**ая** су́мка в магази́не.

6. Э́то _____ плох**о́й** холоди́льник в до́ме.

7. Э́то _____ ста́р**ые** ве́щи в кварти́ре.

8. Э́то _____ хоро́ш**ие** словари́ в библиоте́ке.

8. In addition to describing the most beautiful things you've seen, you might also want to tell your partner what your favorite things are. Use the adjective **са́мый люби́мый**. If there are any words you would like to use but don't know, ask the instructor.

люби́мый = favorite

> — Моя́ са́мая люби́мая³ гру́ппа – «Лед Зепелин»¹.
>
> — А моя́ са́мая люби́мая³ гру́ппа – «Ю-Ту»¹.

1. Моя́ са́мая люби́мая гру́ппа — _____.

2. Мой са́мый люби́мый го́род — _____.

3. Мой са́мый _____ фильм — _____.

4. Моя́ са́мая _____ соба́ка — _____.

5. Моя́ са́мая _____ маши́на — _____.

6. Мой са́мый _____ спорт — _____.

7. Моя́ са́мая _____ кни́га — _____.

8. Мой са́мый _____ журна́л — _____.

9. Мой са́мый _____ рестора́н — _____.

10. Мой са́мый _____ курс — _____.

курс = college class

Adjectives Referring to National Origin

If your favorite class is Russian (or any other foreign language), now you can say it in Russian:

> Мой са́мый люби́мый курс — **ру́сский** язы́к.
>
> **англи́йский** язы́к   **испа́нский** язы́к   **неме́цкий** язы́к
> **францу́зский** язы́к   **япо́нский** язы́к

язы́к = language

9. Using the list above, fill in the appropriate adjectives referring to national origin.

> Брэд Питт — **америка́нский**¹ актёр.³

A. 1. «Битлз» — _____ гру́ппа.

2. Чайко́вский — _____ компози́тор.

3. Рокфе́ллер — _____ бизнесме́н.

4. Наполео́н — _____ импера́тор.

5. Шекспи́р — _____ писа́тель.

6. Эйнште́йн — _____ фи́зик.

7. Ба́рбара Уо́лтерс — _____ журнали́стка.

8. Пика́ссо — _____ худо́жник.

B. 1. Нисса́н — _____ маши́на.

2. Пари́ж — _____ го́род.

3. Гаспа́чо — _____ суп.

4. Макдо́налдс — _____ рестора́н.

5. Столи́чная — _____ во́дка.

6. Мерседе́с — _____ маши́на.

10. A. Describe the movies playing at the Moscow movie theater, «Ко́смос», listed below according to their country of origin.▲

>   1   3   2
> — «Дракула» — э́то **русский** и́ли **американский** фильм?
>   1
> — **Американский**.

> «Аэропо́рт», «А́нна Каре́нина», «Бэ́тмен», «Ма́ленькая Ве́ра», «До́ктор Жива́го», «Фо́ррест Гамп», «Трансфо́рмеры», «Окно́ в Пари́ж», «До́ктор Кто»

▲ Movie theaters in Moscow do not generally have multiple screens. One movie will be shown for a period of two weeks or so, and then another one takes its place. And movie-going is not as popular today as it once was. More and more people watch videos at home.

B. Act out Ке́вин and Та́ня's discussion of one of the movies playing at the «**Ко́смос**» and then discuss a movie of your choice.

Та́ня: — Ты не зна́ешь, «Фо́ррест Гамп» **хоро́ший** фильм?

Ке́вин: — По-мо́ему, **о́чень**.

Та́ня: — Э́то **америка́нский** фильм?

Ке́вин: — Да, **америка́нский**.

Та́ня: — **Интере́сный**?

Ке́вин: — Да, о́чень. О́чень **смешно́й**.

> ру́сский, америка́нский, францу́зский, англи́йский;
> но́вый – ста́рый; хоро́ший – плохо́й;
> смешно́й – серьёзный; интере́сный – неинтере́сный.

смешно́й = funny

серьёзный = serious

1. A. List the names of the characters who appear in the first part of the video.

_____

_____

_____

B. Describe each of the characters using a few adjectives from the following list.

весёлый = cheerful

> 3   1
> По-моему, **Та́ня молода́я и весёлая**.

[
молодо́й – ста́рый, весёлый – невесёлый,
серьёзный – несерьёзный, энерги́чный
– неэнерги́чный, смешно́й – несмешно́й,
интере́сный – неинтере́сный, симпати́чный –
несимпати́чный
]

2. You will be talking about fashion in this unit, so make a list of the clothing items you have learned so far.

_____

_____

_____

3. A. Та́ня asks her mother if she has heard from О́ля, who is out of town on business. What is Та́ня's relationship to О́ля?

- ☐ подру́га
- ☐ сестра́
- ☐ тётя

B. Таня asks her dad, «**Как дела́?**». What is his response?

- ☐ Норма́льно.
- ☐ Пло́хо.
- ☐ Хорошо́.

C. What word does Та́ня use when describing Ке́вин to her father?

- ☐ большо́й
- ☐ симпати́чный
- ☐ мо́дный

D. What is Ке́вин's profession?

- ☐ студе́нт
- ☐ инжене́р
- ☐ фото́граф

4. A. Which of the following items does Та́ня's mother suggest she wear?

- ☐ жёлтое пла́тье
- ☐ джи́нсы
- ☐ си́няя ю́бка

B. What is Та́ня's father's reaction to her final choice?

- ☐ Отли́чно!
- ☐ Ой, как ужа́сно!
- ☐ По-мо́ему, о́чень хорошо́.

«Как дела?»

Everyone likes to keep up with friends and family. Do you remember how Та́ня asks her father, "How are things going?"

> Та́ня: — Приве́т, па́па. **Как дела́?**
> па́па: — Норма́льно.

«**Как дела́?**» is only used in informal conversation between friends, family members, and colleagues. It is inappropriate in official settings or while talking to your professor, someone who is your senior or someone who is in a position of authority.

5. Ask your partner how things are going at work, at home, and at school, using the phrase «**Как дела́?**»

> — Как дела́ **в институ́те?** [2]
> — **Норма́льно.** [1]

на рабо́те, в институ́те, в университе́те, в колле́дже, до́ма

норма́льно, отли́чно, хорошо́, непло́хо, пло́хо, ужа́сно

ужа́сно = terrible

Nationalities			
Country	**Citizenship/Nationality**		**Adjective (какóй?)**
	masculine	**feminine**	
Россúя	рýсский	рýсская	рýсский
Амéрика (США)	американец	американка	американский
Áнглия	англичáнин	англичáнка	англúйский
Гермáния	нéмец	нéмка	немéцкий
Испáния	испáнец	испáнка	испáнский
Фрáнция	францýз	францýженка	францýзский
Япóния	японец	японка	японский

СШÁ /сэшэá/ = USA

Кéвин — **американец**.

Егó сестрá — **американка**.

«Фóррест Гамп» — **американский** фильм.

Кадиллáк — **американская** машúна.

Тáня's father asks where her American friend is:

пáпа: — А где твой американец?
Тáня: — Кéвин? Он дóма.

In Russian, a person's national origin is expressed with a noun (**американец**, **англичáнин**, etc). The only exception is **рýсский**. Nouns and adjectives describing national origin are never capitalized.

6. Fill in the appropriate nouns that indicate a person's nationality. Be sure to choose the correct gender!

> 1 1
> Моя́ подрýга живёт в Токио. Онá японка.

1. Ми́ша живёт в Москве́. Он _____.

2. Мои́ друзья́ живу́т в Пари́же. Они́ _____.

3. Моя́ подру́га живёт в Берли́не. Она́ _____.

4. Мой друг живёт в Ло́ндоне. Он _____.

5. Да́ша живёт в Аме́рике. Она́ не _____,
   она́ _____.

6. Э́тот челове́к живёт в Мадри́де. Он _____.

7. Та́ня's mother is curious about her new American friend. She asks:

ма́ма: — **Ну, как** он, симпати́чный?

Та́ня: — О́чень симпати́чный.

Ну, как он? = So, what is he like?

You have gone on a holiday shopping trip with your roommate. Ask him/her to comment on the items below.

> — Ну, как **кофта?** Краси́вая?
> *(2)* *(3)*
> — По-моему, **очень краси́вая.**
> *(3)* *(1)*

1. Ну, как джи́нсы? Неплохи́е?

2. Ну, как шарф? Краси́вый?

3. Ну, как кроссо́вки? Хоро́шие?

4. Ну, как ту́фли? Мо́дные?

5. Ну, как руба́шка? Неплоха́я?

6. Ну, как пла́тье? Симпати́чное?

7. Ну, как ма́йка? Хоро́шая?

8. Ну, как сви́тер? Симпати́чный?

хотéть "want"		
Present Tense		**Past Tense**
Singular	**Plural**	
я хочу́	мы хоти́м	он хоте́л
ты хо́чешь	вы хоти́те	она́ хоте́ла
он/она́ хо́чет	они́ хотя́т	оно́ хоте́ло
		они́ хоте́ли

The irregular verb **хотéть** is used to express a desire to do something: Я хочу́ **гуля́ть**; он хо́чет **чита́ть**. The verb that follows the conjugated form of хоте́ть is always in the infinitive.

8. Find out what your partner would like to do.

> — Ты хо́чешь **гуля́ть** и́ли **читать**?
>
> — Я хочу́ **гуля́ть**.

1. Ты хо́чешь говори́ть по-англи́йски и́ли по-ру́сски?
2. Ты хо́чешь у́жинать до́ма и́ли в рестора́не?
3. Ты хо́чешь рабо́тать и́ли отдыха́ть?
4. Ты хо́чешь отдыха́ть в Москве́ и́ли Петербу́рге?
5. Ты хо́чешь жить в Вашингто́не и́ли в Нью-Йо́рке?
6. Ты хо́чешь рабо́тать в университе́те и́ли в би́знесе?

9. When А́нна Бори́совна offers Та́ня some dinner, do you remember how Та́ня responds?

А́нна Бори́совна: — У́жин на плите́.¹

Та́ня: — Спаси́бо,² не хочу́.¹

Fill in appropriate replies to the following questions:

— Обе́д в холоди́льнике.

— _____.

— За́втрак на столе́.

— _____.

обе́д = lunch

за́втрак = breakfast

10. Disagree with your partner's outrageous commentary on different articles of clothing.

— По-моему, **э́ти кроссо́вки³ о́чень ста́рые**.¹
— Что ты!² Наоборо́т,² **они́² но́вые**.²

наоборо́т = on the contrary

э́ти ту́фли	ста́рый – но́вый
это пла́тье	мо́дный - немо́дный
э́ти брю́ки	краси́вый - некраси́вый
э́та ю́бка	хоро́ший - плохо́й
э́та ко́фта	коро́ткий - дли́нный
э́тот сви́тер	
э́та ма́йка	
э́ти джи́нсы	
э́тот костю́м	

Ке́вин живёт в э́том до́ме?   Та́ня живёт в э́той кварти́ре?

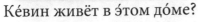

Possessive and Demonstrative Pronouns: Prepositional Case								
Case	Gender	Possessive Pronouns				Demonstrative Pronouns		
Nom.	m.	мой	твой	наш	ваш	э́тот	тот
	n.	моё	твоё	на́ше	ва́ше	э́то	то
	f.	моя́	твоя́	на́ша	ва́ша	э́та	та
Prep.	m./n.	моём	твоём	на́шем	ва́шем	э́том	том
	f.	мое́й	твое́й	на́шей	ва́шей	э́той	той

1. Fill in the missing possessive or demonstrative pronoun.

> 1
> — Да́ша живёт в **э́том** го́роде.

A. 1. Ми́ша рабо́тает в _____ кли́нике.
              this

2. Та́ня живёт в _____ до́ме.
            this

3. Ке́вин живёт в ____э́той____ кварти́ре.
              this

4. А́нна Бори́совна рабо́тает в ____той_____ шко́ле.
                    that

B. 1. Э́тот челове́к живёт в _____ гóроде.

　　　　　　　　　　　　　　　your (plural)

2. Мой словáрь в _____ кóмнате.

　　　　　　　　　　　　your (informal)

3. Егó сестрá рабóтает в _____ университéте.

　　　　　　　　　　　　　　my

4. Твоя́ подрýга хóчет рабóтать в _____ библиотéке.

　　　　　　　　　　　　　　　　　our

5. Э́то Волóдины. Мúша чáсто ýжинает в _____ дóме.

　　　　　　　　　　　　　　　　　　　their

6. Э́то Лéна. Сáша иногдá обéдает в _____ институ́те.

　　　　　　　　　　　　　　　　　her

Nouns ending in -**ий**, -**ия**, or -**ие** take the
prepositional ending -**и** instead of -**е**.

кафетéрий — в кафетéрии
лаборатóрия — в лаборатóрии
общежúтие — в общежúтии

---

2. Where do the following people live or work?

1. Тáня живёт в ___России___.

　　　　　　　　　　　　　　　(Россúя)

2. Рáньше мои́ друзья́ жи́ли ___этои общежитии___.

　　　　　　　　　　　　　　　(э́то общежúтие)

3. Мой брат рабóтал _____.

　　　　　　　　　　　　　　　(нáша лаборатóрия)

4. Моя́ тётя отдыхáла ___во франиуил___.

　　　　　　　　　　　　　　　(Фрáнция)

5. Лéтом моя́ подрýга рабóтала _____.

　　　　　　　　　　　　　　　(А́нглия)

6. Я живý ___в этои___.

　　　　　　　　　　　　　　　(э́то здáние)

3. Using the verb **хотéть** in conjunction with other verbs

Transform the following sentences to indicate what the subject
wants to do.

　　　　　　　　　　　　　　　　1
Он **рабóтает** в лаборатóрии. →

　　　　　　　　　　　　　　　　1
Он **хóчет рабóтать** в лаборатóрии.

---

1. Ке́вин **говори́т** по-ру́сски.

2. А́нна Бори́совна **рабо́тает** в э́той шко́ле.

3. Па́па **отдыха́л** в Герма́нии.

4. Мы **живём** в том общежи́тии.

5. Са́ша **рабо́тает** в твоём институ́те?

6. Э́ти лю́ди **говоря́т** по-ру́сски.

7. Та́ня **чита́ет** по-англи́йски.

8. Мы **у́жинаем** в э́том кафете́рии.

9. Вы **говори́те** по-францу́зски?

10. Ты **живёшь** в э́том зда́нии?

Months	
янва́рь	**в январе́**
февра́ль	**в феврале́**
март	в ма́рте
апре́ль	в апре́ле
май	в ма́е
ию́нь	в ию́не
ию́ль	в ию́ле
а́вгуст	в а́вгусте
сентя́брь	**в сентябре́**
октя́брь	**в октябре́**
ноя́брь	**в ноябре́**
дека́брь	**в декабре́**

In addition to being used to indicate location, **в** plus the prepositional case is also used in some time expressions (**в январе́** = in January). Notice that the fall and winter months (in bold) have ending stress. The names of months are not capitalized.

4. Practicing pronunciation: months

A. Practice pronouncing the months in the nominative and prepositional cases listed above.

If you are listing things, every item except for the last one can be pronounced with IC-3.

B. 1. Мои́ роди́тели не рабо́тали в ма́рте³, в апре́ле³ и в ма́е¹.

2. Моя́ подру́га рабо́тала в кафе́ в сентябре́³, в ноябре́³ и в декабре́¹.

3. Моя́ семья́ отдыха́ла в ию́не³, в ию́ле³ и в а́вгусте¹.

4. Мой брат рабо́тал в магази́не в январе́³, в феврале́³ и в ма́рте¹.

5. Мой друг рабо́тал в библиоте́ке в октябре́³, в ноябре́³ и в декабре́¹.

6. Мы не рабо́тали в апре́ле³, в ма́е³ и в ию́не¹.

5. In what month do the following events occur?

> my father's birthday → **в ноябре́**

1. Thanksgiving
2. New Year's Day▲
3. St. Patrick's Day
4. Memorial Day
5. Independence Day (US)
6. Halloween

▲ The New Year is the biggest celebration of the year in Russia. People decorate a New Year's Tree in their apartment, and on New Year's Eve they put gifts for their family under the tree. The tradition holds that Father Frost (**Дед Моро́з**) has come by and put the presents out for everyone.

7. Labor Day

8. Valentine's Day

9. Your birthday

10. Mother's Day

11. Father's Day

весно́й = in the spring	**ле́том** = in the summer
о́сенью = in the fall	**зимо́й** = in the winter

6. Respond to the following questions based on your own experience. Be sure to say both the month and the season in your answers.

1. Когда́ в ва́шем университе́те кани́кулы?

2. Когда́ в ва́шем университе́те экза́мены?

3. Когда́ вы отдыха́ете?

4. Когда́ вы рабо́таете?

кани́кулы = school vacation

экза́мен = exam

7. Talk about the weather in your city with your partner using the words for the months and the seasons.

> 2
> Когда́ са́мая хоро́шая пого́да **в Москве́**?
>
> 1
> **В Москве́** са́мая хоро́шая пого́да **ле́том**,
>
> 1
> **в ию́не и в ию́ле.**

пого́да = weather

A. Когда́ са́мая хоро́шая пого́да в ва́шем го́роде?

B. Когда́ са́мая плоха́я пого́да в ва́шем го́роде?

8. Imagine that you are at a university job fair looking for a part-time job on campus.

A. Various employers are asking you if you are interested in working for them. Working in groups of three or more, politely accept or decline their proposals.

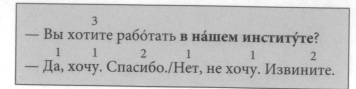

> 3
> — Вы хотите рабо́тать **в на́шем институ́те**?
> 1   1   2   1   1   2
> — Да, хочу. Спаси́бо./Нет, не хочу. Извини́те.

1. Вы хоти́те рабо́тать в на́шей лаборато́рии?
2. Вы хоти́те рабо́тать в на́шем кафете́рии?
3. Вы хоти́те рабо́тать в на́шем общежи́тии?
4. Вы хоти́те рабо́тать в на́шей библиоте́ке?
5. Вы хоти́те рабо́тать в на́шем це́нтре?

B. Now approach the employers yourself and tell them that you wish to work for them. Use the examples from the exercise above to formulate your statements.

> 1
> — Я хочу́ рабо́тать **в ва́шем институ́те**.
> 2   2
> — Отли́чно! А когда́ (вы хоти́те рабо́тать)?
> 1   3   1
> **— Осенью. В октябре́ и в ноябре́.**

C. After you have accepted a job, your prospective employer asks you whether your friend would like to work there, too.

> 1
> — Я хочу́ рабо́тать **в э́той лаборато́рии**.
> 4
> — А ва́ша подру́га?
> 1   1
> — И она́ хо́чет./ А она́ не хо́чет.

> тот центр, э́та библиоте́ка, та лаборато́рия, э́то общежи́тие, э́тот кафете́рий, тот магази́н, э́тот теа́тр, э́тот стадио́н, наш гара́ж, на́ша больни́ца, э́та по́чта

1. A. What time of day did Ле́на and Са́ша drop by to see Та́ня?

- ☐ у́тром
- ☐ днём
- ☐ ве́чером

B. А́нна Бори́совна greets them by saying:

- ☐ До́брое у́тро!
- ☐ До́брый день!
- ☐ До́брый ве́чер!

> до́брый = (here) good
> у́тро = morning
> день = afternoon
> ве́чер = evening

2. Identify the items Ле́на comes to pick up at Та́ня's apartment.

- ☐ ди́ски
- ☐ ю́бка
- ☐ кни́га

3. A. Ле́на tells Та́ня that her new friend Са́ша is a

- ☐ журнали́ст
- ☐ студе́нт
- ☐ архите́ктор

B. How would you characterize Тáня's reaction to Лéна's friend?

☐ angry

☐ positive

☐ disappointed

VIEWING >

4. What does Áнна Борúсовна say before she opens the door?

☐ Кто там?

☐ Кто тут?

☐ Как вас зовýт?

5. A. As a hospitable Russian hostess, Áнна Борúсовна offers her guests:

☐ обéд и чай

☐ бутербрóд и кóфе

☐ вóдка и икрá

B. Лéна

☐ accepts Áнна Борúсовна's offer

☐ asks for water instead

☐ rejects her offer

C. Сáша accepts which of the following?

☐ чай

☐ кóфе

☐ обéд

6. Mark the following statements as true or false. Э́то так úли нет?

	Да	Нет
Лéна doesn't like the red shirt and blue skirt.	☐	☐
Лéна loves all Тáня's outfits.	☐	☐
Тáня doesn't take Áнна Борúсовна's opinions on fashion seriously.	☐	☐

7. Тáня jokes that Сáша's last name is Пýшкин because:

☐ he loves poetry

☐ his first name and patronymic are the same as Пýшкин's

☐ he has curly hair just like Пýшкин

8. «Что де́лать?»

At the end of this episode, Та́ня gets a disturbing call from Ке́вин, who is being questioned by the police. How do you think Та́ня will handle the situation? Will she:

☐ break her date with Ми́ша and go help Ке́вин

☐ send her parents to help Ке́вин

☐ ask the American embassy to represent Ке́вин

Introducing Yourself and Others

You learned how to introduce yourself at the very beginning of this book:

— Здра́вствуйте! Я Са́ша.

To introduce two friends to each other, you would say:

— **Познако́мьтесь**, пожа́луйста. Э́то Са́ша.

In English we would say, "I'd like you to meet my friend Са́ша." When Ле́на's friend Са́ша introduces himself to Áнна Бори́совна, he uses a different construction:

— **Меня́ зову́т** Са́ша. (My name is Саша.)

You can use the same construction to ask someone their name:

— **Как вас зову́т**? (What is your name?)

9. А. In groups of 3 or more, introduce two friends who have never met before. Use the greetings, «До́брое у́тро!», «До́брый день!», and «До́брый ве́чер!»

<pre>
                          2
Жéня: — Дóброе утро!
                          2   2
Вы: — Дóброе утро, Жéня! Познакомьтесь!
                          2   1
Жéня: — Здравствуйте! Меня́ зову́т Женя.
                  1   2
Сáша: — А я Саша. Óчень приятно.
                          2
Жéня: — Óчень приятно.
</pre>

B. Now be brave and approach someone yourself! Spice things up by substituting a famous person's name for your own.

> — Здравствуйте! Как вас зовут?
>
> — Меня́ зову́т **Арнольд**. А как вас зову́т?
>
> — **Сильвестр**. О́чень прия́тно.
>
> — О́чень прия́тно.

10. Russians always invite their friends to join them when they are eating. As you read the following conversation between Са́ша and Ле́на, notice how Са́ша responds to Ле́на's rejection of his offer of food.

> Ле́на: — Что э́то? **Бутербро́д**?
>
> Саша: — Хо́чешь?
>
> Лена: — Спаси́бо, не хочу́.
>
> Саша: — Не хо́чешь? Как хо́чешь.

Now offer a friend in class some food using the above dialogue as a model.

> milk, soup, juice, sandwich, pizza

11. Pretend that you just bought something new. Show it to your partner and get his/her reaction.

> — Вот моя́ но́вая **ко́фта**. Ну, как?
>
> — По-мо́ему, она́ о́чень **краси́вая**.

Не хо́чешь, как хо́чешь.
= (here) Whatever you say.

> skirt, shoes, sneakers, jacket, jeans, scarf, pants,
> men's shirt, sweater, T-shirt

> beautiful, fashionable, nice, funny, interesting

Expressing Your Reactions
To Different Situations

In the video Та́ня and others react to what they hear or see in various ways ranging from approval to disapproval, from surprise to disbelief. Ле́на reacts to Та́ня's outfit by saying:

Здо́рово! (Great! Terrific!)

And Та́ня replies:

Пра́вда? (Really?)

When Та́ня is on the phone with Ке́вин and learns that something has happened, she says:

Не мо́жет быть! (That's impossible!)

Often we combine different reactions in one answer:

Пра́вда? Здо́рово! (Terrific!)
Пра́вда? Как хорошо́! (That's great!)
Пра́вда? Как пло́хо! (That's awful!)

Как хорошо́! and **Как пло́хо!** are used to react to a situation rather than to a concrete object.

12. Practicing pronunciation: intonation in exclamations and questions

1. — Пра́вда? Как интере́сно!

2. — Не мо́жет быть! Как здо́рово!

3. — Ну, как?

   — Отли́чно!

4. — Ну, как?²

   — По-моему, неплохо.¹

5. — Не может быть!²

13. Respond to the following statements using expressions from the preceding exercise.

> — Ке́вин хо́чет жить в Москве́.¹
>
> — Пра́вда?³ **Как интере́сно!**²

А. 1. Ке́вин говори́т по-ру́сски.

2. Да́ша и Та́ня хоро́шие друзья́.

3. Та́ня отдыха́ла на да́че.▲

4. Да́ша живёт в Аме́рике.

5. Ле́на и Та́ня хоро́шие студе́нтки.

6. Та́ня всегда́ опа́здывает.

опа́здывать
(опа́здыв**ай**-) = to be
late

В. 1. Мы не понима́ем по-ру́сски.

2. Э́ти лю́ди не понима́ют по-англи́йски.

3. Мои́ но́вые друзья́ о́чень симпати́чные.

4. Я ча́сто опа́здываю

5. Мои́ друзья́ живу́т в Росси́и.

6. Мой брат (моя́ сестра́) не хо́чет рабо́тать.

7. На́ши де́ти говоря́т по-ру́сски.

14. It's your turn to be the fashion expert. Make statements about fashion using **в мо́де, не в мо́де**. Add some of your own words to the list!

в мо́де = in style

▲ Russian college and university students have a longer school year than Americans. Their summer break is only two months long — July and August, and they have a two-week winter vacation at the end of January.

> 3 1
> — По-моему, **чёрные брю́ки** в моде.
> 1 1 2
> — Да, **чёрные брю́ки** в моде./ Что ты, **чёрные брю́ки**
> 1
> не в моде.

[
long skirts, white jeans, green scarves, short skirts,
black shoes, red sneakers, old things, small backpacks
]

Your words:_____

15. When Та́ня meets Ле́на's new friend, Са́ша, she is
impressed.

> 2
> Та́ня: — А твой Са́ша **ничего́!**
> 1 1
> Ле́на: — Да, он о́чень симпати́чный.

The first line is similar to the English "Your Sasha is not bad!"
Naturally, this is usually said about a person when s/he is not
present.

Using the dialog above as a model, comment on the
following people with a partner.

[
your sister (nice), your brother (interesting), your
friends (nice), Са́ша (handsome), Ле́на
(interesting)
]

16. Ле́на may like Та́ня's outfit, but Та́ня's mother has a
different opinion:

> Та́ня: — Ма́ма так не ду́мает.
> Ле́на: — **Так э́то же** ма́ма!

The second line can be roughly translated as, "Of course – after all, she's your mother!" The words **так это же** are pronounced with only one stress, as if they were one word.

Use this expression to comment on other people.

> 1
> — Да́ша хорошо́ говори́т по-англи́йски.
> 1
> — **Так это же** Да́ша!

1. Ке́вин хоро́ший фото́граф.
2. О́ля отли́чная журнали́стка.
3. Та́ня всегда́ опа́здывает.
4. Ми́ша мно́го рабо́тает.
5. Ке́вин хо́чет хорошо́ говори́ть по-ру́сски.
6. Ми́ша хо́чет рабо́тать в кли́нике.
7. Та́ня не хо́чет у́жинать.

3

Та́ня's friend Да́ша Серге́ева worked for the student newspaper «Зе́ркало» "The Mirror" when she was a student in Moscow. From time to time she sends them materials about her experiences in America. Here's an example.

M о́да на ка́мпусе

Да́ша Серге́ева сейча́с студе́нтка Мэриле́ндского университе́та в Ко́лледж Па́рке. В сентябре́ и в ноябре́ вы чита́ли в на́шей газе́те её репорта́жи о том, где, когда́ и как рабо́тают и отдыха́ют америка́нские студе́нты. Её но́вый репорта́ж о◊ *студе́нческой мо́де.*   about

На ка́мпусе Мэриле́ндского университе́та три цве́та: кра́сный, бе́лый и зелёный. Кра́сный—это кра́сные зда́ния. Бе́лый—бе́лые коло́нны. А зелёный цвет—это трава́◊ и   grass
дере́вья◊. Кста́ти, мо́жет быть не все зна́ют, что   trees
тако́е «ка́мпус». Ка́мпус—это студе́нческий городо́к: библиоте́ки, лаборато́рии, стадио́н, теа́тр, магази́ны, кафе́ и, коне́чно, общежи́тия.

Лю́ди, кото́рые живу́т в Мэриле́нде давно́◊,   for a long time
говоря́т, что о́сенью тут са́мая хоро́шая пого́да◊.   weather
И пра́вда. В октябре здесь тепло́◊ как в а́вгусте   warm
в Москве́ или в Петербу́рге. Студе́нты но́сят◊   wear
ма́йки и шо́рты и́ли коро́ткие ю́бки. Как ле́том!

Что же мо́дно на ка́мпусе? Что там но́сят? Я хочу́ рассказа́ть об одно́м интере́сном парадо́ксе. На ка́мпусе мо́дные ве́щи не в мо́де. Са́мая популя́рная оде́жда, по-пре́жнему◊,   still
джи́нсы и́ли шо́рты, ма́йки и кроссо́вки. Пра́вда,

студе́нты сейча́с ча́сто но́сят не традицио́нные кроссо́вки, а то, что мы всегда́ называ́ли «ке́ды». И, коне́чно, всё ещё популя́рны бейсбо́льные ке́пки◊, кото́рые ча́сто но́сят за́дом наперёд◊. О́чень популя́рны больши́е рюкзаки́. В тако́м большо́м рюкзаке́—кни́ги, уче́бники, за́втрак. А вот и но́вая тенде́нция. Де́вушки но́сят о́чень ма́ленькие, смешны́е рюкзаки́. Что в тако́м рюкзаке́? Ключи́, де́ньги◊, студе́нческий биле́т◊, креди́тная ка́рточка.

money

student ID

О́чень ча́сто ребя́та комбини́руют ра́зные цвета́ в оде́жде: кра́сный и бе́лый, жёлтый и зелёный. А ве́чером са́мый популя́рный цвет - чёрный.

Студе́нческая мо́да—э́то большо́й би́знес в США. Э́то хорошо́ зна́ют таки́е диза́йнерские компа́нии как Ка́лвин Кла́йн, Гес, Бенетто́н, То́мми Хи́лфигер, На́утика, По́ло. Но така́я оде́жда сто́ит о́чень до́рого◊. Поэ́тому студе́нты её ре́дко покупа́ют◊.

expensive

buy

1. Take a guess.

A. Judging from the title, can you guess what this article is about?

_____

_____

B. What kinds of words might you find in an article like this? Get into groups and write down some ideas in Russian.

_____

_____

2. Scan the first paragraph and find out the following information:

A. Who is the author of this article?

_____

B. The author is a

☐ professional writer

☐ student newspaper correspondent

☐ fashion critic

C. What is the article about?

☐ fashions in the U.S.

☐ campus fashions

☐ student designers

D. What university is mentioned by name and why?

_____

3. Read the following questions, then scan the whole text for the requested information. Write down your answers.

1. What is Дáша's definition of the word **кáмпус**? What would this word be in English?

_____

2. Find the place where Дáша describes the University of Maryland campus. List as many details as you can find.

_____

3. Why do you think Дáша finds it surprising that the weather is warm in College Park in October?

_____

4. What clothing is popular among students? Write down as many words as you can find.

_____

5. Find the place in the text where Дáша lists the most popular clothing on campus. Write down what she lists.

_____

6. According to Дáша, what is the function of backpacks?

_____

7. What colors do students prefer to wear during the day? At night?

_____

8. What fashion designers and brand names do you recognize in the text?

   _____

9. What do these designer names have to do with the students?
   ☐ They cater to students' tastes.
   ☐ They used to be students at Maryland.
   ☐ They use student models.

4. A. What do you think about the following statements?

> — Дли́нные пла́тья сейча́с в моде.
> — Да, правда./Что ты! Дли́нные пла́тья не в моде.

Да, пра́вда.
= Yes, this is
true.

1. Чёрный цвет в мо́де.
2. Сейча́с са́мые мо́дные су́мки — рюкзаки́.
3. Са́мая популя́рная оде́жда — джи́нсы и кроссо́вки.
4. Бейсбо́льные ке́пки в мо́де.

B. Now it's your turn to comment on trends on your campus.

> — В на́шем университе́те бейсбо́льные ке́пки в моде.
> — Что ты! Не мо́жет быть!/ Правда? Здорово!

Video Review

1. Put the following mini-episode titles in chronological order. Come up with alternative titles in English.

_____ Вот са́мое хоро́шее пла́тье.

_____ Мили́ция! Что де́лать?

_____ Познако́мьтесь, пожа́луйста. Э́то Са́ша.

_____ Э́то ты, Та́ня?

2. How well do you remember what happens in this episode? Mark the following statements as true or false. If the statements are false, make the necessary corrections.

	Да	Нет
Та́ня's parents are home when she arrives.	☐	☐
А́нна Бори́совна offers Та́ня lunch.	☐	☐
Та́ня decides to wear jeans on her date.	☐	☐
Ле́на and her brother Са́ша drop by to see Та́ня.	☐	☐

Áнна Борисовна offers Cáша some tea.▲   ☐   ☐

Kéвин calls Táня to tell her he is being
questioned by the police.   ☐   ☐

3. Based on Táня's conversation with her parents, put a check
mark by the following phrases if she uses them to describe
Kéвин.

Kéвин:

	Да	Нет
симпатичный	☒	☐
энергичный	☒	☐
серьёзный	☐	☒
молодой	☒	☐
студент	☐	☒
живёт в Бóстоне	☐	☒

4. A. When Áнна Борисовна tries to help Táня pick out an
outfit for her date, we discover that different generations
do not always agree on matters of style. Check Táня's
and her mother's preferences in the following list.

▲ Hot tea is by far the most popular drink in Russia. Russians brew a concentrated tea (called **завáрка**) with
loose tea leaves in small china teapots; they then add hot water to the strong tea in individual cups. Most
Russians also put several teaspoons of sugar into their tea. Iced tea is a rarity.

Та́ня:		А́нна Бори́совна
___	жёлтое пла́тье	___
___	си́няя ю́бка	___
___	бе́лая ко́фта	___
___	кра́сная ко́фта	___
___	зелёные ту́фли	___
___	кра́сные ту́фли	___

B. Circle the outfit that is Та́ня's final choice.

5. A. Listen carefully to the segment in which Ле́на introduces Са́ша to А́нна Бори́совна. Using the following translation as a reference, do a "voice-over" of the segment as you watch it with the sound off.

А.Б.: — Who's there?

Ле́на: — It's me, Lena.

А.Б.: — Good afternoon!

Ле́на: — Good afternoon, Anna Borisovna. I'd like you to meet Sasha.

А.Б.: — Excuse me? What's your name?

Са́ша: — My name is Sasha.

А.Б.: — Nice to meet you.

Са́ша: — Nice to meet you.

B. Based on Ле́на's conversation with Та́ня, mark the following statements about Са́ша as true or false. Correct the statements that are false.

	Да	Нет
His full name is Алекса́ндр Серге́евич Кузнецо́в.	☒	☐
He is a student.	☐	☒
He is an old friend.	☒	☐

6. Describe the relationship between the following pairs of characters from the video.

> Та́ня, Ле́на →
> Ле́на — **её подру́га.**

1. Та́ня, А́нна Бори́совна
   А́нна Бори́совна — _её мама_.

2. Ви́ктор Степа́нович, А́нна Бори́совна
   А́нна Бори́совна — ~~его~~ _его жена_.

3. Та́ня, О́ля
   О́ля — _её сестра_.

4. Та́ня, Ми́ша
   Ми́ша — ~~её~~ _её друг_.

5. Ви́ктор Степа́нович, Та́ня
   Та́ня — _его дочка_.

6. А́нна Бори́совна, Ви́ктор Степа́нович
   Ви́ктор Степа́нович — _её муж_.

7. Са́ша, Ле́на
   Ле́на — _его подруга_.

7. Describe the characters in the video according to the following model.

> 3
> — Ты не зна́ешь, кто **Та́ня**?
> 1   1
> — Она́ **студе́нтка.**/Я то́чно не зна́ю.
> 3   1
> По-моему, она́ **студе́нтка.**

Я то́чно не зна́ю. =
   I don't know for sure.

> Са́ша, Ке́вин, А́нна Бори́совна, О́ля, Ми́ша,
> Ви́ктор Степа́нович

8. You are at the university with a new friend when you bump into someone you know. In groups of three, introduce them using your real names.

> Стив: — Д́оброе у́тро!
>
> Вы: — Д́оброе у́тро, Стив! Познакомьтесь, пожа́луйста.
>
> Стив: — Меня́ зову́т Стив.
>
> Кэ́ти: — А я Кэ́ти. О́чень приятно.
>
> Стив: — О́чень приятно.

> Д́оброе у́тро! Д́обрый день! Д́обрый ве́чер!

9. You are shopping for new clothes. The aggressive salesperson is showing you different items, all of which you hate.

> — Вот о́чень мо́дная руба́шка.
>
> — Кака́я?
>
> — Вот эта, чёрная.
>
> — Что вы! Она́ немодная.

> sweater, jacket, sneakers, dress, pants, jeans, cap, shoes, t-shirt, scarf, suit

> red, white, green, black, yellow

1. A. You and your friend are invited to a "bad taste" party. Create your outfit from the following list.

[
long white skirt, very large orange shoes, short blue dress shirt, short green pants, funny red top, very short old skirt, new brown jeans, ugly old shirt, big black shoes, red scarf, long green sweater, very small yellow t-shirt, gray jacket, favorite old cap
]

_____

_____

B. Now discuss each other's choices.

     2   3
— Ну, как э́та ма́йка, **симпати́чная?**
   3   1   3   1
— По-мо́ему, **симпати́чная**./ По-мо́ему не о́чень.

[
good – bad, beautiful – ugly, interesting – not interesting
]

2. Respond to the following questions about cities.

                 2
— Како́й са́мый большо́й го́род в Росси́и?
   3   3   1
— По-мо́ему, са́мый большо́й го́род в Росси́и — Петербу́рг.
 2   3   1
— Что ты! Са́мый большо́й го́род в Росси́и — Москва́.

1. Какой самый большой город в мире?

2. Какой самый большой город в России?

3. Какой самый большой город в в США?

4. Какой самый красивый город в США?

5. Какой самый большой город в вашем штате?

6. Какой самый красивый город в в вашем штате?

3. You are working on a Russian edition of the "Guinness Book of World Records." Comment on some of the records in the book to your Russian friend. Create your own records.

> высокий человек →
>
> Это **самый высокий человек** в мире.[1]

высокий = tall

[old person, big cat, long bridge, old newspaper, small dog, old building, short book, old hotel]

4. Use the provided statements to create a mini-dialog with your partner.

> Your brother doesn't want to work. →
>
> — Мой брат не хочет работать.[1]
>
> — **Правда?**[3] **Как плохо!**[2]

1. Your friend wants to work in St. Petersburg.

2. Your father is an actor.

3. You want to work at a theater.

4. Your sister lives in Vladivostok.

5. Your sister speaks Russian very well.

6. Your brother works at the zoo.

7. You want to speak Japanese.

zoo = зоопарк

Как хорошо́! Как пло́хо! Как здо́рово! Не мо́жет быть!

5. Imagine that Серге́й decides to take Ке́вин on a personalized tour of the city. Fill in the missing parts of his statements.

1. А́нна Бори́совна рабо́тает _____.
   in this school

2. Мои́ друзья́ живу́т тут, _____.
   in this building

3. Ра́ньше Ми́ша рабо́тал там, _____.
   in that clinic

4. Ра́ньше Са́ша рабо́тал _____.
   at my institute

5. Мы ча́сто обе́даем _____.
   at this cafeteria

6. Мои́ роди́тели ча́сто гуля́ют _____.
   in our park

7. Моя́ подру́га ра́ньше жила́ _____.
   in your building

6. You are a journalist for the popular Russian newspaper «**Изве́стия**». Ask your partner the following questions for your article about life in America.

> — Кака́я **газе́та** в Аме́рике са́мая интере́сная?
> — По-мо́ему, «**Нью-Йорк Таймс**».

1. Како́е метро́ в Аме́рике са́мое большо́е?
2. Како́й го́род в Аме́рике са́мый краси́вый?
3. Кака́я актри́са в Аме́рике са́мая краси́вая?
4. Кака́я ку́хня в Аме́рике са́мая популя́рная?
5. Кака́я оде́жда в Аме́рике са́мая популя́рная?
6. Како́й штат в Аме́рике са́мый ма́ленький?

ку́хня = (here) cuisine

7. Using the following dialog as a model, discuss hotels in your home town with your partner.

Ле́на: — Са́ша, «Евро́па» хоро́шая гости́ница?

Са́ша: — Да, о́чень хоро́шая.

Ле́на: — А но́вая?

Са́ша: — Нет, наоборот, ста́рая. О́чень ста́рая.

По-моему, она́ о́чень краси́вая.

Ле́на: — Э́то больша́я гости́ница?

Са́ша: — Нет, не о́чень.

good, bad, large, small, new, old, beautiful, ugly

Ше́ратон, Хи́лтон, Ко́мфорт Инн, Хо́лидей Инн, Риц

8. You are at your Russian friend Тама́ра's house for dinner. She introduces her to her roommate and then leaves you to get the hors d'oeuvres. Find out the roommate's name, nationality, and occupation. Ask where s/he works.

1. The Nominative Case of Adjectives

Russian adjectives agree in number, gender, and case with their head word. The nominative case endings are presented in the chart below: **-ый** (masculine), **-ая** (feminine), **-ое** (neuter), and **-ые** (plural). Note that in the case of ending-stressed adjectives, the masculine nominate singular form is **-ой**.

	masculine	feminine	neuter	plural
Stem stress	но́вый журна́л	но́вая кни́га	но́вое окно́	но́вые кни́ги
Ending stress	молодо́й челове́к	молода́я семья́	молодо́е живо́тное	молоды́е фи́зики

In Unit I, you learned that the special spelling rules come into play when adding the ending **-и** to stems ending in **к, г, ш, ж** as well as in spelling an unstressed **о** after **ш** and **ж**. The same conditions arise in the spelling of adjectives. The adjectives **ру́сский** and **большо́й** provide good examples of both the **и** and **о** spelling rules. (For a complete list of spelling rules, see Analysis III, 11.)

	masculine	feminine	neuter	plural
Stem stress	ру́сский хоро́ший	ру́сская хоро́шая	ру́сское хоро́шее	ру́сские хоро́шие
Ending stress	большо́й	больша́я	большо́е	больши́е

2. Adjectives Used as Predicates

Э́тот дом но́вый.	This house is new. (…a new one.)
Э́тот дом ста́рый.	This house is old. (…an old one.)
Э́та гости́ница но́вая.	This hotel is new. (…a new one.)
Э́ти ве́щи но́вые.	These things are not new. (…are not new ones.)

Adjectives may be used as predicates, agreeing in number and gender with the subject.

3. The Demonstrative Pronouns э́тот and тот

Note the forms of the demonstrative pronouns **э́тот** and **тот** in the nominative singular and plural.

э́тот (тот) го́род, э́та (та) кни́га, э́то (то) окно́, э́ти (те) кни́ги

The use of **тот** (as opposed to **э́тот**) is more restricted in Russian in comparison with the English "that". **Тот** describes a head word which is markedly removed in space or time from the speaker or is clearly the second element of an opposition. Examine the following Russian-English equivalents; the English "that" very often corresponds to the Russian **э́тот**.

Э́та кни́га моя́, **та** кни́га его́.	*This* book is mine, *that* book is his. (opposition)
Э́та кни́га ста́рая.	*That* book is old.

4. The Indeclinable э́то and the Demonstrative Pronoun э́тот

We have seen that in Russian sentences the subject may be the indeclinable word э́то. (see Analysis I, 1.)

Э́то но́вая кни́га. (subj.) + (pred.)	*This is* a new book.

This indeclinable **э́то** should not be confused with the neuter form of the demonstrative pronoun **э́тот** (**э́то**) used to modify a noun. (see 3 above.)

Э́то окно́.	*This is* a window.
Э́то окно́ большо́е.	*That* window is large.

Examine the use of the indeclinable **э́то** and the demonstrative pronoun **э́тот** in this example:

— Что э́то?	"What is *that*?"
— Э́то магази́н.	"*That* is a store."
— А когда́ рабо́тает э́тот магази́н?	"And when is *that* store open?"

5. The Prepositional Case of Possessive and Demonstrative Pronouns

When a noun in the prepositional case has a possessive, demonstrative or other modifier, keep in mind that the modifier also must be in the prepositional case. The primary endings for all modifiers are **-ом** for masculine and neuter and **-ой/-ей** for feminine.

Case	Endings		masc.	neut.	fem.
Nom.	-ø, -о	-а	э́тот	э́то	э́та
Prep.	-ом	-ой/-ей	э́том		э́той

в э́том до́ме	in this house
в на́шем институ́те	at our institute
в твое́й кварти́ре	in your apartment
в моём го́роде	in my city

6. Time Expressions

As in English, the time when an action takes place can be expressed in Russian with a prepositional phrase, for example, **в** + prepositional case. However, this formula only works for increments of time longer than a week (a month, semester, and year).

в сентябре́	in September
в январе́	in January
в э́том семе́стре	(in) this semester
в э́том ве́ке	(in) this century.

When the time unit involved is part of a day or a season of the year, Russian has a group of special adverbs of time.

у́тром	in the morning	ле́том	in the summer
ве́чером	in the evening	зимо́й	in the winter
днём	in the afternoon	весно́й	in the spring
но́чью	at night (after midnight)	о́сенью	in the fall

7. The Prepositional Case of Nouns Ending in -ий, -ия, -ие

The prepositional case ending of all nouns ending in **-ий, -ия, -ие** is spelled **-и** rather than the expected **-е**.

Gender	Nominative	Prepositional
m.	кафете́рий	в кафете́рии
f.	лаборато́рия	в лаборато́рии
n.	общежи́тие	в общежи́тии

8. The Irregular Verb хоте́ть "want"

Infinitive: хоте́ть

Present

я хочу́	мы хоти́м
ты хо́чешь	вы хоти́те
он/она́ хо́чет	они́ хотя́т

Past

| он хоте́л |
| она́ хоте́ла |
| оно́ хоте́ло |
| они́ хоте́ли |

9. Russian Names

USAGE AND SOCIAL CONVENTION

Unlike in English, it is customary in Russian to address an interlocutor by name on a regualar basis in normal or formal conversation.

Russian names consist of a first name (**и́мя**), patronymic (**о́тчество**) and a last name (**фами́лия**). The normal polite or official form of address is the person's *first name and patronymic*. Use of the last name or the last name preceded by the word **господи́н** (Mr.), **госпожа́** (Ms.) or the word denoting the person's profession, rank, etc. is reserved for formal situations, for people with whom one is not personally acquainted, or for foreigners.

HOW PATRONYMICS ARE FORMED

The patronymic means "son of…" or "daughter of…" and is formed by adding the derivational element **-ов/-ев** to the father's first name, followed by either **-ич** for the son or **-на** for the daughter. For example:

10. Expressions of Nationality

The word **ру́сский** may serve as a noun meaning "Russian" (male), **ру́сская** "Russian" (female), and **ру́сские** "Russians". This usage of an adjective as a noun is not the norm for expressing nationality in Russian. Normally, Russian has separate nouns for male and female natives of a country and also for the name of the country itself. Here is a list of countries, the names of their inhabitants and the adjectives for referring to them.[1] Only the name of the country should be spelled with a capital letter.

---

[1] For a complete list of the Newly Independent States (NIS), see Appendix V.

Country		Masc.	Fem.	Adjective
Аме́рика	America (USA)	америка́нец	америка́нка	америка́нский
Австра́лия	Australia	австрали́ец	австрали́йка	австрали́йский
А́нглия	England	англича́нин	англича́нка	англи́йский
Аргенти́на	Argentina	аргенти́нец	аргенти́нка	аргенти́нский
Герма́ния	Germany	не́мец	не́мка	неме́цкий
Изра́иль	Israel	израильтя́нин	израильтя́нка	изра́ильский
И́ндия	India	инди́ец	индиа́нка	инди́йский
Испа́ния	Spain	испа́нец	испа́нка	испа́нский
Ита́лия	Italy	италья́нец	италья́нка	италья́нский
Кана́да	Canada	кана́дец	кана́дка	кана́дский
Кита́й	China	кита́ец	китая́нка	кита́йский
По́льша	Poland	поля́к	по́лька	по́льский
Фра́нция	France	францу́з	францу́женка	францу́зский
Украи́на	Ukraine	украи́нец	украи́нка	украи́нский
Япо́ния	Japan	япо́нец	япо́нка	япо́нский

The name of the language is always conveyed by the adjective followed by the noun **язы́к**, e.g. **ру́сский язы́к** "Russian," "the Russian language," **испа́нский язы́к** "Spanish," "the Spanish language."

11. Special Spelling Rules

The choice of vowel letter after **ш, ж, ц, ч, щ** and **к, г, х** is arbitrary and requires the knowledge of three special spelling rules. (See also Analysis I, 6.)

After **к, г, х** and **ш, ж, ч, щ** only **и** is spelled (never **ы**).
After **к, г, х** and **ш, ж, ч, щ, ц** only **а** and **у** are spelled (never **я** and **ю**).
After **ш, ж, ч, щ, ц** in the endings of nouns and adjectives the letter **o** may be written only if it is stressed; otherwise the letter **e** should be used.

NOUNS

а́вгуст August
америка́нец American (male)
америка́нка American (female)
англича́нин English (male)
англича́нка English (female)
апре́ль April
архите́ктор architect
бейсбо́льная ке́пка baseball cap
бра́тья (pl.; sing. **брат**) brothers
брю́ки (pl. only) pants
век century
весно́й in the spring
во́дка vodka
гру́ппа group
дека́брь December
детекти́в detective/mystery novel
де́ти (pl.; sing. **ребёнок**) children
друзья́ (pl.; sing. **друг**) friends
жето́н token
живо́тное animal
за́втрак breakfast
зда́ние building
зимо́й in the winter
зоопа́рк zoo
икра́ caviar
импера́тор emperor
испа́нец Spaniard (male)
испа́нка Spaniard (female)
ию́ль July
ию́нь June
кани́кулы school vacation
ка́сса cash register
касси́р cashier (male)
кафете́рий cafeteria
колле́дж college
компози́тор composer
костю́м suit
ко́фе coffee
ко́фта woman's top
кроссо́вки (pl.) sneakers
курс college course
лаборато́рия laboratory

лю́ди pl.; sing. **челове́к**) people
май May
ма́йка t-shirt, sleeveless top
маму́ля mom (affectionate)
март March
мили́ция police station, police
мир world
мо́да style, fashion
мост bridge
не́мец German (male)
не́мка German (female)
ноя́брь November
обе́д lunch
общежи́тие dormitory
оде́жда clothing
октя́брь October
о́сенью in the autumn
оте́ц father
оши́бка mistake
пла́тье dress
плащ raincoat
пого́да weather
ребёнок (sg.; pl. **де́ти**) child
руба́шка shirt
ру́сская Russian (female)
ру́сский Russian (male)
сала́т salad, lettuce
семе́стр semester
сентя́брь September
стул (sg.; pl. **сту́лья**) chair
сюрпри́з surprise
ту́фли (pl.) shoes
у́жин supper
февра́ль February
фильм movie
францу́женка French (female)
францу́з French (male)
футбо́лка T-shirt, sweatshirt, jersey
цвет color
центр center
цирк circus
челове́к (sg.; pl. **лю́ди**) person
шарф scarf
шо́рты (pl. only) shorts
экза́мен exam
ю́бка skirt

язы́к language
янва́рь January
япо́нец Japanese (male)
япо́нка Japanese (female)

PROPER NOUNS

Аме́рика America (USA)
А́нглия England
Герма́ния Germany
Испа́ния Spain
США USA
Фра́нция France
Япо́ния Japan

PRONOUNS

како́й which; what kind of …
тот, та, то that
те those
э́тот, э́та, э́то this
э́ти these

ADJECTIVES

америка́нский American
англи́йский English
бе́лый white
большо́й big
весёлый happy, cheerful
вку́сный tasty, delicious
высо́кий tall
голубо́й light blue
дли́нный long
жёлтый yellow
зелёный green
интере́сный interesting
испа́нский Spanish
кори́чневый brown
коро́ткий short
краси́вый beautiful
кра́сный red
люби́мый favorite
ма́ленький small
мо́дный stylish
молодо́й young
невесёлый not cheerful
невку́сный not tasty
неинтере́сный not interesting
некраси́вый plain, ugly

неме́цкий German
немо́дный unfashionable
неплохо́й not bad
несерьёзный not serious
несмешно́й not funny
неэнерги́чный not energetic
но́вый new
ора́нжевый orange
отли́чный excellent
плохо́й bad
популя́рный popular
са́мый most
серьёзный serious
се́рый gray
симпати́чный nice,
    nice-looking
си́ний blue
смешно́й funny
совреме́нный contemporary
ста́рый old
стра́нный strange
францу́зский French
хоро́ший good
чёрный black
энерги́чный energetic
япо́нский Japanese

VERBS

звони́ть (звони́-) call
хоте́ть (irregular) want

ADVERBS

как how
когда́ when
ла́дно all right
наоборо́т on the contrary
ничего́ not bad, all right
норма́льно OK
ужа́сно terrible
уже́ already

NUMERALS

оди́ннадцать eleven
двена́дцать twelve
трина́дцать thirteen
четы́рнадцать fourteen
пятна́дцать fifteen
шестна́дцать sixteen
семна́дцать seventeen
восемна́дцать eighteen
девятна́дцать nineteen
два́дцать twenty

CONJUNCTIONS

но but

EXPRESSIONS

в мо́де style, fashionable
в э́том году́ this year

до́брое у́тро good morning
до́брый день good afternoon
до́брый ве́чер good evening
здо́рово great, terrific
Как вас зову́т? What's your
    name?
Как дела́? How are things
    going?
Меня́ зову́т … My name is …
мину́тку wait a minute, just a
    minute
не в мо́де out of style
не мо́жет быть that's
    impossible
Не хо́чешь, как хо́чешь.
    Whatever you say.
Ой! Oh! Ouch!
о́чень жаль it's a shame
познако́мьтесь get
    acquainted
пока́ bye
пра́вда true; really
приве́т hi
Так э́то же ма́ма. Of course –
    after all, she's your mother.
Я то́чно не зна́ю. I don't know
    for sure.

UNIT

4

Вот э́то
спекта́кль!

*M*isha and Tanya get into an argument over her being
late to meet him at the theater.

You will learn how to:

- DISCUSS EVENTS THAT HAPPENED IN THE PAST
- RECOGNIZE AND USE LAST NAMES IN RUSSIAN
- BRAG
- TALK ABOUT EVENTS, PEOPLE, AND THINGS
- SAY WHAT YEAR YOU ARE IN COLLEGE (FRESHMAN, ETC.)
- REPLY WITH CONFIDENCE
- HAVE AN INFORMAL CONVERSATION
- EXPLAIN AND INQUIRE WHY THINGS ARE AS THEY ARE
- DESCRIBE AN ACTION THAT BEGAN IN THE PAST AND IS CONTINUING IN THE PRESENT
- EXPRESS SURPRISE
- TALK ABOUT YOUR INTERESTS AND HOBBIES
- DISCUSS ART AND MUSIC
- DESCRIBE THE PLACES WHERE YOU HAVE LIVED
- DISCUSS MOVIES AND TV PROGRAMS
- TALK ABOUT HOW YOU SPEND YOUR FREE TIME, WHERE YOU GO OUT

It was a busy day for Та́ня: after meeting Ке́вин and taking him
to his new apartment, she rushed home to get ready for her date
with Ми́ша at the **Моско́вский худо́жественный теа́тр
(МХТ)**. ▲ Little did she know that her plans would be changed
by Ке́вин's plea for help with his encounter with the police. In
this episode you will find out if Та́ня has enough time to rescue
Ке́вин and still make it to the theater.

1. You may remember that Та́ня mentioned Ми́ша in her
letter to Да́ша. Do you remember anything about him
from Та́ня's letter? Write down at least three sentences
describing Ми́ша using the following verbs: жить,
рабо́тать, отдыха́ть.

_____

_____

_____

_____

▲ Моско́вский худо́жественный теа́тр им. Че́хова (МХТ) — a drama theater in Moscow,
one of the most famous and significant theaters in Russia.

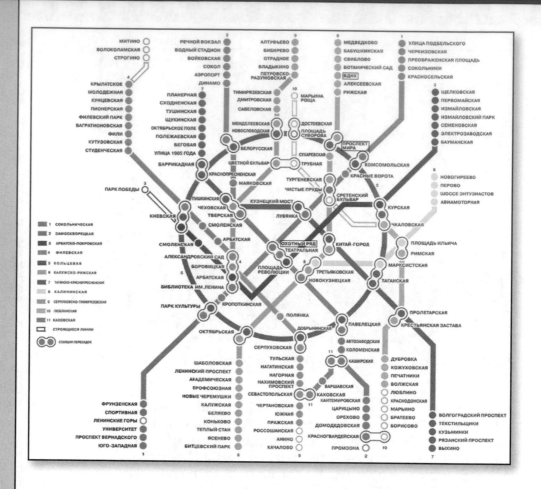

Тáня живёт на стáнции «Проспéкт Мúра».
Кéвин на стáнции «ВДНХ». (вэ-дэ-эн-хá)▲
Москóвский худóжественный теáтр на стáнции
«Охóтный Ряд».

2. This map of the Moscow subway indicates the stations closest
to Тáня's house, where Кéвин had an encounter with the
police, and the **Москóвский худóжественный теáтр.**

▲ ВДНХ (Вы́ставка Достижéний Нарóдного Хозя́йства) – "The Exhibition of Economic
Achievements" was opened in Moscow in 1956. It was created as a monument to Soviet achievements in all
spheres of the economy, culture, education, science, art, agriculture, etc. In 1992 ВДНХ was renamed into
ВВЦ (Всеросси́йский выста́вочный центр) - "The All-Russia Exhibition Center," however the
metro station kept its original name. The Center takes an enormous territory of over 171,600 square meters. Its
basic function nowadays is hosting exhibitions, fairs, festivities, shows and art festivals. (www.vvcentre.ru)

A. How many stops is it from Та́ня's house to Ке́вин's?

_____3_____

B. Approximately how long do you think it will take Та́ня to get there? _____15_____

C. Assuming that Та́ня will spend 20 minutes talking to the police with Ке́вин, how far behind schedule will she be _____?

3. Ми́ша and Та́ня are planning to see «**Ча́йка**», which is a:

☐ бале́т

☐ спекта́кль

☐ дра́ма

☐ о́пера

4. The title of the episode is «**Вот э́то спекта́кль!**» (What a show!) Can you guess what this statement refers to?

▶ Now watch the video with the SOUND OFF.

VIEWING

5. Put these events from the video in the correct order.

A young man approaches Ми́ша. _____

Ми́ша storms off. _____

Ми́ша buys flowers from a vendor. _____

Ми́ша asks Та́ня where she has been. _____

Та́ня gives her flowers to a man. _____

Ми́ша gives Та́ня white flowers. _____

Та́ня finally shows up. _____

Ми́ша gives his tickets to a stranger. _____

A man greets Та́ня. _____

Ми́ша talks to a tourist. _____

6. Ми́ша and the young man who he talks to are

☐ total strangers

☐ old acquaintances

☐ best friends

7. Ми́ша's mood changes drastically while he is waiting for Та́ня. How would you characterize this change?

- ☐ His good mood changes to anger.
- ☐ He is first nervous, then relieved.
- ☐ He becomes increasingly cheerful.

8. How would you characterize Ми́ша's conversation with Та́ня?

- ☐ calm
- ☐ heated
- ☐ flirtatious

9. Та́ня gives her flowers to another man at the end of this episode. What is the man's reaction?

- ☐ He jumps up and down with glee.
- ☐ He throws the flowers in the trash.
- ☐ He is surprised.

▶ Now watch the video with the SOUND ON.

SOUND ON

10. We have divided this episode into four mini-episodes and given them titles. How would you express these titles in English?

Краси́вые цветы́	_____
Где Та́ня?	_____
Э́то я, Васи́льев!	_____
Ми́ша, извини́, пожа́луйста!	_____

11. A woman approaches Ми́ша and asks him about the theater. Who is she?

- ☐ a foreigner
- ☐ an old Muscovite
- ☐ a Russian tourist

12. Ми́ша talks to a young woman at the theater. What is she looking for?

- ☐ телефо́н
- ☐ биле́т
- ☐ соба́ка

цветы́ = flowers

биле́т = ticket

13. A. Judging by the way they act, Ми́ша and the young man he speaks with in the square are not strangers. What in their conversation supports this conclusion? Check all answers that apply.

- ☐ They address each other using **ты**.
- ☐ They hug each other.
- ☐ The young man gives him a free ticket.
- ☐ They know each other's names.

B. What is the young man's name?

- ☐ Пе́тя
- ☐ Васи́лий
- ☐ Оле́г

C. What do Ми́ша and the young man talk about? Check all answers that apply.

- ☐ рабо́та
- ☐ спекта́кль
- ☐ институ́т
- ☐ Та́ня

14. When Та́ня finally arrives, she is very excited to see Ми́ша and tries to explain why she is late.

A. Whose name does Та́ня mention in her explanation?

- ☐ Ке́вин
- ☐ Серге́й
- ☐ Ле́на

B. Though he doesn't say so, Ми́ша appears to be angry at Та́ня. Why?

- ☐ Та́ня caused him miss his favorite play.
- ☐ Та́ня didn't bring him flowers.
- ☐ Та́ня was with another young man.

C. Та́ня tries to remedy the situation by inviting Ми́ша to go: (check all that apply)

- ☐ dancing
- ☐ for a walk
- ☐ to dinner

15. At the end of this episode is an excerpt from «**Чáйка**», the play that Мúша and Тáня missed. Can you guess what «**Чáйка**» is about? Discuss your answer with your classmates.

POSTviewing >

Russian Last Names

Мúша recognizes his old acquaintance Пéтя only after he reminds Мúша of his last name:

Э́то я – **Васúльев.**

Russian last names have two forms: masculine and feminine. To create the feminine form, add the ending **-a** to the end of the masculine form. For example, Пéтя Васúльев's mother's last name is Васúльев**a**. Typical Russian last names end in **-ов(а)/-ев(а)** or **-ын(а)/-ин(а).**

---

16. Look over this list of names of the characters in the video and then fill in the last names of their respective relatives as indicated.

> Тáня Волó**дина**
> Мúша Кóт**ов**
> Сáша Кузнецó**в**
> Лéна Антóн**ова**
> Сергéй Бéлк**ин**
> Пéтя Васúль**ев**
> Кéвин Джéксон

Мúша: Егó мáма – Натáлья Фёдоровна _Kotobr_

Егó пáпа – Ивáн Андрéевич _Kotob_

Пéтя: Егó сестрá – Ирúна Алексáндровна _Bacильebr_

Егó брат – Пáвел Алексáндрович _Bacильes_

Тáня: Её пáпа – Вúктор Степáнович _____

Её мáма – А́нна Борúсовна _____

Лéна: Её пáпа – Алексáндр Ивáнович _____

Её мáма – Валентúна Кирúлловна _____

Сергéй: Егó мáма – Марúна Петрóвна _____

Егó пáпа – Андрéй Михáйлович _____

Past Tense of the Verb Быть "Be"

When Тáня finally arrives at the theater, Мúша asks her twice:

А где ты **былá**?
Ну, где ты **былá**?

As you remember, in Russian there is no present tense of the verb "to be" (**быть**). However, there is a past tense of the verb **быть**, and it is formed just like the past tense of other verbs.

он был
онá былá
онó бы́ло
онú бы́ли

Note the stress shift in the past tense.

17. Insert the correct form of **быть** in the past tense.

1. — Мúша, где ты _____?

   — Я _____ на рабóте.

2. В февралé Óля _____в Петербýрге.

3. — Áнна Борúсовна, вы _____ в теáтре?

   — Да, _____.

4. Ýтром Тáня и Лéна _____ в институ́те.

5. — Дáша, ты _____ в Филадéльфии?

6. Кéвин _____ в библиотéке сегóдня.

7. — Сергéй, где вы _____ лéтом?

   — Мы _____ в Петербýрге.

8. Лéна _____ в кафé.

18. Discuss where you were yesterday morning, yesterday afternoon and yesterday evening.

> — Где ты был(á) **вчерá ýтром**?
> — Я был(á) в библиотеке. А ты?
> — А я был(á) в лаборатории.

1. Кто был на спекта́кле?

Read the following sentences out loud, paying close attention to where the stress falls in the various past tense forms of the verb **быть.**

1. Та́ня и Ми́ша **бы́ли** в теа́тре? [3]

   Нет, они́ **не бы́ли** в теа́тре. [1] [1]

2. А Са́ша **был** на спекта́кле? [3]

   Са́ша **не́ был** на спекта́кле. [1]

3. А Ле́на **была́** в теа́тре? [3]

   Ле́на **не была́** в теа́тре. [1]

   Ле́на и Са́ша **не́ были** в теа́тре. [1]

он был	он не́ был
она́ была́	она́ не была́
они́ бы́ли	они́ не́ были

2. Imagine that you and your partner are planning a trip. Find out whether or not s/he has been to the cities listed below.

— Ты был(á) **в Москве́?** [3]
— Да, был(á)./Нет, не был(не была́). [1] [1] [1] [1] [1]

Москва́, Петербу́рг, Ло́ндон, Пари́ж, Берли́н, Рим, Вашингто́н, Нью-Йо́рк, Бо́стон, Филаде́льфия, Атла́нта, Сиэ́тл

спекта́кль = performance, show

Pay attention to the stress pattern of the verb **быть** in the past tense with negation.

As you know, some nouns require the preposition **на** to express location. This list includes the following three categories of frequently used nouns: points on the compass, gathering places, and some geographical regions.

на ю́ге	на ле́кции	на Ура́ле
на се́вере	на собра́нии	на Кавка́зе
на за́паде	на спекта́кле	на Во́лге
на восто́ке	на бале́те	на Неве́
	на о́пере	на Байка́ле
	на вы́ставке	
	на конце́рте	
	на дискоте́ке	

3. Establish where you and your friends will go tonight by process of elimination. Ask them where they have been.

> 3
> — Ты был(а́) **на конце́рте?**
> 1   1   1   1   1
> — Да, был(а)./Нет, не был(не была́).

вы́ставка, университе́т, о́пера, кинотеа́тр, бале́т, теа́тр, спекта́кль, дискоте́ка, музе́й, ле́кция, клуб, собра́ние, магази́н, стадио́н, рестора́н, по́чта

4. Геогра́фия

Use the map on the insert to identify the geographic location of the cities and places below.

> 2
> — Где Петербу́рг?
> 1
> — **На севере.**

> Ура́л, Москва́, Камча́тка, Росто́в, Сахали́н, Но́вгород, Новосиби́рск, Байка́л, Каспи́йское мо́ре, Арха́нгельск
>
> се́вер, юг, восто́к, за́пад

5. A. Act out the following conversations with your partner.

Та́ня: — Ле́на, ты была́ вчера́ **на собра́нии**?

Ле́на: — Нет, не была́. А ты была́ **на ле́кции**?

Та́ня: — Нет, не была́. А ты?

Ле́на: — А я была́.

Та́ня: — Ми́ша, ты был **на Во́лге**?▲

Ми́ша: — Нет, не был. А ты была́?

Та́ня: — Да, была́.

Ми́ша: — Когда́ ты там была́?

Та́ня: — **Ле́том, в а́вгусте.**

B. Imagine that you are a spy and that your partner is a double-agent. Your innocent conversation reveals that you are both trying to uncover the other's recent whereabouts. Use the preceding two dialogs as models.

6. The following conversation took place between Ле́на and Са́ша on their way to Та́ня's apartment in the third episode of the video. All of the highlighted adjectives are in the prepositional case. Circle their grammatical endings and try to determine which endings are feminine and which are masculine based on the noun that the adjective modifies.

▲ The Volga is the biggest river in Europe (3530 km long). It is the subject of a considerable amount of folk art, especially songs and paintings.

Са́ша: — А где живёт Та́ня?

Ле́на: — Сейча́с она́ живёт в **небольшо́й,** но о́чень **хоро́шей** кварти́ре.

Са́ша: — А в **како́м** до́ме?

Ле́на: — В **большо́м ста́ром** до́ме в це́нтре.

Са́ша: — Она́ и ра́ньше жила́ в це́нтре?

Ле́на: — Нет, ра́ньше она́ жила́ в **но́вом** райо́не, в **большо́м но́вом** зда́нии.

Са́ша: — На **како́м** этаже́ она́ живёт?

Ле́на: — На **тре́тьем.**

район =
neighborhood,
area

эта́ж = floor

Adjectives: Prepositional Case		
Gender	**Endings**	**Examples**
masc. neut.	**-ом**	<u>в **како́м** до́ме, зда́нии?</u> в **большо́м** до́ме в **большо́м** зда́нии
fem.	**-ой**	<u>в **како́й** маши́не?</u> в **кра́сной** маши́не

7. Practicing pronunciation: adjectives and ordinal numerals in the prepositional case

To review the
spelling rules
see Unit III,
Analysis 11.

в но́вом до́ме, в но́вой кварти́ре, в хоро́шем зда́нии, в хоро́шей ко́мнате, на пя́том этаже́, в деся́той кварти́ре

8. You are a freshman having a typical freshman conversation. Use the provided sentences to pinpoint where your partner lives.

>   3
> — Ты живёшь на втор**ом** этаж**é**?
>   1   1   4
> — Нет, я живу́ на перв**ом** этаж**é.** А ты?
>   1   1
> — И я живу́ на пе́рв**ом** этаж**é.**/А я живу́ на тре́ть**ем** этаж**é.**

1. Ты живёшь в краси́вом райо́не?
2. Ты живёшь в хоро́шем общежи́тии?
3. Ты живёшь в ста́ром до́ме?
4. Ты живёшь на пе́рвом этаже́?
5. Ты живёшь в большо́й ко́мнате?

9. The following sentences describe where Ке́вин lives in Moscow. Fill in the appropriate adjectives in the prepositional case based on the video.

1. В како́й кварти́ре живёт Ке́вин? Он живёт в _____ кварти́ре.

2. В како́м до́ме живёт Ке́вин? Он живёт в _____ до́ме.

3. В како́м райо́не живёт Ке́вин? Он живёт в _____ райо́не.

4. На како́м этаже́ живёт Ке́вин? Он живёт на _____ этаже́.

(Remember that Ке́вин lives in apartment 10, there are 4 apartments on each floor and no apartments on the first floor.)

[
large – small, old – new, good – bad, beautiful – ugly;
first - tenth
]

10. Где вы жи́ли ра́ньше?

Using the reference words from the previous exercise, describe places where you used to live.

1. Ра́ньше я жил(а́) в ___в ма́ленькой___ кварти́ре.
2. Ра́ньше я жил(а́) в ___краси́вои___ до́ме.
3. Ра́ньше я жил(а́) в ___хоро́шеи___ ко́мнате.
4. Ра́ньше я жил(а́) в ___ста́рои___ общежи́тии.
5. Ра́ньше я жил(а́) в ___плохои___ зда́нии.
6. Ра́ньше я жил(а́) в ___большои___ го́роде.
7. Ра́ньше я жил(а́) на ___четвёртои___ этаже́.

— Ты **на** как**ом** ку́рсе?ᐟ²   What year are you in?

— Я на перв**ом** ку́рсе.¹   I am a freshman.

Курс, as you might guess from the way it sounds, means course. However, **курс** can also mean "year in college" (freshman, sophomore, etc.)

11. A. What would the English equivalents for the following terms be?

на пе́рвом ку́рсе _____

на второ́м ку́рсе _____

на тре́тьем ку́рсе _____

на четвёртом ку́рсе _____

B. На како́м ты ку́рсе? _____

Ask your classmates this question, then summarize what you have found out.

> Джон, Лесли и Лора³ ³ ³ **на первом ку́рсе.**¹
>
> Ник и Том³ ³ **на втором ку́рсе.**¹

12. Make up exaggerated statements that describe places you could have lived, worked, and visited.

> Я жил(а́) в **самом большо́м до́ме**² в Аме́рике!
>
> Я у́жинал(а) в **самом дорого́м рестора́не**² в ми́ре!

дорого́й = expensive

жить, быть, рабо́тать, у́жинать

краси́вый, интере́сный, симпати́чный, большо́й, хоро́ший, популя́рный, дорого́й, ста́рый, но́вый, са́мый

рестора́н, гости́ница, кварти́ра, теа́тр, го́род, райо́н, страна́, университе́т, музе́й

страна́ = country

О чём дýмает Тáня?
Онá дýмает **о мóде, о балéте,
об одéжде.**

О ком дýмает Тáня?
Онá дýмает **о Мúше,
о Мúше, о Мúше.**

одéжда =
clothing

The Preposition о/об "About"

что → о **чём**
кто → о **ком**

The preposition **о** + the prepositional case is best translated by the word "about". When the noun or adjective immediately following the preposition **о** begins with a vowel, the preposition becomes **об**.

1. Practicing pronunciation: prepositional phrases with **о/об**

Like the prepositions **в** and **на,** the preposition **о/об** is pronounced together with the next word.

> **о Москвé, говорúть о Москвé**
> Тáня и Кéвин говорúли о Москвé.

> **о бúзнесе, читáть о бúзнесе**
> Мúша читáет о бúзнесе.

> **об институýте, спрáшивать об институýте**
> Кéвин спрáшивал об институýте.

> **об обéде, дýмать об обéде**
> Я дýмаю об обéде.

2. The following sentences describe this unit's episode. Provide the missing prepositions and grammatical endings.

1. — О чём э́тот фильм?

   — Э́тот фильм о Та́н__ и Ми́ш__ .

   — Э́тот фильм о теа́тр__ .

2. — О чём говори́ли Ми́ша и Васи́льев?

   — Они́ говори́ли ____ би́знесе и ____ институ́те.

3. — О ком говори́ла Та́ня?

   — Та́ня говори́ла ____ Ке́вин ___ .

3. What were the following conversations about?

   Based on the video, fill in the topics of these different conversations.

   Серге́й и Та́ня говори́ли о Москве́.

1. Ке́вин и Серге́й говори́ли _____

2. А́нна Бори́совна и Та́ня говори́ли _____

3. Ви́ктор Степа́нович и Та́ня говори́ли _____

4. Та́ня и Ке́вин говори́ли _____

5. Ле́на и Са́ша говори́ли _____

6. Ми́ша и Пе́тя говори́ли _____

7. Та́ня и Ми́ша говори́ли _____

   би́знес, Ке́вин, мо́да, у́жин, го́род, кварти́ра, оде́жда, Ми́ша, Та́ня, рабо́та, Аме́рика, институ́т

4. At Russian club meetings, students discuss a wide range of topics. What are some of the things they might talk about?

   1
Студе́нты говоря́т о ру́сской культу́ре.

кухня = cuisine

американский
футбол =
football

русская му́зыка, америка́нский рок, класси́ческая му́зыка, профессиона́льный спорт, но́вый ру́сский фильм, но́вый америка́нский фильм, интере́сная кни́га, ру́сская ку́хня, америка́нский футбо́л

5. Guess what the articles with the following titles are about.

> 2
> — О чём э́та статья́?
>
> 1
> — Э́та статья́ **о спо́рте.**

статья́ = article

Prepositional Plural of Nouns

Gender	Endings	Examples
masc.		в города́х
neuter	-ах/-ях	в зда́ниях
fem.		в ко́мнатах

6. Transform the following phrases from the nominative singular to the prepositional plural.

дом – в дома́х

1. кварти́ра _____
2. общежи́тие _____
3. у́лица _____
4. конце́рт _____
5. вы́ставка _____
6. собра́ние _____
7. ле́кция _____
8. спекта́кль _____

7. A. What are some of the things you usually discuss with your friends?

>   1   4
> — Мы говори́м о **кни́гах.** А вы?
>   1   3   1
> — И мы говори́м о **кни́гах.**/А мы говори́м о спо́рте.

The word **спорт** is always singular.

B. What do you not discuss with your friends?

>   1   4
> — Мы не говори́м об **отметках.**▲ А вы?
>   1   3   1
> — И мы не говори́м об **отме́тках.**/А мы не говори́м о **рабо́те.**

отме́тка = grade

▲ In state run universities and colleges, Russian students do not pay tuition. If they maintain a good grade point average (approximately 3.0), they usually receive a small stipend provided by the administration. In most cases room (but not board) in university dormitories is also free.

книги, фи́льмы, отмéтки, концéрты, музыка́нты, рестора́ны, ба́ры, проблéмы, магази́ны, вéщи, дéньги, роди́тели, друзья́

The -ова- Stem Verbs

Рисова́ть (рис**ова́**-) "draw"

Present tense		Past tense
я рисýю	мы рисýем	он рисова́л
ты рисýешь	вы рисýете	она́ рисова́ла
он/она́ рисýет	они́ рисýют	они́ рисова́ли

The verb **рисова́ть** belongs to the group of **-ова-** stem verbs. This group of verbs is very productive and includes many words with foreign roots. When you read them out loud, you will be surprised how many you can understand without a dictionary.

организ**ова́**ть	тести́р**ова**ть
анализи́р**ова**ть	игнори́р**ова**ть
программи́р**ова**ть	корректи́р**ова**ть
финанси́р**ова**ть	опери́р**ова**ть

8. Suppose you need to make a poster for an upcoming Russian club event. Ask your friends if they know anyone who draws well. Fill in the appropriate form of the verb **рисова́ть.**

1. — Кéвин, ты _____ ?

   — Я в шкóле _____, а сейча́с я не _____.

2. — Та́ня, ты не зна́ешь, Ми́ша хорошó _____?

   — По-мóему, не óчень.

3. — А́нна Бори́совна, вы хорошó _____?

   — Что вы! Я óчень плóхо _____.

4. — Ле́на, студе́нты в твоём институ́те _____?

— Нет, но мой друг Са́ша о́чень хорошо́ _____.
Он архите́ктор.

— Пра́вда? Отли́чно!

9. Где вы бы́ли?

A. You are an interpreter who has just returned from a business trip in Russia. Tell your partner about the many places you visited.

> — Я был(а́) в о́чень интере́сном музее.[1]

> hospital, movie theater, restaurant, museum, theater, concert, exhibit, library, meeting, dance club

> new, old, big, small, interesting, Russian, first, important, excellent

B. Using only the nouns from part A of this exercise, tell your partner *in general* where you have been lately.

> — Где ты был(а́)?[2]
> — Я был(а́) в музеях[3] и в театрах.[1]

PREviewing >

1. A. How would you describe Ми́ша as you saw him in this episode? Choose from the following pairs of antonyms to construct your description.

> 3   1
> По-моему, Ми́ша **молодо́й.**

молодо́й – ста́рый, симпати́чный – несимпати́чный, интере́сный – неинтере́сный, энерги́чный – неэнерги́чный, весёлый – невесёлый, серьёзный – несерьёзный, мо́дный – немо́дный

B. What is Ми́ша wearing? Он:

- ☐ в ку́ртке и джи́нсах
- ☐ в се́ром костю́ме
- ☐ в бе́лом пла́тье

2. You may remember that Ми́ша waits for quite a long time before Та́ня finally shows up. What does he do while he is waiting?

	Да	Нет
smokes a cigarette	☐	☐
buys Táня flowers	☐	☐
talks to a tourist	☐	☐
talks with Пётя Васильев	☐	☐
eats a sandwich	☐	☐
calls Táня	☐	☐
gives away his tickets	☐	☐
buys a newspaper	☐	☐

▶ Read through the following questions and complete as many as you can before you watch the video with the SOUND ON. Finish answering the questions while you watch.

VIEWING

3. A. What kind of flowers does Миша decide to buy for Táня?

☐ красные тюльпаны

☐ жёлтые розы

☐ белые хризантемы

B. How many does Миша buy?▲

☐ три   ☐ пять   ☐ девять

4. When Миша unexpectedly meets his old classmate, Пётя, outside of the theater, what do they talk about after all these years?

Миша и Пётя говорили:

☐ о цветах   ☐ о спектакле   ☐ о билетах

☐ о фильмах   ☐ о книгах   ☐ об институте

☐ о бизнесе   ☐ о Тане   ☐ о собаках

5. Why does Миша give his tickets to a total stranger?

☐ He is feeling generous today.

☐ Táня is so late that they cannot possibly make it to the play.

☐ He decides he would rather go to McDonald's.

▲ When Russians give flowers as gifts, they always give an odd number of flowers. An even number of flowers is only given for funerals.

The young women waiting outside the theater are avid theater fans. They are discussing which performers will be appearing in the upcoming show.

Де́вушка 1: — Ты не зна́ешь, кто сего́дня игра́ет?

Де́вушка 2: — Коне́чно. Э́то мой люби́мый спекта́кль.

игра́ть (игра́й-) = (here) to act

де́вушка = girl, young woman

коне́чно = of course, sure

6. When asked whether she knows who is acting at the show, the second girl replies confidently, **«Коне́чно».**

Reply to your partner's questions using the word **коне́чно** to indicate your confidence.

> 3
> — Ты знаешь, кто Та́ня?
> 2   1
> — **Коне́чно.** Она́ студе́нтка.

1. Ты зна́ешь, где живёт Ми́ша?

2. Ты зна́ешь, о чём говори́ли Ми́ша и Пе́тя?

3. Ты зна́ешь, где жил Ке́вин в Аме́рике?

4. Ты зна́ешь, о чём говоря́т америка́нские студе́нты?

5. Ты зна́ешь, где рабо́тает Ми́ша?

6. Ты зна́ешь, кто Ми́ша?

7. Ты зна́ешь, кто Ке́вин?

8. Ты зна́ешь, в како́й кварти́ре живёт Ке́вин?

> Ми́ша hasn't seen his former classmate Пе́тя for quite a long time, so he asks him how he has been:
>
> Ми́ша: — Ну, **как живёшь?**
> Пе́тя: — Норма́льно.
>
> **«Как живёшь?»** is another way of asking, **«Как дела́?»** Just like **«Как дела́?»**, **«Как живёшь?»** is appropriate only in an informal setting.

7. With your partner, come up with as many responses to the question «**Как живёшь?**» as you can.

Пе́тя is surprised to find Ми́ша alone, so he asks Ми́ша where his girlfriend is.

Пе́тя: — Ты оди́н? А где твоя́ подру́га?
Ми́ша: — Не зна́ю.
Пе́тя: — **Как** не зна́ешь? А кто зна́ет?

"**What do you mean** you don't know", asks Пе́тя. **Как** is used in familiar speech to express surprise and disbelief, and is always pronounced with IC-2.

оди́н (одна́, одно́, одни́)
= alone

8. Practice using **как** in informal exchanges with your partner.

 1
— Ке́вин ру́сский.
 2   2
— **Как** ру́сский? Он америка́нец.

---

1. — Та́ня и Ке́вин бы́ли вчера́ на бале́те.

    — _____ бы́ли? Не́ были.

2. — Та́ня живёт в Вашингто́не.

    — _____ в Вашингто́не? Она́ живёт в Москве́.

3. — Ми́ша рабо́тает в ветерина́рной кли́нике.

    — _____ в кли́нике? Он рабо́тает в би́знесе.

4. — Ми́ша был в Большо́м теа́тре.

    — _____ был? Не́ был.

5. — Ке́вин журнали́ст.

    — _____ журнали́ст? Он фото́граф.

6. — Ми́ша и Пе́тя говори́ли об оде́жде.

    — _____ об оде́жде? Они́ говори́ли о би́знесе.

As you remember from the video, Та́ня and Ми́ша did not end up going to the play together. Frustrated that Ми́ша stormed off, Та́ня decided to go out with other friends. Та́ня, Ле́на and Са́ша decided to go to a club that evening.

Here is an excerpt from their conversation:

но = but

Почему́ ты стои́шь, не танцу́ешь?

Ле́на: — Та́ня, почему́ ты **стои́шь**, не танцу́ешь?

Са́ша: — Хо́чешь танцева́ть?

Та́ня: — Я всегда́ танцу́ю, но сего́дня не хочу́. А ты почему́ **стои́шь?**

Са́ша: — Я пло́хо танцу́ю.

Та́ня: — Не мо́жет быть!

The verb **танцева́ть** (танцева́-) is another -**ова**- verb. Can you explain why танцевать is spelled with **e** instead of **o**?

танцева́ть (танцева́-) "dance"

Present tense		Past tense
я танцу́ю	мы танцу́ем	он танцева́л
ты танцу́ешь	вы танцу́ете	она́ танцева́ла
он/она́ танцу́ет	они́ танцу́ют	они́ танцева́ли

1. Practicing pronunciation

Я хочу́ танцева́ть.   Ле́на танцева́ла.
Мы танцева́ли.   Са́ша не танцева́л.

2. Fill in the missing forms of the verb **танцева́ть.** Be sure to choose the correct tense based on the clues in italics.

1. *Вчера́ ве́чером* Ле́на и Та́ня _____ на дискоте́ке.

2. Та́ня *ча́сто*_____.

3. *В шко́ле* я *иногда́* _____.

4. *У́тром* мы не хоти́м _____.

5. Я не хочу́ _____на дискоте́ке.

6. *Вчера́* мы не _____.

7. Мои́ друзья́ *ре́дко* _____.

8. Ру́сские *ча́сто* _____ до́ма.

3. You are trying to find someone to take a ballroom dancing class with you. Ask them these questions to see if you think they would be a good partner.

1. Do you dance?
2. Where do you like to dance?
3. How often do you dance?
4. How well do you dance?

-жа- stem verbs

Соба́ка **лежи́т** на дива́не.

Милиционе́р **стои́т** на у́лице.

Кни́га **лежи́т** на по́лке.

Кни́ги **стоя́т** на по́лке.

This category of verbs follows the second conjugation. The verb **стоя́ть** is also included in this class.

лежа́ть (лежа́-)
"lie, be in a lying position"

стоя́ть (стоя́-)
"stand, be in a standing position"

Present	Past	Present	Past
я лежу́	он лежа́л	я стою́	он стоя́л
ты лежи́шь	она́ лежа́ла	ты стои́шь	она́ стоя́ла
он/она́ лежи́т	оно́ лежа́ло	он/она́ стои́т	оно́ стоя́ло
мы лежи́м	они́ лежа́ли	мы стои́м	они́ стоя́ли
вы лежи́те		вы стои́те	
они́ лежа́т		они́ стоя́т	

4. Fill in the appropriate forms of the verbs лежа́ть and стоя́ть. Mark on the margin whether the position is vertical (|) or horizontal (—).

1. Кни́га _____ на по́лке.   стоя́ть

2. Бутербро́ды _____ на таре́лке.   лежа́ть

3. Уче́бник _____ на столе́.   лежа́ть

4. Сыр _____ в холоди́льнике.   лежа́ть

5. Чемода́н _____ в ко́мнате.   стоя́ть

6. Что _____ в су́мке?   лежа́ть

7. Где _____ слова́рь?   стоя́ть

8. Ма́йка _____ на сту́ле.   лежа́ть

Here is another excerpt from the conversation at the dance club.

Интере́сно, кто сего́дня игра́ет?

Та́ня: — Са́ша, ты не зна́ешь, кака́я гру́ппа сего́дня **игра́ет?**

Са́ша: — «Руби́новая ата́ка».

Ле́на: — Они́ отли́чно **игра́ют!**

Са́ша: — Так э́то же «Руби́новая ата́ка»!

Ле́на: — А кто **игра́ет на гита́ре?**

Са́ша: — Бори́с Распу́тин. Он са́мый интере́сный гитари́ст в Москве́.

Та́ня: — Пра́вда? Здо́рово!

игра́ть (игра́й-) + на + prep. case = to play (a musical instrument)

руби́новый = ruby

гита́ра = guitar

5. Imagine that you are putting together a band and need to find out which musical instruments your partner plays.

> 3
> — Ты игра́ешь на гита́ре?
> 1
> — Нет.
> 2
> — А на чём ты игра́ешь?
> 1   4
> — **На скри́пке.** А ты?
> 1
> — А я **на гита́ре.**

На чём ты игра́ешь? = What musical instrument do you play?

роя́ль, виолонче́ль, скри́пка, фле́йта, кларне́т, тромбо́н, саксофо́н, бараба́н

роя́ль = (grand) piano

виолонче́ль = cello

скри́пка = violin

бараба́н = drum

6. Part of your auditions for potential musicians for your band includes finding out what kind of people they are. You don't want just anyone to be part of your group. Find out what they do in their free time.

> 1   4
> — Я ча́сто рису́ю. А ты?
> 1
> — А я ча́сто гуля́ю.

танцева́ть на дискоте́ке, гуля́ть, чита́ть (о чём), отдыха́ть, рисова́ть, игра́ть (на чём)

всегда́, ча́сто, ре́дко, иногда́

Here is another excerpt from the same conversation.

На дискотéке

Лéна: — Где Мѝша? Он сегóдня рабóтает?

Тáня: — Нет, не рабóтает.

Сáша: — А где же он?

Тáня: — Я тóчно не знáю. Я не хочý **о нём** говорѝть.

Лéна: — Почемý?

Тáня: — Я не хочý говорѝть **о мойх проблéмах.**

> **О ком** Тáня не хóчет говорѝть?
>
> Тáня не хóчет говорѝть о Мѝше.
>
> Тáня не хóчет говорить **о нём.**

Personal Pronouns: Prepositional Case

Nom.	я	ты	он, онó	онá	мы	вы	онѝ
Prep.	обо мнé	о тебé	о нём	о ней	о нас	о вас	о них

Note how the preposition **о** changes to **обо** when used with **мне: обо мнé**

Remember that the preposition is pronounced together with the word after it as if they were one word: /*абамн*ᵇé/

7. Answer the following questions by filling in the appropriate personal pronouns.

> — Вы говорѝте о Москóвском худóжественном театре?[3]
>
> — Нет, мы говорѝм не **о нём.**[1][1]

1. — Ле́на спра́шивала о Ми́ше?

   — Да, она́ о _____ спра́шивала.

2. — Та́ня хоте́ла говори́ть о Ми́ше?

   — Нет, она́ не хоте́ла о _____ говори́ть.

3. — Са́ша спра́шивал о Та́не?

   — Нет, он о _____ не спра́шивал.

4. — Та́ня говори́ла о Ке́вине?

   — Да, она́ о _____ говори́ла.

5. — Ми́ша спра́шивал о Ке́вине?

   — Нет, он о _____ не спра́шивал.

8. Complete the following sentences by putting the personal pronoun in the correct **case.**

1. Они́ спра́шивают о _____ (ты).

2. Та́ня не хо́чет говори́ть о _____ (он).

3. Я не хочу́ говори́ть о _____ (они́).

4. Мы по́мним о _____ (вы).

5. Ми́ша спра́шивает обо _____ (я)? Интере́сно!

6. Почему́ ты спра́шиваешь о _____ (она́)?

7. Они́ говоря́т о _____ (мы).

8. Я не говорю́ о _____ (они́). Я говорю́ о _____ (ты).

9. Они́ не хотя́т говори́ть о _____ тебе́.

10. Вы по́мните о _____ (они́)? Пра́вда?

по́мнить
(по́мни-) =
to remember

почему́ = why

> Я не хочу́ говори́ть **о мои́х пробле́мах.**
>
> Мои́ роди́тели говоря́т **о но́вых фи́льмах.**

Prepositional Plural of Possessive and Demonstrative Pronouns and Adjectives

| Pronouns | | | | Adjectives |
-их				-ых
Nom. мой твой э́ти чьи				но́вые
Prep. о мои́х о твои́х об э́тих о чьих				о но́вых

9. Complete the following sentences using the appropriate preposition (**в**, **на** or **о/об**) and the prepositional plural case endings.

1. Мы чита́ем _____.
   америка́нские фи́льмы

2. На́ши друзья́ живу́т _____.
   но́вые кварти́ры

3. Мы ча́сто ду́маем _____.
   на́ши роди́тели

4. Та́ня всегда́ танцу́ет _____.
   больши́е дискоте́ки

5. Ты мно́го ду́маешь _____.
   твои́ отме́тки

6. Мои́ друзья́ ча́сто говоря́т _____.
   интере́сные фи́льмы

7. Мы всегда́ у́жинаем _____.
   хоро́шие рестора́ны ▲

8. Я хочу́ чита́ть _____.
   ру́сские студе́нты

9. Я ча́сто ду́маю _____.
   твои́ пода́рки

10. Мы чита́ем _____.
    ста́рые города́

11. Мы не ду́маем _____.
    но́вые дома́

пода́рок = gift, present

го́род (sg.) → города́ (pl.)

дом (sg.) → дома́ (pl.)

▲ The average Russian does not go out to dinner as often as most Americans do. Russians go out to restaurants to mark a special event or celebration. Dinner in a restaurant is usually accompanied by a lot of drinking, smoking, and dancing. Very often there is a live band in the restaurant.

10. Practicing pronunciation: IC-1 and IC-3

A. 1. Мы зна́ем, где живёт Ке́вин.
$\overset{1}{}$

2. Мы зна́ем, где рабо́тал Ми́ша.
$\overset{1}{}$

3. Мы не зна́ем, где рабо́тает Са́ша.
$\overset{1}{}$

4. Мы не зна́ем, где живёт Ле́на.
$\overset{1}{}$

B. 1. Вы не зна́ете, кто сего́дня игра́ет?
$\overset{3}{}$

2. Ты не зна́ешь, где рабо́тает Серге́й?
$\overset{3}{}$

3. Ты не зна́ешь, кака́я э́то гру́ппа?
$\overset{3}{}$

4. Вы не зна́ете, что де́лает Та́ня?
$\overset{3}{}$

The word order in subordinate clauses is the same as in questions.

Где ты живёшь?

Я не зна́ю, где ты живёшь.

11. Pretend that you don't know the answers to the following questions.

> $\overset{2}{}$ $\overset{2}{}$
> — Скажи́те, пожа́луйста, где игра́ет «Руби́новая ата́ка»?
> $\overset{1}{}$
> — Я не зна́ю, где игра́ет «Руби́новая ата́ка».

Subordinate clauses are separated from the main clause by a comma.

1. Скажи́те, пожа́луйста, где Моско́вский худо́жественный теа́тр?
2. Скажи́, пожа́луйста, где живёт Да́ша?
3. Скажи́те, пожа́луйста, где са́мая популя́рная дискоте́ка?
4. Скажи́те, пожа́луйста, кака́я гру́ппа сего́дня игра́ет?
5. Скажи́, пожа́луйста, когда́ сего́дня спекта́кль?
6. Скажи́, пожа́луйста, кто рабо́тает в би́знесе?
7. Скажи́, пожа́луйста, кака́я му́зыка была́ на дискоте́ке?
8. Скажи́, пожа́луйста, почему́ Са́ша не танцу́ет?
9. Скажи́, пожа́луйста, почему́ Ми́ша не хо́чет говори́ть о Ке́вине?

12. You have just regained consciousness in a Moscow hospital and realize that you have total amnesia. Answer the doctor's questions by saying that you don't remember anything.

> 2
> — Как вас зовут?
> 1
> — **Я не помню,** как меня зовут.

1. — Где вы живёте?

   _____

2. — На какой у́лице вы живёте?

   _____

3. — На како́м этаже́ вы живёте?

   _____

4. — В како́м го́роде вы живёте?

   _____

5. — В како́м до́ме вы живёте?

   _____

6. — В како́й кварти́ре вы живёте?

   _____

7. — Где вы рабо́таете?

   _____

8. — Что вы де́лаете в Москве́?

   _____

9. — Что вы де́лаете в кли́нике?

   _____

10. — Хоти́те обе́дать?
    — Хочу́.

13. Find out how creative your partner is. Ask him or her whether s/he used to dance, draw, or play a musical instrument in school and whether s/he continues to do it now. Ask as many different questions as you can.

>   3
> — Ты в шко́ле игра́л(а) на гита́ре?
> 1   1   4
> — Да, в деся́том кла́ссе. А ты?
>   1
> — А я игра́л(а) на фле́йте.
>   4
> — А сейча́с?
>   1   4
> — А сейча́с не игра́ю. А ты?
>   1
> — И я не игра́ю.

кла́сс = grade

PREviewing

1. Вы по́мните о чём говори́ли Та́ня и Ми́ша? Они́ говори́ли:

	Да	Нет
о Моско́вском худо́жественном теа́тре	☐	☐
об у́жине в рестора́не	☐	☐
о спекта́кле	☐	☐
об экза́мене в институ́те	☐	☐
о плохо́м тра́нспорте	☐	☐
об америка́нце Ке́вине	☐	☐
о деньга́х	☐	☐
об их друзья́х	☐	☐
о но́вом би́знесе	☐	☐
о ва́жном де́ле	☐	☐

ва́жное де́ло =
    important matter

▶ Read through the following questions and complete as many as you can before you watch the video with the SOUND ON. Finish answering the questions while you watch.

2. When Та́ня arrives, she says to Ми́ша :

☐ Здра́вствуй, Ми́ша! А вот и я. Ты давно́ здесь стои́шь?

☐ Приве́т! Каки́е краси́вые цветы́! Спаси́бо! Ты давно́ здесь стои́шь?

☐ Приве́т! Ми́ша, извини́, пожа́луйста! Ты давно́ здесь стои́шь?

> давно́ = for a long time

3. Та́ня ду́мает, что

☐ Ми́ша нс по́мнит о Ке́вине.

☐ Ми́ша ревну́ет.

☐ Ми́ша хо́чет гуля́ть в па́рке.

> ревнова́ть (ревнова́-) = be jealous

4. Ми́ша говори́т, что он не хо́чет (check all that apply):

	Да	Нет
рабо́тать в больни́це	☐	☐
говори́ть о Ке́вине	☐	☐
слу́шать, что говори́т Та́ня	☐	☐
танцева́ть	☐	☐
у́жинать	☐	☐
говори́ть о спекта́кле	☐	☐

> слу́шать (слу́шай-) = listen

5. Earlier that evening, Ми́ша runs into an old classmate. What happens when Та́ня has a similar encounter?

When Та́ня arrives, she asks Ми́ша:

— Ты **давно́** здесь стои́шь?

Here, **давно́** indicates a situation that began some time ago and is still going on at the present moment. Compare the Russian phrase to the English: "*Have you been standing here for a long time?*"

6. Practice using **давно́** by answering the following questions.

>   3
> — Та́ня давно живёт в Москве́?
>   1   3   1   2
> — По-мо́ему, нет./По-моему, не очень давно́./ Коне́чно,
>   1
> давно́ ./Я то́чно не зна́ю.

1. Ке́вин давно́ говори́т по-ру́сски?
2. Ми́ша давно́ рабо́тает в би́знесе?
3. Да́ша давно́ живёт в Колле́дж Па́рке?
4. А́нна Бори́совна давно́ рабо́тает в шко́ле?
5. Са́ша давно́ рабо́тает?
6. Ви́ктор Степа́нович давно́ рабо́тает в ба́нке?
7. Серге́й давно́ живёт в Москве́?

> When Та́ня tries to explain why she was late, Ми́ша gets jealous and refuses to talk to her. She asks him:
>
>   — Ну, что ты молчи́шь?
>
> "Why are you so quiet?" (Literally: Why are you silent?) In colloquial Russian, **что** is often used as a synonym for **почему́.** Та́ня could have also said, «**Почему́ ты молчи́шь?**»

молча́ть (молча́-) = be silent

---

7. You have an annoying guest who wants to know why the people at your party aren't talking to him. Give him a polite excuse.

>   2
> — Что **Ва́ня** молчит?
>   1   1   1
> — Я не зна́ю./Он отдыха́ет./Он всегда́ молчи́т.

> твой брат, твоя́ сестра́, ма́ма и па́па, ты, твой
> друзья́

You could say that Ми́ша is a little jealous of Та́ня's new friend, Ке́вин. When Та́ня says that she wants to eat, he replies:

> — Извини́, э́то теа́тр, **а** не рестора́н.

By using a conjunction, **а**, Ми́ша draws attention to the contrast between the theater and a restaurant.

Suppose you are trying to call a theater in Moscow but get the wrong number:

>   2   3
> — Извините, э́то теа́тр?
>   2
> — Э́то ресторан, **а** не теа́тр.

The person answering your call could also have replied:

>   3   1
> — Э́то не театр, **а** ресторан.

Notice how the intonation differs in these two constructions.

The conjunction **а** has a contrastive meaning; it introduces an opposition.

8. The information about the characters provided below is false. Make the necessary corrections to transform them into true statements.

>   1
> Ми́ша рабо́тал **на стадионе.** →
>   2
> Ми́ша рабо́тал **в клинике, а не на стадио́не.**
>   3   1
> or: Ми́ша рабо́тал **не на стадионе, а в клинике.**

1. Ми́ша инжене́р.
2. Та́ня преподава́тельница.
3. А́нна Бори́совна рабо́тает в институ́те.
4. Серге́й живёт в Петербу́рге.
5. Да́ша живёт во Фра́нции.
6. Ке́вин ру́сский.

9. Fill in the appropriate conjunctions to indicate a contrast or a similarity.

и → parallelism of subjects, actions, places, etc.

а → opposition of subjects, etc.

> ¹   ¹
> Та́ня студентка, **и** Серге́й студе́нт.
> ³   ¹
> Та́ня студентка, **а** Ми́ша ветеринар.

1. Та́ня живёт в Росси́и, _____ Да́ша живёт в Аме́рике.

2. Та́ня студе́нтка, _____ Да́ша студе́нтка.

3. Ке́вин фото́граф, _____ Ми́ша ветерина́р.

4. А́нна Бори́совна учи́тельница, _____ Ви́ктор Степа́нович бухга́лтер.

5. Серге́й живёт в Москве́, _____ Ле́на живёт в Москве́.

6. Са́ша живёт до́ма, _____ Ле́на живёт в общежи́тии.

7. Ми́ша рабо́тает, _____ Са́ша рабо́тает.

10. Using the conjunctions **и** or **а**, add information about yourself to what is said about the characters from the video.

> ¹
> Та́ня живёт в квартире. →
> ³   ¹
> Та́ня живёт в квартире, **а я живу́ в доме.**
> ¹   ¹
> or: Та́ня живёт в квартире, **и я живу́ в кварти́ре.**

1. Ми́ша живёт в Москве́.

2. Та́ня живёт в большо́м до́ме.

3. Серге́й ча́сто ду́мает о деньга́х.

4. Ми́ша игра́ет на гита́ре.

5. Cáша всегдá говори́т о спóрте.

6. Ке́вин был в Росси́и.

7. Тáня танцýет на дискотéке.

8. Mи́ша хóчет рабóтать в би́знесе.

9. Лéна мнóго гуля́ет.

10. Ке́вин отдыхáл в январé.

> «Вот э́то да!» is an expression of surprise and awe, similar to the English "Wow!" Can you think of another way to say this in English?

11. Express your surprise at the following statements.

> — Моя́ сестрá – балери́на.¹
>
> — **Вот э́то да!**²

1. Я живý в твоём общежи́тии.

2. Моя́ мáма рабóтает в Бéлом дóме.

3. Моя́ кóшка отли́чно понимáет по-рýсски.

4. Лéтом мы жи́ли в сáмой дорогóй гости́нице в Петербýрге.

5. Я читáл(а) о нáшем профéссоре в газéте.

6. Дáша и Стив ýжинают в сáмых дороги́х рестора́нах в Вашингтóне.

7. Mи́ша рабóтает в би́знесе.

8. В декабрé я был(á) в Москóвском худóжественном теáтре.

9. Мои́ роди́тели рáньше жи́ли в твоéй кварти́ре.

12. Find out where your partner was yesterday and report what you both did to the class.

> — Где ты вчера́ была?
>
> — Я была́ **в кинотеатре.** А ты?
>
> — А я была́ **на работе.**
>
> Вчера́ Ли́нда была́ **в кинотеатре,** а я была́ **на работе.**

13. Your roommate was supposed to meet you somewhere and never showed up. Construct as many mini-dialogs as you can with your partner.

> — Почему́ ты не́ был(а́) **в кинотеатре?**
>
> — Я был(а́) **в библиотеке!**

museum, work, stadium, university, meeting, store, post office, home, lecture

4

DAY 7

Та́ня and Ми́ша didn't make it to the play. However, Та́ня decided to make the best of her evening and joined Ле́на and Са́ша for a night of music and dancing at a local dance club. Below is the advertisement for the club.

И́МПУЛЬС
информацио́нное аге́нтство

Дороги́е друзья́!
Сего́дня в клу́бе «Кора́лл» — но́вая музыка́льная програ́мма

«Энерги́чный май»

Клуб «Кора́лл» — э́то ую́тные ба́ры, конце́рты, да́нсинг

В програ́мме:

Бе́лый зал — конце́рт рок-гру́ппы «Руби́новая ата́ка»
Чёрный зал — дискоте́ка
Да́нсинг весь ве́чер
Веду́щий — диджей Фёдор Петухо́в — о са́мых популя́рных
музыка́льных гру́ппах в ми́ре
В фойе́ и в ба́рах — вы́ставка

А́дрес: Клуб «Кора́лл», ул. Садо́вая, дом 13
метро́ «Пу́шкинская», тролле́йбус 3, 15,
остано́вка «Петро́вка, 8»

Мы рабо́таем — вы отдыха́ете!

Нача́ло 23.00. Цена́ 2500 руб.

руб. = rubles (abbr.)

▲

▲ A trolley looks just like a bus, but it runs on electric power from overhead lines. Because the trolley is dependent on the wires for power, its movement is restricted.

1. Answer the following questions based on the advertisement above.

A. What is the name of the club advertised? _____

B. What is the name of the event? _____

C. What is the address? _____

D. What is the date and time of the event? _____

E. How much does it cost to attend the event? _____

F. List the names of the following items as they appear in the ad:

1. клуб: _____

2. программа: _____

3. рок-группа: _____

4. диджей: _____

Unfortunately, Ми́ша's jealousy prevented him from joining Та́ня, Ле́на and Са́ша at the club. The evening was a true success, just as the ad promised. All Ми́ша could do was read about what he had missed in the local newspaper **«Вече́рняя Москва́».** This is the article he read:

Экстравага́нтный ве́чер в музыка́льном клу́бе «Кора́лл»

Ве́чером в «Кора́лле» - эне́ргия и ритм

*Расска́зывает наш корреспонде́нт **Ива́н Ко́шкин.** Вчера́ он был в клу́бе «Кора́лл» на но́вой музыка́льной програ́мме «Энерги́чный май». Сего́дня мы публику́ем его́ репорта́ж об э́том интере́сном шо́у.*

began

Д́обрый ве́чер, дороги́е друзья́! Вы бы́ли вчера́ в музыка́льном клу́бе «Кора́лл»? Отли́чно! Не́ были? Не мо́жет быть! Тогда́ чита́йте мой репорта́ж. Он начался́◊ в ба́ре.

Интервью́ в ба́ре

Корреспонде́нт: — Д́обрый ве́чер! М́ожно бутербро́д?

beer

Ба́рмен: — Пожа́луйста. Вот пи́во◊, хоти́те?

Корреспонде́нт: — Нет, спаси́бо, я на рабо́те. Скажи́те, а

paintings

кто рисова́л э́ти карти́ны◊, и почему́ они́ здесь, в ба́ре?

| Ба́рмен: | — Худо́жники◊ - мои́ друзья́. Они́ студе́нты в Акаде́мии худо́жеств. О́льга Огурцо́ва, Ю́ра Красно́в, Све́та Руба́шкина. Они́ не о́чень популя́рные худо́жники и о́чень молоды́е, но по-мо́ему, больши́е тала́нты. | artists |
| Корреспонде́нт: | — Да, интере́сные карти́ны ... Абстракциони́зм, пост-модерни́зм. Большо́е спаси́бо. Бутербро́д был о́чень вку́сный. | |

В бе́лом за́ле

В за́ле на сце́не – гру́ппа «Руби́новая ата́ка». Соли́ст Бори́с Распу́тин (кра́сная руба́шка, бе́лые брю́ки) игра́ет на гита́ре. Пе́сня◊: «Жёлтые ро́зы стоя́т на столе́, бе́лые ро́зы лежа́т на песке́◊...» Му́зыка немно́го стра́нная. А вот – но́вый ритм. Втора́я пе́сня – о вампи́рах на мотоци́клах. Музыка́нты игра́ют энерги́чно, танцу́ют на сце́не. Тре́тья пе́сня – соли́ст стои́т на голове́◊. Фанта́стика! Стоя́ть на голове́ – вот э́то да! Тепе́рь и я хочу́ танцева́ть.

song

sand

head

В чёрном за́ле

Весёлые молоды́е лю́ди энерги́чно танцу́ют рок, брейк, рэп. И я (не о́чень молодо́й, но энерги́чный) танцу́ю и танцу́ю. Отли́чная трениро́вка◊! А как же интервью? Вон симпати́чная де́вушка в чёрном пла́тье. «Де́вушка, как вас зову́т?» Она́ не понима́ет, что я говорю́, но смеётся◊. Мо́жет быть◊, я хорошо́ танцу́ю.

exercise

laughs
may be

Ну что, тепе́рь и вы хоти́те танцева́ть в клу́бе «Кора́лл»? Я вчера́ был и на конце́рте, и в ба́ре, и на вы́ставке в музе́е, и на стадио́не ... нет-нет! Я был в клу́бе «Кора́лл»! А вы?

Scan the text one paragraph at a time to answer the following questions.

2. Paragraph 1

    A. Who is the author of this piece?

        ☐ a writer

        ☐ a newspaper correspondent

        ☐ an art critic

B. What is the article about?

☐ a new TV program
☐ a Broadway musical
☐ a music show at the club

C. Write out the title of this event _____

3. Paragraph 2

Does the author encourage his readers to visit the club "Кора́лл"?

☐ да   ☐ нет

4. Paragraph 3

A. Who did the journalist interview?

☐ musician   ☐ bartender   ☐ artist

B. Where did this interview take place? _____

C. Which of the following things does the author not mention in this paragraph?

☐ sandwiches   ☐ beer   ☐ fine art   ☐ rock music

5. Paragraph 4

A. Where does the action in this paragraph take place?

_____

B. Name the person described here. Who is he, and what is he doing at the club?

_____

C. What do yellow roses and vampires on motorcycles have in common?

_____

6. Paragraph 5

A. Where does the action in this paragraph take place?

_____

B. What are people doing there?

_____

C. Who does the correspondent approach?

_____

7. Paragraph 6

This club offers a wealth of experiences similar to which of the following places?

- □ концéрт
- □ бар
- □ дискотéка
- □ музéй
- □ библиотéка
- □ рестора́н
- □ вы́ставка
- □ стадио́н

8. Identify the following statements as true or false. If the statement is false, make the necessary corrections.

The author of this article	Да	Нет
1. …is a young woman	□	□
2. …buys a sandwich and beer.	□	□
3. …thinks the pictures are interesting.	□	□
4. …enjoys the sandwich.	□	□
5. …thinks the music of «**Руби́новая ата́ка**» is strange.	□	□
6. …doesn't like the fast music.	□	□
7. …doesn't dance.	□	□
8. …asks the girl in the black dress what her name is.	□	□

9. Compose a brief description of this article using the provided reference words or your own words.

В статьé кри́тик говори́т о(б) …

стра́нная му́зыка, энерги́чный рок, отли́чный ве́чер, интере́сный клуб, но́вая дискотéка, но́вая програ́мма, вку́сные бутербро́ды, хоро́ший соли́ст, весёлые молоды́е лю́ди, люби́мая гру́ппа, популя́рная му́зыка, симпати́чная де́вушка

10. Как отдыха́ют америка́нские студе́нты? Как вы отдыха́ете?

> $\overset{3}{}$ $\overset{1}{}$
> — По-мо́ему, америка́нские студе́нты мно́го гуля́ют.
> $\overset{2}{}$ $\overset{2}{}$ $\overset{2}{}$
> — Нет, что ты! Америка́нские студе́нты о́чень ма́ло гуля́ют!

> танцева́ть, игра́ть (на чём), рисова́ть, гуля́ть, у́жинать в рестора́не, ду́мать (о чём), говори́ть (о чём), чита́ть (о чём)

11. Tell the class about a concert that you recently attended.

> В ма́е я был(а́) на музыка́льном конце́рте **в Вашингто́не**.
> В програ́мме был **рок**.

> му́зыка «ка́нтри», кла́ссика, джаз, рэп, рок, му́зыка «блю грас», поп-му́зыка, блюз

партéр = orchestra
ряд = row
мéсто = seat

1. Use the pictures above to answer the following questions.

A. What time does the performance begin?

_____

PREviewing

B. Are these good seats?

C. What is the price of the tickets (in rubles and in dollars)? Is this a good price for these seats? Would you expect to pay this much to see a play?

2. A. Listed here are the full names of some of the characters in this episode. What would their close friends or relatives call them?

Михаи́л Ко́тов _____

Пётр Васи́льев _____

Татья́на Воло́дина _____

▲ Except in colloquial speech, Russians measure time according to a 24-hour, rather than a 12-hour, clock. In the 24-hour system, the p.m. hours are indicated by the numbers 13 to 24. So, 1 p.m. is **13 часо́в**, 2 p.m. is **14 часо́в**, etc.

B. What other characters do you recall from the video? Do you know their last names or patronymics? Give both their informal and formal names.

_____   _____

_____   _____

_____   _____

VIEWING

3. Match the characters on the left with the appropriate description.

1. Пе́рвая де́вушка

    A. … спра́шивает, кто сего́дня игра́ет.

2. Втора́я де́вушка

    B. … не зна́ет, где Моско́вский худо́жественный теа́тр.

3. Пе́тя Васи́льев

    C. … говори́т, что э́то её люби́мый спекта́кль.

4. Стра́нный челове́к

    D. … не зна́ет, где его́ подру́га.

5. Ми́ша

    E. … не обе́дала и не у́жинала.

6. Та́ня

    F. … спра́шивает: «Та́ня, ты в теа́тр?»*

7. Ру́сская тури́стка

    G. … говори́т, что Ми́ша капитали́ст.

*This is a colloquial construction with the verb to go omitted.

4. Пе́тя calls Ми́ша a **капитали́ст**, a term that was derogatory until recently. Why does Пе́тя call him that?

Ми́ша рабо́тает в _____

5. Та́ня is trying to make peace with Ми́ша, who is extremely mad at her for being so late. Fill in the blanks in their conversation with the missing verbs.

Ми́ша: — Ну, где ты была́?

Та́ня: — _____, я _____ об америка́нце?
                 remember   spoke

Ми́ша: — О како́м америка́нце?

Та́ня: — О Ке́вине.

Ми́ша: — _____
I don't remember.

Та́ня: — Ну вот, ты ревну́ешь!

Ми́ша: — Почему́ же? Я внима́тельно слу́шаю.

слу́шать (слу́ш**ай**-) = listen

Та́ня: — Нет, _____ . Ми́ша!
you're not listening

Ну что ты _____ ?
(are) silent

6. Listen carefully to the segment in which Та́ня tries to patch things up between her and Ми́ша. Using the following translation as a reference, do a "voice-over" of the segment as you watch it with the SOUND ON.

Ми́ша: — I don't want to talk about your Kevin!

Та́ня: — All right, all right! What do you want (to do)? To dance?

Ми́ша: — I don't want to dance.

Та́ня: — To have dinner?

Ми́ша: — I don't want to have dinner.

Та́ня: — I don't understand; what do you want? You don't want to dance, you don't want to have dinner, you don't want to listen!

Ми́ша: — Yes, I don't want to.

7. Change the following false statements to make them true.

1. Ми́ша не обе́дал и не у́жинал, а Та́ня не хо́чет у́жинать.

2. Ми́ша хо́чет говори́ть о Ке́вине, а Та́ня не хо́чет слу́шать.

3. Ми́ша не спра́шивает, где была́ Та́ня, а Та́ня говори́т, что она́ гуля́ла.

8. Answer the following questions using the phrases «**Я не знáю**», «**Я (не) понимáю**», or «**Я (не) пóмню**».

> ²
> — На каком этажé живёт Сáша? →
> ¹
> — Я не знаю, на какóм этажé живёт Сáша./
> ¹
> Я знаю, на какóм этажé живёт Сáша. Он живёт
> ¹
> **на третьем этажé.**

1. На какóм кýрсе Тáня?
2. На какóм этажé живёт Кéвин?
3. В какóм бизнесе рабóтает Мúша?
4. В какóм теáтре был спектáкль «Чáйка»?
5. В какóй квартúре живёт Кéвин?
6. В какóм гóроде жил Кéвин в Амéрике?
7. В какóм клýбе былá Тáня?
8. В какóм дóме жилá Тáня рáньше?
9. О чём говорúл Пéтя?
10. О ком говорúла Тáня?

9. Imagine you are in a book store and recognize an old friend.

A. Act out your conversation using this one as a model.

> ²   ³
> — Джон, э́то ты?
> ³
> — Извините?
> ²   ³   ¹
> — Джон, ты помнишь? Я – Мэри. Мы же
> ¹
> бы́ли вмéсте **в шкóле в пéрвом клáссе.**
> ²   ²   ²
> — А, Мэри! Извини! Ну, как живёшь?
> ¹   ⁴
> — Нормáльно. А ты как?

вмéсте = together

B. Since you haven't seen each other for such a long time, you and your old friend ask each other what you are doing for a living.

>   2   3
> — Миша, ты работаешь?
>   1   1
> — Да, работаю.
>   2   3
> — Где? **В клинике?**
>   1   1
> — Нет, там я раньше рабо́тал.
>   4
> — А сейчас?
>   1
> — А сейча́с **в бизнесе.**

1. Work in groups of 3 to check your classmates' knowledge of geography. Take turns to ask where the following cities are located.

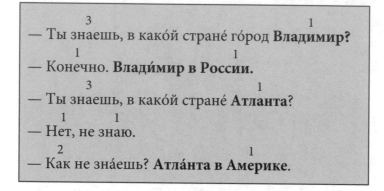

— Ты знаешь, в какой стране́ го́род **Влади́мир?**

— Коне́чно. **Влади́мир в Росси́и.**

— Ты знаешь, в како́й стране́ **Атла́нта?**

— Нет, не зна́ю.

— Как не зна́ешь? **Атла́нта в Аме́рике.**

> Лос-А́нжелес, Воро́неж, Псков, Филаде́льфия, Волгогра́д, Чика́го, Но́вгород, Бо́стон, Пари́ж, Манче́стер, Марсе́ль, Ливерпу́ль

2. Your friend had a party yesterday, and you weren't able to make it. Explain why.

— Где ты был(а́) вчера́?

— Я был(а́) на ва́жном собра́нии.

— Пра́вда? Как интере́сно!/Вот э́то да!/Не мо́жет быть!

> но́вая о́пера, ва́жное собра́ние, Моско́вский худо́жественный теа́тр, интере́сная вы́ставка, ва́жная ле́кция, но́вый францу́зский рестора́н, популя́рный спекта́кль, но́вый бале́т, интере́сная ле́кция

3. Read the following questions with the intonational center on the word prompted by the provided answer.

> 3
> — Ты хо́чешь рабо́тать на Аля́ске?
> 1   1
> — Да, хочу́.

1. — Ты хо́чешь жить в Росси́и?
   — Нет, я хочу́ там отдыха́ть.
2. — Ты хо́чешь рабо́тать в ба́нке?
   — Нет, не хочу́.
3. — Ты был(а́) ле́том в Калифо́рнии?
   — Да, был(а́).
4. — Ты вчера́ рабо́тал(а) в магази́не?
   — Да, рабо́тал(а).
5. — Ты вчера́ был(а́) до́ма?
   — Нет, на рабо́те.
6. — Вы говори́ли о ру́сских фи́льмах?
   — Нет, об америка́нских.

4. Build grammatically correct sentences using the provided parts of speech.

> бе́лые цветы́/ стоя́ть/ на/ ма́ленький стол →
> Бе́лые цветы́ стоя́т на ма́леньком столе́.

1. ру́сский слова́рь/ лежа́ть/ на/ по́лка
2. кни́га/ о/ спорт/ стоя́ть/ в/ моя́ ко́мната
3. бутербро́ды/ лежа́ть/ на/ ку́хня
4. колбаса́/ лежа́ть/ в/ холоди́льник
5. маши́на/ стоя́ть/ в/ гара́ж
6. помидо́ры/ лежа́ть/ на/ стол
7. холоди́льник/ стоя́ть/ на/ ку́хня
8. гита́ра/ лежа́ть/ на/ дива́н
9. ту́фли/ стоя́ть/ в/ спа́льня

5. Act out the following conversations.

A. You meet a professor from Russia at a Russian club party.

Наталья Ивановна: Скажите, пожалуйста, вы уже были в России?

_____

(Tell her whether you have been in Russia. Ask her where she lives.)

Наталья Ивановна: Я живу в Петербурге.

_____

(Say that you know that it's a very beautiful city.)

Наталья Ивановна: Да.

_____

(Ask her where she works in Petersburg.)

Наталья Ивановна: Я работаю в университете. А вы работаете?

_____

(Tell her whether you work, and if you do, where.)

Наталья Ивановна: А где вы живёте, в общежитии?

_____

(Tell her where you live. Give details.)

Наталья Ивановна: А на каком вы курсе?

_____

(Tell her what year you are in.)

B. Наталья Ивановна asks you about the video you have been watching in your Russian class.

Наталья Ивановна: Скажите, пожалуйста, о чём этот фильм?

_____

(Tell her what the video is about. Mention the characters' names.)

Наталья Ивановна: Я не понимаю, этот фильм о русских или об американцах?

_____

(Explain to her which characters are Russians and which one is American.)

Наталья Ивановна: А где живёт Кевин в Москве?

_____

(Tell her about the place where he lives. Give details.)

Ната́лья Ива́новна: А о чём говоря́т геро́и в фи́льме?

_____

(Mention some of the topics they discuss. Specify who talks about what.)

6. Fill in the appropriate forms of the missing personal pronouns. Change the preposition where necessary.

> Та́ня, Ми́ша спра́шивал о (ты). →
> Та́ня, Ми́ша спра́шивал о **тебе́.**

1. А́нна Бори́совна, я ча́сто ду́маю о _____ (вы).

2. Ле́на всегда́ пло́хо говори́т о _____ (я).

3. Э́то гру́ппа «Руби́новая ата́ка». Ты зна́ешь о _____ (она́)?

4. Са́ша был в Большо́м теа́тре, а Та́ня в _____ (он) не была́.

5. Ле́на и Са́ша бы́ли на дискоте́ке, а Ми́ша на _____ (она́) не́ был.

6. Ми́ша ча́сто спра́шивает о _____ (мы).

7. Серге́й был в но́вом америка́нском кафе́, а Ке́вин в _____ (оно́) не́ был.

8. Ле́на, Са́ша всегда́ говори́т о _____ (ты). Как интере́сно!

7. You are filling out an application to study abroad at a Russian university and must demonstrate your ability to write in Russian by providing brief answers to the questions below. Practice your answers orally with your classmates. Feel free to add your own reference words to the given lists.

1. What year are you in college?   **Я на второ́м ку́рсе.**

2. Describe your hobbies.   Я хорошо́ игра́ю на гита́ре.

рисова́ть, танцева́ть, игра́ть (на чём), чита́ть (о чём), гуля́ть

ча́сто, мно́го, непло́хо, хорошо́

3. Describe what you read about (and what you don't read about).

> Я ча́сто чита́ю **об экологи́ческих пробле́мах.**
> Я не чита́ю **о бале́те.**

[америка́нский спорт, пробле́мы в университе́те, класси́ческая му́зыка, но́вые спекта́кли, вы́ставки, америка́нская/ру́сская поли́тика, би́знес, но́вые фи́льмы]

4. What places have you visited in America? In other countries?

> Я был(а́) в шта́те Теха́с.

5. Where have you worked? Where would you like to work in the future?

> Ра́ньше я рабо́тал(а) **в ма́леньком магази́не.**
> Сейча́с я рабо́таю **в на́шей библиоте́ке.**
> Я хочу́ рабо́тать **в большо́м би́знесе.**

 8. Act out the following situations.

A. You are at a party when you run into an old high school classmate who doesn't recognize you. After reminding him who you are, ask him about his life since graduation.

B. You are an agent selling American television shows to a major Russian network. The network, primarily interested in family programming, asks you to describe each show in detail. Describe the shows listed below using the following dialog as a model.

— «Си́мпсонс» - о́чень интере́сная переда́ча.[1]

— Э́то серьёзная переда́ча?[3]

— Нет, что вы! Э́то смешна́я переда́ча.[2][2][2]

— А о чём она́?[2]

— Она́ о семье́. В э́той семье́ па́па рабо́тает на заво́де.[1][1]

— И ма́ма рабо́тает?[3]

— Нет, она́ домохозя́йка.[1][1]

— А де́ти?[4]

— Сын, Барт, в тре́тьем кла́ссе.[1]

— Он хоро́ший шко́льник?[3]

— Нет, не о́чень.[1][1]

передáча = TV show

завóд = plant, factory

домохозя́йка = homemaker

«Меня́ зову́т Эрл», «Геро́и», «О́фис»

1. The Preposition o (об, обо)

The meaning "about" or "concerning" is expressed in Russian by the preposition **o** followed by the prepositional case of the noun in question. The preposition **o** becomes **об** before a vowel sound and **обо** before the pronoun **мне** (see below, 2).

Мы говори́ли **о** письмé.	We spoke about the letter.
Мы говори́ли **о** Тáне.	We spoke about Tanya.
Тáня и её мáма говори́ли **об** одéжде.	Tanya and her mother spoke about clothing.

2. The Prepositional Case of Personal and Interrogative Pronouns

A. The prepositional case forms of the personal pronouns must be memorized.

	Singular		Plural	
	Nom.	**Prep.**	**Nom.**	**Prep.**
1st pers.	я	**обо мнé**	мы	**о нас**
2nd pers.	ты	**о тебé**	вы	**о вас**
3rd pers.	он/онó	**о нём**	они́	**о них**
	онá	**о ней**		

B. The prepositional case forms of the interrogative pronouns must be memorized.

кто → о ком
что → о чём

3. Initial н- in Third-Person Pronouns

Whenever a third-person pronoun (**он, онá, онó, они́**) is the object of a preposition (regardless of case), the pronoun form takes on an initial **н**.

о **н**ём   о **н**ей   о **н**их

4. The Prepositional Case of Adjectives

The prepositional case ending for adjectives is **-ом** for masculine and neuter and **-ой** for feminine (spelled **-ем** and **-ей** after a soft consonant).

Case	Endings			Examples	
	m.	**n.**	**f.**		
Nom.	-ый	-ое	-ая	но́вый, но́вое	но́вая
Prep.		-ом	-ой	но́вом	но́вой

5. The Prepositional Plural of Nouns

The prepositional plural ending for all nouns is **-ах** (spelled **-ях** after a soft consonant).

Nom. Sing.	банк	музе́й	окно́	ка́рта
Prep. Pl.	о ба́нк**ах**	о музе́**ях**	об о́кн**ах**	о ка́рт**ах**

6. The Prepositional Plural of Pronouns and Adjectives

The prepositional plural ending for all types of pronouns and adjectives is **-ых** (**-их**). Compare the following nominative and prepositional plurals:

Nom. Sing.	они́	э́ти	мои́	ва́ши	чьи
Prep. Pl.	о них	об э́тих	о мои́х	о ва́ших	о чьих

Nom. Sing.	-ые	но́вые	молоды́е
Prep. Pl.	-ых	о но́вых	о молоды́х

7. Ordinal Numerals

Like English, Russian distinguishes *cardinal* and *ordinal* numerals. The ordinal numerals function and decline like adjectives. The cardinal numeral **оди́н** changes its form to agree with the noun it precedes: **оди́н ма́льчик, одна́ сестра́, одно́ кре́сло, одни́ де́ти**. The cardinal numeral **два** changes its form only with feminine nouns: **две сестры́** Below is a table of cardinal numerals with the corresponding ordinals from one to ten. These should be memorized.

		masculine	feminine	neuter	
1.	оди́н, одна́, одно́, одни́	пе́рвый	пе́рвая	пе́рвое	first
2.	два (*m.* and *n.*), две (*f.*)	второ́й	втора́я	второ́е	second
3.	три	тре́тий	тре́тья[1]	тре́тье	third
4.	четы́ре	четвёртый	четвёртая	четвёртое	fourth
5.	пять	пя́тый	пя́тая	пя́тое	fifth
6.	шесть	шесто́й	шеста́я	шесто́е	sixth
7.	семь	седьмо́й	седьма́я	седьмо́е	seventh
8.	во́семь	восьмо́й	восьма́я	восьмо́е	eighth
9.	де́вять	девя́тый	девя́тая	девя́тое	ninth
10.	де́сять	деся́тый	деся́тая	деся́тое	tenth

8. The Conjunctions и and а

The Russian conjunction **и** is used to join coordinate subjects and predicates, as does the English conjunction "and". It also introduces clauses in which the speaker wants to express <u>parallelism</u> of actors, actions, places or time segments.

The conjunction **а** introduces clauses containing an <u>opposition</u> of actors, actions, places or time segments, and corresponds to the English conjunctions "and", "whereas", "while".

Compare:

<u>Parallel "и"</u>

Та́ня живёт <u>в го́роде</u>, **и** её роди́тели живу́т <u>в го́роде</u>.

Tanya lives in town and her parents also live in town.

Серге́й отдыха́л <u>на ю́ге</u>, **и** А́нна отдыха́ла <u>на ю́ге</u>.

Sergey vacationed in the south and so did Anna

<u>Oppositional "а"</u>

Ле́на живёт <u>в го́роде</u>, **а** её роди́тели живу́т <u>в дере́вне</u>.

Tanya lives in town and her parents live in the country.

Серге́й отдыха́л <u>на ю́ге</u>, **а** А́нна отдыха́ла <u>на се́вере</u>.

Sergey vacationed in the south and Anna vacationed in the north

---

[1] Note that the ordinal numeral **тре́тий** "third" has the fill vowel **и** in position before the zero-ending only: **тре́тья, тре́тье, тре́тьи** but **тре́тий**.

В ию́не я <u>рабо́тал</u>,
и в а́вгусте я <u>рабо́тал</u>.

В ию́не я <u>рабо́тал</u>,
а в а́вгусте я <u>отдыха́л</u>.

In June I worked and in
August I also worked

In June I worked and in
August I vacationed.

Note that clauses introduced by **и** and **а** must be set off by commas.

9. The Verb быть "to be"

The verb **быть** "to be" is an irregular verb: this means that its conjugation is not entirely predictable from the rules governing stems and endings. You will learn the complete conjugation of this verb in Unit VI. For now, you should memorize the past tense forms of **быть.**

Infinitive:	Past:	Past Tense with Negation:	
быть	он был	он не́ был	/нʲе́был/
	она́ была́	она́ не была́	/нʲибыла́/
	оно́ бы́ло	оно́ не́ было	/нʲе́была/
	они́ бы́ли	они́ не́ были	/нʲе́былʲи/

10. Two Important Classes of Russian Verbs: -жа- and -ова-

As you learned in Unit II, Russian verbs consist of a stem and an ending. The stems are classified according to their final element or suffix. Verb stems with the same suffix share many important features in conjugation, so once you know the rules for a given stem type, you will be able to conjugate almost any verb of that stem type, whether or not you have previously heard it used.

-жа- stem verbs

-жа- stem verbs take second conjugation (II) endings and include any Russian stem ending in -**а** preceded by one of four sibilant sounds: **ж, ш, щ,** and **ч.** Two more verbs with an -**а**- stem preceded by **й,** стоя́ть (стоя́-) "stand" and боя́ться (боя́-ся) "fear", are also considered -жа- stem verbs. There are approximately thirty -жа- stem verbs in Russian, and most of them are intransitive.

лежа́ть (лежа́-) "lie, be in a lying position"

Present		Past
я лежу́	мы лежи́м	он лежа́л
ты лежи́шь	вы лежи́те	она́ лежа́ла
он/она́ лежи́т	они́ лежа́т	оно́ лежа́ло
		они́ лежа́ли

Verbs with the suffix -ова- (-ева-) use <u>first</u> conjugation endings. In present tense conjugation, the -ова- is replaced by -уй-. Note that if the stem suffix (-ова-/-ева-) is stressed, then the present tense form will also stress the syllable -уй-. There are thousands of Russian -ова- stem verbs, and a considerable number of them are built on foreign roots.

рисова́ть (рис**ова́**-) "draw"

Present		Past
я рису́ю	мы рису́ем	он рисова́л
мы рису́ем	вы рису́ете	она́ рисова́ла
он/она́ рису́ет	они́ рису́ют	оно́ рисова́ло
		они́ рисова́ли

танцева́ть (танц**ева́**-) "dance"

Present		Past
я танцу́ю	мы танцу́ем	он танцева́л
ты танцу́ешь	вы танцу́ете	она́ танцева́ла
он/она́ танцу́ет	они́ танцу́ют	оно́ танцева́ло
		они́ танцева́ли

11. Masculine Nominative Plurals Ending in -á

The nominative plural of a small group of masculine nouns is a stressed -**á**, rather than the expected -**ы**. Because nouns in this group are an exception to the basic rule for nominative plurals, they will be identified as exceptions in vocabulary lists.

The stress for these nouns follows what we shall call the AB pattern: that is, stem stress (A) in the singular, but ending stress (B) in the plural.

Examples: го́род   города́

профе́ссор   профессора́

учи́тель   учителя́[2]

---

[2] Note that the stress and the plural ending -á in **учи́тель** are exceptional for nouns with the suffix -**тель**. Compare: **писа́тель – писа́тели, чита́тель – чита́тели.**

The dictionary entries for nouns of this type all look like this: (AB) (á)[3], which refers to the following pattern:

	Singular	Plural (-a)
Nom.	дом	домá
Prep.	о дóме	о домáх

12. Russian and Foreign Names: Formation and Declension

Russian surnames (last names) end in one of a small number of suffixes, the most common of which are **-ов/-ев,** and **-ин.** Masculine surnames decline like nouns, but feminine surnames follow the pronominal declension.

Russian first names and patronymics are always declined like nouns. However, foreign names do not follow the same patterns that Russian names follow. Foreign surnames ending in a vowel sound are indeclinable. Foreign surnames ending in a consonant are declined when they refer to men, and are indeclinable when they refer to women.

Below are some sample declensions of full names in Russian. Pay particular attention to the forms of the surnames.

	Masculine	Feminine
Nom.	Вѝктор Петрóвич Волóдин	Татьѝна Вѝкторовна Волóдина
Prep.	(о) Вѝкторе Петрóвиче Волóдине	(о) Татьѝне Вѝкторовне Волóдин**ой**
Nom.	Уѝльям Шекспѝр	Джéйн Óстин
Prep.	(об) Уѝльяме Шекспѝре	(о) Джéйн Óстин

---

[3] See also Appendix III.

NOUNS

атáка attack
афúша poster (for performance, concert, film, etc.)
балéт ballet
балерúна ballerina
барабáн drum
бúзнес business
билéт ticket
лúшний билéт extra ticket
блю грас blue grass (music)
вéчер evening
виолончéль cello
востóк east
вы́ставка exhibit
геогрáфия geography
гитарúст guitarist
дéвушка girl, young woman
дéло affair, matter, business
дéньги (pl. only) money
джаз jazz
дискотéка dance club
диджей deejay
домохозя́йка housewife
дрáма drama
завóд factory
зáпад west
кáнтри country music
капиталúст capitalist
кларнéт clarinet
класс grade (1st, 2nd, 3rd)
клáссика classical (music)
клуб club
комéдия comedy
концéрт concert
культýра culture
курс year in college; course
кýхня cuisine
лéкция lecture
мéсто seat
милиционéр police officer
мýзыка music
одéжда clothing
óпера opera
отмéтка grade (A, B, C)
партéр orchestra

передáча TV show
подáрок gift, present
полúтика (sing. only) politics
поп-мýзыка pop music
проблéма problem
прогрáмма program
райóн area, neighborhood
рок rock music
рок грýппа rock group
роя́ль (grand) piano
рэп rap music
ряд row
саксофóн saxophone
сéвер north
скрúпка violin
собрáние meeting
солúст soloist, lead singer
спектáкль performance, show
статья́ article
странá country
трáнспорт transportation
тромбóн trombone
тюльпáн tulip
футбóл soccer
америкáнский футбóл football
флéйта flute
хризантéма chrysanthemum
цветы́ (pl.) flowers
этáж floor
юг south

PROPER NOUNS

Аля́ска Alaska
Атлáнта Atlanta
Владúмир Vladimir (city in Russia)
Кавкáз Caucasus (a geopolitical, mountain-barrier region that spreads across Georgia, Armenia, Azerbaijan and part of Southern Russia)
Ливерпýль Liverpool
Манчéстер Manchester

Марсéль Marseilles
Невá Neva
Рим Rome
Сúэтл Seattle
Филадéльфия Philadelphia
Чикáго Chicago

VERBS

быть to be
был, былá, бы́ло was
бы́ли were
волновáться (волновá-ся) worry, be nervous
игрáть (игрáй-) на чём play (a musical instrument)
лежáть (лежá-) lie
молчáть (молчá-) be silent
начинáть (начинáй-) begin
пóмнить (пóмни-) remember
ревновáть (ревновá-) be jealous
рисовáть (рисовá-) draw
слýшать (слýшай-) listen
стоя́ть (стоя́-) stand
танцевáть (танцевá-) dance

ADJECTIVES

вáжный important
ветеринáрный veterinary
дорогóй expensive
голóдный hungry
классúческий classical
музыкáльный musical
небольшóй not large, small
профессионáльный professional
рубúновый ruby
свéжий fresh
экологúческий environmental

ORDINAL NUMERALS

пéрвый first
вторóй second
трéтий third

четвёртый fourth
пя́тый fifth
шесто́й sixth
седьмо́й seventh
восьмо́й eighth
девя́тый ninth
деся́тый tenth

ADVERBS

вме́сте *together*
внима́тельно *attentively*
давно́ for a long time

ещё *still; yet*
опя́ть *again*
про́сто *simply, only*
уже́ *already*

PREPOSITIONS

о, об, обо about

EXPRESSIONS

Вот э́то да! Wow!
Всё! That's it!

Как живёшь? How are you?
Коне́чно. Of course.
оди́н alone
пока́ нет not yet
почему́ why
ско́лько how many; how much
что за + acc. = What kind of
Что ты молчи́шь? Why are
  you (so) quiet?

*T*anya and Misha patch things up and agree to meet. Tanya explains what happened to Kevin.

Ужа́сная исто́рия

You will learn how to:

- FIND OUT A PERSON'S NAME IN BOTH FORMAL AND INFORMAL SETTINGS
- RETELL A STORY IN THE THIRD PERSON
- RENT AN APARTMENT IN MOSCOW (AND HOW NOT TO)
- IDENTIFY YOURSELF AND DESCRIBE WHERE YOU LIVE
- READ A CLASSIFIED AD IN A RUSSIAN NEWSPAPER
- DESCRIBE YOUR TASTES, LIKES AND DISLIKES, AND PERSONAL PREFERENCES
- EXPRESS KINSHIP RELATIONS USING A FAMILY TREE

▶ At the end of the last scene, Та́ня and Ми́ша have an argument. Ми́ша decides to resolve the situation by emailing a letter to Та́ня, but at the last minute decides to slip the letter under her door instead.

1. Answer the following questions using the information from the envelope pictured above.

 A. Write out the full words for the abbreviations in Та́ня's address.

 г. _____ Москва́

 ул. _____ Во́лкова

 д. _____ 6, кв. _____ 12

 B. Comment on the differences in Russian and American addresses. In what order is the information written? Is there anything different about the envelope itself?

2. Here is Ми́ша's letter to Та́ня.

люби́ть (люби́-) = love
ревнова́ть (ревнова́-) = be jealous
волнова́ться (волнова́-ся) = worry

серди́ться (серди́-ся) = be angry

ви́деть (ви́де-) = see

> Танюша, милая, извини
> меня, пожалуйста. Я знаю,
> ты думаешь, что я идиот.
> А я очень люблю тебя и поэтому
> ревную. И ещё я всегда очень
> волнуюсь, когда ты опаздываешь.
> Сердишься? Ну, пожалуйста,
> не сердись. Я очень-очень хочу
> тебя видеть.
>
> Целую тебя, твой Миша.

A. What form of address is the name **Таню́ша?**
- ☐ formal
- ☐ endearing
- ☐ pejorative

B. What kind of letter is this?
- ☐ threatening
- ☐ apologetic
- ☐ self-righteous

C. Why did Ми́ша write it?
- ☐ He forgot Та́ня's birthday.
- ☐ He got mad at Та́ня for being late.
- ☐ He has found another girlfriend.

D. How do you think Та́ня will react to this letter?

- ☐ She will forgive him.
- ☐ She will get even madder.
- ☐ She will find another boyfriend.

VIEWING

▶ In this episode, we will discover how the argument between Ми́ша and Та́ня is resolved and witness some shocking developments involving Ке́вин! Read through the questions below before watching the video with the SOUND OFF.

SOUND OFF

3. Identify the following statements as true or false. Э́то так и́ли нет?

	Да	Нет
When Ми́ша calls, Та́ня hangs up on him.	☐	☐
Та́ня and Ми́ша meet at a museum.	☐	☐
Ке́вин has a housewarming party at his new apartment.	☐	☐
The people in Ке́вин's apartment call the police to come question Ке́вин.	☐	☐
Та́ня shows up to help Ке́вин.	☐	☐

4. Although you will recognize most of the characters in this episode, there will be a few unfamiliar faces. Try to guess who these new characters are.

A. Who are the visitors in Ке́вин's apartment?

- ☐ Ке́вин's relatives from America
- ☐ the neighbors
- ☐ the rightful owners of the apartment

B. What is the man's reaction to Ке́вин?

- ☐ hostile and suspicious
- ☐ warm and friendly
- ☐ indifferent

C. When does the scene with the police take place?

- ☐ while Та́ня and Ми́ша are sitting at the museum
- ☐ two weeks after Ке́вин arrives
- ☐ while Ми́ша is waiting for Та́ня by the theater

D. What is the reason behind the scandal with the police?

☐ Кévин does not have the apartment owners' permission to stay there.

☐ Кévин is wanted for grand theft.

☐ Кévин accidentally took someone's bag at the airport.

5. We have divided this episode into five mini-episodes and given them titles. Now that you have seen the whole video, put the titles in order.

_____ Хэппи энд. Всё хорошо, что хорошо кончается. (All's well that ends well).

_____ Кто вы? Что вы здесь делаете?

_____ Телефонный разговор. (Phone conversation)

_____ Милиция.

_____ В галерее.

▶ Now watch the video with the SOUND ON and see if your predictions were correct.

SOUND ON

6. What is the outcome of Таня's telephone conversation with Миша?

☐ They break up.

☐ They agree to meet.

☐ Миша proposes to Таня.

7. Миша apologizes to Таня: «**Таня, ну извини меня. Я дурак.**» At that point Таня tells Миша:

☐ why she was late to the theater

☐ her plans to leave Moscow and study in America

☐ her criminal record

8. The rightful owners of Кévин's apartment arrive home after a week out of town, and declare that:

☐ Кévин underpaid them by $300

☐ they never rented the apartment to Кévин

☐ they have changed their mind and want Кévин to leave

9. When Та́ня finds out that she and Ке́вин have been swindled, she shifts the responsibility to:

- ☐ faulty advertising
- ☐ her sister
- ☐ a crooked realty firm

10. It looks like Ке́вин may have to find a new place to live! What do you think he will do?

- ☐ move to a hotel
- ☐ move in with Та́ня
- ☐ stay where he is

И́мя, о́тчество, фами́лия

POSTviewing

The son of the owners of Ке́вин's apartment, Ва́ня, is fascinated by the strange American in his apartment. He introduces himself to Ке́вин:

> Меня́ зову́т Ва́ня.

Compare this to the formal introduction Ва́ня's father uses with the police:

> Моя́ **фами́лия** Смирно́в.

In very formal situations, «**Фами́лия?**», «**И́мя?**», and «**О́тчество?**» are used in place of «**Как вас зову́т?**» In written form this is abbreviated as **Ф.И.О.**

фами́лия	и́мя	о́тчество
Смирно́в▲	Васи́лий	Петро́вич
Смирно́ва	Гали́на	Ива́новна
Смирно́в	Ива́н (Ва́ня)	Васи́льевич

▲ There are 80,000 people in the city of Moscow with the last name of **Смирно́в**. The most widespread last name, **Ивано́в**, outnumbers this by approximately 20,000.

11. **A.** Pretend that you are the police officer in the video. Ask the Смирно́вы for their names.

B. Ask your partner his/her name in as many different ways as you can: formal, polite, and informal. Make up your **о́тчество** based on your father's name, i.e. David would become Дави́довна or Дави́дович, etc.

12. The misunderstandings in this episode led to some name-calling. Here are the names you heard today, plus a few more.

дура́к (m.)/ ду́ра (f.)= fool

идио́т/ идио́тка = idiot

хулига́н/ хулига́нка = hoodlum

жу́лик = swindler

хам = rude, obnoxious person

Come up with a list of famous characters (fictional or real) who fit the description above.

> Барт Си́мпсон **хулига́н.**

Чья э́то сестра́?
Э́то сестра́ Та́ни.

Чей э́то фотоаппара́т?
Э́то фотоаппара́т Ке́вина.

The Genitive Case				
	Nominative		**Genitive**	
masc.	-ø (-ь)	брат, учи́тель	-а (-я)	бра́та, учи́теля
neut.	-о (-е)	окно́, общежи́тие	-а (-я)	окна́, общежи́тия
femin.	-а (-я)	сестра́, Та́ня	-ы (-и)	сестры́, Та́ни

1. Change the following nouns from the nominative to genitive case.

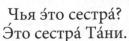

друг — дру́га

подру́га, го́род, до́чка, ию́ль, ма́ма, зда́ние, сын,
преподава́тель, музе́й, мили́ция, па́па, письмо́, апре́ль,
собра́ние, ча́шка

2. Answer the following questions about possession using the words
in parentheses in the genitive case.

> 2
> — Чей э́то паке́т? (Та́ня) →
> 1
> — Э́то паке́т **Та́ни**.

1. Чей э́то компью́тер? (подру́га)
2. Чьи э́то де́ньги? (сестра́)
3. Чьи э́то ве́щи? (друг)
4. Чьё э́то пла́тье? (О́ля)
5. Чья э́то гита́ра? (брат)
6. Чей э́то рюкза́к? (Серге́й) *Серей*
7. Чьи э́то роди́тели? (Ле́на)
8. Чьи э́то пробле́мы? (Та́ня)
9. Чьи э́то биле́ты? (Михаи́л)
10. Чья э́то маши́на? (милиционе́р)

3. What places can you find in your friend's collection of maps of the world?

> — Кака́я э́то ка́рта?
>
> — Э́то ка́рта **Нью-Йо́рка**.

> Москва́, Петербу́рг, А́фрика, Росси́я, Аме́рика, Крым, Кавка́з, Вашингто́н, Евро́па, А́зия, Пари́ж, Кана́да, Ло́ндон

4. Ask the salesperson the subjects of the different textbooks you see in a Russian bookstore, and then ask him/her to show you the books.

> — Како́й э́то уче́бник?
>
> — Э́то уче́бник **биоло́гии**.
>
> — Мо́жно?
>
> — Пожа́луйста.

5. Below is a table of the Commonwealth of Independent States (CIS) and their current capitals. Use the information in the table below to state the capital of each country.▲

> 3   1
> Киев – столица **Украины**.

Страна	Столица	Страна	Столица
Азербайджан	Баку	Молдавия	Кишинёв
Армения	Ереван	Россия	Москва
Белоруссия	Минск	Таджикистан	Душанбе
Грузия	Тбилиси	Туркменистан	Ашхабад
Казахстан	Астана	Узбекистан	Ташкент
Киргизстан	Бишкек	Украина	Киев

6. You have just arrived in Russia on a study abroad program, and your host family wants to know where you live in America. Describe the area where you live.

> Я живу в штате Мэриленд, на востоке Америки. Столица штата — Аннаполис. Я живу в маленьком городе на юге штата.

7. Later in the evening Ваня shows Кевин pictures of his whole family. Discuss the following diagram of Ваня's family.

▲ The USSR (Union of Soviet Socialist Republics) existed from 1922 to 1991 and consisted of 15 constituent republics. After the collapse of the Soviet Union, many of the newly independent states formed the Commonwealth of Independent States (CIS), which now includes 11 republics of the former Soviet Union. Turkmenistan discontinued permanent membership in 2005 and is now an associate member.

Пётр Алексеевич [3] — муж **Екатери́ны Викторовны** [1].

Пётр Алексеевич [3] — де́душка **Вани** [1].

Смирно́вы

Пётр Алексеевич	Екатерина Викторовна

Юрий Петрович	Ирина Петровна

Маша (Мария Юрьевна)

Го́лубевы

Наталия Сергеевна	Иван Николаевич

Василий Петрович	Галина Ивановна

Ваня (Иван Васильевич)

дя́дя (uncle), тётя (aunt), де́душка (grandfather), ба́бушка (grandmother), двою́родный брат (male cousin), двою́родная сестра́ (female cousin)

Possessive and Demonstrative Pronouns: Genitive Case		
	Masculine	**Neuter**	**Feminine**
Nom.	э́тот, наш, мой	э́то, на́ше, моё	э́та, на́ша, мо**я́**
Gen.	э́т**ого**, на́ш**его**, мо**его́**	э́т**ого**, на́ш**его**, мо**его́**	э́т**ой**, на́ш**ей**, мо**е́й**

8. Combine the two sentences provided, using the genitive case to indicate possession.

Э́то мой брат. А э́то его́ ко́шка [1]. →

Э́то ко́шка **моего́ брата** [1].

1. Вот наш профéссор. А э́то егó кабинéт.

   Э́то кабинéт _____.

   кабинéт = office

2. Вот моя́ подрýга. А э́то её собáка.

   Э́то собáка _____.

3. Вот мой друг. А э́то егó маши́на.

   Э́то маши́на _____.

4. Вот моя́ сестрá. А э́то её муж.

   Э́то муж _____.

5. Вот наш студéнт. А э́то егó общежи́тие.

   Э́то общежи́тие _____.

6. Вот мой друг. А э́то егó рюкзáк.

   Э́то рюкзáк _____.

9. А́нна Бори́совна's school has finished for the day, but some parents have not arrived to pick up their children. She is outside looking for their parents.

> 2
> **Где роди́тели э́того мáльчика?**

[э́та дéвочка, э́тот ребёнок, э́тот шкóльник, э́тот хулигáн, э́та шкóльница]

10. You are living in an apartment where your neighbors are always leaving things in the middle of the hallway. Ask different people who these things belong to.

> 2
> — Чей э́то велосипéд? (твой сосéд) →
> 1
> — Э́то велосипéд **твоегó сосéда**.

велосипéд = bicycle

сосéд = neighbor (male)

сосéдка = neighbor (female)

1. Чьи э́то газе́ты? (ва́ша сосе́дка)
2. Чей э́то дива́н? (наш сосе́д)
3. Чьи э́то ве́щи (наш сын)
4. Чья э́то су́мка? (твой сосе́д)
5. Чьё э́то ра́дио? (твоя́ до́чка)
6. Чьи э́то кроссо́вки? (ваш сын)
7. Чей э́то му́сор? (твоя́ сосе́дка)
8. Чья э́то ко́шка? (наш сосе́д)
9. Чей э́то скейтбо́рд? (мой сын)
10. Чья э́то гита́ра? (моя́ до́чка)

му́сор = trash

скейтбо́рд = skateboard

11. Your friend and family members have loaned you lots of nice things for your new apartment. Tell your roommate who the things belong to.

> — Э́то не мой телефо́н. [1]
>
> — А чей он? [2]
>
> — Э́то телефо́н **моего́ дя́ди**. [1]
>
> — Да? Интере́сно!/ Здо́рово! [3] [2] [2]

тётя, дя́дя, де́душка, ба́бушка, брат, сестра́, друг, подру́га

плеер = mp3 player

то́стер = toaster

плеер, дива́н, кре́сло, таре́лки, ла́мпа, компью́тер, ра́дио, стол, то́стер, телеви́зор, сту́лья, холоди́льник

Ке́вин чита́ет **кни́гу**.

Subject (Nom.)   Direct Object (Acc.)

Inanimate Nouns: Accusative Case		
	Nominative	**Accusative**
masc.	**-ø** (-ь) чемода́н, слова́рь	**-ø** (-ь) чемода́н, слова́рь
neut.	**-o** (-e) окно́, пла́тье	**-o** (-e) окно́, пла́тье
femin.	**-a** (-я) кни́га, фотогра́фия	**-y** (-ю) кни́гу, фотогра́фию

The accusative case is the case of the direct object. *Inanimate* masculine and neuter nouns have the **same ending** in the accusative and nominative cases. Feminine nouns in the accusative case take the ending –y (-ю).

1. Change the following nouns from the nominative to the accusative case.

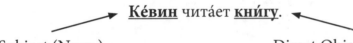

ла́мпа → ла́мпу

пакéт, лéкция, спектáкль, истóрия, письмó, здáние, билéт, кварти́ра, фотоальбóм, маши́на, лаборатóрия, рáдио

2. How well do you know the subjects listed below?

> Я **не óчень хорошó** знáю **физику**.

кинó (indecl.) = film, cinema

эконóмика, теáтр, мýзыка, литератýра, кинó, матемáтика, статистика, истóрия, геогрáфия, компьютер, политика, футбóл

хорошó, плóхо, óчень хорошó, óчень плóхо, не óчень хорошó, неплóхо

3. Accept or reject the following offers of food.

> 3
> — Хочешь **банáн?**
> 3   1   3   1   1
> — **Банáн?** Хочу./ **Банáн?** Спасибо, не хочу.

морóженое = ice cream

конфéта = (piece of) candy

гáмбургер, пицца, колбасá, помидóр, банáн, апельсин, морóженое, шоколáд, бутербрóд, конфéта

Animate Nouns: Accusative Case			
	Nominative		**Accusative**
masc.	-ø (-ь)	брат, Сергéй	-а (-я) брáта, Сергéя
femin.	-а (-я)	сестрá, Тáня	-у (-ю) сестрý, Тáню

Note that the accusative case of animate masculine nouns is the same as the genitive case of these nouns.

4. Change the following nouns from the nominative to the accusative case.

> милиционéр → **милиционéра**

Ви́ктор Петро́вич, А́нна Бори́совна, муж, жена́, бизнесме́н, Ва́ня Смирно́в, друг, подру́га, тётя, дя́дя, ба́бушка, де́душка

	Personal and Interrogative Pronouns: Accusative and Genitive Case								
	Personal Pronouns							**Interrogative Pronouns**	
Nom.	я	ты	он/оно́	она́	мы	вы	они́	кто	что
Acc.	меня́	тебя́	его́	её	нас	вас	их	кого́	что
Gen.	меня́	тебя́	его́	её	нас	вас	их	кого́	чего́

Note that accusative and genitive forms of personal pronouns coincide.

5. Кто зна́ет кого́?

Let's discuss which characters in the video know each other. Guess if you are not sure.

> 3
> — Та́ня знает **Ми́шу?**
> 1   1
> — Да, она́ **его́** знает.

1. Ми́ша и А́нна Бори́совна
2. Серге́й и Ми́ша
3. Та́ня и Ва́ня
4. Ми́ша и Ке́вин
5. Ке́вин и А́нна Бори́совна

6. Ми́ша и Ва́ня
7. Ва́ня и Серге́й
8. Ке́вин и Васи́лий Петро́вич
9. Та́ня и Гали́на Ива́новна
10. Ва́ня и А́нна Бори́совна

6. Express surprise at what your partner says.

> 1
> — Ты **меня́** не понима́ешь.
> 3
> — **Тебя́?**
> 1   1
> — Да, **меня́**.

Both the first name and the patronymic take accusative case endings.

Nominative → Accusative

Гали́на Ива́новна → Гали́ну Ива́новну

Васи́лий Петро́вич → Васи́лия Петро́вича

1. Я вас знáю.
2. Мы тебя́ пóмним.
3. Ты меня́ не слу́шаешь.

4. Они́ нас не понимáют.
5. Он тебя́ не пóмнит.
6. Я тебя́ не понимáю.

слу́шать
   (слу́шай-) =
   listen

любúть (люби́-) "love"

Note the stress
shift and
consonant
mutation

(б → бл) in the
first person
singular of the
verb люби́-.

Present Tense			
я	люблю́	мы	лю́бим
ты	лю́бишь	вы	лю́бите
он/онá	лю́бит	они́	лю́бят

Past Tense
он люби́л
онá люби́ла
онó люби́ло
они́ люби́ли

7. Что вы лю́бите?

Now let's talk about everyone's favorite subject: food!
What food do you like?

— Ты лю́бишь **морóженое?** ▲

— **Морóженое?** Люблю́./ **Морóженое?** Не люблю́.

кéтчуп =
   ketchup

майонéз =
   mayonnaise

пи́цца, колбасá, морóженое, шоколáд, молокó, чай, кóфе,
сок, икрá, кéтчуп, майонéз, суп, хлеб, мáсло, сáхар

8. Talking about personal preferences and tastes

A. Find out what your neighbor likes and dislikes.

— Ты лю́бишь **му́зыку?**

— Да, люблю́. А ты?

— И я люблю́. / А я не люблю́.

▲ Russians love ice cream and eat ice cream throughout the entire year, even in the bitter cold. On the other hand, they believe that you can catch a cold by eating ice cream and drinking cold drinks. So ice cream becomes a taboo if you have a sore throat.

музыка, театр, опера, балет, спорт, литература, кино, природа, история, баскетбол, бейсбол, футбол, море, политика, теннис

природа = nature

B. You would like to buy your Russian friend some music as a birthday present, but aren't sure what s/he likes. Find out.

> ³
> — Ты слушал(а) **Аллу Пугачёву?**
> ³   ¹
> — **Аллу Пугачёву▲?** Слушал(а).
> ²
> — Ну, и как?
> ³   ¹
> — Знаешь, я **её** (не) люблю.

Майкл Джексон, группа «Грин Дей», группа «Роллинг Стоунз», Мадонна, Джоньи Кеш, группа «Битлз», группа «Серебро», группа «Аквариум», группа «А-Студио», Дима Билан

9. Correct the following sentences according to the model.

> Машина любит **Сергея**. →
> Сергей любит **машину**.

1. Пицца любит Кевина.
2. Театр любит Таню.
3. Велосипед любит Ваню.
4. Колбаса любит Анну Борисовну.
5. Футбол любит Василия Петровича.

▲ **Алла Пугачёва** has been one of the most popular Russian pop singers since the early 1980s.

6. Зоопа́рк лю́бит Ми́шу.
7. Молоко́ лю́бит милиционе́ра.
8. Исто́рия лю́бит студе́нта.
9. Моро́женое лю́бит меня́.
10. Кино́ лю́бит вас.

10. Create sentences with the words in this table.

> Ви́тя по́мнит Ми́шу.

Ви́тя	по́мнить	Ми́ша
Ке́вин	не понима́ть	милиционе́р
я	хоте́ть	конфе́та
Ке́вин	фотографи́ровать	го́род
мы	люби́ть	спо́рт
Ми́ша	не слу́шать	Та́ня
А́нна Бори́совна	не люби́ть	литерату́ра
Воло́дины	слу́шать	ра́дио
Ми́ша	ревнова́ть	Та́ня
Смирно́вы	не понима́ть	Ке́вин

фотографи́ровать
(фотографи́**рова**-)
= take a picture of

ревнова́ть
(ревн**ова́**-)
+ acc. = be
jealous

11. Ask your little brother/sister what s/he is drawing.

> $\overset{2}{}$
> — **Что** ты рисуешь?
> $\overset{1}{}$
> — Я рису́ю **апельсин**.
> $\overset{2}{}$
> — **Кого́** ты рисуешь?
> $\overset{1}{}$
> — Я рису́ю **брата**.

кни́га, дом, ла́мпа, мо́ре, велосипе́д, друг, брат, подру́га,
маши́на, семья́, ты, мы

PREviewing

1. Today we will take another look at the first three mini-episodes of «Ужа́сная исто́рия» ("A terrible story"). Match the mini-episode titles on the left with the key sentences on the right.

A. Телефо́нный разгово́р

1. We don't understand you, and you don't understand us.

B. В галере́е

2. Forgive me, I'm a fool.

C. Кто вы?
Что вы здесь де́лаете?

3. I really want to see you.

2. Fill in the missing pronoun.

1. We don't understand **you**, and you don't understand **us**.

Мы не понима́ем _____, вы не понима́ете _____.

2. Forgive **me**, I'm a fool.

Извини́ _____, я дура́к.

3. I really want to see **you**.

Я о́чень хочу́ _____ ви́деть.

ви́деть (ви́де-) = see

3. Answer the following questions based on the video.

> $\overset{3}{—}$ Ми́ша лю́бит Та́ню?
> $\overset{1}{—}$ $\overset{1}{Да}$, он её лю́бит.

1. Ми́ша понима́ет Та́ню?
2. Та́ня лю́бит Ми́шу?
3. Смирно́вы зна́ют Ке́вина?
4. Ке́вин понима́ет Гали́ну Ива́новну и Васи́лия Петро́вича?
5. Ке́вин зна́ет Ва́ню?

▶ Read through the following questions and complete as many as you can before you watch the video with the SOUND ON. Finish answering the questions while you watch.

4. Below we have reproduced some key lines from the video. Identify: (a) the speaker, and (b) the person being addressed.

— Я о́чень хочу́ тебя́ ви́деть.

a. _____

b. _____

— Я тебя́ всегда́ ревну́ю.

a. _____

b. _____

— Как тебя́ зову́т?

a. _____

b. _____

— Меня́ зову́т Ва́ня. А вас?

a. _____

b. _____

— Вы не понима́ете нас,

a. _____

мы не понима́ем вас.

b. _____

5. Mark the following statements as true or false. Это так и́ли нет?

	Да	Нет
Та́ня не чита́ла письмо́ Ми́ши.	☐	☐
Та́ня и Ми́ша бы́ли на вы́ставке.	☐	☐
Та́ня ревнова́ла Ми́шу.	☐	☐
Та́ня и Ми́ша говори́ли о му́зыке.	☐	☐
Ва́ня – брат Та́ни.	☐	☐
Ва́ня – студе́нт.	☐	☐
Ва́ня говори́т по-англи́йски.	☐	☐
Смирно́вы хорошо́ понима́ют Ке́вина.	☐	☐
Ке́вин – хулига́н.	☐	☐

POSTviewing

6. Restate the following quotes from the video in the third person.

> Ми́ша: «Я хочу́ тебя́ ви́деть». →
> **Ми́ша хо́чет ви́деть Та́ню.**

1. «Я тебя́ всегда́ ревну́ю».
2. «Вы не понима́ете нас, мы не понима́ем вас».

> Ми́ша (Та́ня), Гали́на Ива́новна и Васи́лий Петро́вич (Ке́вин)

7. As we have seen, misunderstandings are a pretty common occurrence. Гали́на Ива́новна says to Ке́вин:

> «Вы не понима́ете **нас**, мы не понима́ем **вас**».

Using this sentence as a model, write similar sentences about misunderstandings between the people listed below.

> мы—вы, он—она́, вы—он, она́—ты, ты—мы, Ми́ша—Та́ня, Та́ня—Ке́вин, А́нна Бори́совна—Та́ня

Demonstrative and Possessive Pronouns: Accusative Case

	Masculine	Neuter	Feminine
Nom.	э́тот/ мой/ наш дом э́тот/ мой/ наш друг	э́то/ моё/ на́ше письмо́	э́та/ моя́/ на́ша кни́га э́та/ моя́/ на́ша сестра́
Acc. (inanimate)	э́тот/ мой/ наш дом	э́то/ моё/ на́ше письмо́	э́ту/ мою́/ на́шу́ кни́гу
Acc. (animate)	э́того/ моего́/ на́шего дру́га	—	э́ту/ мою́/ на́шу сестру́

8. Complete the following sentences placing the words in parentheses in the accusative case.

> Мы хорошо́ зна́ем _____ (твоя́ ма́ма).
> Она́ о́чень симпати́чная. →
>
> Мы хорошо́ зна́ем **твою́ ма́му**.
> Она́ о́чень симпати́чная.

1. Я не понима́ю _____. (наш преподава́тель) Он о́чень бы́стро говори́т.

2. Ты по́мнишь _____? (моя́ подру́га) Она́ студе́нтка в твоём университе́те.

3. Я люблю́ _____. (литерату́ра) Я мно́го чита́ю.

4. Я зна́ю _____. (твой друг) Он живёт в на́шем до́ме.

5. Я читала _____. (твоё письмо́) Оно́ о́чень интере́сное.

6. Я хорошо́ зна́ю _____. (э́тот райо́н) Я там ра́ньше жил(а́).

7. Вы по́мните _____? (э́тот челове́к) Он жил в ва́шем до́ме.

8. Я люблю́ _____. (э́та ма́йка) Она́ о́чень симпати́чная.

9. Мы по́мним _____. (ваш профе́ссор) Он ру́сский?

You can now recognize the accusative case in the phrase Кéвин uses to ask one of the strangers in the apartment what his name is.

— Как **тебя** зовут?
                2

— **Меня** зовут Ваня. А **вас**?
     1   4

— А я Кевин.
     1

The literal translation of the question «Как вас зовут?» is "How do (they) call you?"

9. A. Answer the following questions that the police officer might have asked Кéвин and the owners of the apartment.

Как зовут э́того ма́льчика?

Э́того ма́льчика _____

Как зовут э́ту же́нщину?

_____

Как зовут э́того мужчи́ну?

_____

Как зовут э́того америка́нца?

_____

Как зовут подру́гу Кéвина?

_____

же́нщина = woman

мужчи́на = man

Татья́на, Ва́ня, Гали́на Ива́новна, Кéвин,
Васи́лий Петро́вич

B. Your friend Воло́дя has invited you to a party at his place. Since you don't know anyone there, ask Воло́дя to identify the people at the party.

> 3
> — Ты не знаешь, кто э́то?
>
> 1
> — Э́то **подру́га мое́й сестры́**.
>
> 2
> — Как её зову́т?
>
> 1
> — **Ла́ра**.

[
Лёша (my brother's neighbor), Ле́на и Са́ша
(Ла́ра's friends), Ве́ра (Лёша's sister), Ли́за и Ви́ка
(my sister's friends)
]

Adjectives: Accusative and Genitive Case

	Masculine	Neuter	Feminine
Nom.	*Како́й?* **-ый/-ой** но́в**ый** рюкза́к хоро́ш**ий** друг молодо́**й** учи́тель	*Како́е?* **-ое/-ее** но́в**ое** общежи́тие хоро́ш**ее** зда́ние	*Кака́я?* **-ая** но́в**ая** ле́кция хоро́ш**ая** подру́га
Acc.	(Inanim.) *Како́й?* **-ый/-ой** но́в**ый** рюкза́к (Anim.) *Како́го?* **-ого/-его** хоро́ш**его** дру́га молодо́**го** учи́теля	*Како́е?* **-ое/-ее** но́в**ое** общежи́тие хоро́ш**ее** зда́ние	*Каку́ю?* **-ую** но́в**ую** ле́кцию хоро́ш**ую** подру́ту
Gen.	*Како́го?* **-ого/-его** но́в**ого** рюкзака́ хоро́ш**его** дру́га молодо́**го** учи́теля	*Како́го?* **-ого/-его** но́в**ого** общежи́тия хоро́ш**его** зда́ния	*Како́й?* **-ой/-ей** но́в**ой** ле́кции хоро́ш**ей** подру́ти

1. Imagine that you have gone to the store with your sister to buy her a present. Find out what she likes.

> — Хочешь э́ту ко́фту?
>   2
> — Каку́ю?
>   1
> — **Кра́сную.**
>   1   1   1   1
> — Да, хочу./ Нет, не хочу.

кра́сный, чёрный, бе́лый, голубо́й, жёлтый,
ора́нжевый, се́рый, кори́чневый, дли́нный, коро́ткий

юбка, кофта, платье, рубашка, шарф, свитер, майка, костюм

2. You are working for a joint venture and invite your Russian partner to dinner. Find out what your partner likes to eat and drink.

пиво = beer

> 2
> — Какое пиво вы любите?
> 1
> — Американское пиво.

вино = wine

вино (французское, итальянское, американское, красное, белое)

фруктовый = fruit (adj.)

чай (зелёный, чёрный, фруктовый)

икра (красная, чёрная)

хлеб (белый, чёрный)

кухня (итальянская, американская, китайская, мексиканская, русская)

3. Describe the occupations of the Смирнов family members using the following chart.

> 3   1
> Ваня — школьник московской школы.

Гали́на Ива́новна	дире́ктор	небольша́я компа́ния
Васи́лий Петро́вич	преподава́тель	институ́т эконо́мики
Пётр Алексе́евич	соли́ст	Большо́й теа́тр
Екатери́на Ви́кторовна	дире́ктор	музыка́льная шко́ла
Ири́на Петро́вна	студе́нтка	Моско́вский университе́т
Ю́рий Петро́вич	ме́неджер	но́вый магази́н

Consonant Mutation

-и- stem люби́ть (люби́-)	-е- stem ви́деть (ви́де-)	-а- stem писа́ть (писа́-)
▪ я люблю́ — б → бл	▪ я ви́жу — д → ж	▪ я пишу́ — с → ш
▫ ты лю́бишь	▫ ты ви́дишь	▪ ты пи́шешь
▫ он лю́бит	▫ он ви́дит	▪ он пи́шет
▫ мы лю́бим	▫ мы ви́дим	▪ мы пи́шем
▫ вы лю́бите	▫ вы ви́дите	▪ вы пи́шете
▫ они́ лю́бят	▫ они́ ви́дят	▪ они́ пи́шут

4. Fill in the missing verbs. Watch for consonant mutation and shifting stress.

> — Я пишу́ упражнение.
> — А он **пишет?**
> — Да, **пишет.**/Нет, не **пишет.**

1. — Я смотрю́ телеви́зор.

   — А твой брат _____?

   — Да (Нет), _____.

smotré́tь
(смотрé-) =
watch

2. — Я перевожу́ статью́.

   — А твоя́ подру́га _____?

   — Да (нет), _____.

переводи́ть
(переводи́-)
= translate

3. — Я пишу́ письмо́.

   — А твой друг _____?

   — Да (Нет), _____.

4. — Я люблю́ моро́женое.

   — А твой сын _____?

   — Да (нет), _____.

5. — Я ви́жу Ка́тю.

   — А Ка́тя _____ тебя́?

   — Да (нет), _____.

сиде́ть (сиде́-)
= sit

6. — Де́вушки сидя́т на дива́не.

   — А па́па _____?

   — Да (нет), _____.

5. Imagine yourself talking about a group of couch potatoes (of which you are a part). Describe their behavior.

> Я опя́ть **не рабо́таю, сижу́ и смотрю́ телеви́зор**.

опя́ть = again

Он опя́ть _____.

Она́ опя́ть _____.

Они́ опя́ть _____.

Мы опя́ть _____.

Ты опя́ть _____.

Вы опя́ть _____.

6. Looking for something/somebody

A. Our characters are trying to locate each other and are asking for help. Act out their conversations with a partner.

> 3
> — Ты не видел(а) **Áнну Борúсовну?**
> 1   1
> — Вúдел(а). Онá **в библиотéке**.

> Тáня и Лéна, Лéна и Сáша, Мúша и Лéна, Тáня и Áнна Борúсовна, Галúна Ивáновна и Васúлий Петрóвич

> библиотéка, столóвая, пéрвый этáж, вторóй этáж, лаборатóрия, дискотéка, милúция, кафé, бар, кинотеáтр

> Keep in mind that words like **столóвая**, **вáнная**, etc. that have adjectival endings are declined like adjectives

B. You are getting ready to go out and can't find what you need. Ask your roommate whether s/he has seen it.

> 3
> — Ты не вúдела **мою́ большу́ю сýмку?**
> 1   1
> — Вúдел(а). Онá **на кýхне**.

> стáрый учéбник, мáленький рюкзáк, крáсная рýчка, нóвый журнáл, нóвая кнúга, бéлая кóфта, любúмая чáшка, рýсский словáрь, длúнный шарф

> стол, спáльня, вáнная, туалéт, стул, дивáн, пóлка, шкаф, кóмната, гарáж, холодúльник, плитá

7. You would like to go to a movie, but would first like to find out if the film is worth seeing, so you ask your partner.

Note how titles of films, books, newspapers, etc. are declined if they stand alone, but not declined if they are preceded by a noun.

> 3
> — Ты видел(а) «Бэ́тмена»?
>
> 3   1
> — «Бэтмена»? Видел(а).
>
> 2
> — Ну, и как?
>
> 2
> — Отличный фильм.

> 3
> — Ты видел(а) фильм «Бэ́тмен»?
>
> 3   1
> — Фильм «Бэтмен»? Видел(а).
>
> 2
> — Ну, и как?
>
> 2
> — Отличный фильм.

«Война́ и мир» = *War and Peace*

> «Касабла́нка», «Суперме́н», «Тарза́н», «А́нна Каре́нина», «Идио́т», «Термина́тор», «Робоко́п», «Га́млет», «Фи́рма», «Клие́нт», «Преда́тор», «Война́ и мир», «До́ктор Нет»

8. Что ты де́лаешь?

Call your old friend to find out what s/he is doing.

> 2
> — Что ты делаешь?
>
> 1
> — Я пишу́ упражнение.
>
> 1
> — А я чита́ю статью.

упражне́ние = exercise

> чита́ть, писа́ть, переводи́ть, смотре́ть

> упражне́ние, текст, кни́га, журна́л, статья́, уче́бник, газе́та, телеви́зор, кино́, письмо́

студе́нт пе́рвого ку́рса	= freshman▲
студе́нт второ́го ку́рса	= sophomore
студе́нт тре́тьего ку́рса	= junior
студе́нт четвёртого ку́рса	= senior

9. A. Та́ня's best friend Ле́на, who lives in the dormitory, can't seem to find her student ID to show to the guard at the front door. He asks another student to verify Ле́на's identity.

          ³
— Вы зна́ете э́ту де́вушку?

     ¹   ¹   ¹
— Да, зна́ю. Её зову́т Ле́на.

       ³
— Она́ студе́нтка?

    ¹   ¹
— Да, она́ студе́нтка **второ́го курса**.

      ⁴
— А вы кто?

                              ¹
— Я сту́дентка **истори́ческого факульте́та**.

¹
Вот мой студе́нческий биле́т.

B. Та́ня — студе́нтка второ́го ку́рса истори́ческого факульте́та. А вы?

[
математи́ческий, хими́ческий, физи́ческий, инжене́рный, экономи́ческий, истори́ческий, филологи́ческий, факульте́т би́знеса, факульте́т полити́ческой нау́ки, факульте́т ру́сского языка́
]

C. Та́ня — студе́нтка Междунаро́дного университе́та. А вы?

истори́ческий факульте́т = history department

студе́нческий биле́т = student i.d.

филологи́ческий факульте́т = philology department

▲ This translation is not precise because of a difference in educational systems between Russia and the U.S. In Russia one usually declares a major when applying to the university.

«Мину́точку, мину́точку…»

PREviewing

1. Answer the following questions in Russian.

   A. Where does the last part of this episode take place?

   _____

   B. Which characters appear in these two mini-episodes?

   _____

2. Apparently there has been a serious misunderstanding about Кéвин's apartment. Let's go back to the very beginning of the story and try to figure out where things went wrong.

	Да	Нет
Дáша asks Тáня to help Кéвин find a place to stay in Moscow.	☐	☐
Тáня asks her father to find an apartment for Кéвин.	☐	☐

Continued

	Да	Нет
Та́ня and her sister О́ля meet Ке́вин at the airport and bring him back to his apartment.	☐	☐
Та́ня had never been to Ке́вин's apartment before.	☐	☐
The Смирно́вы had not agreed to rent their apartment to Ке́вин.	☐	☐
The Смирно́вы think that Ке́вин is an intruder.	☐	☐
Та́ня blames her father for the whole fiasco.	☐	☐
The police officer comes to the conclusion that Ке́вин has been swindled by someone pretending to be the owner of the Смирно́вы's apartment.	☐	☐

3. Here are some new words that you will hear in this portion of the video:

> хозя́ин (m.), хозя́йка (f.) = owner
> хозя́ева (pl.)

In this episode хозя́ин is used by the police officer to mean "owner"; this word can also be used to mean "host" or "landlord".

▶ Read through the following questions and complete as many as you can before you watch the video with the SOUND ON. Finish answering the questions while you watch.

VIEWING

4. What is the first piece of information that the Смирно́вы give the police officer?
   ☐ фами́лия и но́мер телефо́на
   ☐ но́мер телефо́на и а́дрес
   ☒ фами́лия и а́дрес

5. Ке́вин is described in several different ways. Which character describes him as:

америка́нец ___мӑn___

хулига́н ___Mɪn___ ~~tatiana~~ Хозя́йка

фото́граф ___Кевин___

6. Та́ня explains to the policeman that her sister О́ля made the arrangements for Ке́вин's apartment. Why isn't О́ля there?

☐ Она́ в больни́це.

☐ Она́ на рабо́те.

☒ Она́ в командиро́вке.

в командиро́вке = away on business

7. Та́ня relates the outcome of the apartment mix-up to Ми́ша.

A. Place the lines in Ми́ша and Та́ня's conversation in the correct order.

М	_5_	Ну, не зна́ю. В гости́нице?
Т	_2_	А ты как ду́маешь?
М	_1_	Где тепе́рь Ке́вин?
Т	_6_	Да! Ва́ня лю́бит англи́йский язы́к, Ке́вин — америка́нец. Они́ говоря́т по-англи́йски.
М	_3_	Ну да!
Т	_4_	А вот и нет. Ке́вин живёт там, в той кварти́ре.

B. Based on this conversation, which of the following things can we say about Ми́ша?

☒ He is still jealous of Ке́вин.

☒ He is curious about where Ке́вин will live now.

☐ He wants Ке́вин to move in with him.

C. In the end, why do the Смирно́вы decide to let Ке́вин stay?

☒ Ке́вин would be the perfect English tutor for Ва́ня.

☐ The Смирно́вы need a little extra money.

☐ Гали́на Ива́новна needs someone to do the housework.

POSTviewing

8. Following standard procedure, the police officer asked Ке́вин to write down his version of the incident at the Смирно́вы's apartment. Poor Ке́вин was so exhausted and frustrated that he forgot how to say some things in Russian and simply wrote them in English. Help him by reading his report aloud, translating the English words into Russian as you go along.

I am sitting дóма и смотрю́ фотоальбóм. Я — фотóграф и мнóго take pictures. Это óчень интерéсный альбóм. In this альбóме фотогрáфии Москвы́, пáпы, мáмы и their son, дóма в дерéвне, grandmother and grandfather, их собáки и кóшки. I love смотрéть стáрые фотогрáфии. Я смотрю́ и дýмаю о моéй семьé, о мои́х parents, о мои́х friends. I wonder, что они́ сейчáс дéлают. Мóжет быть, дýмают about me?

И вдруг I see: в кóмнате стоя́т these people. Я их не знáю, я их рáньше не ви́дел, а они́ не знáют me и не понимáют, что я дéлаю in their apartment. «Я здесь живу́», - говорю́ я. «Нет», - say они́. – «Это нáша кварти́ра. Мы живём in it.» Знáчит, они́ не сдавáли эту apartment. Прóсто они́ бы́ли на дáче и didn't know, что в их кварти́ре is living чужóй человéк. Óчень неприя́тно.

в дерéвне = in the country

мóжет быть = maybe

знáчит = (here): so
сдавáть = rent
прóсто = simply
чужóй человéк = stranger
неприя́тно = unpleasant

As you probably noticed in the video, the word **минýточку** (nominative case **минýточка**) is rather useful. For example, as everyone is trying to state their case to the policeman, the officer says:

Минýточку-минýточку.
Hold on a minute./Just a minute.

Минýточка is the diminutive form of the word for "minute" (**минýта**): **минýточку** literally means "Wait one little minute." Diminutive forms are frequent in conversational Russian. Here are just a few more examples.

кóфт**очка**   кóш**ечка**
секýнд**очка**   Лён**очка**

---

9. А. Act out the phone conversation below in groups of 3.

Кéвин:	— Алло, мóжно Тáню?
мáма Тáни:	— **Минýточку.**
Тáня:	— Да?
Кéвин:	— Привéт, Тáня. Это Кевин.
Тáня:	— Ой, здрáвствуй, Кéвин!

When you ask to speak to someone on the phone, use **мóжно** + the person's name in the accusative case:

Мóжно **Тáню?**
May I speak to Тáня?

B. You need to find a book at the library. Ask the librarian for help.

— Извини́те, где **рома́н Толсто́го «А́нна Каре́нина»?**▲
— **«А́нна Каренина»?** Минуточку. Вот, пожалуйста.
— Спасибо.

пье́са Че́хова «Три сестры́», «Севасто́польские расска́зы» Толсто́го, рома́н Достое́вского «Бра́тья Карама́зовы», стихи́ Ахма́товой, рома́н Бе́лого «Петербу́рг», рома́н Пастерна́ка «До́ктор Жива́го»

C. Ask the store clerk to show you certain items.

— Извините, можно **бе́лую ма́йку?**
— Какую вы хоти́те?
— Вон ту.
— Минуточку. Вот, пожалуйста.
— Спасибо.

кори́чневый костю́м, э́тот ча́йник, чёрная руба́шка, се́рая ма́йка, зелёный рюкза́к, бе́лая ке́пка, ма́ленький калькуля́тор, чёрный плащ, э́та ку́ртка, большо́й фотоальбо́м, э́то ра́дио

▲ There were three prominent writers in the history of Russian literature by the name of Tolstoy: Lev, Alexey, and Konstantin. If the first name is not mentioned, it is implied that the writer in question is Lev Tolstoy, the most famous among them.

Ми́ша is glad that he and Та́ня are back together again. At the end of the episode, he asks Та́ня to confirm that everything is all right:

Ми́ша:	— Всё хорошо́?
Та́ня:	— По-мо́ему, всё отли́чно!

всё = everything

10. Practice this very typical exchange with your partner.

$$\overset{3}{—\ \text{Всё хорошо́?}}$$
$$\overset{1}{—\ \text{Да,}}\ \overset{1}{\text{всё нормально.}}/\ \overset{1}{\text{Нет,}}\ \overset{1}{\text{всё ужасно.}}$$

отли́чно, хорошо́, норма́льно, пло́хо, ужа́сно

5

Pictured here are some examples of advertisements

A. What information is given in the advertisements for apartments? How are these ads different from typical American ads for apartments? Finding an apartment in Moscow is not an easy job, as Ке́вин and Та́ня discovered. Today you will read the story of a man who loses everything to a swindler.

Как Борис Бездо́мный покупа́л кварти́ру

Пи́шет наш корреспонде́нт
Ники́та Соба́кин.
Газе́та «Коммерса́нт»

Случи́лось э́то◊ ле́том. Молодо́й бизнесме́н Бори́с Бездо́мный хоте́л купи́ть◊ но́вую кварти́ру. Он жил в но́вом райо́не, но о́чень люби́л центр го́рода, Ста́рую Москву́. Он хоте́л жить то́лько◊ в Ста́рой Москве́, а кварти́ры там о́чень дороги́е◊. Кварти́ра—э́то де́ньги. Больши́е де́ньги. Что де́лать?

this happened

buy

only

expensive

Друг Бори́са ви́дел в ли́фте◊ объявле́ние◊ о кварти́ре. В объявле́нии бы́ли телефо́н и и́мя: Арка́дий К. Бори́с не знал Арка́дия, не знал его́ репута́цию и не знал, что де́лать— звони́ть или не звони́ть. Рискова́ть и́ли не рискова́ть? Бори́с звони́т◊ ему́. Арка́дий говори́т, что он эмигри́рует и поэ́тому продаёт◊ кварти́ру бы́стро и недо́рого. Кварти́ра в ста́ром до́ме на Тверско́м бульва́ре. Бори́с и Арка́дий оформля́ют докуме́нты. И вот наш геро́й уже́ живёт в но́вой кварти́ре. Всё ря́дом◊: метро́, теа́тры, магази́ны, рестора́ны и да́же кинотеа́тр—всё отли́чно!

elevator | information

calls

is selling

close by

Но вдруг◊ неприя́тный сюрпри́з. 29 а́вгуста Бори́с у́жинает и смо́трит телеви́зор. Открыва́ется◊ дверь и … о, у́жас! Э́то хозя́ева кварти́ры—Во́лковы. Они́ бы́ли на да́че, возвраща́ются◊ и кого́ же они́ ви́дят? Они́ ви́дят в кварти́ре чужо́го челове́ка◊. Коне́чно, они́ ду́мают, что э́то банди́т. Вы хорошо́ понима́ете, что тут бы́ло: сканда́л, мили́ция. Что же случи́лось?

suddenly

opens

return

stranger

Ле́том Во́лковы жи́ли на да́че, а кварти́ру сдава́ли◊. В э́том году́ их кварти́ру в ию́не, ию́ле и а́вгусте снима́л◊ Арка́дий, а Во́лковы, как всегда́◊, жи́ли на да́че. Жу́лик «эмигра́нт» про́дал◊ их кварти́ру Бори́су. Где сейча́с

rent out

rented

as usual

sold

аферист◊ Аркадий? Говорят, что он теперь живёт и «работает» в Санкт-Петербурге, но его видели в Москве.

А Борис Бездомный теперь живёт в однокомнатной квартире мамы, на первом этаже без◊ телефона, без балкона в районе Бибирево, очень далеко от◊ центра и от метро. Так что, если◊ вы планируете сдавать, продавать или покупать квартиру, помните о Борисе и не рискуйте!

1. Read the title and the heading of today's reading.

   A. Who is the author?
- ☐ a real estate agent
- ☑ a newspaper correspondent
- ☐ a frustrated customer

   B. The author's name is: _Никита Собакин_

2. Scan the first paragraph for the following information.

   A. What is Борис's profession? _____

   B. Where did he previously live? _____

   C. Борис wants an apartment that:

	Да	Нет
is downtown	☐	☐
is on Arbat Street	☐	☐
is on the first floor	☐	☐
has a large kitchen	☐	☐
has a balcony	☐	☐

3. Scan the second paragraph for the following information.

   A. How did Борис finally find a new apartment?
- ☐ He used a real estate agent.
- ☐ He got a tip from a friend who saw an ad.
- ☐ He got a call from a seller.

B. The seller wanted to get rid of the apartment because he:
- ☐ was getting married and needed a bigger place
- ☐ was planning to leave the country permanently
- ☐ needed money to launch a business venture

C. What was one of the selling points of his apartment?
- ☐ It had new furniture.
- ☐ It was in a new building.
- ☐ The location was convenient.

4. Scan the third paragraph for the following information.

A. What was Борис doing in his apartment on August 29th?
- ☐ writing a novel
- ☐ watching TV
- ☐ sleeping

B. What was the unpleasant surprise that greeted Борис?
- ☐ The house was scheduled to be demolished.
- ☐ His ex-wife moved in with him.
- ☐ The owners of the apartment came back.

5. Scan the fourth paragraph for the following information.

A. The deal fell through because the seller
- ☐ changed his mind about emigrating and wanted his apartment back
- ☐ decided to get more money for his apartment
- ☐ was a scam artist

B. What became of the seller?
- ☐ He is back on the streets.
- ☐ He took the money and ran away to Germany.
- ☐ He was arrested and sent to jail.

6. Scan the fifth paragraph for the following information.

A. Где Борис живёт сейчас? Он живёт:
- ☐ в квартире жены
- ☑ в квартире мамы
- ☐ на улице
- ☐ в гостинице
- ☐ в машине

B. How would you describe Бори́с's new home?

☐ на тре́тьем этаже́

☐ в це́нтре го́рода

☒ в райо́не Би́бирево

C. What is the author's recommendation on how to buy an apartment in Moscow?

☒ Do not take risks.

☐ Deal only with people you know personally.

☐ Avoid dealing with friends.

7. The name Бори́с Бездо́мный contains a pun. The prefix **без** in Russian means "without" in English. How would you translate the full name? The preposition **без** is followed by the genitive case. Reread the last paragraph and find two examples of **без**. Translate the whole sentence into English.

8. Read the text again.

A. Underline all the features of a good apartment.

B. Describe the following in Russian:

1. What did Бори́с consider to be a good apartment?

2. What is a good apartment in your mind?

3. What is more important and what is less important when you try to rent or buy an apartment?

 9. You would like to rent an apartment in Moscow. Explain to the real estate agent exactly what you are looking for.

> 2
> — Каку́ю кварти́ру вы хоти́те?
> 1
> — Я хочу́ небольшу́ю кварти́ру.
> 3   2
> — Вы хоти́те кварти́ру в це́нтре и́ли в но́вом райо́не?
> 1
> — В це́нтре.
> 2
> — А на како́м этаже́?
> 2   1
> — Пожа́луйста, не на пе́рвом.

Final Review

PREviewing

1. The title of this episode is «Ужáсная истóрия».

   A. Who makes the statement «Ужáсная истóрия»? What is s/he referring to?

   B. Write down your own title for this episode in Russian and compare it with your classmates' ideas.

---

2. Match the titles of the following mini-episodes in «Ужáсная истóрия» to the corresponding lines. Check your answers when you watch the video.

   1. Телефóнный разговóр

   2. Кто вы? Что вы здесь дéлаете?

   3. Хэ́ппи энд. Всё хорошó, что хорошó кончáется (All's well that ends well.)

   A. Э́то нáша квартúра.

   B. По-мóему, всё отлúчно!

   C. Я хочý тебя́ вúдеть.

VIEWING >

▶ Read through the questions below and try to answer as many as you can before you watch this episode for the last time.

3. Fill in the names of the characters from the video who are described by the following statements. Hint: some names will appear more than once.

_____ Он всегда́ ревну́ет Та́ню.

_____ Она́ чита́ла письмо́ Ми́ши.

_____ Он ду́мает, что хозя́ин кварти́ры жу́лик.

_____ Они́ живу́т в деся́той кварти́ре на у́лице Королёва.

_____ Он шко́льник и лю́бит говори́ть по-англи́йски.

_____ Он не хулига́н, он фото́граф.

_____ Она́ не понима́ет Ке́вина.

_____ Они́ бы́ли на да́че.

_____ Он смотре́л фотоальбо́м.

> Та́ня Воло́дина, Ми́ша Ко́тов, Ке́вин Джэ́ксон, Гали́на Смирно́ва, Васи́лий Смирно́в, Ва́ня Смирно́в, милиционе́р

POSTviewing >

4. Russians often name streets, squares, and other places after their favorite writers, composers, scientists, etc. The streets where Та́ня and Ке́вин live are good examples of this:

у́лица Королёва   у́лица Во́лкова

Korolyov street   Volkov street

A. What are the names of the city streets which pay honor to the following writers:

> Купри́н — у́лица Куприна́
> Бе́лый — у́лица Бе́лого
> Ахма́това — у́лица Ахма́товой

Чéхов, Пýшкин, Гóголь, Блок, Пастернáк, Булгáков, Лéрмонтов, Толстóй, Достоéвский

B. During the Soviet period, streets were also named after political leaders. At various times in recent history hardly a single major city in all of Russia would not have at least some of the following street names:

ýлица Лéнина, ýлица Стáлина, ýлица Хрущёва, ýлица Брéжнева, ýлица Андрóпова, ýлица Горбачёва, ýлица Éльцина

Who is the public figure for whom each of the previous streets is named?

C. You have just set up the provisional government in your new country. Rename the city streets to honor the heroes of your revolution.

5. Кéвин and Смирнóвы resolved their conflict peacefully and the Смирнóвы even offered to let Кéвин live with them. Can you imagine what this conversation might have sounded like? Using this English model as a guide, construct your own version of Кéвин's «хэ́ппи энд».

Смирнóв: — Кéвин, this is terrible.

                _____

Смирнóва: — You are a really nice guy.

                _____

Вáня: — You're American, you speak English,
                and I love English.

                _____

Смирнóва: — Do you want to live in our apartment?

                _____

Ке́вин: — Great!

_____

Смирно́в: — Everything's okay!

_____

6. Ва́ня's English teacher assigned an original adventure story that each student was to compose on their own in English for next time. Ва́ня came up with an interesting idea for the story in Russian, but did not have time to get it all translated by the deadline. Try to reconstruct the original Russian version of Ва́ня's story, based on his half-done assignment. (Fortunately for you, the words he uses are all familiar.)

Working in small groups, complete the assignment by translating the English words back into Russian.

Мы бы́ли на да́че.

Я люблю́ <u>to vacation</u> на да́че. Там <u>in the spring</u> живу́т <u>grandmother</u> и де́душка, <u>our dog</u> Ла́йка и ко́шка Му́рка. Люблю́ наш дом, ре́ку, <u>our</u> сосе́дку тётю Ню́ру и <u>her</u> коро́ву Ла́сточку, наш сад и огоро́д. Но ма́ма и па́па не лю́бят <u>the dacha</u>. Они́ <u>say</u>, что я здесь отдыха́ю, а они́ рабо́тают. Они́ лю́бят <u>Moscow</u>. Они́ <u>think</u>, что Москва́ — <u>the most</u> хоро́ший го́род <u>in the world</u>.

И вот мы до́ма. Наш подъе́зд, наш эта́ж, <u>our apartment</u>, коридо́р, ко́мната…. Но что э́то? <u>What do we see</u>? В ко́мнате челове́к, <u>is sitting</u> на на́шем <u>sofa</u>, смо́трит фотоальбо́м. <u>I think</u>, он о́чень симпати́чный. Но кто э́то? <u>What is he doing in our apartment</u>? Он говори́т, что он <u>an American</u> и что он здесь живёт. Не мо́жет быть! Э́то на́ша кварти́ра. Но я зна́ю, что он америка́нец. Мы <u>spoke English</u>.

7. Meanwhile, at the police station, the officer on duty asked witnesses to a robbery to identify people in a line-up. Act out his exchanges with the various witnesses.

> 3
> — Вы зна́ете **э́того мужчи́ну?**
> 3 1   1   2   2
> — **Его́?** Нет, не зна́ю./ Да, зна́ю.

река́ = river
коро́ва = cow
сад =garden
огоро́д = vegetable
    garden

человéк, мужчи́на, жéнщина, врач, учи́тельница, дéвушка, мáльчик, студéнт, студéнтка, мéнеджер, бухгáлтер

8. As a result of a misunderstanding you are being questioned by the police. The police officer on duty asks you for your name and passport number, and wants to know what you are doing in Moscow. Act out your encounter with the officer.

1. You are having lunch with your good friend who also happens to be a real busybody. Answer his/her questions.

> — Что лю́бит ва́ша ма́ма? (весёлая му́зыка) →
> — Она́ лю́бит **весёлую му́зыку**.

1. Кого́ ты здесь зна́ешь? (э́тот бизнесме́н)
2. Что перево́дит э́тот журнали́ст? (коро́ткий ру́сский текст)
3. Что лю́бит твой друг? (америка́нская литерату́ра)
4. А что лю́бит его́ сестра́? (геогра́фия, матема́тика, исто́рия)
5. Кого́ ты там ви́дишь? (ма́ленький ма́льчик и его́ ма́ма)
6. Что он рису́ет? (большо́й кот и ма́ленькая ко́шка)
7. Что ты писа́л у́тром? (дли́нное письмо́)
8. Что он пи́шет? (статья́ о шко́ле)

2. Discuss the following topics.

1. Како́го америка́нского писа́теля вы лю́бите?
2. Каку́ю му́зыку вы лю́бите слу́шать?
3. Каку́ю оде́жду вы лю́бите?
4. Каку́ю ку́хню вы лю́бите?

3. Separate the words in each sentence with a slash, then read the sentences aloud. Insert the appropriate punctuation, stress marks, and capitalization.

1. Япомнючтотаняживётвмоскве
2. Янепомнюкакзовутновогодругалены
3. Тызнаешьчтокевинделаетвмоскве
4. Мишаписалчтооноченьхочетвидетьтаню
5. Пётралексеевичэтомужекатеринывикторовны
6. Танястуденткавторогокурсакиноведческогофакультета

4. Match the questions with the appropriate answers.

1. Что ты де́лаешь?
2. Твоя́ сестра́ сейча́с до́ма?
3. Вы лю́бите ко́фе?
4. Ты зна́ешь э́ту де́вушку?
5. Чья э́то кни́га?
6. Где вы бы́ли ле́том?

A. Да, её зову́т Ле́на.
B. Я пишу́ статью́.
C. Мое́й но́вой подру́ги.
D. Мы бы́ли в Кана́де.
E. Да, о́чень люблю́.
F. Нет, она́ на рабо́те.

5. Вы лю́бите чита́ть? А что вы чита́ли?

> ^{3}
> — Ты чита́л(а) «Оди́н день Ива́на Дени́совича» Солжени́цына?
> ^{1} ^{1} ^{1} ^{1}
> — Да, чита́л(а)./ Нет, не чита́л(а).

«А́нна Каре́нина» Толсто́го, «О́ливер Твист» Ди́ккенса, «Ю́рский парк» Кра́йтона, «До́ктор Жива́го» Пастерна́ка, «Идио́т» Достое́вского, «Макбе́т» Шекспи́ра, «Евге́ний Оне́гин» Пу́шкина, «После́дний тайку́н» Фицджера́льда

6. A. Here are some newspapers and periodicals that Ке́вин has been reading. Now you can answer the question, «**Что он чита́ет?**»

B. What newspapers and periodicals do you read? Compare your choice with others in your group.

> — Какую газе́ту ты лю́бишь чита́ть?
>
> — Я чита́ю «Вашингто́н Пост». А ты?
>
> — А я люблю́ «Нью-Йо́рк Таймс».

7. Са́ша decides to call Ле́на at the dormitory and invite her to see a movie. He has to talk to the person on duty at the front desk to find her.

A. Unscramble the lines in their conversation by placing a number next to each line. Check yourself by reading the conversation aloud with your partner.

1. _____ — Мину́точку.

   _____ — Каку́ю Ле́ну?

   _____ — Извини́те, Ле́ну Анто́нову.

   _____ — В ко́мнате 25.

   ____1____ — Я вас слу́шаю.

   _____ — Мо́жно Ле́ну?

   _____ — В како́й она́ ко́мнате?

2. _____ — Ле́на, э́то ты?

   _____ — Приве́т, э́то Са́ша.

   ____1____ — Алло́.

   _____ — Да, я.

   _____ — Приве́т, Са́ша!

B. Work as a class to translate the rest of their conversation.

— How are you?

— I'm fine. What are you doing now?

— I'm translating an article about the history of American film.

— Wow! You are a really good student.

— What are you talking about? The dean says I'm a bad student and I work too little. So what are you doing today?

— I read in the paper that "Spider-Man 3" is at our movie theater. Have you seen it?

— No.

— Would you like to?

— Not today.

— Please, it's a great movie!

— Goodbye, Sasha.

— Okay, Lena. Goodbye.

8. Situations

1. Someone on campus asks you for directions; apologize and explain that you don't know the campus very well.

2. You and your Russian friend are invited to the wedding anniversary of Пётр Алексéевич and Екатери́на Ви́кторовна. Identify the people present to your friend. (Refer to the family tree in day 2, exercise 7.)

> — Вон Ири́на. Она́ тётя Ва́ни.
>   ³
> — А э́то её муж?
>   ²   ²   ¹   ²
> — Нет, что ты! Э́то Васи́лий, брат Ири́ны.

3. You bring your Russian friend home for Thanksgiving. Show him/her around your house.

> — Вон кóмната моéй сестры́.
>   ²   ²
> — Краси́во. А чьи э́то кни́ги?
>   ¹
> — Э́то кни́ги моегó дéдушки.

папа, мáма, брат, сестрá, дéдушка, бáбушка, дя́дя, тётя

гитáра, роя́ль, компью́тер, учéбники, кни́ги, одéжда, фотогрáфии, игру́шки, вéщи, плéер, кóмната

игру́шка = toy

1. The Genitive Case

The genitive case in Russian expresses possession or inherent connection (for example, part of a whole). The genitive case typically corresponds to English possessives in 's (s') or prepositional phrases beginning with "of."

Это нача́ло **сло́ва**.	This is the beginning *of the word*.
На стене́ виси́т ка́рта **Росси́и**.	A map *of Russia* hangs on the wall.
Это кварти́ра **Ке́вина**.	This is *Kevin's* apartment.
Это фами́лия **журнали́ста**.	This is the *journalist's* last name.
Они́ говори́ли о рабо́те **студе́нта**.	They spoke about *the student's* work.
Столи́ца **Украи́ны** — Ки́ев.	The capital *of Ukraine* is Kiev.

Note that in Russian the word or phrase in the genitive case usually *follows* the noun denoting the thing possessed:

Это ко́мната **сы́на**.	This is the *son's* room.
Это ко́мната **сы́на Васи́лия Петро́вича**.	This is *Vasiliy Petrovich's son's* room.

Later we shall see how the genitive case is also required in expressions of quantity.

2. Formation of the Genitive of Nouns

Masculine/Neuter (First Declension)[1]				
Case	Endings	Examples		
Nom.	-ø (-ь)/ -о (-е)	студе́нт	писа́тель	окно́	зда́ние
Gen.	-а (-я)	студе́нт**а**	писа́тел**я**	окн**а́**	зда́ни**я**

In the genitive singular, first declension nouns take the ending **-а** (-я), i.e. the nominative singular **-ø** (-ь) or **-о** (-е) in such nouns is replaced by **-а** (-я).

Feminine (Second Declension)				
Case	Endings	Forms		
Nom.	-а (-я)	карти́на	река́	у́лица	дере́вня
Gen.	-ы (-и)	карти́н**ы**	рек**и́**	у́лиц**ы**	дере́вн**и**

---

[1] Masculine and neuter declensions are usually referred to as the first declension; feminine (-a nouns) are called second declension nouns.

In the genitive singular, second declension nouns take **-ы** (**-и**). Note that in keeping with the spelling rules (cf. Analysis III, 11) **и** must be spelled after **к, г** and **х** and after all sibilants (i.e. **ш, ж, щ, ч**) except **ц**.

3. The Accusative Case

Use of the Accusative

A noun that is the *direct object* of the verb in a given sentence requires the accusative case. Verbs that take a direct object are called *transitive verbs*.

Да́ша	пи́шет	письмо́.	
Subject + (nom.)	Predicate + (trans. verb)	Object (acc.)	Dasha is writing *a letter*.
Ми́ша	чита́ет	кни́гу.	Misha is reading *a book*.

4. Formation of the Accusative Case of Nouns

First Declension (Masculine/Neuter)					
Case	**Endings**	**Examples**			
Nom.	**-ø** (**-ь**)/ **-о** (**-е**)	дом	друг	писа́тель	окно́	зда́ние
Acc. (inanim.)	**-ø** (**-ь**)/ **-о** (**-е**)	дом			окно́	зда́ние
(anim.)	**-а** (**-я**)		дру́га	писа́теля		

The accusative case of first declension nouns is identical to the nominative case, except for masculine nouns denoting animals (including humans – hereafter referred to as **animate nouns**). The ending of the accusative of animate first declension nouns is **-а** (-я) (this coincides with the first declension *genitive* ending).

Second Declension (Feminine)		
Case	**Endings**	**Examples**
Nom.	**-а** (**-я**)	шко́ла	дере́вня
Acc.	**-у** (**-ю**)	шко́лу	дере́вню

The accusative singular of second declension nouns is **-у** (-ю). Study the following examples:

Ва́ня слу́шает **му́зыку.**	Vanya is listening to *music*.
Ле́на хорошо́ зна́ет **го́род.**	Lena knows *the city* well.
Я зна́ю **Ке́вина Дже́ксона.**	I know *Kevin Jackson*.
Та́ня **чита́ет письмо́.**	Tanya is reading *a letter*.

5. Summary of Noun Endings

Case	First Declension					Second Declension	
	Masculine			**Neuter**		**Feminine**	
	Endings			Endings		Endings	
Nom.	-ø (-ь)	áдрес	брáт	-о (-е)	окнó	-а (-я)	газéта
Acc.	-ø (-ь)	áдрес		-о (-е)	окнó	-у (-ю)	газéту
(anim.)	-а (-я)		брáта				
Gen.	-а (-я)	áдреса	брáта	-а (-я)	окнá	-ы (-и)	газéты
Prep.	-е	áдресе	брáте	-е	окнé	-е	газéте

6. The Genitive and Accusative Cases of Personal and Interrogative Pronouns

Examine and learn the forms of the personal and interrogative pronouns summarized in the following chart. Note that with the exception of the interrogative pronoun что, the genitive and accusative forms in these two cases are identical.

Case	Personal Pronouns							Interrogative Pronouns	
Nom.	я	ты	он/онó	онá	мы	вы	они	кто	что
Acc.	меня́	тебя́	его́	её	нас	вас	их	когó[2]	что
Gen.	меня́	тебя́	его́	её	нас	вас	их	когó	чегó[2]
Prep.	обо мнé	о тебé	о нём	о ней	о нас	о вас	о них	о ком	о чём

Study the following examples:

— **Когó** онá лю́бит?　　　　　　　"*Who* does she love?"
— Онá лю́бит **тебя́.**　　　　　　　"She loves *you*."

Он знáет **меня́,** а онá знáет **вас.**　　　He knows *me* and she knows *you*.

Мы ви́дели **его́** в Москвé.　　　　　We saw *him* in Moscow.

The genitive forms of the pronouns **я, ты, мы, вы** and **кто** are never used to denote possession.

---

[2] The pronominal and adjectival genitive ending **-ого** is invariably pronounced as though the consonant were **в**, rather than **г**.

7. The Genitive and Accusative Cases of Demonstrative and Possessive Pronouns

Demonstrative and possessive pronouns must agree with the word they modify in number, gender, and case. The accusative forms of the masculine demonstrative and possessive pronouns are identical with the genitive forms when they modify an animate noun; otherwise they are identical with the nominative forms.

The Genitive and Accusative Cases Of Demonstrative and Possessive Pronouns											
Masculine/Neuter											
Nom.	э́тот	э́то	наш	на́ше	ваш	ва́ше	мой	моё	твой	твоё	чей	чьё
Acc. (anim.)	э́тот	э́то	наш	на́ше	ваш	ва́ше	мой	моё	твой	твоё	чей	чьё
	э́того		на́шего		ва́шего		моего́		твоего́		чьего́	
Gen.	э́того		на́шего		ва́шего		моего́		твоего́		чьего́	
Prep.	э́том		на́шем		ва́шем		моём		твоём		чьём	

Feminine					
Nom.	э́та	на́ша	ва́ша	моя́	чья
Acc.	э́ту	на́шу	ва́шу	мою́	чью
Gen.	э́той	на́шей	ва́шей	мое́й	чьей
Prep.	э́той	на́шей	ва́шей	мое́й	чьей

Remember that the third-person possessive pronouns (**его́, её, их**) never change (cf. Analysis II, 10). Here are a few examples of agreement between pronouns and their head word:

Э́то дом **моего́ преподава́теля.**   This is *my teacher's* house.
Мы говори́ли **о ва́шей жене́.**   We were speaking *about your wife*.
Я зна́ю **э́того челове́ка.**   I know *that man*.
О чьей рабо́те говори́ла Ма́ша?   *Whose work* was Masha talking about?

But:

Он говори́л **о её сестре**   He was talking *about her sister*
и **об их кварти́ре** в Москве́.   and *their apartment* in Moscow.

8. The Genitive and Accusative Cases of Adjectives

Adjectives agree in number, gender, and case with the word they modify. As was the case with demonstrative and possessive pronouns, Russian adjectives also distinguish animate from inanimate accusative masculine. In ending-stressed possessive pronouns (see #7 above) the stress always falls on the final syllable, whereas in ending-stressed adjectives the stress falls on the penultimate syllable; cf. **моего́** but **дорого́го.**

	Stem-stressed			Ending-stressed		
	Masculine	**Neuter**	**Feminine**	**Masculine**	**Neuter**	**Feminine**
Nom.	но́вый	но́вое	но́вая	молодо́й	молодо́е	молода́я
Acc.	но́вый	но́вое	но́вую	молодо́й	молодо́е	молоду́ю
Anim.	но́вого			молодо́го		
Gen.	но́вого		но́вой	молодо́го		молодо́й
Prep.	но́вом		но́вой	молодо́м		молодо́й

Мы ви́дели то́лько нача́ло **э́того** о́чень **интере́сного фи́льма.**	We saw only the beginning *of that very interesting film.*
Я не зна́ю **э́того молодо́го челове́ка.**	I don't know *that young man.*
Кто а́втор **э́того но́вого рома́на?**	Who is the author *of this new novel?*

9. The Russian Verb – Verb Classifier

In studying and conjugating Russian verbs, we have centered our attention so far on combining stems with endings. In Unit IV we began to study the shape of the stem itself, identifying stems terminating in **-жа-, -ай-, -ова-.** In this unit, we will continue the analysis of stems, in order to master most of the important stem types. Since the process of learning Russian verbs is cumulative and systematic, we will include here and elsewhere stem types previously learned alongside new ones. The current unit will bring the total number of stem types learned to eight out of eleven types in all of Russian.

The stem consists of a *root* (CVC)[3] with or without prefixes and is followed by a *suffix,* which we call the verb *classifier.*

---

[3] Roots in Russian are represented by the formula "CVC", in which "C" represents any consonant or consonant cluster and "V" represents any vowel. Most Russian roots are monosyllabic.

повтори́ть "repeat" повтори́-

stem			+	ending
по (prefix)	втор (root) CVC	й suffix or verb classifier		ть

In all, there are eleven verb classifiers in Russian: **-и-**, **-е-**, **-жа-**, **-а-**, **-ова-**, **-ай-**, **-ей-**, **-авай-**, **-ну-**, **-о-**, and **-ø-** (which indicates the absence of a suffix after the root). Of these, only three (**-и-**, **-ова-**, **-ай-**) are "productive", that is, only three classifiers are used to form new verbs entering the modern language.

In reviewing some familiar stems we can readily identify the verb classifier in each:

"read"	чита́й-	чит + а́й-
"speak"	говори́-	говор + и́-
"live"	жи́в-	жи́в + ø-

The analysis of Russian verbs according to verb classifiers has immediate practical consequences for predicting conjugation. The verb classifier determines which present tense vowel (i.e. the first conjugation **-ет** or **-ут** or the second conjugation **-ит** or **-ят**)[4] a verb requires. Moreover, the classifier enables one to anticipate the two other processes which may occur in the formation of Russian verbs: (1) *alternation* of the final root consonant, and (2) *shift of stress*. Once the rules for each classifier are learned, you will be able to conjugate any regular basic stem in Russian, regardless of whether or not you have previously encountered that particular verb.

10. Classes of Verbs

Only three classes of verbs in Russian take second conjugation endings: **-и-**, **-е-** and **-жа-** verbs; the remaining eight classes take first conjugation endings. All classes except **-ø-** class may have stress shift in the *present* tense; only "zero" verbs may have stress shift in the *past* tense.

Let's analyze the three second conjugation classes more closely.

Second Conjugation Verbs

1. Verb Classifier **-и-**

   The final root consonant *alternates*[5] before the

   проси́- "ask (a favor)"
   проси́ть
   прошу́ (прос-и-у; с → ш before у)

---

[4] See Analysis II, 1.

[5] See Analysis V, 12.

first person singular –у.
This is a productive group,
numbering thousands of
verbs, mostly transitive.

про́сишь
про́сит   проси́л
про́сим   проси́ла
про́сите   проси́ло
про́сят   проси́ли

2.   Verb Classifier -**e**-

The final root consonant
alternates before the first
person singular –**y**.
This is a group of about 50 verbs,
mostly intransitive.

ви́де- "see"
ви́де**ть**
ви́**жу** (вид-е-у; д → ж before у)
ви́д**ишь**
ви́д**ит**   ви́дел
ви́д**им**   ви́дела
ви́д**ите**   ви́дело
ви́д**ят**   ви́дели

3.   Verb Classifier -**жа**-

In this group -**жа**- represents the
suffix -**a**- preceded by a sibilant:
жа, ша, ща, ча (and also -**я**-
in two exceptional cases: боя́ться
"fear" and стоя́ть "stand".

This is a group of more than
30 verbs, most of which are
intransitive.

лежа́- "lie", "be in a lying position"

лежа́**ть**
лежу́
лежи́**шь**
лежа́**т**

     лежа́л
     лежа́ла
     лежа́ло
     лежа́ли

First Conjugation Verbs

All other regular verbs take first conjugation endings. Among these are verbs with the
classifiers -**ай**- and -**ø**- as well as the classifiers -**a**- and -**ова**.

4.   Verb Classifier -**a**-

The final root consonant
alternates before *all vocalic
endings* (thus throughout the
present tense).
Approximately 60 verbs.

писа-ˣ "write
писа́**ть**
пишу́ (пис-а-у; с → ш before у)
пи́ш**ешь**
пи́ш**ут**   писа́л
         писа́ла
         писа́ло
         писа́ли

5. Verb Classifier **-ова-**

   The **-ова-** is replaced by **-уй-** before *all vocalic endings*. Note that in verbs with stressed **-ова-** the stress shifts back to **-уй-**. Thousands of verbs, mostly with foreign verbs.

   диктова́- "dictate"
   диктова́ть
   дикту́ю
   дикту́ешь
   дикту́ют   диктова́л
        диктова́ла
        диктова́ло
        диктова́ли

6. Verb Classifier **-ай-**

   Thousands of verbs, mostly imperfective.[6]

   чита́й- "read"
   чита́ть
   чита́ю
   чита́ешь
   чита́ют   чита́л
        чита́ла
        чита́ло
        чита́ли

7. Verb Classifier **-ø-**

   About 80 verbs in all (unprefixed). This group will be analyzed in greater detail in subsequent units. Stress may shift in the past tense only.

   жи́в- "live"
   жить
   живу́
   живёшь
   живу́т   жил
        жила́
        жи́ло
        жи́ли

11. Stress in the Verb

The majority of Russian verbs have fixed stress, i.e. their stress falls on the same syllable in all conjugated forms. Stress may be fixed on the root or on the syllable immediately following the root (the "post-root" syllable). As you remember from Analysis II, 8, fixed stress is indicated by the sign ´ placed over the appropriate syllable of the basic stem in the verb stem notation.

Fixed Stress

root (CVC)		post-root	
ви́де-"see"	ста́н- ø "become"	чита́й- "read"	говори́- "speak", "say"
ви́жу	ста́ну	чита́ю	говорю́
ви́дишь	ста́нешь	чита́ешь	говори́шь

---

[6] For an explanation of imperfective verbs, see Analysis VI.

ви́дит	ста́нет	чита́ет	говори́т
ви́дим	ста́нем	чита́ем	говори́м
ви́дите	ста́нете	чита́ете	говори́те
ви́дят	ста́нут	чита́ют	говоря́т
ви́деть	стать	чита́ть	говори́ть
ви́дел	стал	чита́л	говори́л
ви́дела	ста́ла	чита́ла	говори́ла
ви́дело	ста́ло	чита́ло	говори́ло
ви́дели	ста́ли	чита́ли	говори́ли

Shifting Stress

A number of Russian verbs, including some of the most common, have shifting stress. The stress shift always proceeds from the post–root syllable onto the root. There are but two patterns of stress shift in Russian verbs: present and past tense. If one has learned the two patterns, one can predict the proper stress for any form of any basic stem. Shifting stress is indicated by an ˣ placed over the basic stem: писǎ-.

In verbs with suffixes other than -ø-, present tense stress shift affects all present tense forms except the first person singular.

Past tense shift occurs only in verbs with the -ø- classifier and affects all past tense forms except the feminine.[7]

		писǎ-		жǐв- ø	
	root	post-root syllable	root	post-root syllable
я		пишу́		живу́
ты	пи́шешь			живёшь
он/она́	пи́шет			живёт
мы	пи́шем			живём
вы	пи́шете			живёте
они́	пи́шут			живём
		писа́ть	жи́ть	
		писа́л	жи́л	
		писа́ла		жила́
		писа́ло	жи́ло	
		писа́ли	жи́ли	

---

[7] Later we will have occasion to contrast the present tense shift (always a one-syllable shift to the left) with past tense movement, which may shift the stress as far to the left in the word as it can go. The negative past tense of жǐв- provides an example: óн нé жил /нʲéжыл /, она́ не жила́ /нʲижыла́ /, онó нé жило, они́ нé жили. The same stress pattern occurs in the negative past tense forms of the verb бы́ть. (See Analysis IV, 9.)

12. Consonant Alternations

Final root consonant (CVC) alternation occurs at predictable points in the conjugation of Russian verbs. It also occurs in the formation of comparative adjectives as well as in word-building. Note that not every consonant undergoes alternation, nor are all the alternations listed below of equal importance or frequency. Those listed in light type are infrequent and are included here to aid the student at more advanced levels of study.

Dentals (hard or soft)

д → ж
т → ч
з → ж
с → ш
ст → щ
ск → щ
ц → ч

Labials (hard or soft)

б → бл^ь
п → пл^ь
м → мл^ь
в → вл^ь
ф → фл^ь

Velars (hard or soft)

г → ж
к → ч
х → ш

Church Slavonic

д → дж
т → щ

13. Verb Summary

In addition to the rules for joining verb stems and endings discussed in Unit II, there are three other factors which need to be taken into consideration if one is to be able to conjugate any Russian verb fully:

1. Choice of present tense vowel (i.e. first or second conjugation type);

2. Whether or not a consonantal alternation occurs;

3. Whether or not the stress is fixed or mobile, and if mobile, whether the shift occurs in the present or past tense.

The *verb classifier* determines the outcome of the conjugation. Only three classes of Russian verbs have second conjugation endings: **-и-**, **-е-** and **-жа-** types. All other stems are first conjugation.

Alternation occurs before the first person singular ending **-у** (**-ю**) of all **-и-** and **-е-** verbs, and before any vocalic ending for stems in **-а-** and **-ова-**. While most verbs in Russian have fixed stress (e.g. читáй-, говорú-), there are two types of shifting stress in Russian verbs: past tense (affecting -ø- suffixes) and present tense (affecting suffixes other than -ø-).

14. Apposition

When a noun (together with its modifiers) is in apposition with another noun, i.e., when it specifies or explains that noun with a different noun, there are two possibilities in Russian:

1. If the first noun denotes a person, there is *strict apposition* and both nouns (or noun phrases) take the same case.

Та́ня говори́ла о **сестре́ О́льге**.	Tanya spoke about her *sister Olga*.
Ле́кцию чита́ет **профе́ссор Кузнецо́в**.	The lecture is being read by *Professor Kuznetsov*.
Я зна́ю **милиционе́ра Петро́ва**.	I know *police officer Petrov*.
Я ви́дел **Анто́нова, на́шего врача́**.	I saw *Antonov, our doctor*.

2. If the first noun does not denote a person, there is non-strict apposition, and the second noun (or noun phrase) is in the nominative case.

Я ви́дел дра́му **«Ива́нов»**.	I saw the play *"Ivanov"*.
Кто геро́й рома́на **«А́нна Каре́нина»**?	Who is the hero of the novel *"Anna Karenina"*?

In conversational Russian, the first identifying noun may be omitted, in which case the noun of apposition will be in the appropriate grammatical case.

О́льга рабо́тала в журна́ле **«Но́вый мир»**.	Olga worked at the magazine *"New World"*.

And:

И мой друг то́же рабо́тал в **«Но́вом ми́ре»**.	My friend also worked *at "New World"*.

NOUNS

а́лгебра algebra
ба́бушка grandmother
баскетбо́л basketball
бейсбо́л baseball
биле́т ticket
студе́нческий биле́т student I.D.
биоло́гия biology
брат brother
двою́родный брат cousin (male)
велосипе́д bicycle
ви́део video
вино́ wine
геогра́фия geography
геоме́трия geometry
грамма́тика grammar
де́душка grandfather
дере́вня village, country
дире́ктор director
диске́тка computer diskette
до́ктор doctor, Dr.
дура́к (m.; f. ду́ра) fool
же́нщина woman
жизнь life
жу́лик swindler, thief
звоно́к phone call, bell
знако́мый friend, acquaintance
идио́т (m; f. идио́тка) idiot
и́мя (first) name
исто́рия story; history
кабине́т office
ке́тчуп ketchup
кино́ (indecl.) film, cinema
конфе́та (piece of) candy
ку́хня cuisine; kitchen
лимо́н lemon
лингви́стика linguistics
литерату́ра literature
майоне́з mayonnaise
ма́льчик boy
матема́тика mathematics
милиционе́р police officer
мо́ре sea
моро́женое ice cream
мужчи́на man

му́сор trash
о́тчество patronymic
пи́во beer
пле́ер mp3 player
предме́т subject (in school)
приро́да nature
прия́тель friend
пье́са play
разгово́р conversation
рисова́ние drawing
рома́н novel
сестра́ sister
двою́родная сестра́ cousin (female)
скейтбо́рд skateboard
сосе́д (pl. сосе́ди) neighbor (male)
сосе́дка neighbor (female)
стати́стика statistics
стихи́ poems
столи́ца capital
текст text
те́ннис tennis
то́стер toaster
упражне́ние exercise
факульте́т department
инжене́рный~ engineering dept.
истори́ческий~ history dept.
математи́ческий~ mathematics dept.
физи́ческий~ physics dept.
филологи́ческий~ philology dept.
хими́ческий~ chemistry dept.
экономи́ческий~ economics dept.
факульте́т би́знеса business dept.
факульте́т полити́ческой нау́ки dept. of political science
факульте́т ру́сского языка́ dept. of Russian language
фами́лия surname
фи́зика physics
физкульту́ра physical education
фотоальбо́м photo album

футбо́л soccer
хам rude, obnoxious person
хи́мия chemistry
хозя́ин (pl. хозя́ева) owner, landlord, host
хозя́йка owner, landlady, hostess
хулига́н (m.; f. хулига́нка) hooligan, hoodlum
шофёр driver
эконо́мика economics
язы́к language

PROPER NOUNS

Азербайджа́н Azerbaijan
А́зия Asia
Астана́ Astana (capital of Kazakhstan)
Арме́ния Armenia
А́фрика Africa
Ашхаба́д Ashkhabad (capital of Turkmenistan)
Баку́ Baku (capital of Azerbaijan)
Белару́сь Belarus
Бишке́к Bishkek (capital of Kyrgyzstan)
Гру́зия Georgia
Душанбе́ Dushanbe (capital of Tajikistan)
Евро́па Europe
Ерева́н Yerevan (capital of Armenia)
Казахста́н Kazakhstan
Кана́да Canada
Киргизста́н Kyrgyzstan
Кишинёв Chisinau/Kishinev (capital of Moldova)
Крым Crimea (peninsula in the Black Sea)
Молда́вия Moldova
Таджикиста́н Tajikistan
Ташке́нт Tashkent (capital of Uzbekistan)
Тбили́си Tbilisi (capital of Georgia)
Туркмениста́н Turkmenistan

ADJECTIVES

друго́й other, different
за́нят busy
италья́нский Italian
кита́йский Chinese
мексика́нский Mexican
рад glad
сча́стлив happy
телефо́нный phone
фрукто́вый fruit
чужо́й (челове́к) stranger

VERBS

ви́деть (ви́де-) see
возвраща́ться (возвраща́й-ся) return
зна́чит (it) means
люби́ть (люби́-) love
мочь (irreg.) be able(to)
переводи́ть (переводи́-) translate
писа́ть (писа́-) write

представля́ть (представля́й-) imagine
проси́ть (проси́-) ask, beg
ревнова́ть (ревнова́-) be jealous
сдава́ть (сдава́й-) rent
серди́ться (серди́-ся) be angry
сиде́ть (сиде́-) sit
слы́шать (слы́ша-) hear
смея́ться (смея́-ся) laugh
смотре́ть (смотре́-) watch, look at
фотографи́ровать (фотографи́рова-) take a picture of
целова́ть (целова́-) kiss

ADVERBS

вдруг suddenly
про́сто simply
сра́зу at once
тепе́рь now

тогда́ then
то́же also

EXPRESSIONS

в командиро́вке away on business
Всё хорошо́? Is everything okay?
Всё хорошо́, что хорошо́ конча́ется. All's well that ends well.
Мину́точку! Just a minute!
мо́жет быть maybe
цель пое́здки purpose of trip
час дня one o'clock p.m.
Что случи́лось? What happened?

Что же случилось

~~сразу~~ сразу

сразу

*T*anya and Misha run into Kevin at the mall, and Misha and Kevin finally get acquainted. They have lunch in a restaurant and talk about Misha's plans to start his own veterinary business. Kevin offers to help.

За на́ше
бу́дущее!

You will learn how to:

- Make a toast russian style
- Read a russian calendar
- Discuss a menu and order food in a restaurant
- Talk about your tastes in books and television
- Indicate intentions
- Describe how you spend free time
- Express reservation
- Express your likes and dislikes
- Discuss past and future events
- Talk about a sequence of actions
- Discuss and buy a pet

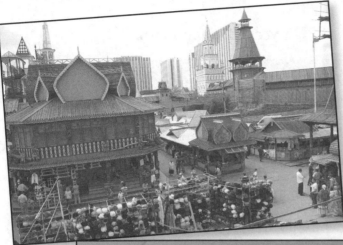

Making a Toast

PREviewing

The title of this episode is a toast: **За на́ше бу́дущее!** (To our future!) To make a toast in Russian you need some wine, good company, and most importantly the preposition **за** + the accusative case. Here are some examples.

За тебя́! За вас!
За твою́ но́вую рабо́ту!
За ма́му!
За дру́жбу!
За на́ше знако́мство!

How would you make a toast to Та́ня, Ми́ша, or Ке́вин?
How would you say the toast "To us!"?

дру́жба = friendship

знако́мство = acquaintance

За на́ше знако́мство! = To our (first) meeting!

Today you are going to see how Та́ня and Ми́ша spent their Sunday.

Ру́сский календа́рь ▲

2009

Январь

ПН		5	12	19	26
ВТ		6	13	20	27
СР		7	14	21	28
ЧТ	1	8	15	22	29
ПТ	2	9	16	23	30
СБ	3	10	17	24	31
ВС	4	11	18	25	

Февраль

ПН		2	9	16	23
ВТ		3	10	17	24
СР		4	11	18	25
ЧТ		5	12	19	26
ПТ		6	13	20	27
СБ		7	14	21	28
ВС	1	8	15	22	

Март

ПН		2	9	16	23	30
ВТ		3	10	17	24	31
СР		4	11	18	25	
ЧТ		5	12	19	26	
ПТ		6	13	20	27	
СБ		7	14	21	28	
ВС	1	8	15	22	29	

Апрель

ПН		6	13	20	27
ВТ		7	14	21	28
СР	1	8	15	22	29
ЧТ	2	9	16	23	30
ПТ	3	10	17	24	
СБ	4	11	18	25	
ВС	5	12	19	26	

Май

ПН		4	11	18	25
ВТ		5	12	19	26
СР		6	13	20	27
ЧТ		7	14	21	28
ПТ	1	8	15	22	29
СБ	2	9	16	23	30
ВС	3	10	17	24	31

Июнь

ПН	1	8	15	22	29
ВТ	2	9	16	23	30
СР	3	10	17	24	
ЧТ	4	11	18	25	
ПТ	5	12	19	26	
СБ	6	13	20	27	
ВС	7	14	21	28	

Июль

ПН		6	13	20	27
ВТ		7	14	21	28
СР	1	8	15	22	29
ЧТ	2	9	16	23	30
ПТ	3	10	17	24	31
СБ	4	11	18	25	
ВС	5	12	19	26	

Август

ПН		3	10	17	24	31
ВТ		4	11	18	25	
СР		5	12	19	26	
ЧТ		6	13	20	27	
ПТ		7	14	21	28	
СБ	1	8	15	22	29	
ВС	2	9	16	23	30	

Сентябрь

ПН		7	14	21	28
ВТ	1	8	15	22	29
СР	2	9	16	23	30
ЧТ	3	10	17	24	
ПТ	4	11	18	25	
СБ	5	12	19	26	
ВС	6	13	20	27	

Октябрь

ПН		5	12	19	26
ВТ		6	13	20	27
СР		7	14	21	28
ЧТ	1	8	15	22	29
ПТ	2	9	16	23	30
СБ	3	10	17	24	31
ВС	4	11	18	25	

Ноябрь

ПН		2	9	16	23	30
ВТ		3	10	17	24	
СР		4	11	18	25	
ЧТ		5	12	19	26	
ПТ		6	13	20	27	
СБ		7	14	21	28	
ВС	1	8	15	22	29	

Декабрь

ПН		7	14	21	28
ВТ	1	8	15	22	29
СР	2	9	16	23	30
ЧТ	3	10	17	24	31
ПТ	4	11	18	25	
СБ	5	12	19	26	
ВС	6	13	20	27	

1. Practicing pronunciation: days of the week

> понеде́льник
> вто́рник
> среда́
> четве́рг
> пя́тница
> суббо́та
> воскресе́нье

▲ Russian days of the week are not capitalized. On a Russian calendar, the first day of the week is Monday, and the dates are listed vertically. Until 1918, Russia followed the Julian calendar, which was thirteen days behind the western Gregorian calendar. In February 1918, the Russian civil calendar was adjusted to the European system; the Russian Orthodox Church, however, never officially accepted the change and continues to use the old style.

2. Календа́рь

А. Use the calendar to identify dates that correspond to the following days of the week.

> 2
> — **Како́е число́** пе́рвый понеде́льник ма́я?
> 3 1
> — Пе́рвый понеде́льник мая – **4-ое число́.**

число́ = date

> второ́е воскресе́нье, тре́тья пя́тница, пе́рвая среда́, пя́тый четве́рг

В. Ask your partner on which days of the week the following dates fall.

> 2
> — Како́й день **9-ое ма́я▲?**
> 3 1
> — **9-ое мая – суббо́та.**

In dates the month is used in the genitive case: девя́тое **ма́я** = the ninth of May.

> 1-ое, 20-ое, 14-ое, 10-ое, 23-ье, 13-ое, 4-ое, 26-ое ма́я

С. What day is it today? What is the date today?

> 2
> — Како́й сего́дня день?
> 1
> — Сего́дня понеде́льник.
> 2
> — Како́е сего́дня число́?
> 1
> — Сего́дня 11-ое число́.

▲ In May Russians celebrate two big holidays: Labor Day on the first, and Victory Day on the ninth. Labor Day was established in 1889 by an international workers' organization to celebrate the solidarity of the proletariat. Victory Day commemorates the victory over fascist Germany in 1945.

3. Read the following advertisement for the place where Та́ня and Ми́ша spent their Sunday after leaving the mall.

прекра́сный = wonderful
о́тдых = rest, relaxation

карти́на = picture

ждём вас = (here)
looking forward to
seeing you

> **РЕКОМЕНДУЕМ ПРЕКРАСНЫЙ ОТДЫХ!**
> **В СУББОТУ И ВОСКРЕСЕНЬЕ В ИЗМАЙЛОВО**
>
> СУВЕНИРЫ
> КАРТИНЫ СОВРЕМЕННЫХ ХУДОЖНИКОВ
> МУЗЫКАЛЬНЫЕ ИНСТРУМЕНТЫ
> КАССЕТЫ И ДИСКИ СОВРЕМЕННОЙ МУЗЫКИ
>
> НА ТЕРРИТОРИИ ПАРКА
>
> КАФЕ, РЕСТОРАНЫ, БАРЫ
> АТТРАКЦИОНЫ
> КАРУСЕЛИ
>
> # ЖДЁМ ВАС В ИЗМАЙЛОВО!

Где бы́ли Ми́ша и Та́ня в воскресе́нье?

☐ в кинотеа́тре   ☐ в па́рке

☐ в музе́е   ☐ в кафе́

☐ на вы́ставке   ☐ в магази́не

☐ на конце́рте   ☐ в библиоте́ке

VIEWING

▶ Now watch the video with the SOUND OFF.

SOUND OFF

4. Put the following events in order.

_____3_____ Ми́ша, Та́ня, and Ке́вин have lunch at a café.

_____1_____ Ми́ша and Та́ня are browsing at the mall.

_____2_____ Ми́ша and Та́ня run into Ке́вин.

_____5_____ Ми́ша proposes a toast.

_____4_____ The waitress takes their orders.

5. Что де́лали Ми́ша, Та́ня и Ке́вин в торго́вом це́нтре?

торго́вый центр = shopping center

☑ гуля́ли   ☐ слу́шали му́зыку

☑ отдыха́ли   ☐ покупа́ли сувени́ры

☐ рабо́тали   ☐ танцева́ли

☑ обе́дали в кафе́   ☐ смотре́ли фи́льмы

покупа́ть (покупа́й-) = to buy

6. Check off the food and drinks that Ми́ша, Та́ня, and Ке́вин have for lunch.

☐ ice cream sundae   ☑ salad

☐ steak   ☐ chicken

☐ coffee   ☑ water

☐ hot dogs   ☐ pizza

☐ hamburgers   ☐ fish

☑ meat   ☐ beer

☐ rice   ☑ potatoes

☑ wine   ☐ cake

7. You may remember that Та́ня's friendship with Ке́вин caused friction between Ми́ша and Та́ня. How does Ми́ша react when he finally meets Ке́вин?

	Да	Нет
Is Ми́ша still jealous?	☑	☐
Have Ми́ша and Та́ня resolved their conflict?	☑	☐
Does Ми́ша get along with Ке́вин?	☑	☐

▶ Now watch the video with the SOUND ON.

SOUND ON

8. Name the item Ми́ша offers to buy Та́ня.

☐ су́мка   ☑ брасле́т   ☐ цветы́

9. Та́ня is surprised to find Ке́вин at the mall and asks him: «**Что ты тут де́лаешь?**» How does Ке́вин reply?

☑ Гуля́ю, фотографи́рую, покупа́ю сувени́ры.

☐ Рабо́таю в кафе́.

☐ Отдыха́ю и покупа́ю но́вую оде́жду.

10. What food and drinks do Та́ня, Ми́ша, and Ке́вин order for lunch?

Они́ зака́зывают:

☐ спаге́тти   ☐ бефстро́ганов   ☑ ку́рицу

☐ борщ   ☐ чай   ☐ фру́кты

☑ зелёный сала́т   ☒ бифште́кс   ☑ моро́женое

☑ ры́бу   ☐ жа́реную   ☐ торт

☑ вино́   карто́шку   ☐ га́мбургер

☑ во́ду

> **зака́зывать**
> (зака́зыв**ай**-) = order

11. Кто Ми́ша?

☐ Он студе́нт.

☐ Он бухга́лтер.

☐ Он ме́неджер.

☑ Он ветерина́р.

12. Put the following mini-episodes in order.

Пла́н Ми́ши	4
Обе́д в кафе́	3
Краси́вые ве́щи	1
Тост	5
«Познако́мьтесь, пожа́луйста!»	2

POSTviewing

> **Ру́сские сувени́ры** лежа́т в рюкзаке́.
>
> Ке́вин лю́бит **ру́сские сувени́ры.**
>
> The accusative plural of inanimate nouns and their modifiers is the same as the nominative plural.

13. Что Ке́вин ви́дел в Москве́?

Ке́вин, being a photographer, loves to take pictures of everything in Moscow. Name the places that Ке́вин saw on the first day using the reference words in the plural form.

> **совреме́нный** = modern, contemporary

> 1
> Ке́вин ви́дел в Москве́ **совреме́нные зда́ния.**

> старый, новый, интересный, смешной, (не) красивый, современный, большой, маленький

> дом, гостиница, здание, театр, институт, банк, парк, улица, больница, машина, ресторан, кафе, библиотека, кинотеатр, почта

14. Таня, Миша и Кевин обедали в кафе.

A. Интересно, Миша и Таня часто обедают в кафе?

Они обедают в кафе:

- ☐ каждый день
- ☐ каждую субботу
- ☐ каждую неделю
- ☐ каждый месяц

> Time expressions with **каждый** (every) take the accusative case:
>
> каждую среду = every Wednesday

> неделя = week
>
> месяц = month

B. How do you think Миша and Таня usually spend their free time? Discuss the following questions with your partner, using the word **каждый** in your answers.

> — Миша и Таня часто обедают в кафе?
>
> — Я думаю, Миша и Таня обедают в кафе
>
> **каждую неделю.**

1. Миша и Таня часто танцуют на дискотеке?
2. Они часто гуляют в Измайлово?
3. Они часто смотрят балеты?
4. Они часто ужинают в ресторане?

15. How often do you do each of the activities listed below?

— Ка́ждую неде́лю я рабо́таю в библиотеке. А ты?
— А я не рабо́таю в библиотéке.

  Ка́ждую неде́лю я рабо́таю в рестора́не.

упражне́ние = exercise

писа́ть упражне́ния, отдыха́ть, писа́ть
по-ру́сски, смотре́ть телеви́зор, танцева́ть,
обе́дать, за́втракать, у́жинать, чита́ть, слу́шать
му́зыку, рабо́тать, гуля́ть

ка́ждый де́нь, ка́ждый ве́чер, ка́ждое у́тро,
ка́ждую неде́лю, ка́ждую суббо́ту, ка́ждое
воскресе́нье

16. А чита́ть вы лю́бите? Что вы чита́ете?

— Ты ча́сто чита́ешь **ко́миксы**?
— О́чень. Ка́ждый день./ Не о́чень. Не ка́ждый день.

ко́миксы (pl.) = comics
рома́н = novel
расска́з = story
стихи́ = poems
кла́ссика (sg.) = classics
нау́чная фанта́стика =
  science fiction

ко́миксы, журна́лы, газе́ты, рома́ны, уче́бники,
пи́сьма, статьи́, детекти́вы, расска́зы, стихи́,
кла́ссика, нау́чная фанта́стика

Days of the Week

понеде́льник	в понеде́льник
вто́рник	во вто́рник
среда́	в сре́ду
четве́рг	в четве́рг
пя́тница	в пя́тницу
суббо́та	в суббо́ту
воскресе́нье	в воскресе́нье

в сре́ду
(acc.) = on
Wednesday

1. В понеде́льник, во вто́рник, в сре́ду …

A. Где Та́ня была́ в суббо́ту?

В понеде́льник, во вто́рник, в сре́ду, в четве́рг и в пя́тницу Та́ня была́ в институ́те. Нет, э́то оши́бка! **В сре́ду** она́ не была́ в институ́те. Она́ была́ в Шереме́тьево. (И дека́н зна́ет об э́том!) **В понеде́льник и во вто́рник** она́ обе́дала в институ́тской столо́вой (о́чень вку́сно!), а у́жинала до́ма. **В сре́ду** ве́чером она́ танцева́ла на дискоте́ке. **В четве́рг** она́ была́ в спорти́вном за́ле. **В пя́тницу** Та́ня писа́ла курсову́ю рабо́ту в университе́тской библиоте́ке. **В воскресе́нье** Та́ня и Ми́ша гуля́ли в Изма́йлово.

А **в суббо́ту**? Как вы ду́маете, где была́ Та́ня в суббо́ту?

B. Practicing pronunciation

> **в понеде́льник**
> **во вто́рник**
> **в сре́ду**
> **в четве́рг**
> **в пя́тницу**
> **в суббо́ту**
> **в воскресе́нье**

C. Discuss with your partner what you did last week.

> 2
> — Что ты де́лал(а) в понеде́льник?
> — В понеде́льник я рабо́тал(а) в университе́тской
> 　　1　　　　4
> 　столо́вой. А ты?

писа́ть пи́сьма, игра́ть на гита́ре, смотре́ть но́вый фильм, танцева́ть на мое́й люби́мой дискоте́ке, чита́ть неинтере́сную дли́нную кни́гу, переводи́ть ру́сский текст, смотре́ть телеви́зор, у́жинать в италья́нском рестора́не

оши́бка = mistake

дека́н = dean

столо́вая = dining hall, cafeteria

спорти́вный зал = gym

курсова́я рабо́та = term paper

2. Каки́е журна́лы и газе́ты вы чита́ете?

A. Fill out this questionnaire about which periodicals you read; add your favorite publications below.

	ка́ждый день	ка́ждую суббо́ту	ка́ждое воскресе́нье	ка́ждую неде́лю	ка́ждый ме́сяц
газе́та «Нью-Йо́рк Таймс»					
газе́та «Файнэ́ншал Таймс»					
журна́л «Нью Йо́ркер»					
журна́л «Таймс»					
журна́л «Ньюсуи́к»					
журна́л «Ри́дерс Да́йджест»					
университе́тская газе́та					

B. Discuss the following questions with your classmates.

1. Что вы чита́ете ча́сто, а что – ре́дко?

2. Что вы чита́ете ка́ждый день?

3. Что вы чита́ете ка́ждое воскресе́нье?

4. Что вы чита́ете ка́ждую неде́лю?

C. Pictured on the following page are some Russian newspapers and magazines.▲ Which ones would you be interested in reading?

> ²
> — Что ты хо́чешь чита́ть?
>
> ¹
> — Я хочу́ чита́ть **газе́ту «Аргуме́нты и фа́кты»**.
>
> ⁴
> А ты?
>
> ¹
> — А я хочу́ чита́ть **журна́л «Автопилот»**.

▲ Russian daily newspapers are short, usually 8-12 pages long, but they are enormously varied. You may purchase a subscription to a newspaper or buy one on the street at a newspaper kiosk or from a vendor near a metro station.

3. Вы ча́сто смо́трите телеви́зор? Что вы смо́трите ча́сто? А что ре́дко? Что вы смо́трите ка́ждый ве́чер? Ка́ждый понеде́льник, вто́рник … ?

переда́ча =
TV show

— Я смотрю́ **музыка́льные переда́чи** ка́ждый день.
А ты?
— А я ре́дко смотрю́ **музыка́льные переда́чи.**/
И я смотрю́ музыка́льные переда́чи ка́ждый день.

международные новости, музыкальные программы,
мультфильмы, фильмы, передача «60 минут», передача
20/20, передача «Симпсоны», спортивные передачи

Nouns: Dative Case

	Endings	1st declension	Endings	2nd declension
Nom.	-ø (-ь), -o (-e)	друг, писатель, общество	-a (-я)	подруга, тётя
Dat.	-y (-ю)	другу, писателю, обществу	-e	подруге, тёте

The dative case is the case of the indirect object (the indirect receiver of
the action of a verb).

The following verbs take an indirect object (dative case).

звонить (звони-) "telephone"   Кевип звонил Тане.

отвечать (отвечай-) "answer"   Таня отвечала милиционеру.

помогать (помогай-) "help"   Таня помогает Кевину.

The following verbs take two objects: a direct object (accusative case)
and an indirect object (dative case).

готовить (готови-) "prepare, cook"   Анна Борисовна готовит
                                     семье ужин.

писать (писа-) "write"   Сергей пишет другу письма.

покупать (покупай-) "buy"   Миша покупает Тане
                                     подарки.

4. Put the nouns indicated into the dative case to complete the
following sentences.

  1. Таня часто помогает _____.
                              (Кевин)

  2. Даша пишет _____ каждый месяц.
                    (Таня)

3. Та́ня всегда́ отвеча́ет _____.

   (Да́ша)

4. Та́ня иногда́ звони́т _____.

   (Серге́й)

5. Са́ша звони́т _____ ка́ждый день.

   (Ле́на)

6. Ке́вин пи́шет _____ ка́ждую неде́лю.

   (брат)

7. А́нна Бори́совна помога́ет _____.

   (дире́ктор)

8. Ми́ша покупа́ет _____ цветы́.

   (ба́бушка)

5. Respond to the following situations using the words in parentheses.

> Ва́ня лю́бит моро́женое. (Гали́на Ива́новна, покупа́ть) →
> **Гали́на Ива́новна покупа́ет Ва́не моро́женое.**

1. Ва́ня хо́чет говори́ть по-англи́йски. (Ке́вин, помога́ть)

2. Та́ня лю́бит цветы́. (Ми́ша, покупа́ть)

3. Та́ня лю́бит чита́ть пи́сьма Да́ши. (Да́ша, писа́ть)

4. Ма́ма гото́вит обе́д. (па́па, помога́ть)

5. Ке́вин хо́чет есть. (Та́ня, гото́вить бутербро́ды)

6. Милиционе́р спра́шивает Ке́вина. (Ке́вин, отвеча́ть)

7. Та́ня лю́бит бале́т. (Ми́ша, покупа́ть биле́ты)

есть = eat

Personal Pronouns: Dative Case

Nom.	я	ты	он/оно́	она́	мы	вы	они́
Dat.	**мне**	**тебе́**	**ему́**	**ей**	**нам**	**вам**	**им**

6. A. Pretend that you can't hear what your partner says. Ask him/her to repeat what s/he has told you.

dative case of кто → кому

> — Та́ня помога́ет **Ке́вину.**
>   ¹
>   ³
> — **Кому́?**
>   ¹
> — **Ке́вину.**

1. Са́ша ка́ждый день звони́т **дру́гу и подру́ге.**
2. Ма́ма гото́вит **Ва́не.**
3. Ва́ня ча́сто помога́ет **ма́ме.**
4. Да́ша ка́ждый ме́сяц пи́шет **Та́не.**
5. Та́ня всегда́ отвеча́ет **Да́ше.**
6. Серге́й всегда́ помога́ет **Та́не и Ле́не.**
7. Ка́ждый ве́чер Та́ня звони́т **Ми́ше.**

B. Replace the noun(s) highlighted in the previous sentences with a personal pronoun.

> Та́ня помога́ет **Ке́вину.** → Та́ня помога́ет **ему́.**

7. Fill in the blanks with the appropriate verb or personal pronoun in the dative case.

> — Почему́ ты ре́дко мне **звони́шь?**
>   ²
>   ²   ¹   ¹
> — Что ты! Наоборо́т. Я ча́сто звоню́ **тебе́.**

1. — Почему́ ты нам не _____?

   — Что ты! Наоборо́т. Я ча́сто помога́ю _____.

2. — Почему́ па́па не хо́чет нам _____?

   — Что ты! Наоборо́т. Он ча́сто гото́вит _____.

3. — Почему́ ты мне не _____?

— Что ты! Наоборо́т. Я ча́сто звоню́_____.

4. — Почему́ твой друг тебе́ не _____?

— Что ты! Наоборо́т. Он ча́сто пи́шет _____.

8. A. Here are some excerpts from a TV guide in the Russian newspaper «Анте́нна». Use the following information about the video characters' tastes to predict which shows they watch.

> Та́ня лю́бит му́зыку. → **Ка́ждый вто́рник** она́ смо́трит **переда́чу** «**Му́зыка на за́втрак**».

1. Ми́ша лю́бит поли́тику.
2. Са́ша лю́бит рок.
3. Ва́ня лю́бит мультфи́льмы.
4. Серге́й лю́бит де́ньги.
5. Смирно́вы лю́бят америка́нское кино́.
6. Ле́на лю́бит америка́нские телесериа́лы.
7. Ви́ктор Петро́вич лю́бит спорт.
8. А́нна Бори́совна лю́бит бале́т.

телесериа́л = TV series

B. Which programs sound interesting to you?

> — Я хочу́ смотре́ть **спорти́вную програ́мму**
> 1   4
> «**Футбо́л россии**». А ты?
> 1
> — А я хочу́ смотре́ть «**Адвока́т**».

РОССИЯ ТЕЛЕКАНАЛ

ТВ ЦЕНТР

НТВ

КУЛЬТУРА ТЕЛЕКАНАЛ

СПОРТ ТЕЛЕКАНАЛ

Канал 1
Канал приносит извинения за перерыв в работе в связи с профилактикой до 11.45
11.45 ЕРАЛАШ
12.00 НОВОСТИ
12.20 «УБОЙНАЯ СИЛА» Сериал
13.20 ДЕТЕКТИВЫ
14.00 ДРУГИЕ НОВОСТИ
14.30 ПОНЯТЬ. ПРОСТИТЬ
15.00 НОВОСТИ
15.20 «ПОХОЖДЕНИЕ ГЕНИАЛЬНОГО АФЕРИСТА»
16.00 «ОГОНЬ ЛЮБВИ» Сериал
17.00 ФЕДЕРАЛЬНЫЙ СУДЬЯ

РОССИЯ
Канал приносит извинения за переры в связи с работе в связи с профилактикой до 11.50
11.50 «ЧАСТНЫЙ ДЕТЕКТИВ» Сериал
Бибигон представляет
12.45 «ВОЗВРАЩЕНИЕ БЛУДНОГО ПОПУГАЯ» «ЦАРЕВНА-ЛЯГУШКА» Мультфильмы
14.00 ВЕСТИ
14.20 МЕСТНОЕ ВРЕМЯ ВЕСТИ–МОСКВА
Бибигон представляет
14.40 «МАЧЕХА». Сериал
15.35 СУД ИДЕТ
16.30 КУЛАГИН И ПАРТНЕРЫ
17.00 ВЕСТИ
17.30 МЕСТНОЕ ВРЕМЯ ВЕСТИ-МОСКОВСКАЯ ОБЛАСТЬ
17.50 ВЕСТИ ДЕЖУРНАЯ ЧАСТЬ

ТВ ЦЕНТР
6.00, 7.30 НАСТРОЕНИЕ
8.30, 11.30, 14.30, 17.30 СОБЫТИЯ
8.45 ПЕТРОВКА, 38
8.55, 14.45 «ИСТОРИЯ ГОСУДАРСТВА РОССИЙСКОГО»
9.00 «СИЛЬНЫМ ДУХОМ» 1-я серия
10.45 ДЕТЕКТИВНЫЕ ИСТОРИИ «Таблетки смерти»
11.15 ПЕТРОВКА, 38
11.45 «ПОСТСКРИПТУМ» с Алексеем Пушковым
12.55 «МОРСКОЙ УЗЕЛ» Фильм из цикла «ДОКАЗАТЕЛЬСТВА ВИНЫ»
13.45 ЛИНИЯ ЗАЩИТЫ
14.50 «ИСПОЛНЕНИЕ ЖЕЛАНИЙ». Мультфильм
16.30 НОВОЕ «ВРЕМЕЧКО»
17.55 ДЕЛОВАЯ МОСКВА

3

7.00 БИЗНЕС ПЕРСОНА
7.25 ПОГОДА
15.30 ГОРОД. НОВОСТИ
15.40 ЦЕНА ВОПРОСА
16.20 ЛЮДИ ДЕЛА
16.25 ПОГОДА

НТВ
6.00 СЕГОДНЯ УТРОМ
9.00 СЛЕДСТВИЕ ВЕЛИ...
10.00 СЕГОДНЯ
10.20 ЧРЕЗВЫЧАЙНОЕ ПРОИСШЕСТВИЕ ОБЗОР ЗА НЕДЕЛЮ
10.55 «КУЛИНАРНЫЙ ПОЕДИНОК» С Михаилом Пореченковым
11.55 КВАРТИРНЫЙ ВОПРОС
13.00 СЕГОДНЯ
13.30 «АДВОКАТ» Сериал
15.30 ОБЗОР ЧРЕЗВЫЧАЙНОЕ ПРОИСШЕСТВИЕ
16.00 СЕГОДНЯ
16.30 «УЛИЦЫ РАЗБИТЫХ ФОНАРЕЙ» Сериал

КУЛЬТУРА
7.00 ПРОГРАММА КАНАЛА «ЕВРОНЬЮС»
10.00 НОВОСТИ КУЛЬТУРЫ
10.20 «В ГЛАВНОЙ РОЛИ...» у Юлиана Макарова
10.40 ПРОГРАММА ПЕРЕДАЧ
10.50 Классика кино «ПУТЕВКА В ЖИЗНЬ»
12.40 ЛИНИЯ ЖИЗНИ Юлий Ким
13.35 ПЯТОЕ ИЗМЕРЕНИЕ
14.05 Из Золотой коллекции телетеатра А. П. Чехов «В НОМЕРАХ»
15.25 «ДОКУМЕНТАЛЬНАЯ ИСТОРИЯ» с Кириллом Андерсоном «Давид Рязанов: инакомыслящий соратник»
15.55 ПОРЯДОК СЛОВ
Бибигон представляет
16.00 «НОВЫЕ ПРИКЛЮЧЕНИЯ МЕДВЕЖОНКА ПАДДИНГТОНА»
16.20 «КТО Я ТАКОЙ?»
16.30 АНДЫ ВСЕРЬЕЗ»
16.55 ЭНЦИКЛОПЕДИЯ
17.05 «ПУТЕШЕСТВИЕ В ЦАРСТВО ЖИВОТНЫХ»
17.35 ПЛОДЫ ПРОСВЕЩЕНИЯ ПЛЕННИЦЫ СУДЬБЫ Лариса Рейснер

СПОРТ
4.40 ФУТБОЛ. Премьер-лига
6.45, 9.00, 13.35, 17.20 ВЕСТИ–СПОРТ
Бибигон представляет
7.00, 8.00 ЗАРЯДКА С ЧЕМПИОНОМ
7.15 ПРИКЛЮЧЕНИЕ КОТА ЛЕОПОЛЬДА» «ДВА ВЕСЕЛЫХ ГУСЯ»
8.15 МИР ДЕТСКОГО СПОРТА
8.45 МАСТЕР СПОРТА
9.10 ВЕСТИ–СПОРТ МЕСТНОЕ ВРЕМЯ
9.15 ЛЕТОПИСЬ СПОРТА
9.45 БАСКЕТБОЛ Чемпионат России Женщины. 1/4 финала
11.35 РЫБАЛКА С РАДЗИШЕВСКИМ
11.50 ГАНДБОЛ Лига чемпионов Женщины. 1/2 финала «Лада» (Россия) — «Хипо» (Австрия)
13.45 АВТОСПОРТ. Чемпионат мира по ралли
14.20 ФУТБОЛ. Премьер-лига ЦСКА — «Локомотив»
16.15 ФУТБОЛ РОССИИ
17.35 ФУТБОЛ. Лига чемпионов. 1/4 финала «Ливерпуль» (Англия) — «Арсенал» (Англия)

7

5.05, 4.30 ВЕСЕЛЫЕ СТАРТЫ
6.05 МУЗЫКАЛЬНЫЙ ТРЕК
6.15 ЗАРЯДКА ДЛЯ СТРАНЫ
6.30 МУЛЬТФИЛЬМЫ
7.00 7 НОВОСТЕЙ
7.05 ФЕХТОВАНИЕ
8.05 «15:00». Сериал
8.30 «ПЛЯЖ, ЭКСТРИМ И ВСЕ ТАКОЕ»
9.05, 21.20, 4.05 NHL
9.20, 14.05, 21.05, 4.15 NBA LIVE!
9.35 АВТОСПОРТ РОССИИ
10.05 СПОРТ СОБАК
10.20 ЖЕНЩИНЫ В СПОРТЕ
11.05, 22.35 МИР ПОДВОДНОЙ ОХОТЫ
11.20, 23.35 АКАДЕМИЯ НАХЛЫСТА
11.35, 23.05 ПРЕДЕЛЬНАЯ ГЛУБИНА
12.05, 23.20 ДИАЛОГИ О РЫБАЛКЕ
12.20 TOTAL РЕГБИ
13.05, 19.05 X-TREME 99,9
14.20 КИБЕРСПОРТ
14.35 GAME SPORT
15.05 GOLF TODAY
15.35 СВОБОДНЫЙ ПОЛЕТ
16.05 ВОКРУГ СВЕТА
16.20 SPORTS WATCH
17.05, 18.05, 21.35 OUTRAGEOUS AND COURAGEOUS
17.20 КЛАССИКА ФУТБОЛА
18.20 INDYCAR
20.05 KOTV: КЛАССИКА БОКСА
22.05 РАЛЛИ-РЕЙДЫ РОССИИ
22.20 НАСТОЛЬНЫЙ ХОККЕЙ
0.05 ДАРТС
1.05 НОЧНОЙ ВЫИГРЫШ
2.05, 3.05 СПОРТМАНИЯ

МУЗ-ТВ

5.00, 8.55, 12.55, 0.40, 3.00 МУЗ-ТВ ХИТ
6.00, 10.00, 2.00 НАШЕ
7.00, 16.25, 23.30 ТВОЙ ВЫБОР
11.00 ЗВЕЗДЫ ПОД ПРИЦЕЛОМ
11.55 БЛИЖЕ К ЗВЕЗДАМ Дима Билан
12.25, 19.00 PRO-ОБЗОР
14.50 АЛФАВИТ
15.00, 21.00 ЗВЕЗДЫ ЗАЖИГАЮТ
16.00 ZOOM
17.25, 23.00 SMESH.NO
18.00 ЗВЕЗДНЫЕ ФАБРИКАНТЫ Дайджест
18.30 «ЛЮБОВЬ НЕ ШОУ-БИЗНЕС-2» Сериал
19.30 «Я МЕЧТАЮ»
20.00 МУЛЬТЯШКА
20.25 СТИЛИСТИКА
22.00 ЗВЕЗДНЫЕ ФАБРИКАНТЫ
22.25 БЛОНДИНКА В ШОКОЛАДЕ
22.50 PRO-НОВОСТИ

MTV

6.00 МУЗЫКА НА ЗАВТРАК
10.00 News Блок Weekly с Александром Анатольевичем
10.30 Звездная жизнь: из грязи в князи
11.30 Делаем кино: 21
12.00 Пятеро в отрыве
13.00 МУЗЫКА НАВСЕГДА
15.00 Русская 10-ка Хит-парад
16.00 Пятеро в отрыве
17.00 Тачку на прокачку
17.30 Стоп! Снято: Mariah Carey «Touch My Body»
18.00 Концертный зал: Лучшие выступления на Киноградах
19.00 Гид по стилю
19.30 Киночарт
20.00 Звезда в кубе
20.30 Тачку на прокачку: Madonna's Ride
21.00 «КЛУБ». Сериал 4-й сезон
22.00 «КЛИНИКА!» Сериал
22.30 Южный парк
23.00 Чудаки
23.30 Копы под прицелом
0.00 News Блок Daily с Ярославом Александровичем
0.15 МУЗЫКА НАВСЕГДА
1.00 «Поймай удачу!» Интерактивная игра

СТОЛИЦА

6.00 ОГНИ БОЛЬШОГО ГОРОДА
6.35 МУЗЫКА НА КАНАЛЕ
7.00 МУЛЬТФИЛЬМЫ
7.30 МОСКОВСКОЕ УТРО
9.30, 3.40 «ПЛЮС БЕСКОНЕЧНОСТЬ»
10.30, 13.30, 16.30, 19.30, 21.30, 1.00 НОВОСТИ
10.40, 22.20 АФИША
11.00 «ХИТ-ПАРАД ДИКОЙ ПРИРОДЫ»
12.00 БУДНИ СТОЛИЦЫ
12.55 ВАШ РЕЦЕПТ
13.05 ПОХУДЕНИЕ БЕЗ ЗАПРЕТОВ
13.20, 19.20 ОПЕРАТИВНАЯ СТОЛИЦА
13.45 ЦЕНТР «ЛИК»
13.50, 5.35 «ТАЙНЫ ЗАТОНУВШИХ КОРАБЛЕЙ»
14.30 МОЛОДЕЖНАЯ ТРИБУНА
15.00 КРАСОТКА
15.15 ГОРОЖАНКА
15.45 ОТДЕЛ КАЧЕСТВА
16.00 ГОРОЖАНИН
16.45 НЕОТЛОЖНАЯ ПОМОЩЬ
16.55 ГЕРОЙ ГОРОДА
17.40, 22.25 МОСКВА-2008
18.05 ДЕНЬ ГОРОДА
18.50 КУ-КО-НЯ
19.05 НАРОДНЫЙ КОНТРОЛЬ
22.05 ЕСТЬ МНЕНИЕ
22.40 НОЧНОЙ РАЗГОВОР Зинаида Кириенко
23.30 НОЧНОЙ КАНАЛ
1.30 «НОВЫЙ ФРАНКЕНШТЕЙН»

ЗВЕЗДА

6.00 «МОЯ СТРАНА»
6.15, 19.30 НАСТОЯЩЕЕ ВРЕМЯ
6.30 МУЛЬТФИЛЬМЫ
7.00 ЗВЕЗДА ОНЛАЙН
9.00, 13.00, 16.00, 18.00, 22.00 НОВОСТИ
9.15 «ЗАВЕЩАНИЕ МАРКО РОТКО» Док. фильм из цикла «ТАЙНАЯ ИСТОРИЯ ИСКУССТВА»
10.00 «БАРМЕН ИЗ «ЗОЛОТОГО ЯКОРЯ». Фильм
11.25 «ЗИМНИЙ ВЕЧЕР В ГАГРАХ». Фильм
13.15 ВХОД ВОСПРЕЩЕН
13.45 ЗВЕЗДЫ ВООРУЖЕННЫХ СИЛ
14.20, 3.20 «ГОРОД ЗАЖИГАЕТ ОГНИ»
18.20, 1.55 Звезды экрана «А ВЫ ЛЮБИЛИ КОГДА-НИБУДЬ?»
18.30, 5.10 «СТАЛИНГРАД ВЫСТОЯЛ» Док. фильм из цикла «НЕИЗВЕСТНАЯ ВОЙНА»
19.45 Любимые фильмы без рекламы «ЕХАЛИ В ТРАМВАЕ ИЛЬФ И ПЕТРОВ»
20.00, 4.20 «ВИЗИТ К МИНОТАВРУ»
21.00 «КРЫЛЬЯ РОССИИ»
22.30 «ПОСЛЕДНИЙ БРОНЕПОЕЗД». 5-я серия
23.15 «ДЕТЕКТИВ МОНК»
0.10 БОЛЬШОЕ ЖЮРИ
0.55 «НОВЫЕ ТЕХНОЛОГИИ ВОЙНЫ»

ЧИТАЙТЕ В АПРЕЛЬСКОМ НОМЕРЕ «КИНО ПАРКА»

УТОЛИ НАШИ ПЕЧАЛИ, НАТАЛИ

Что мы знаем о Натали Портман? В 13 лет она сыграла у Люка Бессона девочку с фикусом. Еще она долго отказывалась от роли Лолиты, не желая «плодить пошлость на экране». Она вегетарианка и, возможно, лесбиянка... Но за линейкой журналистских штампов кроется немало тайн самой стильной брюнетки Голливуда, о которых мы все как-то забывали рассказать. Настало то самое время.

Verbal Aspect

Today we will discuss the topic of *aspect:* what aspect means and how it is central to understanding Russian verbs. Although English does not have a special grammatical category called aspect, you can still see aspect at work in English. We will use the following email from Kevin to his brother Steve to illustrate the concept of aspect through English verbs.

Dear Steve,

Have you ever been confronted by the police? You know me – I was the one who never broke curfew, saved my allowance for two and a half years to buy my first car, etc., etc. Well I've seen it all, now that I have been interrogated by a Moscow police office.

Picture this: I'm bombarded with questions from a policeman while a bunch of Russians claim that I'm a "hooligan." All my knowledge of Russian flew right out of the window as **I was standing** there in front of all these people accusing me of breaking into their apartment! Tanya's sister Olya is the one who got the place for me, and apparently whoever took her money (my money!) for the apartment was NOT the real owner. Living space is at such a premium here; they said that this happens all the time – can you believe that? People will rent out a place that doesn't belong to them. Amazing.

So I'm sitting here in the apartment, thinking I'm going to get thrown into some retro-Soviet prison and never be heard from again. Fortunately, I had Tanya's number and was able to catch her before she went out for the evening. **I called** and she came right down; she helped me clear things up with the family. They were really pretty cool about the whole thing, and I've ended up staying at their place.

Now on to more mundane topics. It really is a totally different world here. I don't know if it was my jet lag or the city itself, but the landscape seemed surreal on the drive from the airport to "my" apartment. When Tanya and I got to the apartment, she showed me where everything was. **I kept asking questions** because every little thing is so different here. **Have you ever made tea** with the loose tea leaves in a tiny little pot? Well, Russians do! The kitchen is not modern at all – no disposal in the sink and no microwave; what they call a sandwich is a single piece of bread with butter and some meat or cheese on it; and the bathroom is separated into two rooms – one for the shower and another for the john. But I'm actually getting used to it now that I've been here for a few days. I've even started taking off my shoes when I come into the apartment – I feel like I'm in Japan or something.

I've got to go now. Take it easy.

Kevin

1. Read through the highlighted verb phrases in the text one more time and assign each phrase to one of the following categories.

   A. An isolated event in the past (possibly remote) that has no direct bearing on the present situation

   B. An event that took place in the past on more than one occasion (possibly repeatedly)

   C. A one-time action that went for a while

   D. A single, complete event in the past that led to another action or a change in the situation – an event/action that made a difference

Congratulations – you have successfully completed your first analysis of aspect! Aspect is all about identifying *different types of action*. There are only two aspects in Russian: the **perfective** and the **imperfective**. The perfective aspect, illustrated in example D, expresses one very specific kind of action. The imperfective aspect, illustrated in examples A, B, and C, expresses all other kinds of action not covered by the perfective aspect.

The following chart illustrates the 3 features of an action that comprise aspect.

Action	Aspect	Examples
+ single + complete + of consequence	**Perfective aspect** Result Completion	Та́ня **написа́ла** письмо́. Вот оно́.
- single + complete + of consequence	**Imperfective aspect** Repetition	Зимо́й Та́ня ча́сто **писа́ла** пи́сьма Да́ше.
+ single - complete + of consequence	**Imperfective aspect** Process	Та́ня до́лго **писа́ла** письмо́.
+ single + complete - of consequence	**Imperfective aspect** Statement of fact	Да́ша **писа́ла** Та́не. А Та́ня **писа́ла** Да́ше?

Most imperfective verbs have perfective counterparts. These pairs of verbs are called "aspectual pairs". Often aspectual pairs look very similar; in some rare cases they look completely different. Examine the list of aspectual pairs below and comment on the similarities between the imperfective forms and their perfective counterparts.

IMPERFECTIVE	PERFECTIVE
писа́ть (писа̌-)	написа́ть (написа̌-)
звони́ть (звони́-)	позвони́ть (позвони́-)
обе́дать (обе́дай-)	пообе́дать (пообе́дай-)
слу́шать (слу́шай-)	послу́шать (послу́шай-)
смотре́ть (смотре̌-)	посмотре́ть (посмотре̌-)
чита́ть (чита́й-)	прочита́ть (прочита́й-)
де́лать (де́лай-)	сде́лать (сде́лай-)
гото́вить (гото́ви-)	приготовить (пригото́ви-)
отвеча́ть (отвеча́й-)	отве́тить (отве́ти-)
реша́ть (реша́й-)	реши́ть (реши́-)
покупа́ть (покупа́й-)	купи́ть (купи̌-)
помога́ть (помога́й-)	помо́чь (irreg.)
говори́ть (говори́-)	сказа́ть (сказа̌-)

All of the verbs you have learned so far have been *imperfective* verbs. From now on you will learn verbs in *pairs*, with the imperfective verb listed first.

2. Fill in the blanks with a verb in the past tense. Identify the contextual clues which indicate repetition, process, or result.

A. Repetition

Ка́ждую неде́лю Та́ня **смотре́ла** фи́льмы.

1. Ка́ждый де́нь Ва́ня ___*delal gelaen*___ (де́лай-/сде́лай-) матема́тику.

2. Та́ня и Ми́ша ча́сто ___*govorili*___ (говори́-/сказа̌-) о ветерина́рной кли́нике.

3. Та́ня ре́дко ___*pokupala*___ (покупа́й-/купи̌-) проду́кты.

4. Серге́й иногда́ ___*zvonit*___ (звони́-/позвони́-) Та́не.

5. Ра́ньше Та́ня и Ле́на всегда́ ___*obedali*___ (обе́дай-/пообе́дай-) в институ́тской столо́вой.

6. В Аме́рике Ке́вин _____ слу́шай-/послу́шай-) но́вости ка́ждое у́тро.

7. Ви́ктор Степа́нович обы́чно _____ (гото́ви-/пригото́ви-) за́втрак.

Adverbs **всегда́, иногда́, ча́сто, ре́дко, обы́чно** and time expressions like **ка́ждую неде́лю** indicate *repetition* and require an *imperfective* verb.

проду́кты (pl. only) = groceries

обы́чно = usually

B. Process

дóлго = for a long time

> В пя́тницу Та́ня до́лго **писа́ла** курсову́ю рабо́ту.

Adverbs like **до́лго** indicate process and also require an *imperfective* verb.

1. Да́ша до́лго _____ (писӑ-/написӑ-) письмо́ Та́не.
2. Вчера́ Та́ня до́лго _____ (чита́й-/прочита́й-) письмо́ Да́ши.
3. Вчера́ А́нна Бори́совна до́лго _____ (смотрӗ-/посмотрӗ-) телеви́зор.
4. Ле́на до́лго _____ (де́лай-/сде́лай) упражне́ние.
5. Ва́ня до́лго _____ (реша́й-/реши́-) зада́чу.
6. Серге́й сиде́л до́ма и до́лго _____ (слу́шай-/послу́шай-) му́зыку.

C. Result

> 3
> — Ты **купила** но́вые кроссо́вки?
> 1   1   1
> — Да, **купила**. Вот они́.

1. — Ты _прочитал_ (чита́й-/прочита́й-) мой журна́л?
   — Да, _прочитал_ (чита́й-/прочита́й-). Вот он.
2. — Ты _решил_ (реша́й-/реши́-) вчера́ зада́чу?
   — Да, _решил_ (реша́й-/реши́-). Отве́т – 10.

зада́ча = as-signment, problem

3. — Ты ~~написал~~ Написал (писӑ-/написӑ-) письмо́ де́душке?
   — Да, _Написал_ (писӑ-/написӑ-). Вот оно́.

отве́т = answer

4. — Ты вчера́ _купил_ (покупа́й-/купи́-) но́вую су́мку?
   — Нет, не _покупал_ (покупа́й/купи́-).
5. — Твои́ роди́тели ~~купили~~ купи́ли (покупа́й-/купи́-) тебе́ но́вый компью́тер?
   — Да, ~~купи́л~~ купи́ли (покупа́й-/купи́-). Вот он. Хо́чешь посмотре́ть?

3. A. Comment on the use of aspect in the following phone conversation between Та́ня and Ле́на.

Ле́на: — Алло! Э́то ты, Та́ня? [2] [3]

Та́ня: — Да, привет, Ле́на! Как дела? [1] [2] [2]

Ле́на: — Нормально. Что ты **делаешь?** [1] [2]

Та́ня: — **Пишу́** курсову́ю рабо́ту. [1]

Ле́на: — Правда? Не мо́жет быть! А я её уже́ **написа́ла.** [3] [2] [1]

Та́ня: — Когда? [2]

Ле́на: — В четве́рг ве́чером. [1]

Та́ня: — А ты долго её писа́ла? [3]

Ле́на: — Да, о́чень до́лго. [1] [2]

B. Using the previous conversation as a model, call one of your classmates and find out if s/he has already completed the work assigned by your professor.

> реша́ть зада́чу, чита́ть статью́, писа́ть рабо́ту, де́лать упражне́ния

4. Rewrite the following sentences using the word **ча́сто,** changing the aspect of the verb as needed.

> Да́ша <u>написа́ла</u> письмо́ Та́не. (perfective) →
> Она́ **ча́сто** <u>пи́шет</u> пи́сьма Та́не (imperfective)

1. Ви́ктор Петро́вич <u>прочита́л</u> статью́ о би́знесе.
2. Ва́ня <u>реши́л</u> тру́дную зада́чу.
3. Ле́на <u>написа́ла</u> хоро́ший докла́д.
4. А́нна Бори́совна <u>купи́ла</u> интере́сную кни́гу.

5. Ке́вин <u>посмотре́л</u> но́вый фи́льм.

6. Гали́на Ива́новна <u>пригото́вила</u> вку́сный обе́д.

5. You and your friend have been invited to a wedding. Discuss your ideas for a wedding gift.

>   2
> — Како́й подарок ты хо́чешь купи́ть Джо́ну и А́нне?
>   1   4
> — Я хочу́ купи́ть им **краси́вые ложки.** А ты?
>   1
> — А я хочу́ купи́ть им **лампу.**

plates, cups, spoons, forks, knives, picture, lamp, teakettle

Today you are going to watch the first two mini-episodes of the video: «Краси́вые ве́щи» and «Познако́мьтесь, пожа́луйста!»

1. Are the following statements about the video true or false? Это так и́ли нет? Correct all false statements according to the model.

> Ми́ша хоте́л купи́ть Та́не **карти́ну.** →
>
> Нет. Он хоте́л купи́ть ей **браслет.**

	Да	Нет
Ми́ша хоте́л купи́ть Та́не рюкза́к.	☐	☐
Та́ня купи́ла Ми́ше кроссо́вки.	☐	☐
Ми́ша купи́л Та́не шарф.	☐	☐
Та́ня лю́бит брасле́ты.	☐	☐
Ке́вин купи́л ка́рту и откры́тки.	☐	☐
Та́ня хоте́ла обе́дать.	☐	☐

> ка́рта = map
> откры́тка = postcard

Here are some new words and expressions you will hear today.
тебе́ нра́вится/нра́вятся = do you like

Тебе́ нра́вится **Москва́**?
Do you like Moscow?
(lit.: Is **Moscow** pleasing *to you*?)

Тебе́ нра́вятся **ру́сские сувени́ры**?
Do you like Russian souvenirs?
(lit.: Are **Russian souvenirs** pleasing *to you*?)

The *person doing the liking* goes in the *dative case*; **who or what the person likes** goes in the **nominative**.

2. Using the verb **нра́виться,** name things or characteristics from the video that you like or don't like.

> Мне нра́вятся **друзья́ Та́ни**.
>
> Мне не нра́вится **Шереме́тьево**.

[
кварти́ра Ке́вина, соба́ка Та́ни, Большо́й теа́тр, роди́тели Та́ни, маши́на Серге́я, эпизо́д в мили́ции, Изма́йлово, чёрное пла́тье Та́ни, хозя́ева Ке́вина, карти́ны на вы́ставке.
]

3. A. Why does Ми́ша show Та́ня a bracelet?

☐ It's identical to the one she has.

☐ He would like to buy it for her.

☐ He wants her opinion on how much it's worth.

B. Та́ня makes it clear that she:
- ☐ would love to have the bracelet
- ☐ hates bracelets
- ☐ will not accept presents from Ми́ша

C. Why is Та́ня reluctant to accept the silk scarf?

до́рого = expensive

- ☐ О́чень до́рого.
- ☐ Ша́рфы не в мо́де.
- ☐ Она́ не лю́бит кра́сный цвет.

D. Ми́ша dismisses Та́ня's reservations by saying:

ерунда́ = (here) nonsense

- ☐ Ерунда́!
- ☐ Пра́вда?
- ☐ Что ты!

E. Ми́ша asks Та́ня if she likes the scarf: «**Он тебе́ нра́вится?**» How does she reply?
- ☐ Да, о́чень.
- ☐ Нет, не о́чень.
- ☐ Не нра́вится.

VIEWING ▷

4. A. Which of the following does Ке́вин not mention in response to Та́ня's question, «**Что ты тут де́лаешь?**»
- ☐ Гуля́ю.
- ☐ Фотографи́рую.
- ☐ Покупа́ю сувени́ры.
- ☐ Отдыха́ю.

B. Ми́ша asks Ке́вин if he likes it in Moscow: «**Вам нра́вится в Москве́?**» What is Ке́вин's reply?
- ☐ Коне́чно! Тут де́вушки краси́вые.
- ☐ Да, здесь о́чень краси́во.
- ☐ Да, Москва́ о́чень краси́вый го́род.

5. In this episode, Ми́ша finally gets to meet Ке́вин.

Та́ня: — Познако́мьтесь, пожа́луйста. Вот э́то Ке́вин. А э́то мой друг Ми́ша.

Using the previous sentence as a model, introduce Ми́ша and Та́ня to your sister, brother, mother, and father.

6. Express your interest in an item and ask the salesperson if it is expensive.

> — Кака́я интере́сная маши́на! Дорого?
>   (2)   (3)
> — Нет, что вы! О́чень дёшево.
>   (2)   (2)   (1)

дёшево = cheap

> ма́ленький компью́тер, большо́й нож, краси́вая
> соба́ка, интере́сные сувени́ры, ста́рые кни́ги

7. Respond to your partner's questions using the phrase **ерунда́**.

POSTviewing

> — Ты слушал(а) гру́ппу «Спайс Гёрлз»?
>   (3)
> — Да.
>   (1)
> — Ну, и как?
>   (2)
> — Ерунда.
>   (1)

ерунда́ = (here) "It's nothing special".

1. Ты обе́дал(а) в но́вом рестора́не?
2. Ты смотре́л(а) переда́чу «Дэ́йли Ньюз»?
3. Ты был(а́) в университе́тском теа́тре?
4. Ты чита́л(а) сего́дня ко́миксы?

Possessive Pronouns and Adjectives: Dative Case

Nominative	мой но́вый друг	моя́ но́вая подру́га
Dative	мое**му́** но́в**ому** дру́гу	мо**е́й** но́в**ой** подру́ге

8. Supply continuations to the following sentences.

> Я говори́л(а) мое́й подру́ге **о Та́не и Ке́вине.**

1. Я купи́л(а) ка́рты Аме́рики _____
   мой ру́сский друг

2. Я прочита́л(а) письмо́ ма́мы _____
   моя́ подру́га

3. Я написа́л(а) запи́ску _____
   наш сосе́д

4. Мы помогли́ _____
   ва́ша но́вая студе́нтка

5. Я вчера́ позвони́л(а) _____
   твой брат

6. Мы пригото́вили суп▲ _____
   на́ша ба́бушка

запи́ска = note

> Ке́вину нра́**вится** его́ но́вая кварти́ра.
> Та́не нра́**вится** зелёный шарф.
> Ми́ше нра́**вятся** соба́ки и ко́шки.

9. Make statements about what the following people like.

> Ке́вин (ру́сские сувени́ры) →
> **Ке́вину** нра́вятся **ру́сские сувени́ры.**

▲ Soup is an obligatory component of the average Russian's daily diet. They consider it very healthy and nutritious food. The majority of people (especially children under pressure from their parents) eat soup every day.

Táня (америкáнские фи́льмы), Вáня (англи́йский язы́к), Ми́ша (но́вая ветерина́рная кли́ника), Лéна (Сáша), Сáша (собáка Тáни), Сергéй (его́ но́вая маши́на), Дáша (америкáнские дискотéки), моя́ сосéдка (нáша ко́шка), мой друг (ру́сские писáтели)

Вáне нрáвится читáть по-англи́йски.
Ему́ не нрáвится решáть задáчи.

10. What kinds of things do you enjoy doing **in your free time**? What <u>don't</u> you like to do? Discuss these questions with your partner.

— Мне нрáвится **смотрéть телесериалы.** [1]

— Не мо́жет быть! А мне нрáвится **читáть комиксы.** [2] [1]

— Прáвда? Здо́рово! [3] [2]

— Мне не нрáвится **рабóтать вéчером.** [1]

— А мне не нрáвится **жить в общежи́тии.** [1]

гото́вить, дéлать тру́дные упражнéния, смотрéть но́вые фи́льмы, переводи́ть дли́нные ру́сские тéксты, покупáть но́вые вéщи, писáть доклáды, игрáть на гитáре, слу́шать му́зыку, гуля́ть на кáмпусе, обéдать в университéтской столо́вой, читáть газéту, покупáть проду́кты, покупáть одéжду

When Ми́ша asks Ке́вин whether he likes Moscow, Ке́вин comments on how nice Muscovites are:

Ке́вин: — Лю́ди здесь о́чень симпати́чные.
Ми́ша: — **Лю́ди как лю́ди.**

"They're just ordinary people", Ми́ша responds. This response indicates reservation about a particular subject, and can only be used with nouns.

11. You are at a fast food restaurant with a Russian friend who is a fast food fanatic. Express your reservations about his/her comments on the delicious food there.

> — Ой, кака́я вку́сная **кури́ца!**
> — **Ку́рица** как **кури́ца.**

[га́мбургер, сала́т, чи́збургер, конфе́ты, шокола́д, моро́женое, бутербро́ды, пи́цца]

12. Что тебе́ нра́вится?

A. Your friend has dragged you along for a back-to-school shopping trip. Exchange opinions about the different things you see in the store.

> — Тебе́ нравится **э́тот рюкза́к?**
> — Да, о́чень. А тебе́?
> — И мне нра́вится./ А мне не нравится.
> — Тебе́ нравятся **э́ти кроссо́вки?**
> — Нет, не о́чень.
> — И мне не нра́вятся./ А мне нра́вятся.

B. You are in a store with your mother, who has some very strange ideas about fashion. Disagree with her statements about the items you see.

мáма: — Ой, какáя красотá!

вы: — Тебé нрáвится **эта куртка?**

мáма: — Да, очень. А тебé?

вы: — **Кýртка** как **куртка.**

мáма: — Ой, **какие симпатичные кроссовки!**

Вы: — Да ну, ерунда!

мáма: — А мне **они** нравятся.

Какáя красотá! = Как красиво!

красотá = beauty

bag, postcards, pens, jacket, raincoat, pants, jeans, t-shirt, bracelet, picture, souvenirs, pins, shoes, backpack, poster

—Приве́т, Ва́ня!

—Приве́т, Ната́ша! Что ты сего́дня **бу́дешь де́лать?**

—**Я бу́ду смотре́ть** фильм. А ты?

—А я **бу́ду де́лать** уро́ки.

Imperfective Aspect

Past	Present	Future
Я **писа́ла** письмо́.	Я **пишу́** письмо́.	Я **бу́ду писа́ть** письмо́.

Future Imperfective

я	бу́ду	
ты	бу́дешь	
он/она́	бу́дет	
мы	бу́дем	} писа́ть
вы	бу́дете	
они́	бу́дут	

1. Что бу́дут де́лать на́ши геро́и ве́чером в понеде́льник? Use the future imperfective in your answers.

Та́ня **бу́дет писа́ть** письмо́ Да́ше.

Ке́вин, Ми́ша, Ва́ня, Ле́на, А́нна Бори́совна

чита́ть статью́, реша́ть зада́чу, покупа́ть пода́рки, смотре́ть телеви́зор, фотографи́ровать, гото́вить обе́д

Perfective Aspect

Past	Present	Future
Я **написа́ла** письмо́.	—	Я **напишу́** письмо́.

Future Perfective

я	напишу́
ты	напи́ш**ешь**
он/она́	напи́ш**ет**
мы	напи́ш**ем**
вы	напи́ш**ете**
они́	напи́ш**ут**

Imperfective stem + present tense endings → *present imperfective*

Perfective stem + present tense endings → *future perfective*

2. Complete the following dialogs using the future perfective.

> 3
> — Ты сказала па́пе об экза́мене?
> 1   1   1
> — Нет, не сказала, **скажу́** завтра.

1. — Ты пригото́вил обе́д?

   — Нет, не пригото́вил, _____ ве́чером.

2. — Вы позвони́ли Та́не?

   — Нет, не позвони́ла, _____ у́тром.

3. — Ва́ня, ты реши́л зада́чу?

   — Нет, не реши́л, _____ за́втра.

4. — Твои́ роди́тели купи́ли соба́ку?

   — Нет, не купи́ли, _____ в суббо́ту.

5. — Та́ня написа́ла письмо́ Да́ше?

   — Нет, не написа́ла, _____ в воскресе́нье.

6. — Ты пообе́дал?

   — Нет, не пообе́дал, _____ ве́чером.

7. — Да́ша перевела́ статью́?

   — Нет, не перевела́, _____ в сре́ду.

8. — Ви́ктор Петро́вич, вы прочита́ли статью́?

   — Нет, не прочита́л, _____ в понеде́льник.

перевести́ (перевёд-́)

Future Tense		Past Tense	
я	переведу́	он	перевёл
ты	переведёшь	она́	перевела́
он/она́	переведёт	они́	перевели́
мы	переведём		
вы	переведёте		
они́	переведу́т		

переводи́ть
(переводи̭-)/
перевести́
   (перевёд-́)
= translate

3. Make up sentences that describe when these people are going to complete their actions using the words in the columns.

Ми́ша прочита́ет статью́ за́втра ве́чером.

Ми́ша	написа́ть письмо́	за́втра ве́чером
Ке́вин	пригото́вить обе́д	в понеде́льник
Ва́ня	прочита́ть статью́	во вто́рник
Та́ня	перевести́ текст	в сре́ду
Ле́на	купи́ть пода́рок	в четве́рг
Са́ша	реши́ть зада́чу	в пя́тницу
А́нна Бори́совна	сде́лать упражне́ние	в суббо́ту

4. A. Find out what your partner will be doing after the following events.

по́сле = after

по́сле концерта = after the concert

Note that the preposition **по́сле** takes the genitive case.

> 2
> — Что ты бу́дешь делать **по́сле конце́рта?**
>
> 1
> — **По́сле конце́рта** я бу́ду ужинать.

> ле́кция, семина́р, обе́д, у́жин, экза́мен, собра́ние, дискоте́ка

> обе́дать, у́жинать, отдыха́ть, покупа́ть проду́кты, смотре́ть телеви́зор, чита́ть газе́ту

B. Procrastinate! Tell your partner that you will do whatever s/he wants you both to do after another event.

> 2
> — Когда́ мы бу́дем **обедать?**
>
> 1
> — Мы бу́дем обе́дать **по́сле концерта.**

5. What do you think each of the three characters will do after their lunch together?

> ³
> Я думаю, после обеда в кафе **Кевин будет покупать**
> ¹ ⁴
> **продукты.** А ты, как думаешь?

— Лена, что ты делала вчера вечером?	"Lena, what did you do last night?"
— **Покупала** подарок.	"I was shopping for a present."
— Ну, и как, **купила?**	"So, did you buy anything?"
— Нет, не купила.	"No, I didn't."

In the first question, the speaker asks Лена what she did last night: what *activity* she was engaged in. Лена answers using the imperfective aspect. (**Покупала** подарок.) Once the speaker is armed with this information, s/he then is able to ask Лена if the activity (shopping) produced a *result* (the purchase of a present). (Ну, и как, **купила?**)

---

6. Complete the following dialogs.

> ²
> — Что ты делал(а) вчера вечером?
> ¹
> — Покупал(а) подарок.
> ² ³
> — Ну, и как, **купил(а)?**
> ¹ ¹ ¹ ¹
> — **Да, купил(а)./ Нет, не купил(а).**

1. — Что ты делал(а) вчера утром?

   — Переводил(а) статью.

   — Ну, и как, _____?

   — _____.

2. — Что ты де́лал(а) вчера́ у́тром?
   — Писа́л(а) письмо́.

   — Ну, и как, _____?

   — _____.

3. — Что ты де́лал(а) вчера́ ве́чером?
   — Реша́л(а) зада́чу.

   — Ну, и как, _____?

   — _____.

4. — Что ты де́лал(а) вчера́ ве́чером?
   — Чита́л(а) кни́гу.

   — Ну, и как, _____?

   — _____.

5. — Что ты де́лал(а) вчера́ ве́чером?
   — Покупа́л(а) телеви́зор.

   — Ну, и как, _____?

   — _____.

6. — Что ты де́лал(а) вчера́ ве́чером?
   — Переводи́л(а) текст.

   — Ну, и как, _____?

   — _____.

[
покупа́ть/купи́ть, переводи́ть/перевести́, писа́ть/
написа́ть, реша́ть/реши́ть, чита́ть/прочита́ть
]

7. Find out what your partner did on different days last week and
whether s/he completed it.

есть/съесть
(irreg.) = eat

есть

Present Tense				Past Tense	
я	ем	мы	еди́м	он	ел
ты	ешь	вы	еди́те	она́	е́ла
он/она́	ест	они́	едя́т	они́	е́ли

пить/вы́пить
= drink

пить

Present Tense				Past Tense	
я	пью	мы	пьём	он	пил
ты	пьёшь	вы	пьёте	она́	пила́
он/она́	пьёт	они́	пьют	оно́	пи́ло
				они́	пи́ли

8. Practicing pronunciation

Я пью. Я пью молоко́.

Ты пьёшь. Ты пьёшь во́ду.

Он пьёт. Он пьёт сок.

Она́ пьёт. Она́ пьёт чай.

Мы пьём. Мы пьём ко́фе.

Вы пьёте. Вы пьёте вино́.

Они́ пьют. Они́ пьют ко́ка-ко́лу.

> Ми́ша **ест** мя́со ка́ждый день.
> Та́ня ре́дко **ест** мя́со.

9. А. А что еди́те вы? Вы ча́сто еди́те мя́со?

> — Что ты ешь? Ты часто ешь **мя́со?**
>   2   3
> — Я ем **мя́со** ка́ждую неде́лю.
>   1

мя́со, ры́ба, карто́шка, суп, сала́т, хлеб, сыр, колбаса́

> Ке́вин обы́чно **пьёт** во́ду.
> Ми́ша и Та́ня ча́сто **пьют** ко́ка-ко́лу.

В. А что вы обы́чно пьёте? Что вы ре́дко пьёте?

> — Я ча́сто пью **молоко́**. А ты?
>   1   4
> — И я ча́сто./А я ре́дко.
>   1   1

вино́, пи́во, вода́, спрайт, молоко́, чай, ко́фе, ко́ка-ко́ла, сок

С. Что вы е́ли и пи́ли сего́дня у́тром? А что вы е́ли и пи́ли вчера́ ве́чером?

> — Что ты е́л(а) и пил(а́) сего́дня у́тром?
>   2
> — Сего́дня у́тром я е́л(а) **бутербро́д** и пил(а́) **ко́фе**.
>   3   1

хлеб, ма́сло, сыр, колбаса́, икра́, помидо́р, огуре́ц, сала́т, суп, борщ, мя́со, карто́шка, макаро́ны, жа́реная ку́рица, бефстро́ганов, бифште́кс, моро́женое, бана́н

вода́, спрайт, молоко́, чай, ко́фе, ко́ка-ко́ла, сок, бе́лое вино́, кра́сное вино́, пи́во

10. Где вы бу́дете в суббо́ту? А в воскресе́нье?

Find out where your partner is planning to be over the weekend.

> ² — Где ты бу́дешь в суббо́ту?
> ¹   ⁴
> — Я бу́ду **на даче.**▲ А ты?
> ¹
> — А я бу́ду **дома.**

11. Что вы бу́дете де́лать за́втра?

Find out your partner's plans for tomorrow.

> ² — Что ты бу́дешь де́лать за́втра?
> ¹   ⁴
> — Я бу́ду **рабо́тать.** А ты?
> ¹   ¹
> — И я бу́ду **рабо́тать.**/ А я бу́ду **гото́вить обе́д.**

▲ A **да́ча** is a summer house, usually located from thirty minutes to two hours drive from the city. Owners go there for weekends and summer vacations. Most people not only relax there, but also plant vegetable gardens, and grow tomatoes, cucumbers, squash, parsley, dill, potatoes, strawberries, etc. Frequently children stay at the **да́ча** for the whole summer, provided they have someone (their **ба́бушка**, for example) to stay with them.

БЛИНЫ́▲

ПЕЛЬМÉНИ▲▲

ЩИ▲▲▲

▲ **Блины́** were a major dish at pagan Slavs' holidays, associated with the beginning of spring. They were baked round and yellow to symbolize the sun. Later, the Russian Orthodox Church incorporated pagan holidays into its calendar, so **блины́** has survived as a special dish at certain celebrations and as a type of everyday food. They are served with herring, salmon, caviar, sour cream, butter, jams, honey, and almost anything else you can think of.

▲▲ **Пельмéни** is one of the most popular Russian dishes. They resemble either dumplings or ravioli with meat. **Пельмéни** originated in Siberia (the word in one of the Siberian dialects means "bread ear") where they were cooked in huge numbers and frozen to last a long time. It takes about five minutes to boil them to perfection. **Пельмéни** are traditionally served with sour cream, butter, vinegar, or mustard.

▲▲▲ **Щи** is a traditional Russian cabbage soup. It can be made with fresh cabbage or sauerkraut with the addition of carrots, onions, parsley, and sometimes potatoes and tomatoes. **Щи** can be vegetarian or made with meat or mushroom broth and is served with sour cream and chopped dill and parsley.

1. After running into each other at the торго́вый центр, Ке́вин, Та́ня, and Ми́ша go and get a bite to eat.

PREviewing

A. A typical Russian menu lists food according to the following categories:

холо́дные заку́ски (appetizers) _фру́кты_
сала́т

пе́рвые блю́да (soups; lit. _борщ_
"first courses") _щи_

вторы́е блю́да (entrees; lit. _пи́цца_
"second courses") _спаге́тти_

десе́рты (desserts) _моро́женое_
экле́р

напи́тки (beverages) _во́дка_
~~Вод~~ _Вода́_

Can you guess in which categories the following food and drinks would be listed?

[
~~борщ~~, пи́цца, га́мбургер, фру́кты, шокола́д,
щи, ~~моро́женое~~, экле́р, пельме́ни, шампа́нское,
помидо́ры, во́дка, апельси́ны, пи́во, вино́,
минера́льная вода́, котле́ты, ~~спаге́тти~~, плов,
наполео́н, сала́т, блины́
]

B. Translate the following list of words associated with eating out into Russian.

_____

_____

_____

restaurant, café, menu, waiter, waitress, to order, fork, knife▲, spoon, cup, plate, delicious, breakfast, lunch, dinner, cuisine

VIEWING

2. **A.** Why does Кéвин give the menu to Тáня?

☐ He doesn't have his glasses.

☑ He can't read Russian well.

☒ He doesn't know much about Russian cuisine.

B. The first dish Тáня recommends is **холóдный борщ.** What kind of dish is this?

холóдный = cold

☑ суп

☐ закýска

☐ вторóе блю́до

3. **A.** How does Мúша summon the waitress?

☐ Официáнтку, пожáлуйста!

☑ Мóжно вас?

☐ Мы хотúм есть!

B. How does she respond?

☐ Что вы хотúте?

☑ Слýшаю вас.

☐ Что вы бýдете?

C. Match the name of the character with what s/he orders.

Кéвин — рыба
Тáня — кýрица
Мúша — бифштéкс

Кéвин — бéлое винó
Тáня — водá
Мúша — сок

▲ In Russia, it is considered proper etiquette to use both a fork and a knife while eating, even if the food is soft enough to be eaten with just a fork. It is considered bad manners to put your hands under the table during a meal; and, naturally, no elbows on the table!

D. Although each character orders a different entrée and drink, they all agree on dessert! Write down what they order for dessert.

ice cream

4. Are the following statements about the video true or false? Это так и́ли нет?

	Да	Нет
1. The conversation at lunch centers around politics.	☐	☑
2. Ми́ша wants to start his own veterinary business.	☑	☐
3. Ке́вин's sister is a businesswoman.	☑	☐
4. Her company is called "Birds of a Feather".	☐	☑
5. Ке́вин promises to contact his sister about the possibility of doing business with Ми́ша.	☑	☐

5. A. What toast does Ми́ша propose?

☐ За Ке́вина!

☐ За нас!

☑ За на́ше знако́мство!

What is the English equivalent for this toast?

_To_

B. The title of this episode is a toast, «**За на́ше бу́дущее!**» Which character proposes this toast? How would you express this toast in English?

_____

_____

6. It looks like Ке́вин and Ми́ша are quickly becoming friends. Which of the following statements about their conversation supports this conclusion?

☐ They address each other using **ты**.

☐ Ми́ша says that he wants to be friends.

☐ Ке́вин tells Ми́ша that he is a great guy.

To order food in Russian you need to read your menu carefully and use the following expression:

я бу́ду + the accusative form of the desired dish or drink.

As you can see, the verbs **есть** and **пить** can be omitted.

7. A. You are having dinner at the café shown in the video. Using the menu on the following page as a reference, discuss what you are going to order.

>   2   1
> — Ну, что мы бу́дем есть? Я бу́ду **ку́рицу.**
>   1   1
> — А мне не нра́вится **ку́рица.** Я бу́ду **бифште́кс.**
>   2
> А что бу́дем пить?
>   1
> — Я бу́ду **кра́сное вино́.**
>   1   3
> — А я бу́ду **ко́ка-ко́лу.** А десе́рт бу́дешь?
>   2   1
> — Спаси́бо, не хочу́.

Меню

Салаты и закуски

Салат «Цезарь» лёгкий	182	220 р.
Салат "Цезарь" с куриной грудкой	230	255 р.
Салат "Цезарь" с сёмгой-гриль	226	265 р.
Салат «Греческий»	310	245 р.
Овощной салат микс с куриной печенью	185	245 р.
Селедочка с отварной картошечкой	50/70/13	70 р.

Блины и оладьи

Блинчики с грибами и сырным соусом	155/50	145 р.
Блинчики с мясом	210/50	155 р.
Блины с сёмгой	80/80/15	165 р.
Оладьи	126/30	75 р.

Первые блюда

Борщ	330/20/20/1	140 р.
Суп из белых грибов	350/20/20/1	130 р.
Лапша куриная	350/20/1	120 р.
Пельмени с куриным бульоном	25 шт./120/20/1	145 р.
Суп грибной	300	150 р.
Суп из морепродуктов	300/20/1 шт.	190 р.

Горячие блюда

Котлеты мясные с картофельным пюре	115/125/15	165 р.
Котлеты куриные с картофельным пюре	140/125/15	165 р.
Картошечка жареная с грибами	200/50/45	145 р.
Тушёная говяжья печень с картофельным пюре	140/200/25	180 р.
Рёбрышки свиные барбекю с картофелем фри	250/100/50	285 р.

Гарниры

Гречка	100	45 р.
Рис с овощами	100	45 р.
Капуста тушеная	150	45 р.
Картофель отварной	150	45 р.
Картофельное пюре	100	60 р.

Десерты

Штрудель яблочный	150/5/2	120 р.
Штрудель вишневый	110/5/2	115 р.
Торт шоколадный с хрустящим пралине	92/10/15	125 р.
Мороженое	130/20	95 р.

Горячие напитки

Кофе Эспрессо	60	65 р.
Кофе Капучино	150	120 р.
Кофе Американо	140	110 р.
Кофе Глиссе	230	120 р.
Чай чёрный	150/5	55 р.
Чай зеленый	150	55 р.

Безалкогольные напитки

Квас	250 / 500 / 1000	50 / 80 / 140 р.
Сок	250	75 р.
Свежевыжатый сок	250	150 р.
Молочный коктейль	200	90 р.
Пепси, Пепси Лайт, Миринда, Сэвен Ап, Тоник	600	80 р.
Холодный чай «Липтон»	600	90 р.
Минеральная вода «Аква Минерале»	600	75 р.
Минеральная вода «Эвиан»	330	110 р.

Вино красное

Столовое (Италия)	150	120 р.
«Шампрео» полусладкое (Франция)	150	145 р.
«Бержерак Руж» АОС (Франция)	150 / 750	160 / 710 р.
«Шато Кайе Бордо» АОС (Франция)	150 / 750	170 / 800 р.

Вино белое

Столовое (Италия)	150	120 р.
«Шампрео» полусладкое (Франция)	150 / 750	145 / 670 р.
«Бордо Шеваль Канкар» АОС (Франция)	150 / 750	160 / 745 р.

B. Now summon the waiter/waitress and order your meal.

— Мо́жно вас? [3]

— Слу́шаю вас. [1]

— Я бу́ду **ку́рицу.** [1]

— А я бу́ду **бифште́кс.** [1]

— Хорошо́, а что вы бу́дете пить? [1] [2]

— Я бу́ду **кра́сное вино́.** [1]

— А я бу́ду **ко́ка-ко́лу.** [1]

— А на десе́рт? [4]

— **Моро́женое,** пожа́луйста. [1]

C. After the meal arrives, propose a toast.

— За **на́ше знако́мство!** [2]

на́ше знако́мство, дру́жба, ты, мы

8. Да́ша is preparing an article that contrasts American and Russian eating habits for her university newspaper in Moscow. Compare Да́ша's survey; discuss your answers with your partner.

	за́втрак	обе́д	у́жин
Где вы еди́те?			
Где едя́т ва́ши роди́тели?			
Где ест ваш брат?			
Где ест ва́ша сестра́?			
Где едя́т ва́ши друзья́?			

> 　　　　　　　　　 1
> — Я ем за́втрак **дома.**
> 　　 1　　　　　　　　　　　 1
> — И я ем за́втрак **до́ма.**/ А я ем за́втрак
> 　　　　　　　　 1
> **в университете.**

9. You are an exchange student from Russia and have returned home from the university with a stomachache. Your Russian host mom is anxious to discover the culprit; she knows you had breakfast at home, so she asks you what you ate for lunch and dinner.

на обе́д = for lunch

на у́жин = for dinner

> 　　　　　　　　　　　 2
> — Что ты е́л(а) на обед?
> 　　　　　　　 1
> — На обе́д я е́л(а) **пиццу.**
> 　 3　　　　 2　　　　　　　　　　　　　 2
> — **Пиццу?** Ужасно! А что ты е́л(а) на ужин?
> 　　　　　　　　　 1
> — На у́жин я е́л(а) **суп.**
> 　　　　 1
> — Хорошо.

> пи́цца, о́вощи, плов, спаге́тти, жа́реная ку́рица, борщ, га́мбургер, сала́т, суп, бефстро́ганов, ры́ба, торт

Ми́ша is delighted when he discovers that Ке́вин's sister is the director of the pet food company «**Кот и пёс**». He offers to help her company establish contacts in Moscow:

«Мы мо́жем им **помо́чь**».

"We can help them." **Помо́чь,** the perfective form of помога́ть, is an irregular verb.

помо́чь

Present Tense				Past Tense	
я	помогу́	мы	помо́жем	он	помо́г
ты	помо́жешь	вы	помо́жете	она́	помогла́
он/она́	помо́жет	они́	помо́гут	оно́	помогло́
				они́	помогли́

10. Complete the following dialogs by filling in the appropriate form of the verb помо́чь.

> — Я пло́хо чита́ю по-английски. Ты не **помо́жешь?**
> — Обяза́тельно **помогу́.**

обяза́тельно = certainly, definitely

1. — Мой брат пло́хо понима́ет матема́тику, а за́втра экза́мен. Вы не _____?

   — Обяза́тельно _____.

2. — Та́ня о́чень пло́хо гото́вит. А́нна Бори́совна не _____?

   — Обяза́тельно _____.

3. — Ке́вин не понима́ет меню́. Та́ня и Ми́ша не _____?

   — Обяза́тельно _____.

4. — Сего́дня мы бу́дем покупа́ть проду́кты. Ты не _____?

   — Обяза́тельно _____.

5. — Ва́ня пи́шет письмо́ по-английски. Ке́вин не _____?

   — Обяза́тельно _____.

6. — Я перевожу́ о́чень дли́нный ру́сский текст.

   Ты не _____?

   — Обяза́тельно _____.

> Та́ня ча́сто звони́т **подру́гам**.
> Ке́вин ча́сто звони́т **роди́телям** в США.
> Ми́ша ча́сто звони́т **колле́гам ветерина́рам**.

колле́га (*m. or f.*) = colleague

Dative Plural

Nouns	Pronouns and Adjectives
-ам (-ям) инжене́рам подру́г**ам** общежи́ти**ям**	**-ым** (-им) на́**шим** ста́**рым** подру́гам мои́**м** но́**вым** друзья́м

11. Complete the following sentences using the dative plural.

> Ке́вин позвони́л **роди́телям**.

1. Та́ня купи́ла пода́рки _____.   подру́ги

2. Ми́ша говори́л о ветерина́рной кли́нике _____.   колле́ги

3. Гали́на Ива́новна говори́ла о Ке́вине _____.   сосе́ди

4. Ке́вин помо́г _____ прочита́ть англи́йскую статью́.   друзья́

5. Ва́ня говори́л _____ о семье́ Ке́вина.   роди́тели

12. A Russian sociologist doing research on eating habits is interviewing Americans in Moscow. Describe your family's eating habits.

> Мы ре́дко еди́м су́ши.
> Мы ча́сто еди́м спаге́тти.
> Мы всегда́ еди́м моро́женое.
> Мы иногда́ еди́м пи́ццу.
> Мы не еди́м га́мбургеры.

13. You are a nutritional advisor for Russian kindergartens. Ask kindergarten teachers what the children have been eating and give comments.

>   2
> — Что де́ти едя́т на первое?
>   1
> — На пе́рвое де́ти едя́т **суп.**
>   1   4
> — Хорошо. А на второе?
>   1
> — А на второ́е **пиццу.**
>   1   2
> — Плохо. А что де́ти едя́т на десерт?
>   1   3   1
> — **Фрукты – апельсины, бананы.**
>   2
> — Отли́чно!

borsch, salad, tomatoes, potatoes; sandwiches, steak, fish, chicken, omelet, hamburgers; candy, ice cream, chocolate

UNIT   Чте́ние

6

DAY 7

лáпа = paw

1. Answer the following questions based on the advertisement from the newspaper «**Четы́ре лáпы**» below.

A. Write down the Russian equivalents for the following terms in the nominative case.

stray ("homeless") animals _____

first shelter in Moscow _____

Fund for the Protection of Animals _____

Благотворительный фонд защиты животных «**БИМ**»▲	*Charity Fund for the Protection of Animals* **"BIM"**

Это – просьба о **ПОМОЩИ**, обращение в Вашему доброму сердцу, умению сострадать. Наша общая с Вами боль – это **БЕЗДОМНЫЕ ЖИВОТНЫЕ,** бессловесные скитальцы наших улиц. Мы, пытаясь помочь им, начали строительство **ПЕРВОГО** в Москве **ПРИЮТА** для бездомных животных на земле, переданной нам городом.
Нужны средства...

СПАСИБО.

Адрес: 121552 Москва, ул. Академика Павлова, 40-1-62. Тел.: (495) 249-63-55
Реквизиты: Р/с 700001 в филиале «Кутузовский», К/с 890641 в КБ «Российский Кредит», т. Москва К/с 103161900 в ЦРКЦ ГУ ЦБ РФ по МО код. уч. С3 МФО 211004
Текущий валютный счет: 000070 KTZ 012/001 в филиале «Кутузовский», к.с. 890141 в КБ «Российский кредит» г. Москва

живóтное = animal

прию́т = shelter

срéдства = (here) donations

B. The purpose of this advertisement is to:

☐ publicize an upcoming animal show

☐ get financial support for an animal shelter

☐ announce the opening of a new animal shelter in Moscow

Was this plea for donations successful? Read about the first veterinary center in Moscow in the following article, which appeared in «**Кот и пёс**».

▲ Many Russians recognize «**Бим**»as the title character of a book «**Бéлый Бим чёрное ýхо**» and a movie based on it. This very popular book, written by the Russian author **Троепóльский** (1905–1995), tells the story of a special bond between a man and his dog, **Бим,** a white spaniel with a black ear.

Пе́рвый в Москве́

Что де́лать, е́сли ваш симпати́чный котёнок потеря́л° аппети́т и да́же не хо́чет смотре́ть на еду°? Ваш энерги́чный пу́дель лежи́т и не хо́чет гуля́ть? Какаду́ ничего́ не говори́т, да́же когда́ его́ зову́т? Коро́че°, что де́лать, е́сли ва́ше люби́мое дома́шнее живо́тное° заболе́ло°? Нужна́ по́мощь ветерина́ра. И хоро́шего ветерина́ра!

has lost

food

in short

pet | has gotten sick

О́чень ско́ро в Москве́ бу́дет но́вый це́нтр, где специали́сты помо́гут ва́шему больно́му° дру́гу. Э́то бу́дет пе́рвый, уника́льный ветерина́рный центр в на́шем го́роде. Почему́ уника́льный? Об э́том я спроси́ла ме́неджера це́нтра Серге́я Па́вловича Самохва́лова. Вот, что он мне рассказа́л.

sick

Журнали́ст:	Чья э́то иде́я организова́ть в Москве́ тако́й ветерина́рный центр?
Самохва́лов:	В пе́рвый раз я услы́шал об э́той иде́е от моего́ дру́га, Михаи́ла Ко́това. Тогда́ я поду́мал, что э́то про́сто фанта́зия. Но Михаи́л так ве́рил°, что э́то реа́льно, что я то́же пове́рил. А пото́м пове́рили и други́е.

believed

Журнали́ст:	Кто рабо́тает в ва́шем но́вом коллекти́ве, и́ли, как тепе́рь говоря́т, в ва́шей кома́нде°?

team

Самохва́лов:	Мы все о́чень молоды́е. Наш сре́дний во́зраст° — 25 лет.

age

Журнали́ст:	Все говоря́т, что ваш центр уника́льный. Почему́?
Самохва́лов:	Понима́ете, ветерина́рные кли́ники бы́ли в на́шем го́роде и ра́ньше. Но наш но́вый центр – э́то большо́й ко́мплекс. Он бу́дет помога́ть всем живо́тным – и больны́м, и здоро́вым°. В ко́мплексе бу́дут ветерина́рная кли́ника, сало́н, магази́н, пансиона́т и прию́т.

healthy

Журнали́ст:	Ну, ветеринарна́я кли́ника – э́то я понима́ю. А каки́е фу́нкции бу́дут у сало́на?
Самохва́лов:	В сало́не бу́дут рабо́тать лу́чшие специали́сты – парикма́херы°. Там вы ку́пите шампу́нь, аэрозо́ль, крем и́ли лосьо́н для° ва́шей соба́ки и́ли ко́шки.

here: groomers

for

	Журнали́ст:	А что мо́жно бу́дет купи́ть в ва́шем магази́не?
canned food	Самохва́лов:	Во-пе́рвых, еду́, ра́зные консе́рвы◊. И, коне́чно, в магази́не бу́дут са́мые ра́зные витами́ны – ведь э́то о́чень ва́жный элеме́нт в дие́те ка́ждого дома́шнего живо́тного.
	Журнали́ст:	Четвёртый компоне́нт ва́шего це́нтра – пансиона́т. Расскажи́те, пожа́луйста, как он бу́дет рабо́тать.
cannot without	Самохва́лов:	Мне ча́сто звони́т мой прия́тель. Он гео́лог. Сего́дня он в Москве́, а за́втра во Владивосто́ке, и́ли на Байка́ле. А его́ бульдо́г, Арту́р▲, не мо́жет◊ жить оди́н. Ка́ждый раз мой прия́тель до́лжен реша́ть пробле́му, где Арту́р бу́дет жить без◊ него́. И мы реши́ли: организу́ем пансиона́т.
	Журнали́ст:	Вы сказа́ли, что в ва́шем це́нтре бу́дет прию́т. Расскажи́те о нём.
stray probably fate adopt | are afraid	Самохва́лов:	Вы когда́-нибу́дь ви́дели на у́лице бездо́мную◊ соба́ку и́ли ко́шку? Наве́рное◊, да. Вы ду́мали об их судьбе́◊? О́чень ча́сто москвичи́ хотя́т взять◊ таку́ю соба́ку и́ли ко́шку, но боя́тся◊. Мо́жет быть, она́ больна́я? В на́шем прию́те бу́дет специа́льное аге́нтство. Е́сли вы хоти́те взять соба́ку и́ли ко́шку, вы мо́жете позвони́ть в э́то аге́нтство. Мы бу́дем гаранти́ровать, что все на́ши живо́тные здоро́вы.
open	Журнали́ст:	И после́дний вопро́с. Когда́ вы плани́руете откры́ть◊ ваш центр?
advertisement	Самохва́лов:	В декабре́ и́ли в январе́, е́сли всё бу́дет норма́льно. Вот на́ша рекла́ма◊.
	Журнали́ст:	Отли́чно! Спаси́бо. До свида́ния.

Мари́на Умно́ва

▲ Many Russian dogs are given foreign-sounding names like **Бра́ун** or **Бест**. The use of Russian personal names for animals is avoided.

2. Scan the entire text for the following information.

A. What is the name of the piece?

☐ interview

☐ fiction

☐ essay

☐ review

B. Who takes part in the discussion?

☐ Сергей Павлович Самохвалов

☐ Марина Умнова

☐ Артур

☐ Бим

Write down their names and identify their line of work.

имя	профессия

C. What is the main topic of discussion?

☐ comprehensive animal care

☐ the housing shortage in Moscow

☐ the needs of veterinarians in Russia

☐ nutrition for pets

D. The title of this piece, «Первый в Москве», refers to the first:

☐ animal shelter

☐ pet store

☐ comprehensive veterinary clinic

3. Label the journalist's questions (A, B, C, …), then scan the text one question at a time to provide the necessary information.

A. The name Михаил Котов is mentioned because he is:

☐ the founder of the veterinary center

☐ Самохвалов's main competitor

☐ the person who came up with the idea to build a veterinary center

☐ a prominent proponent of animal rights

B. 25 years refers to:

☐ the average age of the center's employees

☐ the average life expectancy of pets in Russia

☐ the length of time it would take to make such a center self-supportive

☐ the amount of time it took to build the center

C. List the five components of the new center.

пе́рвый компоне́нт _____

второ́й компоне́нт _____

тре́тий компоне́нт _____

четвёртый компоне́нт _____

пя́тый компоне́нт _____

D. List four products you can buy at the **сало́н** in the veterinary center.

1. _____ 3. _____

2. _____ 4. _____

E. Canned food and vitamins are mentioned because they

☐ can be purchased in the center's store

☐ are hard to obtain in Russia

☐ will be produced on the premises

F. What is the best definition for the word «**пансиона́т**»?

☐ kennel

☐ grooming services

☐ animal shelter

☐ pet store

G. According to the manager, the «**прию́т**» component of the center is intended for:

☐ paying clients only

☐ all stray animals

☐ sick animals

☐ abused and abandoned pets

H. In what month will the center open?

В _____ и́ли в _____.

4. Scan the whole text one more time to find the following information.

A. Write down the adjectives used to describe the center.

_____

B. Самохва́лов mentions his friend's pet in the interview. Write down its breed and name.

_____

Продаются щенки родезийского риджбека. Привиты, приучены к туалету. Т. 740-6460, 364-8228, www.rodridg.ru

☐ таксы 392–23–94
☐ щенки кавказской овчарки, азиатской овчарок (4 месяца). Недорого. Солнечногорск. Т. 8–903–717–27–50
☐ щенки колли с хорошей родословной Т. 8–916–564–24–77
☐ щенки лабрадора. (495) 735–82–61

ПРОПАЛ ЙОРК-ТЕРЬЕР, МАЛЬЧИК. Золотисто-серый, стриженый, без ошейника, клеймо в паху ОХЕ и цифры. 6 лет. В районе: д. Дарьино, 2-е Рублево-Успенское, Можайское шоссе - 14.04.2008 г. Вознаграждение или щенок йорка. Т. 8-903-597-6985, 723-1915

5. You have come to Самохва́лов's new pet store to buy a dog. Although they don't have the breed of dog you would like, the salesperson recommends looking through the advertisements in the popular newspaper «Четы́ре ла́пы».

A. Write down the telephone numbers you would call if you wanted to buy the following dogs.

Dachshund _____

Labrador _____

Collie _____

Asian Shepherd _____

Rhodesian Ridgeback _____

Yorkshire Terrier _____

B. Talk about your plans and obtain the phone number from your partner.

> — Я хочу́ купи́ть соба́ку.
> — Пра́вда? А каку́ю?
> — Мне нра́вятся таксы.
> — Вот но́мер телефо́на: 360-40-40.

6. One partner plays a salesperson in the new veterinary center's pet store, while the other partner is a customer who wants to buy a dog. Begin your conversation using the following model.

у́мный = intelligent

до́брый = kind

> — Я хочу́ купи́ть соба́ку.
> — А каку́ю соба́ку вы хоти́те?
> — Симпати́чную, у́мную, до́брую…
> — Вот, познако́мьтесь, э́то Бра́ун.

Continue your conversation using questions for reference.

поро́да = breed

Salesperson: — Кого́ вы хоти́те купи́ть?

— Како́й поро́ды соба́ку вы хоти́те купи́ть?

— Вы хоти́те купи́ть большу́ю и́ли ма́ленькую соба́ку?

Customer: — Кака́я э́то поро́да?

— Что он (она́) ест? Она́ мно́го ест?

— Что он (она́) лю́бит? Что он (она́) не лю́бит?

— Что ему́ (ей) нра́вится? Что ему́ (ей) не нра́вится?

бульдо́г, та́кса, терье́р, ча́у-ча́у, пу́дель, ко́лли

вку́сная еда́, мя́со, колбаса́, моро́женое, специа́льная еда́, шокола́д, витами́ны, консе́рвы, фру́кты, бифште́кс

есть, спать, танцева́ть, игра́ть, гуля́ть

спать = sleep

2/2008
МАРТ

КОТ и ПЁС

PREviewing

кот = cat (male)

пёс = dog (male)

Final Review

Pictured here is **«Кот и пёс»,** a popular magazine for dog and cat lovers. Coincidentally, this is also the Russian translation of the name of the American pet food company "Cats and Dogs". As you watch the video, try to identify the importance of the company **«Кот и пёс».**

1. The title of this episode is **«За на́ше бу́дущее!»** What is Та́ня referring to when she makes this toast?

☐ her upcoming marriage to Ми́ша

☐ the proposed business partnership between Ми́ша and Ке́вин's sister

☐ Та́ня's plan to move to America

2. Discuss whether the following statements about this episode are true. Correct all false statements.

> — Э́то пра́вда, что Ке́вин купи́л шарф Та́не?
>   ³   ¹
> — Нет, что ты! Ми́ша купи́л шарф Та́не.
>   ²   ²   ²

1. В воскресе́нье Та́ня и Ми́ша гуля́ли.
2. Ми́ша хоте́л купи́ть пода́рок Та́не.
3. Та́ня лю́бит дороги́е ве́щи.
4. Ми́ша купи́л Та́не зелёный шарф.
5. В торго́вым це́нтре Ми́ша и Та́ня ви́дели Ке́вина.
6. Ке́вин рабо́тал в кио́ске.
7. Та́ня, Ми́ша и Ке́вин обе́дали в столо́вой.
8. Ми́ша и Ке́вин говори́ли о Та́не.

3. Вы по́мните, что Та́ня, Ми́ша и Ке́вин е́ли на обе́д? А что они́ пи́ли?

Та́ня е́ла _____

Та́ня пила́ _____

Ми́ша ел _____

Ми́ша пил _____

Ке́вин ел _____

Ке́вин пил _____

кио́ск = kiosk

4. A. Fill in the missing pronouns in the dative case.

Ми́ша: — Хо́чешь, я куплю́ _____ э́тот брасле́т?

Та́ня: — Нет, спаси́бо. Ты же зна́ешь, я не люблю́ брасле́ты.

Ми́ша: — Та́ня, _____ нра́вится вот э́тот ша́рфик. Мо́жно, я _____ его́ куплю́?

Та́ня: — Что ты, Ми́ша, э́то о́чень до́рого.

Ми́ша: — Да ну, ерунда́! Скажи́, он _____ нра́вится?

Та́ня: — Да, о́чень.

> VIEWING

B. Та́ня was a little nervous when she introduced Ке́вин to Ми́ша. Do you remember how it went? Fill in the names of the characters.

_____ — Приве́т, Ке́вин! Что ты тут де́лаешь?

_____ — Как что? Гуля́ю, фотографи́рую, покупа́ю сувени́ры.

_____ — Ну, и что ты купи́л?

_____ — Да так, ерунду́. Ка́рту, откры́тки.

_____ — Ой, вы же незнако́мы! Познако́мьтесь, пожа́луйста. Вот э́то Ке́вин. А э́то мой друг Ми́ша.

незнако́мы = not acquainted

C. As you know, when Russians discuss what they are going to order from a menu they use two different expressions: **Ты бу́дешь ... ?** (Will you have ... ?) and **Ты хо́чешь ... ?** (Would you like ... ?). Fill in the missing verbs.

Та́ня: — Ну, что мы _____ есть? Ке́вин, хо́чешь посмотре́ть меню́?

Ке́вин: — Спаси́бо. Лу́чше ты. Я не понима́ю в меню́.

Та́ня: — _____ холо́дный борщ?

Ке́вин: — А что э́то тако́е? Ты мо́жешь перевести́ э́то на англи́йский?

Та́ня: — Я не зна́ю, как э́то по-англи́йски. Это тако́й суп.

Ке́вин: — Суп? Нет, спаси́бо, не на́до.

Та́ня: — Мо́жет быть, зелёный сала́т?

Ке́вин: — О́чень хорошо́. Зелёный сала́т и ...

Ми́ша: — Ну, что тут ещё?

Та́ня: — _____ ры́бу, бифште́кс, и́ли ку́рицу? Я _____ ры́бу.

Ке́вин: — А я _____ бифште́кс.

Ми́ша: — А я _____ ку́рицу.

Ми́ша: — Мо́жно вас?

Официа́нтка: — Слу́шаю вас.

Ми́ша:	— Да́йте нам, пожа́луйста, зелёный сала́т.	
Официа́нтка:	— Помидо́ры, огурцы́ … Что ещё?	
Ми́ша:	— Ры́бу, ку́рицу и бифште́кс.	
Официа́нтка:	— Ры́ба, ку́рица, бифште́кс. Отли́чно. А что вы бу́дете пить?	
Та́ня:	— Я _____ сок.	
Ми́ша:	— Да́йте нам, пожа́луйста, буты́лку бе́лого вина́.	
Официа́нтка:	— Вино́ бе́лое …	
Ке́вин:	— Мо́жно мне воды́?	
Официа́нтка:	— Каку́ю во́ду вы _____ ? Боржо́ми? Нарза́н?▲	
Ке́вин:	— Я _____ про́сто во́ду.	
Официа́нтка:	— Про́сто во́ду? Хорошо́! А на десе́рт?	
Ми́ша:	— А на десерт моро́женое.	

Да́йте нам, пожа́луйста = Please give us

буты́лка = bottle

D. Unscramble the transcript of the last part of Та́ня, Ми́ша and Ке́вин's conversation. Put the sentences in the correct order. The first and the last ones are done for you.

_____	Ми́ша:	— Ну, и отли́чно! Вы́пьем за на́ше знако́мство!
_____	Ке́вин:	— Большо́е спаси́бо. Я ей обяза́тельно позвоню́.
_____	Ми́ша:	— Ну и отли́чно! Вы́пьем за наше знакомство!
___1___	Ми́ша:	— Мо́жет быть, им нужны́ конта́кты? Мы мо́жем им помо́чь. Мы бы́ли бы о́чень ра́ды помо́чь ва́шей сестре́.
___9___	Та́ня:	— И за на́ше бу́дущее!
	Ке́вин:	— Да, мо́жет быть.
_____	Та́ня.	— Прекра́сно. Мо́жет, вы бу́дете на «ты»?

▲ «Боржо́ми» and «Нарза́н» are popular brands of mineral water named after the towns containing the springs where the water is collected. They are rich in minerals and considered to be very healthy. Resorts or spas that specialize in the treatment of certain ailments are often located near these kinds of mineral springs.

_____ Та́ня: — Мо́жет быть, и она́ мо́жет помо́чь Ми́ше.

_____ Ке́вин: — Хорошо́.

5. You would like to buy a pet and were lucky enough to find a coupon for a free ad in the magazine «**Четы́ре ла́пы**». The text of the ad may not be more than 15 words, including the phone number. Fill out the coupon.

КУПОН НА БЕСПЛАТНОЕ ОБЪЯВЛЕНИЕ

Ф.И.О. ....

Адрес ....

Телефон ....

Профессия ....

Текст объявления (не более 15 слов, включая № телефона):

_____

_____

_____

_____

_____

Просим писать печатными буквами!

Куплю́ молодо́го шна́уцера, до́брого и весёлого. Не о́чень до́рого. Мой телефо́н 156-24-38.

---

6. A. On Monday, the day after Та́ня, Ми́ша, and Ке́вин had lunch together, Та́ня told her friend Ле́на how she spent Sunday. Act out their conversation.

Та́ня: — Вчера́ мы бы́ли в торго́вом це́нтре.

Ле́на: — А что вы там де́лали?

Та́ня: — Гуля́ли, обе́дали.

Лёна:	— Краси́вый?
Та́ня:	— Да, о́чень краси́вый. А ещё мы там ви́дели Ке́вина. Он покупа́л сувени́ры.
Лёна:	— И что он купи́л?
Та́ня:	— Ка́рту и откры́тки. Я познако́мила Ми́шу и Ке́вина.
Лёна:	— Ну, и как?
Та́ня:	— Всё бы́ло отли́чно! Я ужа́сно боя́лась, ты зна́ешь, Ми́ша немно́го ревну́ет. Но Ке́вин ему́ о́чень понра́вился. По-мо́ему, и Ми́ша понра́вился Ке́вину. Мы пообе́дали в кафе́.
Лёна:	— А что вы е́ли?
Та́ня:	— Зелёный сала́т, ры́бу, ку́рицу и бифште́кс. А на десе́рт – моро́женое. Всё бы́ло вку́сно и недо́рого.
Лёна:	— А о чём вы говори́ли?
Та́ня:	— Ми́ша и Ке́вин говори́ли о ветерина́рном це́нтре и о сестре́ Ке́вина. Его́ сестра́ – дире́ктор большо́й компа́нии. Ке́вин позвони́т сестре́. Мо́жет быть, она́ помо́жет Ми́ше. Пра́вда, здо́рово?

а ещё = also

познако́мить = introduce

я боя́лась = I was afraid

B. Discuss the events on Sunday as if you were:

   a. Ке́вин и Ва́ня

   b. Ми́ша и Серге́й

   c. Лёна и Са́ша

7. Сего́дня ве́чером

   A. Speculate as to what Та́ня, Ми́ша and Ке́вин will do Sunday night after they meet at the mall.

              3   1   4
    — Я ду́маю, Ми́ша бу́дет смотре́ть телеви́зор. А ты?

   B. А вы? Что вы бу́дете де́лать сего́дня ве́чером? Find out what your partner has planned.

— Что ты бу́дешь де́лать сего́дня ве́чером?
— Ещё не знаю. Наве́рное, я бу́ду **переводи́ть текст.** А ты?
— А я бу́ду **рабо́тать.**

чита́ть статью́, рабо́тать, отдыха́ть, писа́ть письмо́, писа́ть упражне́ния, чита́ть кни́гу, смотре́ть телеви́зор, слу́шать му́зыку, переводи́ть текст, гото́вить у́жин, чита́ть журна́л, покупа́ть проду́кты

1. Ка́ждый день, ка́ждую неде́лю, ка́ждый ме́сяц …

How did you spend your free time last year? Fill out the following
questionnaire and discuss it with your classmates.

	ка́ждый день	ка́ждую суббо́ту	ка́ждое воскресе́нье	ка́ждую неде́лю	ка́ждый ме́сяц
1. Вы смотре́ли телеви́зор					
2. Вы бы́ли в кино́					
3. Вы бы́ли на конце́рте					
4. Вы бы́ли в теа́тре					
5. Вы обе́дали в рестора́не					
6. Вы у́жинали в рестора́не					
7. Вы покупа́ли оде́жду					
8. Вы покупа́ли кни́ги					
9. Вы покупа́ли еду́					
10. Вы чита́ли газе́ты и́ли журна́лы					
11. Вы слу́шали ра́дио					

> ```
>               3
> — Ты часто смотрел(а) телевизор?
>        1            4
> — Каждую субботу. А ты?
> ```

2. **Find out about your partner.**

   A. Вы часто пишете письма? Кому вы пишете?

   > ```
   >               3
   > — Ты часто пишешь письма?
   >    1  1
   > — Да, часто.
   >               2
   > — А кому ты пишешь?
   >                   1        4
   > — Бабушке и другу. А ты?
   >       1
   > — А я редко пишу письма.
   >       2
   > — Кому ты пишешь?
   >       1
   > — Подруге.
   > ```

   B. Вы часто звоните по телефону? Кому вы звоните?

по телефону =
on the
telephone

   > ```
   >               3
   > — Ты часто звонишь по телефону?
   >    1  1
   > — Да, часто.
   >               2
   > — А кому ты звонишь?
   >    1       4
   > — Маме. А ты?
   >       1
   > — А я редко звоню по телефону.
   >       2
   > — А кому ты звонишь?
   >       1
   > — Другу и подруге.
   > ```

3. You bump into a friend at the mall. Ask your friend what s/he is doing there.

> — Что ты тут де́лаешь?
>
> — Хочу́ купи́ть **карти́ну** мое́й **сестре́.** А ты?
>
> — А я хочу́ купи́ть **сувени́ры** мое́й **подру́ге.**

4. A. Find out the telephone number of the institute, hotel, post office, and police station.

> — Вы не зна́ете но́мер телефо́на **рестора́на «Москва́»?**
>
> — Зна́ю. **Сто со́рок семь, два́дцать во́семь, де́сять.**

B. Say your phone number. Make another person write it down and dictate it back to you.

5. Discuss your activities every day of last week.

> — Что ты де́лал(а) в понеде́льник?
>
> — Я был(а́) в университете. А по́сле ле́кции я был(а́) в библиотеке.
>
> — А ве́чером?
>
> — Ве́чером я был(а́) в общежитии.
>
> — А что ты де́лал(а)?
>
> — Я писа́л(а) доклад.
>
> — Ну, и как, написал(а)?
>
> — Нет, я написа́л(а) его́ в среду.

6. What are your plans for the winter break? Discuss them with your partner.

7. Ask your friend what s/he is eating or drinking.

> — Что ты ешь?
>
> — **Бифштекс** Хочешь?
>
> — Спасибо, я уже ел(а).

> — Что ты пьёшь?
>
> — **Сок.** Хочешь?
>
> — Нет, спасибо.

candy, sandwiches, ice cream, borsch, steak, fish, chicken, omelet, pizza, potatoes

juice, water, beer, coke, milk, tea, wine, coffee

8. Scan the following short synopses of programs on Russian TV from the magazine **«ТВ Парк».** Which programs would you like to watch? Which ones you would not watch? Justify your answer.

> — Я хочу́ посмотре́ть «Шрек». Мне нра́вятся мультфи́льмы.

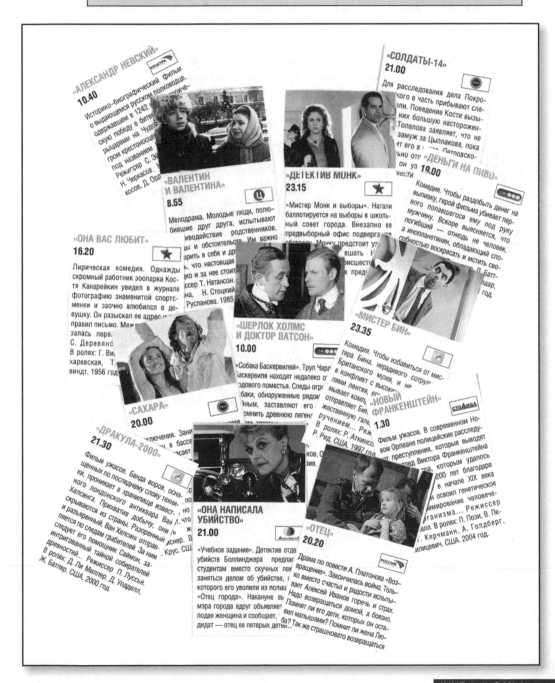

9. Study the results of this poll of members of the Moscow club for dog owners, **«Элита»**. Note that the German Shepherd took first place in both categories: "I own ..." (**владею**) and "I dream about..." (I would like to own) (**мечта́ю**).

Моя́ любо́вь – неме́цкая овча́рка

Гла́вный кино́лог-психо́лог моско́вского клу́ба «Эли́та» Влади́мир Грице́нко провёл опро́с среди́ чле́нов своего́ клу́ба. Бы́ло за́дано два вопро́са – «Како́й соба́кой вы владе́ете?» и «Соба́ка ва́шей мечты́?» Бы́ло опро́шено две́сти пятьдеся́т челове́к. Места́ распредели́лись так.

ВЛАДЕЮ	МЕЧТАЮ
Неме́цкая овча́рка	Неме́цкая овча́рка
Дог	Дог
Ризеншна́уцер	Ротве́йлер
Эрдельтерье́р	Ко́лли
Ротве́йлер	Среднеазиа́тская овча́рка
Ко́лли	Восточноевропе́йская овча́рка
Чёрный терье́р	Ризеншна́уцер
Среднеазиа́тская овча́рка	Доберма́н
Миттельшна́уцер	Афга́нская борза́я
Доберма́н	Эрдельтерье́р

Таки́м о́бразом, ещё раз подтверди́лась всепланéтная любо́вь челове́чества к неме́цкой овча́рке. И что они́ в ней нашли́?

A. Каки́е соба́ки са́мые популя́рные?

B. Каки́е соба́ки нра́вятся вам?

10. Situations

A. You are interviewing a 110-year old person. Find out about his/her habits. What does s/he eat and drink? What does s/he like? What doesn't s/he like?

B. You are in Novgorod and decide to have lunch at the café **«Самова́р»**. Order food and drinks.

C. You have decided to buy a cat or a dog. Talk to the salesperson at the pet store.

1. Verbal Aspect

The Meaning of Aspect

Every Russian verb belongs to one of two aspectual types, imperfective aspect or perfective aspect. In a standard Russian dictionary almost every verb listing shows not one stem but a pair of stems, the perfective and imperfective. Russian speakers must decide each time they use a verb which aspectual form of the verb best conveys the idea they want to express.

The perfective aspect is highly specified regarding the types of situations in which it can be used. The imperfective is much more open-ended and can express many different types of notions.

The perfective form of a verb characterizes its action as 1) completed, 2) taking place "at one go", and 3) relevant to the speaker at the moment of speech. By contrast, imperfective verbs reveal a wide variety of meanings. Only an imperfective verb can express a single action *in progress* (a non-completed action) or an action performed *on more than one occasion* and *completed* on each occasion. In addition, a speaker of Russian uses an imperfective verb to refer to a completed action simply to verify whether the action ever took place. (Did it happen or didn't it happen?)

To summarize, the perfective form is used only when *all* of the three conditions are met-when the action is *completed*, on *one occasion*, and *relevant to the speaker* at the time of its expression. In all other cases the imperfective form is used. The majority of the verbs you have encountered up to this point have been *imperfective*. Imperfective verbs far outnumber perfective verbs in frequency of occurrence.

In order to understand Russian and express yourself freely in that language, it is essential to master both the perfective and imperfective forms of each verb. Study the choice of aspect, paying particular attention to the role played by context. Begin by comparing verbal aspects in the following sentences. Note how words like **всегда** "always" or **каждый день** "every day" bring out the *repetitive* meaning in the imperfective verb.

Лётом Ва́ня ка́ждый день **смотре́л** телеви́зор. (*Imperfective: repeated action*)	In the summer Vanya watched TV every day.

The imperfective aspect is used for actions *in progress*, where the notion of process can be indicated by expressions of duration, such as for a long time, for two hours, all night long, etc., or by another action in progress.

— Вéчером Тáня дóлго **писáла** курсовýю рабóту, а Мúша **читáл** журнáл «Кот и пёс». *(Imperfective: process)*

In the evening Tanya worked on a term paper for a long time, and Misha read the journal "Cat and Dog."

The imperfective aspect in the conversation segment that follows provides a context where the speaker is simply verifying whether or not an action took place.

— Вáня, ты не пóмнишь, мы **дéлали** упражнéние № 5?

(Imperfective: main concern is verification of exercise number, rather than its successful completion).

"Vanya, do you remember – did we do exercise 5?"

— Нет, не дéлали.

"No, we didn't do it."

The perfective aspect in the following model expresses an action which is single, complete, relevant to the speaker, and has an impact on the present situation (i.e. result is evident.)

— Тáня, ты хóчешь есть?
— Óчень. А ты ужé **приготóвила** ýжин?
— Да, ýжин на столé. *(Perfective: result is at hand)*

"Tanya, do you want to eat?"
"Yes. Have you already made dinner?"
"Yes, it's on the table."

2. Aspect and Tense

The one-time, finalized nature of a perfective action is incompatible with the Russian conception of present time. A perfective action is possible only in the past or future. In the chart below perfective actions are represented by small circles, while imperfective actions are indicated by line segments. If the horizontal (left to right) line is a time vector upon which a perpendicular line marks the present moment (*now*), then every perfective action must necessarily fall to the left (past tense) or to the right (future tense) of the *now* line. Imperfective verbs, on the other hand, can refer to actions in progress (perhaps intermittently), in the past (i.e. wholly to the left of the *now* line), in the future (i.e. wholly to the right of the *now* line), or in the present (i.e. crossing the *now* line). The present tense is expressed by imperfective verbs only.

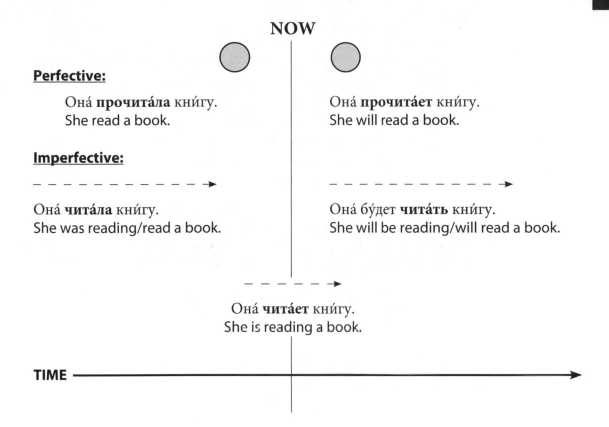

NOW

Perfective:

Она́ **прочита́ла** кни́гу.
She read a book.

Она́ **прочита́ет** кни́гу.
She will read a book.

Imperfective:

Она́ **чита́ла** кни́гу.
She was reading/read a book.

Она́ бу́дет **чита́ть** кни́гу.
She will be reading/will read a book.

Она́ **чита́ет** кни́гу.
She is reading a book.

TIME

3. Future Tense

The future tense endings of perfective verbs are identical in form to those of the present of imperfective verbs. Do not confuse perfective future (**я прочита́ю** "I will read, will have read, will finish reading") and imperfective present.

Perfective future: прочита́ть (прочита́й-)

я	прочита́ю	мы прочита́ем
ты	прочита́ешь	вы прочита́ете
он/она́	прочита́ет	они́ прочита́ют

Imperfective future requires the appropriate form of the verb **быть** "be" (agreeing with the subject) followed by the imperfective infinitive. For example, **я бу́ду чита́ть** "I will be reading, I will read".

Imperfective Future: читáть (читáй-)

я	бýду читáть	мы бýдем читáть	
ты	бýдешь читáть	вы бýдете читáть	
он/онá	бýдет читáть	онú бýдут читáть	

The use of aspect in the future tense is, for the most part, similar to that of the past. Study the following examples, taking particular care to distinguish imperfective *present*, perfective *future* and imperfective *future*.

— Лéна, что ты **бýдешь дéлать** лéтом? (*Imperfective: process*)
— Лéтом я **бýду отдыхáть** на юге. (*Imperfective: process*)

"Lena, what will you be doing this summer?"
"This summer I will be vacationing in the south."

— Что сейчáс дéлает Мúша?
— Он пúшет статью́.
— Он скóро её **напúшет?** (*Perfective: result*)
— Нет, он **бýдет** её дóлго **писáть.** (*Imperfective: process*)

"What is Misha doing right now?"
"He is writing an article."
"Will he finish it soon?"

"No, he will be writing it for a long time."

Смирнóвы óчень любят дáчу. Я дýмаю, что онú бýдут отдыхáть там кáждое лéто. (*Imperfective: repeated action*)

The Smirnovs are very fond of the summer house. I think they will vacation there every summer.

4. Formation of Aspect

Verbal aspectual pairs are differentiated by one of three means:

a. *Suffixation* (with possible alternation of final root consonant).

Imperfective		**Perfective**	
отвечáй-	"answer"	отвéти-	"answer"
решáй-	"solve", "decide" "attempt to solve"	решú-	"solve", "decide" "obtain a solution"

b. *Prefixation* (which does not affect conjugation)

Imperfective		**Perfective**	
писа́-	"write"	написа́-	"get written"
чита́й-	"read"	прочита́й-	"finish reading"
де́лай-	"do"	сде́лай-	"get done"

c. *Suppletion* (verbs of the aspectual pair have different roots; this formation is rare)

Imperfective		**Perfective**	
говори́-	"say", "tell"	сказа́-	"say", "tell"

At a later stage in your study of Russian, you will learn rules for deriving certain types of perfective verbs from their imperfective counterparts and vice versa.

Examples of the Use of Aspect

Я до́лго **чита́л** э́ту кни́гу, но ещё **не прочита́л** её.
(Imperfective: process / Perfective: result)

I *have been reading* this book for a long time, but still *have not finished* it.

Мы до́лго **реша́ли** зада́чу и наконе́ц **реши́ли** её.
(Imperfective: process / Perfective: result)

We *worked* on the problem for a long time and finally *solved* it.

Мы **не реши́ли** э́ту зада́чу.
(Negated perfective: failed to obtain a solution, negative result)

We *did not solve* this problem.

Мы **не реша́ли** э́ту зада́чу.
(Negated imperfective: statement that no action took place)

We *did not work* on this problem.

Ке́вин, что ты **сде́лал?** Э́то же ра́ковина. А му́сор там.
(Perfective: complete action)

Kevin, what *have you done?* That's the sink, and the trash is over there.

— Та́ня, что ты **бу́дешь де́лать** сего́дня ве́чером?
(Imperfective: process)

"Tanya, what *will* you *be doing* tonight?"

— Я **бу́ду смотре́ть** телеви́зор. Сего́дня ве́чером бу́дет переда́ча о Ча́рли Ча́плине.
(Imperfective: process)

"I *am going to watch* television. A program about Charlie Chaplin is on tonight."

Here is an example from classical Russian literature:

Что же **де́лал** Бе́льтов в продолже́ние 10 лет? Всё, и́ли почти́ всё. Что он **сде́лал?** Ничего́ и́ли почти́ ничего́. *(Imperfective: process / Perfective: result)*	What did Beltov do during the 10 years? Everything, or almost everything. What *did* he *achieve?* Nothing, or almost nothing. (Herzen, *Who Is Guilty?*)

5. Consecutive and Simultaneous Actions

Two or more perfective verbs in the same sentence convey consecutive actions, one following the other. Imperfective verbs may convey actions overlapping in time.

Вчера́ ве́чером я, **прочита́л** статью́, **написа́л** упражне́ния и **перевёл** текст. *(Perfective/perfective/perfective: consecutive, completed actions)*	Yesterday evening I *read* an article, *wrote* exercises, and *translated* a text.
Та́ня **посмотре́ла** на браслéт и **сказа́ла:** «Нет, спаси́бо, я его́ не куплю́.» *(Perfective/perfective: consecutive, completed actions)*	Tanya *glanced* at the bracelet and *said,* "No, thank you, I won't buy it."
Ке́вин **сиде́л** до́ма и **смотре́л** фотоальбо́м. *(Imperfective/imperfective: overlapping actions)*	Kevin *stayed* at home and *looked* at a photo album.
Когда́ Та́ня **гото́вила** обе́д, она́ **слу́шала** му́зыку. *(Imperfective/imperfective: overlapping actions)*	As Tanya *fixed* dinner, she *listened* to music.

6. The Verb быть "be"

The verb **быть** "be" is an irregular imperfective verb. In the case of an irregular verb it is necessary to learn more than one stem. In the given verb, the irregularity appears in the unpredictable alternation of the root vowel from **у** in the future tense to **ы** in the past tense and the infinitive. (Note also the root stress in the future tense.)

Infinitive: быть

Past Tense:	Present Tense:	Future Tense:			
он был	(none)	я	бу́ду	мы	бу́дем
она́ была́		ты	бу́дешь	вы	бу́дете
оно́ бы́ло		он/она́/оно́	бу́дет	они́	бу́дут
они́ бы́ли					

Negated Past Tense:

он не́ был	/н^ье́был/
она́ не была́	/н^ьибыла́/
оно́ не́ было	/н^ье́былə/
они́ не́ были	/н^ье́был^ьи/

— Вы **бу́дете** на ле́кции сего́дня? "Will you be at the lecture today?"
— Да, обяза́тельно **бу́ду**. "Yes, I will be there for sure."

А́нна Бори́совна **была́** на рабо́те вчера́ и **бу́дет** на рабо́те за́втра. Anna Borisovna was at work yesterday and will be at work tomorrow.

7. Non-Suffixed Verbs with Stems Terminating in -д/-т

There are 9 different types of non-suffixed (ø) verb stems, each of which contains one or two special formation features. Stems which have a final consonant of either -д or -т, for example, replace the -д/-т with -с before the -ти́ infinitive ending (e.g. перевёд-´ → перевести́). The deletion д + л = л in past tense forms follows the normal truncation rules, where C1 + C2 = C2 (See Analysis II, 7).

перевести́[1] (перевёд-´) "translate" (perfective)

Past Tense:	Present Tense:		Future Tense:	
он перевёл	(none)	я	переведу́	мы переведём
она́ перевела́		ты	переведёшь	вы переведёте
оно́ перевело́		он/она́	переведёт	они́ переведу́т
они́ перевели́				

8. Days of the Week

The days of the week are:

понеде́льник	"Monday"
вто́рник	"Tuesday
среда́	"Wednesday"
четве́рг	"Thursday"
пя́тница	"Friday"
суббо́та	"Saturday"
воскресе́нье	"Sunday"

Note first that the Russian week starts on Monday, and, secondly, that the days of the week are never capitalized in Russian.

---

[1] Note that the stress falls on the post-root syllable throughout. In the case of non-suffixed verbs with this pattern the infinitive ending is -**ти́**.

Какой сегодня день?

In the expression «**Какой сегодня день?**», the subject of the sentence is **день;** therefore, in the answer the name of the day of the week determines the form of the verb, since the subject always agrees with the verb in gender and number.

— Какой вчера был день?	"What day was yesterday?"
— Вчера была среда.	"Yesterday was Wednesday."
— Вчера было воскресенье.	"Yesterday was Sunday."
— Вчера был четверг.	"Yesterday was Thursday."
— Какой сегодня день?	"What day is today?"
— Сегодня четверг.	"Today is Thursday."

Какое сегодня число?

— Какое сегодня число?	"What is today's date?"
— Сегодня второе (число).	"Today is the second."

Note that the date of a month is expressed by the noun **число** and requires neuter agreement. The word «**число**,» however, is frequently omitted.

Expressing "Time When"

For increments of time less than a week always use the preposition **в** plus the **accusative case.**

— Когда будет лекция?	"When will the lecture be?"
— Лекция будет в пятницу.	"The lecture will be on Friday."
В эту минуту Таня увидела Кевина.	At that moment Tanya saw Kevin.
В эту секунду Миша позвонил Тане.	At that second Misha called Tanya.

9. The Dative Case of Nouns

The dative case is used to designate an *indirect* receiver of the action of a verb, the object of certain intransitive verbs (i.e. verbs which do not take a direct object) and the logical subject of impersonal sentences (See Analysis VIII). In subsequent units, the use of the dative with prepositions will be discussed.

THE DATIVE SINGULAR OF NOUNS

All first declension nouns take -у (-ю) in the dative; the dative of second declension nouns is identical with the prepositional.

First Declension

Case	Endings	Examples			
Nom.	-ø(-ь) / -о(-е)	муж	писа́тель	сло́во	зда́ние
Dat.	-у(-ю)	му́жу	писа́телю	сло́ву	зда́нию

Second Declension

Case	Endings	Examples	
Nom.	-а(-я)	подру́га	тётя
Dat.	-е	подру́ге	тёте

Second declension nouns ending in -ия take the ending -и in the dative case:

исто́рия → исто́рии

THE DATIVE PLURAL OF NOUNS

The dative plural ending for all Russian nouns is -ам (-ям). Stress in the dative plural is the same as in other oblique case (gen., prep., etc.) forms.

Case	Endings	1st Decl.			2nd Decl.
Nom. Pl.	-ы(-и) /-а(-я)	студе́нты	роди́тели	о́бщества	ба́бушки
Dat. Pl.	-ам(-ям)	студе́нтам	роди́телям	о́бществам	ба́бушкам

10. The Dative Case of Pronouns and Adjectives

THE DATIVE SINGULAR

The dative singular pronoun and adjective endings are: -ому (-ему) for the masculine and the neuter, and -ой (-ей) for the feminine. In ending-stressed adjectives the stress in the dative falls on the penultimate syllable of the ending молодо́му; in ending-stressed pronouns the stress in the dative falls on the final syllable of the ending: моему́.

Masculine/Neuter

Case	Examples				
Nom.	мой	наш	э́тот, э́то	но́вый, но́вое	молодо́й, молодо́е
Dat.	моему́	на́шему	э́тому	но́вому	молодо́му

Feminine

Case	Examples				
Nom.	моя́	на́ша	э́та	но́вая	молода́я
Dat.	мое́й	на́шей	э́той	но́вой	молодо́й

THE DATIVE PLURAL

The dative plural ending of pronouns and adjectives is **-ым** (-им).

Case	Examples				
Nom. Pl.	э́ти	мои́	ва́ши	но́вые	больши́е
Dat. Pl.	э́тим	мои́м	ва́шим	но́вым	больши́м

The dative plural forms of the pronouns **те** "those" and **все** "all", "everyone" are **тем** and **всем** respectively.

Compare the following dative singular and plural forms.

Я уже́ позвони́л **твое́й сестре́.**	I have already called up *your sister.*
Я уже́ позвони́л **твои́м сёстрам.**	I have already called up *your sisters.*
Ке́вин купи́л сувени́ры **хоро́шему дру́гу** в Аме́рике.	Kevin bought souvenirs *for a good friend in America.*
Ке́вин купи́л сувени́ры **хоро́шим друзья́м** в Аме́рике.	Kevin bought souvenirs *for good friends* is America.

11. The Dative Case of Personal and Interrogative Pronouns

Nom.	я	ты	он/оно́	она́	мы	вы	они́	кто	что
Dat.	**мне**	**тебе́**	**ему́**	**ей**	**нам**	**вам**	**им**	**кому́**	**чему́**

12. Uses of the Dative

An *indirect object* denotes the indirect receiver of the action of the verb, the person for whom or on whose behalf an action is performed.

Áнна Бори́совна пригото́вила обе́д **му́жу и до́чке.**	Anna Borisovna cooked dinner *for her husband and daughter.*
Ми́ша рассказа́л **нам** интере́сную исто́рию.	Misha told *us* an interesting story.
Мы сказа́ли **на́шим друзья́м** об э́том.	We told *our friends* about it.

Like their English counterparts, a number of Russian verbs may take both accusative and dative objects: **покупа́ть/купи́ть** "to buy", **гото́вить/пригото́вить** "to cook".

Гали́на Ива́новна купи́ла <u>сы́ну</u>   Galina Ivanovna bought her son a new
                        dat.   camera.

<u>но́вый фотоаппара́т.</u>
        acc.

Са́ша пригото́вил <u>Ле́не</u> <u>вку́сный у́жин.</u>   Sasha cooked a delicious dinner for Lena.
                  dat.   *acc.*

Серге́й показа́л <u>Ми́ше</u> <u>но́вую маши́ну.</u>   Sergey showed the new car to Misha.
                dat.   *acc.*

13. Special Verbs Governing the Dative

A small group of intransitive verbs governs the dative. Verbs belonging to this group must be memorized, since there is no parallel construction in modern English. (If you know German or Latin, you will notice some parallels.)

звони́ть (звони́-)/позвони́ть (позвони́-)	"call"
отвеча́ть (отвеча́й-)/отве́тить (отве́ти-)	"answer"
помога́ть (помога́й-)/помо́чь (irreg.)	"help"

Я вам позвоню́ за́втра ве́чером.	I will call you tomorrow night.
Милиционе́р отве́тил Ке́вину.	The police officer answered Kevin.
Ми́ша нам ча́сто помога́ет.	Misha often helps us.

14. The Verb нра́виться/понра́виться

The verb **нра́виться/понра́виться** "to be pleasing to" + dative case is used to express liking for a person or thing. It is a very commonly used verb in Russian.

Э́то мне нра́вится. I like this.

Он ей понра́вился. She liked him.

Я зна́ю, что э́тот фильм вам понра́вится. I know you will like this movie.

Note carefully that the logical subject (experiencer) in the above construction is in the *dative case;* whereas the thing or person that is liked is in the nominative.

15. The Accusative Plural

The accusative plural of all inanimate nouns is identical with the nominative plural. Accusative plural nouns denoting animals (including humans) have the same form as the genitive plural (see Analysis VIII).

16. The Irregular Verb есть/съесть "Eat"

This pair of verbs belong to the small group of high-frequency verbs in Russian which are irregular. Their forms must be memorized.

Present				Past	
я	ем	мы	еди́м	он	ел
ты	ешь	вы	еди́те	она́	е́ла
он/она́	ест	они́	едя́т	оно́	е́ло
				они́	е́ли

The perfective form is conjugated the same way as the imperfective: **я съем, ты съешь… они́ съедя́т; он съел, она́ съе́ла, они́ съе́ли.** No basic stems are provided for irregular verbs in the vocabulary.

17. The Verb пить/вы́пить "Drink"

The verb **пить** "drink" is one of five non-syllabic stems in Russian ending in **-й.** For now, you should memorize the forms.

Present				Past	
я	пью	мы	пьём	он	пил
ты	пьёшь	вы	пьёте	она́	пила́
он/она́	пьёт	они́	пью́т	оно́	пи́ло
				они́	пи́ли

The perfective is formed with the stressed prefix **вы́пить: я вы́пью; он вы́пил, она́ вы́пила,** etc.

18. The interrogative pronoun какой and the demonstrative pronoun такой

The interrogative pronoun **какой** "what (kind of)", "which" and the demonstrative pronoun **такой** "that kind of", "such" have the same endings as ending-stressed adjectives.

какой журнал, какая книга, какое общежитие, какие газеты

The pronoun **какой** occurs in various interrogative sentences.

— Какой это город?	"What city is this?"
— Это Киев.	"This is Kiev."
— Какая это квартира?	"Which apartment is this?"
— Это вторая квартира.	"This is apartment #2."
— Какое это здание?	"What kind of building is this?"
— Это старое здание.	"This is an old building."
— Какие это студенты?	"What students are they?"
— Это историки.	"They are history students."

The pronoun **такой** is often used after the interrogative pronoun **что** "what", in which case it has a specifying meaning.

— Что это такое?	"What can that be?"
— Это новое кафе.	"It's a new café."

When used after **что,** the pronoun invariably takes the neuter gender singular.

Что такое «борщ»?	What is a "borsch"?

NOUNS

аппарату́ра *equipment*
аттракцио́н *amusement park ride*
бефстро́ганов beef Stroganoff
бифште́кс steak
блин crepe, pancake
блю́до dish
борщ borsch (beet soup) BB
  браслéт bracelet
бу́дущее *future*
буты́лка bottle
ве́чер evening AB (-á)
витами́н vitamin
вода́ water CC
  минера́льная ~ mineral water
воскресе́нье Sunday
вто́рник Tuesday
геро́й hero
дека́н dean
десе́рт dessert
дире́ктор director AB (-á)
диск compact disc
день day
докла́д presentation, report
дру́жба friendship
еда́ food
зада́ча assignment, problem
заку́ска appetizer
запи́ска note
знако́мство acquaintance
инструме́нт instrument
календа́рь calendar BB
карто́шка (sg.) potato(es)
карти́на picture
карусе́ль carousel
кио́ск kiosk
кла́ссика classics
колле́га (m. or f.) colleague
ко́миксы (pl.) comics
компа́ния company
ко́мплекс complex
компоне́нт component
консе́рвы canned food
конта́кт contact
кот cat (male)
котле́та burger, cutlet BB

ку́рица chicken
ла́па paw
лека́рство medicine
макаро́ны (pl.) pasta
меню́ (indecl. neut.) menu
ме́сто place AB
ме́сяц month
мультфи́льм (му́льтик) cartoon
мя́со meat
напи́ток drink
наполео́н Napoleon (pastry)
неде́ля week
но́вости (pl.) news C
о́бщество society
о́вощи vegetables C
огуре́ц cucumber BB
омле́т omelet
отве́т answer
о́тдых rest, relaxation
откры́тка postcard
оши́бка mistake
пельме́ни (pl. only) dumplings
переда́ча TV show BB
пёс dog (male)
плака́т poster
план plan
плов pilaf
пода́рок gift, present
понеде́льник Monday
поро́да breed
прию́т shelter
програ́мма program
проду́кты (pl. only) groceries
пя́тница Friday
рабо́та paper
  курсова́я рабо́та – term paper
расска́з story
рома́н novel
ры́ба fish
сала́т lettuce, salad
сало́н salon, (here) pet grooming service
семина́р seminar
сочине́ние essay
спаге́тти spaghetti
среда́ Wednesday CC

стихи́ (pl. only) poems B
столо́вая dining hall, cafeteria
суббо́та Saturday
сувени́р souvenir
су́ши sushi
телесериа́л TV series
террито́рия territory
торго́вый це́нтр shopping center
торт cake
тост toast
упражне́ние exercise
успе́х success
у́тро morning
фанта́стика (нау́чная) science fiction
филиа́л branch office
фи́рма firm, company
худо́жник artist
четве́рг Thursday BB
число́ date, number BA
шампа́нское champagne
щи (pl. only) cabbage soup
эклéр éclair
эпизо́д episode

PROPER NOUNS

Изма́йлово Izmailovo (region in Moscow) (indeclinable)

ADJECTIVES

до́брый kind, good
жа́реный fried
институ́тский institute
италья́нский Italian
ка́ждый every
междунаро́дный international
музыка́льный music
незнако́м not acquainted
прекра́сный wonderful
рад glad
совреме́нный modern, contemporary
специа́льный special
спорти́вный sports
  ~ зал gymnasium
тру́дный difficult

у́мный intelligent
университе́тский university
холо́дный cold
це́лый whole

VERBS

говори́ть (говори́-)/**сказа́ть**
(сказа̌-) speak, say, tell
гото́вить (гото́ви-) /
пригото́вить
(пригото́ви-) cook, prepare
дава́ть (*дава́й-*)/*дать*
(*irregular*) *give*
де́лать (де́лай-)/**сде́лать**
(сде́лай-) do
есть/съесть (irregular) eat
зака́зывать (зака́зывай-) /
заказа́ть (заказа̌-) order
зака́нчивать (зака́нчивай-) /
зако́нчить(зако́нчи-)
graduate, finish
звони́ть (звони́-)/ **позвони́ть**
(позвони́-) call (by phone)
мечта́ть (*мечта́й-*) (*imp.*)
dream
мочь (*irreg., imp.*) *be able to,*
can
называ́ться (*называ́й-ся*)
(*imp.*) *be called*
нра́виться (нра́ви-ся) (imp.)
like
обе́дать (обе́дай-) /**пообе́дать**
(пообе́дай-) have lunch
организова́ть (*организова́-*)
(*imp.*) *organize*

переводи́ть (переводи̌-) /
перевести́ (перевёд́-)
translate
писа́ть (писа̌-) /**написа́ть**
(написа̌-) write
пить/вы́пить drink
покупа́ть (покупа́й-) /
купи́ть (купи̌-) buy
помога́ть (помога́й-) /
помо́чь (irregular) help
рекомендова́ть
(*рекомендова́-*) (*imp.*)
recommend
реша́ть (реша́й-) /**реши́ть**
(реши̌-) solve, decide
смотре́ть (смотре̌-) /
посмотре́ть (посмотре̌-)
watch, look at
учи́ться (*учи̌-ся*) (*imp.*) *study*
(*at a university or school*)
чита́ть (чита́й-) / **прочита́ть**
(прочита́й-) read

ADVERBS

дёшево cheap
до́лго for a long time
до́рого expensive
ещё still, else
за́втра tomorrow
лу́чше better
наве́рное probably
непро́сто difficult
обяза́тельно certainly,
definitely
обы́чно usually

пра́вильно correct
прекра́сно wonderful
симпати́чно nice
тру́дно difficult
уже́ already

PREPOSITIONS

за + accus. to … (used when
making a toast)
на + accus. for (breakfast,
dinner, etc.)
по́сле + gen. after

EXPRESSIONS

Большо́е спаси́бо. Thanks a
lot.
Да́йте, пожа́луйста, …
Please give (me) …
ерунда́ junk, nothing special
Ждём вас. Looking forward to
seeing you.
Кака́я красота́! How lovely!
Как э́то по-англи́йски? How
do you say that in English?
Лю́ди как лю́ди. They're just
ordinary people.
Не на́до. It is not necessary
нужны́ конта́кты (here) you
need business contacts
Ну и что? So what?
по телефо́ну on the telephone
са́мое гла́вное the main thing
Что э́то тако́е? What's that?
Что ещё? What else?

The Russian Alphabet

Cyrillic Letter		Name of Letter	Cyrillic Letter		Name of Letter
А а	*А а*	a	П п	*П п*	pe
Б б	*Б б*	be	Р р	*Р р*	er
В в	*В в*	ve	С с	*С с*	es
Г г	*Г г*	ge	Т т	*Т т*	te
Д д	*Д д*	de	У у	*У у*	u
Е е	*Е е*	ye	Ф ф	*Ф ф*	ef
Ё ё	*Ё ё*	yo	Х х	*Х х*	kha
Ж ж	*Ж ж*	zhe	Ц ц	*Ц ц*	tse
З з	*З з*	ze	Ч ч	*Ч ч*	che
И и	*И и*	i	Ш ш	*Ш ш*	sha
Й й	*Й й*	i kratkoye (short i)	Щ щ	*Щ щ*	scha
К к	*К к*	ka	ъ	*ъ*	tvyordi znak (hard sign)
Л л	*Л л*	el	ы	*ы*	yeri
М м	*М м*	em	ь	*ь*	myagkiy znak (soft sign)
Н н	*Н н*	en	Э э	*Э э*	e oborotnoye (reversed e)
О о	*О о*	o	Ю ю	*Ю ю*	yu
			Я я	*Я я*	ya

Summary Tables of Noun Endings

Singular

	First Declension			Neuter		Second Declension	
	Masc.Inanimate/Masc.Animate					Feminine	
Nom.	теа́тр	словáрь	мáльчик	окнó	мóре	газéта	ку́хня
Acc.	теа́тр	словáрь	мáльчика	окнó	мóре	газéту	ку́хню
Gen.	теа́тра	словаря́	мáльчика	окнá	мóря	газéты	ку́хни
Prep.	теа́тре	словарé	мáльчике	окнé	мóре	газéте	ку́хне
Dat.	теа́тру	словарю́	мáльчику	окнý	мóрю	газéте	ку́хне
Instr.	теáтром	словарём	мáльчиком	окнóм	мóрем	газéтой	ку́хней

Plural

	First Declension			Neuter		Second Declension	
	Masc.Inanimate/Masc.Animate					Feminine	
Nom.	теáтры	словари́	мáльчики	óкна	моря́	газéты	ку́хни
Acc.	теáтры	словари́	мáльчиков	óкна	моря́	газéты	ку́хни
Gen.	теáтров	словарéй	мáльчиков	óкон	морéй	газéт	ку́хонь
Prep.	теáтрах	словаря́х	мáльчиках	óкнах	моря́х	газéтах	ку́хнях
Dat.	теáтрам	словаря́м	мáльчикам	óкнам	моря́м	газéтам	ку́хням
Instr.	теáтрами	словаря́ми	мáльчиками	óкнами	моря́ми	газéтами	ку́хнями

Summary Tables of Pronoun Declension

Personal Pronouns

	я	ты	он/оно	она	мы	вы	они
Nom.	я	ты	он/оно	она	мы	вы	они
Acc.	меня	тебя	его	её	нас	вас	их
Gen.	меня	тебя	его	её	нас	вас	их
Prep.	обо мне	о тебе	о нём	о ней	о нас	о вас	о них
Dat.	мне	тебе	ему	ей	нам	вам	им
Instr.	*мной*	*тобой*	*им*	*ей*	*нами*	*вами*	*ими*

Interrogative Pronouns

Nom.	кто	что
Acc.	кого	что
Gen.	кого	чего
Prep.	о ком	о чём
Dat.	кому	чему
Instr.	*кем*	*чем*

Demonstrative and Possessive Pronouns

Masculine and Neuter Singular

Nom.	этот	это	наш	наше	мой	моё	чей	чьё	весь	всё	тот	то
Acc.	этот	это	наш	наше	мой	моё	чей	чьё	весь	всё	тот	то
Gen.	этого		нашего		моего		чьего		всего		того	
Prep.	этом		нашем		моём		чьём		всём		том	
Dat.	этому		нашему		моему		чьему		всему		тому	
Instr.	*этим*		*нашим*		*моим*		*чьим*		*всем*		*тем*	

Feminine Singular

Nom.	эта	наша	моя	чья	вся	та
Acc.	эту	нашу	мою	чью	всю	ту
Gen.	этой	нашей	моей	чьей	всей	той
Prep.	этой	нашей	моей	чьей	всей	той
Dat.	этой	нашей	моей	чьей	всей	той
Instr.	*этой*	*нашей*	*моей*	*чьей*	*всей*	*той*

Plural

	эти	наши	мой	чьи	все	те
Nom.	эти	наши	мой	чьи	все	те
Acc.	эти/этих	наши/наших	мой/мои́х	чьи/чьих	все/всех	те/тех
Gen.	этих	наших	мои́х	чьих	всех	тех
Prep.	этих	наших	мои́х	чьих	всех	тех
Dat.	этим	нашим	мои́м	чьим	всем	тем
Instr.	э́тими	на́шими	мои́ми	чьи́ми	все́ми	те́ми

Summary of Adjective Endings

	Stem-Stressed			Ending-Stressed		
	Masculine/ Neuter	Feminine	Plural	Masculine/ Neuter	Feminine	Plural
Nom.	но́вый но́вое	но́вая	но́вые	молодо́й молодо́е	молода́я	молоды́е
Acc. inan.	но́вый но́вое	но́вую	но́вые	молодо́й молодо́е	молоду́ю	молоды́е
anim.	но́вого		но́вых	молодо́го		молоды́х
Gen.	но́вого	но́вой	но́вых	молодо́го	молодо́й	молоды́х
Prep.	но́вом	но́вой	но́вых	молодо́м	молодо́й	молоды́х
Dat.	но́вому	но́вой	но́вым	молодо́му	молодо́й	молоды́м
Instr.	но́вым	но́вой	но́выми	молоды́м	молодо́й	молоды́ми

На Nouns	
на ю́ге	на заня́тии
на се́вере	на ку́рсе
на за́паде	на ле́кции
на восто́ке	на пра́ктике
	на репети́ции
на Байка́ле	на семина́ре
на Во́лге	на собра́нии
на Неве́	на факульте́те
на Кавка́зе	
на Ура́ле	на бале́те
	на вы́ставке
на да́че	на дискоте́ке
на ку́хне	на конце́рте
на по́чте	на спекта́кле
на рабо́те	
на у́лице	

Stress Patterns in Russian Nouns

Shifting stress in inflections (i.e. declensions, conjugations, etc.) is a characteristic feature of Russian. Most Russian words (about 96 percent of the Russian vocabulary) have fixed stress. However, there are many words with shifting stress, i.e. words in whose declension, conjugation, changing for the degrees of comparison, etc. the stress shifts from the stem to the ending or vice versa.

Nouns have eight shifting stress patterns in their declensional paradigm. Two of these patterns apply only to a few words.

The main types of shifting stress patterns in the noun declensional paradigm reflect the accentual opposition between the singular and the plural: fixed stress on the stem (A) in the singular vs. fixed stress on the ending (B) in the plural: **мо́ре** "sea" – **моря́** "seas" (this pattern covers only masculine and neuter nouns); fixed stress on the ending (B) in the singular vs. fixed stress on the stem (A) in the plural: **письмо́** "letter" – **пи́сьма** "letters", **окно́** "window" - **о́кна** "windows" (this pattern covers masculine, feminine and neuter nouns).

Shifting stress (C) in the singular is not typical of nouns: there are only 31 feminine nouns belonging to this pattern. The pattern represents an opposition between the accusative and the other cases: the stress on the stem in the accusative vs. the stress on the ending in all the other forms: **рука́** "hand and/or arm"), **руки́, руке́, ру́ку, руко́й, о руке́**. Shifting stress in the plural (C) reflects the opposition between the nominative (and the accusative of inanimate nouns), which has stem stress, and the oblique cases, which have end stress: **го́ры** "mountains", **гор, гора́ми, о гора́х.**

Stress in Russian serves to differentiate between the forms of a word, e.g. **го́рода** "of a city" – **города́** "cities", **мо́ря** "of the sea" – **моря́** "seas", **письма́** "of a letter" – **пи́сьма** "letters", **руки́** "of the hand and/or the arm" – **ру́ки** "hands and/or arms". There are several hundred nouns whose genitive singular and nominative plural are distinguished only by stress.

As a rule, shifting stress occurs in unsuffixed, commonly used words with a monosyllabic or disyllabic stem. Rarely used suffixed words, recently borrowed suffixed words, and suffixed words with polysyllabic stems generally have fixed stress.

There are six basic shifting stress declensional patterns: AB, BA, AC, BC, CA, and CC. A two-place symbol will be used to designate each type of stress pattern: the first place refers to the singular; the second place to the plural. Within each place:

A indicates stress fixed on the stem[1].

B indicates stress fixed on the ending.

C indicates the one possible shift of stress in the singular or plural:

singular – stress is shifted to the root (initial syllable) in the *feminine accusative only.*

plural - stress is shifted to the root (initial syllable) in the *nominative* (and the *accusative* if the latter is identical with the nominative) *only.*

In all other forms stress remains fixed on the post-root syllable.

Thus, there are logically nine possible types, of which eight actually exist in Russian:

	AA	AB	AC
Nom.	кни́га	сад	гость
Acc.	кни́гу	сад	го́стя
Gen.	кни́ги	са́да	го́стя
Prep.	кни́ге	са́де	го́сте
Dat.	кни́ге	са́ду	го́стю
Instr.	кни́гой	са́дом	го́стем
Nom.	кни́ги	сады́	го́сти
Acc.	кни́ги	сады́	госте́й
Gen.	книг	садо́в	госте́й
Prep.	кни́гах	сада́х	гостя́х
Dat.	кни́гам	сада́м	гостя́м
Instr.	кни́гами	сада́ми	гостя́ми

---

[1] Stem stress in the plural that is opposed to ending stress in the singular (i.e. types BA and CA) always falls on the final stem syllable, not counting the inserted vowel of the genitive plural. Thus: высота́ — высо́ты, меньшинство́ — меньши́нства; письмо́ — пи́сьма — пи́сем, ремесло́ — ремёсла — ремёсел.

	BA	BB	BC
Nom.	жена́	язы́к	губа́
Acc.	жену́	язы́к	губу́
Gen.	жены́	языка́	губы́
Prep.	жене́	языке́	губе́
Dat.	жене́	языку́	губе́
Instr.	жено́й	языко́м	губо́й
Nom.	жёны	языки́	гу́бы
Acc.	жён	языки́	гу́бы
Gen.	жён	языко́в	губ
Prep.	жёнах	языка́х	губа́х
Dat.	жёнам	языка́м	губа́м
Instr.	жёнами	языка́ми	губа́ми

	CA	CB	CC
Nom.	зима́	No nouns of	рука́
Acc.	зи́му	this stress type	ру́ку
Gen.	зимы́	are attested in	руки́
Prep.	зиме́	Russian.	руке́
Dat.	зиме́		руке́
Instr.	зимо́й		руко́й
Nom.	зи́мы		ру́ки
Acc.	зи́мы		ру́ки
Gen.	зим		рук
Prep.	зи́мах		рука́х
Dat.	зи́мам		рука́м
Instr.	зи́мами		рука́ми

Pattern AB

а́дрес (-а́)	ме́сто (-а́)	сло́во (-а́)
го́род (-а́)	мо́ре (-я́)	суп
де́ло (-а́)	мост	сын (*nom. pl.* сыновья́)
дире́ктор (-а́)	муж (*nom. pl.* мужья́)	сыр
до́ктор (-а́)	но́мер (-а́)	учи́тель (-я́)
дом (-а́)	профе́ссор (-а́)	хлеб (-а́)
друг (*nom. pl.* друзья́)	ряд	цвет (-а́)
и́мя (*nom. pl.* имена́)	сад	час

Pattern BA

вино́	окно́	семья́
жена́	письмо́	сестра́ (*gen. pl.* сестёр)
		страна́

Pattern AC

год (and AB)	дере́вня	о́вощи *pl.*
гость	но́вость *f.*	соль *f.*

Pattern BB

врач	рубль
дека́брь	сентя́брь
день	слова́рь
звоно́к (*gen. sing.* звонка́)	статья́
каранда́ш	стол
нож	февра́ль
ноя́брь	четве́рг
октя́брь	эта́ж
певе́ц (*gen. sing.* певца́)	язы́к
плащ	янва́рь
продаве́ц (*gen. sing.* продавца́)	

Pattern CA   Pattern CC

вода́	голова́
	доска́
	среда́

Numerals

1. Cardinal Numerals

1	оди́н, одна́, одно́	18	восемна́дцать	80	во́семьдесят
2	два, две	19	девятна́дцать	90	девяно́сто
3	три	20	два́дцать	100	сто
4	четы́ре	21	два́дцать оди́н	200	две́сти
5	пять	22	два́дцать два	300	три́ста
6	шесть	23	два́дцать три	400	четы́реста
7	семь	24	два́дцать четы́ре	500	пятьсо́т
8	во́семь	25	два́дцать пять	600	шестьсо́т
9	де́вять	26	два́дцать шесть	700	семьсо́т
10	де́сять	27	два́дцать семь	800	восемьсо́т
11	оди́ннадцать	28	два́дцать во́семь	900	девятьсо́т
12	двена́дцать	29	два́дцать де́вять	1000	ты́сяча
13	трина́дцать	30	три́дцать	2000	две ты́сячи
14	четы́рнадцать	40	со́рок	3000	три ты́сячи
15	пятна́дцать	50	пятьдеся́т	4000	четы́ре ты́сячи
16	шестна́дцать	60	шестьдеся́т	5000	пять ты́сяч
17	семна́дцать	70	се́мьдесят		

a. Spelling rule: Numerals up to 40 have **ь** at the end; those after 40 have **ь** in the middle of the word: пятна́дцать – пятьдеся́т, пятьсо́т, семна́дцать – се́мьдесят, семьсо́т.

b. 21, 32, 43, etc. are formed by adding the digit to the ten: два́дцать оди́н (одна́, одно́), три́дцать два (две), со́рок три, etc.

c. **Ты́сяча** "thousand" is a regular feminine noun; further thousands are regular too: две ты́сячи, три ты́сячи, пять ты́сяч, со́рок ты́сяч.

d. **Миллио́н** "million" and **миллиа́рд** (or **биллио́н**) "thousand million" are regular masculine nouns and decline accordingly: два миллио́на, пять миллио́нов; три миллиа́рда, девяно́сто миллиа́рдов.

e. Remember that in writing numerals, a comma is used in Russian where a decimal point is used in English. Thus, 32,5 means "thirty-two and a half" in Russian. Thousands are marked off either by a period or by a space. For example: 6.229.315 or 6 229 315 (cf. the English 6, 229, 315).

2. Ordinal Numerals

1	пе́рвый	14	четы́рнадцатый	90	девяно́стый
2	второ́й	15	пятна́дцатый	100	со́тый
3	тре́тий	16	шестна́дцатый	200	двухсо́тый
4	четвёртый	17	семна́дцатый	300	трёхсо́тый
5	пя́тый	18	восемна́дцатый	400	четырёхсо́тый
6	шесто́й	19	девятна́дцатый	500	пятисо́тый
7	седьмо́й	20	двадца́тый	600	шестисо́тый
8	восьмо́й	30	тридца́тый	700	семисо́тый
9	девя́тый	40	сороково́й	800	восьмисо́тый
10	деся́тый	50	пятидеся́тый	900	девятисо́тый
11	оди́ннадцатый	60	шестидеся́тый	1000	ты́сячный
12	двена́дцатый	70	семидеся́тый		
13	трина́дцатый	80	восьмидеся́тый		

a. The Russian ordinal numerals corresponding to 21st, 32nd, 43rd, etc, are composed of the *cardinal* representing the ten and the *ordinal* representing the digit: два́дцать пе́рвый (-ое, -ая, -ые), три́дцать второ́й, со́рок тре́тий; семь ты́сяч семьсо́т седьмо́й, etc.

b. The Russian 2000th, 3000th, etc. are formed on the pattern of the hundreds: двухты́сячный, трёхты́сячный, пятиты́сячный, шеститы́сячный, etc.

New Independent States (NIS)[1]

COUNTRY				
Азербайджа́н	Azerbaijan	азербайджа́нец	азербайджа́нка	азербайджа́нский
Арме́ния	Armenia	армяни́н	армя́нка	армя́нский
Белору́сь	Belarus	белору́с	белору́ска	белору́сский
Гру́зия	Georgia	грузи́н	грузи́нка	грузи́нский
Казахста́н	Kazakhstan	каза́х	каза́шка	каза́хский
Киргизста́н	Kyrgyzstan	кирги́з	кирги́зка	кирги́зский
Молда́вия	Moldova	молдава́нин	молдава́нка	молда́вский
Таджикиста́н	Tajikistan	таджи́к	таджи́чка	таджи́кский
Туркмениста́н	Turkmenistan	туркме́н	туркме́нка	туркме́нский
Узбекиста́н	Uzbekistan	узбе́к	узбе́чка	узбе́кский
Украи́на	Ukraine	украи́нец	украи́нка	украи́нский

Some of the Larger Republics within the Russian Federation[2]

REPUBLIC				
Башкортоста́н	Bashkortostan	башки́р	башки́рка	башки́рский
Буря́тия	Buryatia	буря́т	буря́тка	буря́тский
Саха́ (Яку́тия)	Sakha (Yakutia)	яку́т	яку́тка	яку́тский
Татарста́н	Tatarstan	тата́рин	тата́рка	тата́рский
Тува́	Tuva	туви́нец	туви́нка	туви́нский
Чува́шия	Chuvash Republic	чува́ш	чува́шка	чува́шский

---

[1] The New Independent States (NIS) is a Western designation for Russia and 11 other former Soviet republics (excluding the Baltic States). While Russian is not the official state language of most of the new nations, it continues to serve as an official language of communication within and among these states. For example, when Belarus and Uzbek officials or business people communicate with one another, they are very likely to use Russian for that purpose.

[2] Russia (also officially known as the Russian Federation) consists of Moscow, St. Petersburg, and 86 regions (oblasts), some of which have the status of republics within the Russian Federation. The above examples reflect some of the most well-known republics and the words used to refer to members of the ethnic groups after which they are named. As a rule, these republics include several ethnic groups (including Russians); the titular group often represents only a minority within the given republic.

A. Russian Consonants

The Russian phonetics system contains two sets of consonant pairs: hard/soft consonants and voiced/voiceless consonants.

1. HARD AND SOFT CONSONANTS

There are 15 pairs of soft and hard consonants in Russian:

/п/ — /пʲ/	/б/ — /бʲ/	/м/ — /мʲ/	/ф/ — /фʲ/	/в/ — /вʲ/
/т/ — /тʲ/	/д/ — /дʲ/	/с/ — /сʲ/	/з/ — /зʲ/	/к/ — /кʲ/
/г/ — /гʲ/	/х/ — /хʲ/	/л/ — /лʲ/	/н/ — /нʲ/	/р/ — /рʲ/

The remaining six consonants cannot be separated into hard/soft pairs. Three are always hard — /ш, ж, ц/ — and three are always soft — /щ, ч, й/.

The choice of a hard or soft consonant can affect a word's meaning. Compare:

у́гол /у́гал/ "corner" — у́голь /у́галʲ/ "coal"

говори́т /гавар ʲи́т/ "s/he speaks" — говори́ть /гавар ʲи́тʲ/ "to speak"

рад /рат/ "glad" — ряд /рʲат/ "row"

лук /лук/ "onion" — люк /лʲук/ "manhole"

Soft consonants are pronounced in the same way as their hard counterparts with one important difference: in a soft consonant, the tongue arches toward the middle of the roof of the mouth (the palate), as it does in the pronunciation of the vowel /и/. Because of the similarity in formation, Russian soft consonants are often described by phoneticians as having an "/и/ nuance". Students will find it easier to produce a soft consonant if they begin by pronouncing it in position between two /и/ - vowels, for in this case the middle part of the tongue will already be in the correct position.

This distinction between soft and hard consonants does not exist in English. Therefore, to many speakers of English, a palatalized consonant before the vowels /a/, /o/, and /y/ may sound something like the corresponding hard consonant plus the consonant /й/ ("yot"). Actually, this "yot" is inseparable from the consonant.

Failure to distinguish a soft consonant from a soft consonant + /й/ can lead to some confusion in meaning. Compare:

се́мя /сʲе́мʲa/ "seed" – семья́ /сʲимʲйа́/ "family"
лёд /лʲо́т/ "ice" – льёт /лʲйо́т/ "(s/he) pours"

2. VOICED AND VOICELESS CONSONANTS

There are 11 pairs of voiced and voiceless consonant sounds in Russian:

Voiceless:	/п/ /пᵇ/	/ф/ /фᵇ/	/с/ /сᵇ/	/т/ /тᵇ/	/ш/	/к/ /кᵇ/
Voiced:	/б/ /бᵇ/	/в/ /вᵇ/	/з/ /зᵇ/	/д/ /дᵇ/	/ж/	/г/ /гᵇ/

The remaining consonants cannot be separated into voiced/voiceless pairs. Nine consonant sounds are always voiced: /м, мᵇ, н, нᵇ, л, лᵇ, р, рᵇ, й/, and four are always voiceless:

$$/ч, ц, х, щ/.$$

As in English, the correct pronunciation of voiced and voiceless consonants is crucial to the differentiation of words and their meaning in Russian. The voiceless/voiced pair *p — b* distinguishes the words "pit" and "bit", for example. Compare the following pairs of words in Russian:

том "tome"	дом "house"
корá "tree bark"	горá "mountain"
икрá "caviar"	игрá "game"
пар "vapor"	бар "bar"

Voiced consonants are produced with the vibration of the vocal cords, while voiceless consonants are not. The difference between the Russian and English consonants lies in the fact that Russian voiced consonants are voiced throughout the entire length of the sound, whereas English voiced consonants are semi-voiced: only the end of the sound is voiced. That is, the vocal cords begin vibrating only at the end of the articulation of the sound.

Two basic rules govern the phonetic behavior of Russian voiced and voiceless consonants.

1. Voiced consonants become devoiced in word final position, therefore the word зуб "tooth" is pronounced /зуп/ and rhymes with суп "soup". Similarly:

дог /док/ "Great Dane"	rhymes with док "dock"
код /кот/ "code"	rhymes with кот "cat"
муж /муш/ "husband"	rhymes with душ "shower"

2. Within a consonant cluster, the voicing quality of the final consonant determines the voicing of the entire cluster. A voiceless consonant becomes voiced when followed by a voiced consonant, and a voiced consonant becomes voiceless when followed by a voiceless consonant. Compare the spelling and the phonetic transcriptions of the following words:

Voiceless to Voiced	Voiced to Voiceless
рюкзáк /рᵇугзáк/ "backpack"	автóбус /афтóбус/ "bus"
сдать /здать/ "hand in"	лóжка /лóшка/ "spoon"
футбóл /фудбóл/ "soccer"	

However, remember that Russian unpaired voiced consonants — /р, рᵇ, л, лᵇ, м, мᵇ, н, нᵇ/, and /й/ - do *not* cause voicing in a preceding voiceless consonant:

слой "layer" — злой "malicious"

икра́ "caviar" — игра́ "game"

пра́во "law" — бра́во "bravo"

The hard/soft pair /в/ — /вᵇ/ can change to /ф/ — /фᵇ/, but, like those listed above, will not cause a preceding consonant to become voiced.

Compare the phonetic value of /в/ — /вᵇ/ before a voiceless consonant:

в шкафу́ pronounced as one word /**фш**кафу́/ "in the cupboard", ав**т**о́бус /а**фт**о́бус/ "bus", Ка**вк**а́з /ка**фк**а́с/ "Caucasus"

and after a voiceless consonant:

твой /**тв**ой/ "yours", Мос**кв**а́ /ма**скв**а́/ "Moscow"

Note that in normal, rapid speech voicing and devoicing may occur at word junctures:

на**ш д**ом /на**жд**о́м/ "our home"
то**т д**руг[1] /то**дд**ру́к/ "that friend"
Но**ж т**ут. /но**шт**у́т/ "The knife is here."

3. ARTICULATION OF RUSSIAN CONSONANTS

The mouth is relaxed when pronouncing consonant sounds in Russian; in English the mouth is not relaxed.

The Consonants /м, ф, в, п, б, г, к/

The consonants /м, ф, в, п, б, г, к/ differ very little from their American English counterparts /m, f, v, p, b, g, k/. The only major difference lies in the consonants /п/ and /к/ which are always pronounced *without aspiration* in Russian. Compare the non-aspirated p's and k's in "spark", "skate", and "apple" and their aspirated counterparts in "park", "pot", "Kate", and "caught", pronounced with a noticeable puff of air.

The Consonants /н, т, д, с, з/

The Russian consonants /н, т, д, с, з/ are dental sounds, pronounced with the tip of the tongue lowered and touching the lower front teeth and the front part of the tongue pressed against the upper teeth. The English counterparts of these consonants — /n, t, d/ — are pronounced differently, with the tip of the tongue pressed against the alveolar palate. The Russian /т/, unlike its English counterpart, is pronounced without aspiration, and the Russian /н/ is never velar; cf. "thing" versus **танк**.

---

[1] Note that the double consonant is pronounced as *one* long sound.

Pronouncing Russian dental consonants /н, т, д/ with the tip of the tongue raised upwards hinders the softening of soft consonants.

The Consonants /ш, ж/

The Russian consonants /ш/ and /ж/ are always hard. In pronouncing them, the tongue assumes a "spoon-like" position with both the tip and the back part of the tongue raised, and the middle part of the tongue lowered. The lips protrude. The Russian /ш/ and /ж/ sound less soft than their English counterparts.

Consonants /ш/ and /ж/ are hard; although the spelling rules require that the letter **и** be written after them, it is always pronounced as /ы/. In addition, the sound /ш/ is spelled by the letter **ч** in the words **ч**то /**ш**то/ "what", скý**ч**но /скý**ш**на/ "(one is) bored", коне́**ч**но /кане́**ш**на/ "of course", and in a small number of others.

The Consonants /л/ and /лʲ/

The consonants /л/ and /лʲ/ are especially difficult for the native speakers of English because the pronunciation of the English /l/ lies somewhere between them: it is softer than /л/ and harder than /лʲ/. The tongue position between these two consonants can be compared to a spoon with its bottom up for the hard /л/ and its bottom down for the soft /лʲ/. To pronounce the hard /л/, the tip of the tongue should be lowered toward the lower teeth; it is helpful to place it in between the upper and the lower teeth. The back part of the tongue is raised and retracted. For the soft /лʲ/, the tongue arches upward; the tip and the front part of the tongue touch the hard palate.

The Consonant /р/

The tip of the tongue vibrates near the alveolar palate in order to pronounce /р/ in the initial position. By contrast, the initial /r/ in American English is pronounced with the front part of the tongue bent downward, relatively tense and immobile. To achieve the Russian /р/, the tip of the tongue must be relaxed and able to vibrate freely. Combinations of /р/ with the consonants /т/ and /д/, such as **тра** and **дра**, may help develop this free vibration.

The Consonant /й/ ("yot")

The consonant /й/ is pronounced with more tension than its English counterpart in the words **y**es and **y**ellow.

The Consonant /х/

The consonant /х/ is produced like /к/, but with the tongue lowered slightly. The tip of the tongue is near the lower teeth but does not touch them, and the throat is relaxed. The Russian /х/ resembles the Scottish "ch" in "lo**ch**." Since the tongue is raised to the same height as in the articulation of the vowel /у/, careful practice of this vowel will help you to master pronunciation of the Russian /х/.

The Consonant /ч/

The consonant /ч/ is an unpaired soft consonant. It is softer than the corresponding English sound.

The Consonant /щ/

The consonant /щ/ is produced with the tip of the tongue moved more forward and down, the front part of the tongue more flattened than in the articulation of /ш/, and the lips protruding. The consonant /щ/ is a soft, long sound. It is designated by the letter **щ** and sometimes by the consonant clusters **сч, зч,** and **жч** (unless they occur at morpheme junctures): **сча́стье** /ща́сʲтʲйа/ "happiness", **счёт** /щот/ "score", **мужчи́на** /мущи́на/ "man." Cf.: **счита́ть** /щита́тʲ/ "count", but **счита́ть** /счита́тʲ/ "compare a copy with the original text".

The Consonant /ц/

The consonant /ц/ is a complex sound that begins as /т/ and then turns into a /с/. It is a single, fused sound and not a combination of the sounds /т/ and /с/ as in the English word "its."

In addition to the letter ц, the sound may also be represented by the consonant clusters **тц, дц, тс, дс,** and **тьс.** For example:

два́дцать "twenty," де́тский "children's," городско́й "city," "urban," боя́ться "to fear."

    Take note of the following consonant clusters which include silent consonants:

вств /ств/ — здра́вствуйте /здра́ствуйтʲи/ "hello"
                          чу́вствовать /чу́стваватʲ/ "feel"
здн /зн/ — по́здно /по́зна/ "late"
               пра́здник /пра́знʲик/ "holiday"
стн /сн/ — гру́стно /гру́сна/ "sadly"
стл /сл/ — счастли́вый /щислʲи́вый/ "happy
лнц /нц/ — со́лнце /со́нца/ "sun"

B. Russian Vowels

1. ARTICULATION OF RUSSIAN VOWELS

The vowel /а, о, у/ can follow either hard or soft consonants.

The vowel /а/ is pronounced with the tip of the tongue flattened and placed behind the lower teeth.

The vowel /о/ is pronounced with the lips protruding and rounded. The back part of the tongue is raised toward the back palate, the tip of the tongue retracted. Hence, the Russian /о/ is further back than the corresponding English vowel.

The vowel /y/ requires that the lips be still more rounded and protruding than for the Russian /o/. Note that in pronouncing the Russian vowel sequence /o/ — /y/, the tongue and the lips move in opposite directions: the tongue moves back, while the lips move forward. The tongue retracts further back than in the pronunciation of the English **oo** in "boot."

The vowel /ы/ follows only hard consonants. In pronouncing /ы/, the tongue is raised high and retracted. Practice the sound /ы/ by saying the Russian vowel /y/ with your lips held in the position you would use to pronounce the vowel /и/.

In normal, rapid speech, when the letter /и/ occurs word-initially, it is pronounced /ы/ when the preceding word ends in a hard consonant:

сын Ива́н /сын**ы**ва́н/, в институ́те /**вы**нстʲиту́тʲи/.

The vowel /и/ follows only soft consonants. The vowel /и/ differs little from the first sound in the English word "each."

The vowel /e/ follows only soft consonants. It is similar to "e" in the English word "vet."

The vowel /э/ does not occur after soft consonants. It is pronounced with the mouth open wider than for the corresponding vowel /e/.

The vowel /э/ is pronounced:

1) in place of the orthographic э:

    э́тот

2) in place of /e/ in the following instances:

    a) after hard consonants /ш, ж, ц/

      шесть /шэстʲ/
      жест /жэст/
      це́ны /цэ́ны/

    b) in a few borrowed words:

      пане́ль /панэ́лʲ/
      анте́нна /антэ́на/

2. STRESS AND VOWEL REDUCTION

Except for little grammatical words (particles, prepositions), every Russian word has one stressed syllable which is pronounced louder, stronger, and with more emphasis than the other syllables. Vowels in unstressed syllables are usually weaker, shorter, more quiet, and have a less distinct quality.

карада́ш
1 2　3

In the word **каранда́ш** "pencil", only the stressed /a/ (in the syllable «даш») has a typical Russian /a/-like timbre. In the syllable «ран», /a/ resembles rather the English vowel in the word "but", in the syllable «ка» /a/ sounds even less /a/-like; it is close to the final sound in the English word "sofa".

You will gradually get used to the Russian rhythm which in general terms can be expressed numerically as

1, 2, 3́, 1

This means that in the first part of the word before stress (pre-tonic part), the closer vowels are to the stressed syllable, the stronger the vowels become. However, after the stressed syllable (post-tonic part), vowels are short and weak. Because Russian does not have fixed stress (i.e. all the words have stress on the last syllable, as in French), any syllable can be stressed. Therefore, the proposed formula describes only a general tendency. A special symbol /a/ will be used in phonetic transcription for the unstressed a's. Study the examples below:

маши́на "car"   катастро́фа "catastrophe"   бана́н "banana"
2 3 1   1 2   3 1   2 3

Some Russian vowels change their sound quality when they are unstressed. Thus, the Russian letter **o** is pronounced as /o/ only under stress. In the unstressed position the letter **o** undergoes same reduction as **a: хорошо́** is pronounced as /харашо́/.

The three Russian vowels /у, ы, и/ do not change their quality in the unstressed position. The chart below illustrates the changes in other vowels.

Vowel Reduction				
After hard consonants		**After soft consonants**		
Letters	*Sounds*	*Letters*	*Sounds*	*Exceptions*
а	/*a*/	я	/*и*/	Grammatical endings: /*a*/ тётя /т^ьо́т^ь*a*,/ учи́ться /учи́тц*a*/
o	/*a*/	—	—	—
э	/*ы*/	e	/*и*/	Endings of neuter nouns and adjectives in the nominative case: /*a*/ Чёрное мо́р*e* /чо́рн*айа* мо́р^ь*a*/

C. RUSSIAN SENTENCE INTONATION

In contemporary spoken Russian there are seven basic intonational constructions (IC): IC-1, IC-2, IC-3, IC-4, IC-5, IC-6, and IC-7. The last three intonational constructions, IC-5, IC-6, and IC-7, are used in emphatic speech and designate emotions: approval, disapproval, admiration, irony, etc. Each intonational construction is made up of a pretonic, a stressed (tonic), and a post-tonic part.

Each intonational construction is characterized by a particular pitch movement, which coincides with the point of emphasis of each sentence (the intonational center). The intonational center falls on the stressed syllable of the most important word within the sentence. After describing the contours of each intonational construction, we will use only the numerical superscript of the appropriate IC to identify the intonational centers.

Intonational Construction 1 (IC-1)

IC-1 designates the intonational contour characteristic of the Russian declarative sentence:

Э́то ма́ма.   This is (my) mom.

IC-1 is characterized by an intonational center pronounced with a sharply falling tone.

The portion of the sentence preceding the intonational center (pre-tonic) is pronounced with a level, medium tone, smoothly and without pauses. The portion of the sentence after the intonational center, (post-tonic) remains on a low pitch.

The intonational center of IC-1 can be on any word that clarifies the meaning of the sentence. Compare:

$$\overset{1}{\text{Э́то мой дом.}}$$ This is my house.

$$\overset{1}{\text{Э́то мой дом.}}$$ This is *my* house.

$$\overset{1}{\text{Э́то мой дом.}}$$ *This* is my house.

Intonational Construction 2 (IC-2)

IC-2 is used in interrogative sentences that contain a question word.

Кто э́то?   Who is it?

The stressed part is pronounced with a falling tone and greater emphasis (denoted by the thick line). The post-tonic part is pronounced on a low pitch with a slight fall on the last syllable (as in IC-1). The intonational center is not necessarily on the question word; it can be at any other word that clarifies the meaning of the sentence:

$$\overset{2}{\text{Где ма́ма?}}$$ Where is mother?

Do not raise the tone of the post-tonic part.

Intonational Construction 3 (IC-3)

IC-3 is used in interrogative sentences which do not contain a question word.

Мáма дóма?   Is mom at home?

The pre-tonic part is pronounced with a level medium tone. At the stressed part the tone rises sharply from a higher than mid level. The post-tonic part is pronounced at a low pitch with a slight fall at the last syllable.

A sharp rise of the tone of the stressed part in questions of this type presents great difficulty for English speakers, who tend to pronounce the stressed part of the question with an insufficiently high and sharp rise. English speakers also tend to raise the tone of the post-tonic part.

The position of the intonational center in IC-3 is determined by the meaning of the question.

— Э́то ваш сын? — Да, сын.   "Is it your *son*?" "Yes, it is my son."

— Э́то ваш сын? — Да, мой.   "Is it *your* son?" "Yes, it is *my* son."

Intonational Construction 4 (IC-4)

IC-4 is used in interrogative sentences with the conjunction **a**.

— Сегóдня вéчером я рабóтаю. **А ты?**   "I am working tonight. And how about you?"

The portion of the sentence before the intonational center (pre-tonic) is pronounced on a medium pitch, sometimes with a slight fall. At the intonational center, the tone starts on a lower pitch and then gradually rises within the syllable.

This type of intonation presents no problem for English speakers, since a gradual rise of tone is characteristic of English questions without a question word.

┌─────────────────── KEY ───────────────────┐

acc.	accusative		*m.*	masculine
colloq.	colloquial		*neut.*	neuter
f.	feminine		*nom.*	nominative
gen.	genitive		*perf.*	perfective
impf.	imperfective		*pl.*	plural
indecl.	indeclinable		*prep.*	prepositional
inf.	infinitive		*sg.*	singular
irreg.	irregular			

└──┘

The number in parentheses at the end of each entry indicates the chapter where the word first appears.

The following information about nouns is indicated in parenthesis:

1. Gender, if it is not clear from the nominative form, e.g. дéдушка (*m.*), и́мя (*n.*)

2. Irregular nominative plurals, e.g. друг (*nom. pl.* друзья́)

3. Stress shifts, e.g. áдрес AB

4. Indeclinable nouns, e.g. кинó (*indecl.*)

5. на-nouns, e.g. зáпад (на)

A small subset of Russian verbs is irregular, as indicated below, e.g. хотéть (*irreg.*). The remaining verbs are given with the verb stem in italics, e.g. читáть *читáй-.*

Some verbs take objects in a certain case. The case required is indicated after the verb, by the appropriate interrogative pronoun, e.g. **давáть** *давáй-* / **дать** (*irreg.*) **что, кому́** (to give **something** to **someone**).

А

а¹ and (1)
а² but (1)
а́вгуст August (3)
авто́бус bus (1)
а́дрес AB (*nom. pl.* адреса́) address (1)
Азербайджа́н Azerbaijan (5)
А́зия Asia (5)
актёр actor (1)
актри́са actress (1)
а́лгебра algebra (5)
алло́ hello (on the telephone) (1)
Астана́ Astana (capital of Kazakhstan) (5)
Аля́ска Alaska (4)
Аме́рика America (USA) (3)
америка́нец American (male) (3)
америка́нка American (female) (3)
америка́нский American (3)
англи́йский English (3)
англича́нин English (male) (3)
англича́нка English (female) (3)
А́нглия England (3)
антропо́лог anthropologist (1)
апельси́н orange (2)
аппарату́ра equipment (6)
апре́ль April (3)
Арба́т Arbat (street in Moscow) (2)
Арме́ния Armenia (5)
Арха́нгельск Arkhangelsk (city in Russia) (1)
архите́ктор architect (3)
ата́ка attack (4)
Атла́нта Atlanta (4)
аттракцио́н amusement park ride (6)
А́фрика Africa (5)
ах oh (2)
Ашхаба́д Ashkhabad (capital of Turkmenistan) (5)
аэропо́рт airport (1)

Б

ба́бушка grandmother (5)
бага́ж (*sg. only*) luggage (1)
Байка́л Lake Baikal (1)
Баку́ Baku (capital of Azerbaijan) (5)
бале́т (на) ballet (4)
балери́на ballerina (4)
Балтимо́р Baltimore (2)
бана́н banana (1)
банк bank (1)
бар bar (1)
бараба́н drum (4)
Белору́сь Belarus (5)

бе́лый white (3)
Берли́н Berlin (2)
бефстро́ганов beef Stroganoff (6)
библиоте́ка library (1)
би́знес business (4)
бизнесме́н businessperson (1)
биле́т ticket (4)
    ли́шний ~ extra ticket (4)
    студе́нческий ~ student ID (5)
био́лог biologist (1)
биоло́гия biology (5)
бифште́кс steak (6)
Бишке́к Bishkek (capital of Kyrgyzstan) (5)
блин BB crepe, pancake (6)
блю грас blue grass (4)
блю́до dish (6)
больни́ца hospital (1)
большо́й big (3)
борщ BB borsch (beet soup) (6)
Бо́стон Boston (2)
брасле́т bracelet (6)
брат (*nom. pl.* бра́тья) brother (1)
    двою́родный ~ cousin (male) (5)
брю́ки (*pl. only*) pants (3)
бу́дущее (noun) the future (6)
бутербро́д sandwich (2)
буты́лка bottle (6)
бухга́лтер bookkeeper, accountant (1)
был, была́, бы́ло, бы́ли was, were (4)
бы́стро fast, quickly (2)

В

в¹ (+ *prep.*) in, at (2)
в² (+ *acc.*) on (with days of the week) (6)
ва́жный important (4)
ва́нная (*noun*) bathroom (2)
ваш, ва́ша, ва́ше, ва́ши your(s) (1)
Вашингто́н Washington (2)
вдруг suddenly (5)
век century (3)
велосипе́д bicycle (5)
весёлый happy, cheerful (3)
весно́й in the spring (3)
ветерина́р veterinarian (1)
ветерина́рный veterinary (4)
ве́чер AB (*pl.* вечера́) evening (4)
    до́брый ~ good evening (3)
    до ве́чера see you in the evening (5)
ве́чером in the evening (2)
ве́щи (*pl.*) things (1)
ви́део video (5)

видеока́мера video camera (1)
ви́деть *виде-* /уви́деть кого - что see (5)
ви́за visa (1)
ви́лка fork (2)
вино́ BA wine (5)
виолонче́ль cello (4)
витами́н vitamin (6)
вку́сно tasty, delicious (2)
вку́сный tasty, delicious (3)
Влади́мир Vladimir (4)
вме́сте together (4)
внима́тельно attentively (4)
вода́ CA water (6)
   минера́льная ~ mineral water (6)
во́дка vodka (3)
возвраща́ться *возвраща́й-ся* (*impf.*) return (5)
Во́лга (на) the Volga River (1)
Волгогра́д Volgograd (city in Russia) (1)
волнова́ться *волнова́-ся* (impf.) worry, be nervous (4)
вон (over) there (1)
Воро́неж Voronezh (city in Russia) (1)
воскресе́нье Sunday (6)
восемна́дцать eighteen (3)
во́семь eight (1)
восьмо́й eighth (4)
восто́к (на) east (4)
вот here (is/are) (1)
   Вот э́то да! Wow! (4)
врач BB doctor (1)
всё¹ everything (1)
Всё!² That's it! (4)
всегда́ always (2)
встре́ча (на) meeting (5)
вто́рник Tuesday (6)
второ́й second (4)
вчера́ yesterday (2)
вы you (1)
вы́пить (6) see пить
высо́кий tall (3)
вы́ставка (на) exhibit (4)

Г

газе́та newspaper (1)
га́мбургер hamburger (1)
гара́ж (BB) garage (1)
где where (1)
геогра́фия geography (4)
гео́лог geologist (1)
геоме́трия geometry (5)
Герма́ния Germany (3)

геро́й hero (6)
гита́ра guitar (1)
гитари́ст guitarist (4)
говори́ть¹ *говори-* о ком - о чём (*impf.*) speak (2)
говори́ть² *говори-* / сказа́ть *сказа́-* что, кому́, о чём say, tell (4)
Голливу́д Hollywood (1)
голова́ CC head (1)
голо́дный hungry (4)
голубо́й light blue (3)
гори́лла gorilla (1)
го́род AB (*nom. pl.* города́) city (1)
гости́ная (*noun*) living room (2)
гости́ница hotel (1)
гость AC guest (2)
гото́вить *гото́ви-* / пригото́вить что, кому́ cook, prepare (6)
грамма́тика grammar (5)
Гру́зия Georgia (5)
гру́ппа group (3)
гуля́ть *гуля́й-* (*impf.*) go for a walk (2)

Д

да yes (1)
дава́ть *дава́й-* / дать (*irreg.*) что, кому́ give (6)
   Да́йте, пожа́луйста ... Please give (me) ... (6)
давно́ for a long time (4)
дать (6) see дава́ть
да́ча (на) dacha (cottage) (2)
два two (1)
два́дцать twenty (3)
двена́дцать twelve (3)
де́вушка girl, young woman (4)
девятна́дцать nineteen (3)
де́вять nine (1)
девя́тый ninth (4)
де́душка (*m.*) grandfather (5)
дека́брь BB December (3)
дека́н dean (6)
де́лать *де́лай-* / сде́лать что do (2)
де́ло AB affair, matter, business (4)
день BB day (1)
   до́брый ~ good afternoon (3)
де́ньги (*pl. only*) money (4)
де́сять ten (1)
деся́тый tenth (4)
детекти́в detective/mystery novel (3)
де́ти (*pl.; sg.* ребёнок) children (3)
Детро́йт Detroit (2)
дёшево cheap (6)
джаз jazz (4)

джи́нсы (*pl. only*) jeans (1)
Джорджта́ун Georgetown (1)
дива́н sofa (2)
диджéй DJ (4)
Дина́мо Dinamo (here: stadium in Moscow) (1)
дирéктор AB (*nom. pl.* директора́) director (5)
диск compact disk (6)
дискéтка computer diskette (5)
дискотéка (на) dance club (4)
дли́нный long (3)
днём in the afternoon (2)
до́брый kind (6)
докла́д presentation, report (6)
до́ктор AB (*pl.* доктора́) doctor, Dr. (5)
до́лго for a long time (6)
дом AB (*nom. pl.* дома́) house, building (1)
домохозя́йка home-maker (4)
до́рого expensive (6)
дорого́й expensive (4)
до свида́ния goodbye (1)
доска́ CC blackboard (1)
до́чка daughter (2)
дра́ма drama (4)
друг AB (*nom. pl.* друзья́) male friend (1)
друго́й other, different (5)
дру́жба friendship (6)
ду́мать *ду́май-* / поду́мать о ком – о чём
    think (2)
дура́к BB fool (5)
Душанбе́ Dushanbe (capital of Tajikistan) (5)
дя́дя (*m.*) uncle (1)

Е

Евро́па Europe (5)
его́ his (2)
еда́ food (6)
её her(s) (2)
Ерева́н Yerevan (capital of Armenia) (5)
ерунда́ junk, nothing special, nonsense (6)
есть / съесть (*irreg.*) eat (6)
ещё still; yet (4)

Ж

жа́реный fried (6)
Ждём вас. Looking forward to seeing you. (6)
жена́ BA wife (1)
же́нщина woman (5)
жето́н token (3)
жёлтый yellow (3)
живо́тное (*noun*) animal (3)
жизнь (*f.*) life (5)

жить *жи̌в-* (*impf.*) live (2)
жу́лик swindler (5)
журна́л magazine (1)
журнали́ст journalist (male) (1)
журнали́стка journalist (female) (1)

З

за (+ *acc.*) to … (used when making a toast) (6)
заво́д (на) factory (4)
за́втра tomorrow (6)
    до за́втра until tomorrow, goodbye (2)
за́втрак breakfast (3)
за́втракать *за́втракай-* / поза́втракать have
    breakfast (2)
зада́ча assignment, problem (6)
заказа́ть (6) see зака́зывать
зака́зывать *зака́зывай-* / заказа́ть *заказа̌-* что
    order (6)
зака́нчивать *зака́нчивай-* / зако́нчить *зако́нчи-*
    что graduate, finish (6)
заку́ска appetizer (6)
за́нят busy (5)
за́пад (на) west (4)
запи́ска note (6)
звони́ть *звони́-* / позвони́ть кому́ call (3)
звоно́к BB telephone call (5)
зда́ние building (3)
здесь here (1)
здо́рово great, terrific (3)
здра́вствуй(те) hello (1)
зелёный green (3)
зимо́й in the winter (3)
знако́мство acquaintance (6)
знако́мый (*noun*) friend, acquaintance (5)
знать *знай-* (*impf.*) кого - что know (2)
    Вы не зна́ете … (Ты не зна́ешь …)?
    Do you happen to know …? (2)
    Я то́чно не зна́ю. I don't know for sure. (3)
зна́чит (it) means (5)
зоопа́рк zoo (3)

И

и and (1)
игра́ть *игра́й-* (*impf.*) на чём play (a musical
    instrument) (4)
игру́шка toy (2)
извини́(те) I'm sorry, excuse (me) (1)
Изма́йлово Izmailovo (region in Moscow) (6)
икра́ BA caviar (3)
и́ли or (2)
импера́тор emperor (3)

и́мя АВ (*neut.; gen.sg.* и́мени) first name (5)
инжене́р engineer (1)
иногда́ sometimes (2)
институ́т institute (1)
инструме́нт instrument (6)
интере́сно[1] interestingly (2)
интере́сно[2] I wonder (2)
интере́сный interesting (3)
испа́нец Spaniard (male) (3)
Испа́ния Spain (3)
испа́нка Spaniard (female) (3)
испа́нский Spanish (3)
исто́рик historian (1)
исто́рия[1] story (5)
исто́рия[2] history (5)
италья́нский Italian (5)
их their(s) (2)
ию́ль July (3)
ию́нь June (3)

К

кабине́т office (5)
Кавка́з (на) Caucasus (Mountainous area to the south of Russia) (4)
ка́ждый every (6)
Казахста́н Kazakhstan (5)
как how (3)
    Как вас зову́т? What's your name? (3)
    Как дела́? How are things going? (3)
    Как же так? How come? (2)
    Как живёшь? How are you? (4)
    Как интере́сно! How interesting! (1)
    Как э́то по-англи́йски? How do you say that in English? (6)
како́й which; what kind of (3)
    Кака́я красота́! How lovely! (6)
календа́рь BB calendar (6)
калькуля́тор calculator (2)
Камча́тка Kamchatka (peninsula in the far east of Russia) (1)
кани́кулы (*pl. only*) school vacation (3)
ка́нтри country (music) (4)
капитали́ст capitalist (4)
Капито́лий Capitol (2)
каранда́ш BB pencil (1)
ка́рта map (1)
карти́на picture (6)
карто́шка potato(es) (6)
Каспи́йское мо́ре Caspian Sea (1)
ка́сса cash register (3)
кассе́та cassette (3)
касси́р cashier (3)

кафе́ (*indecl.*) café (1)
кафете́рий cafeteria (3)
кварти́ра apartment (1)
ке́пка cap (2)
    бейсбо́льная ~ baseball cap (3)
Ки́ев Kiev (capital of Ukraine) (2)
кино́ (*indecl.*) film (5)
кинотеа́тр movie theater (1)
Киргизста́н Kyrgyzstan (5)
кита́йский Chinese (5)
Кишинёв Kishinev/Chisinau (capital of Moldova) (5)
кларне́т clarinet (4)
класс grade (1st, 2nd, 3rd) (4)
кла́ссика[1] classical (music) (4)
кла́ссика[2] classics (literature) (6)
класси́ческий classical (4)
кли́ника clinic (2)
клуб club (4)
ключ BB key (2)
кни́га book (1)
когда́ when (3)
ко́ка-ко́ла Cola-Cola (1)
колбаса́ BA salami, sausage (2)
колле́га (*m. & f.*) colleague (6)
колле́дж college (2)
Колле́дж Парк College Park (1)
командиро́вка business trip (5)
ко́миксы (*pl.*) comics (6)
коме́дия comedy (4)
ко́мната room (1)
компа́ния company (6)
ко́мплекс complex (6)
компози́тор composer (3)
компоне́нт component (6)
компью́тер computer (1)
коне́чно of course (4)
консе́рвы canned food (6)
конта́кт contact (6)
конфе́та piece of candy (5)
конце́рт (на) concert (4)
кори́чневый brown (3)
коро́ткий short (3)
ко́рпус АВ (-á) building (1)
Кострома́ Kostroma (city in Russia) (1)
костю́м suit (1)
кот BB cat (male) (6)
котле́та burger (6)
ко́фе (*m., indecl.*) coffee (3)
ко́фта woman's top (3)
ко́шка cat (female) (1)
краси́во beautiful (1)

красивый beautiful (3)
красный red (3)
Кремль BB Kremlin (1)
кресло armchair (2)
кроссовки (pl.) sneakers (3)
Крым Crimea (peninsula on the Black Sea famous for its resorts) (5)
ксерокс photocopier (2)
кто who (1)
культура culture (4)
купить (6) see покупать
курица chicken (6)
курс¹ college course (3)
курс² (на) year in college (4)
куртка jacket (1)
кухня¹ (на) kitchen (2)
кухня² cuisine (4)

Л

лаборатория laboratory (3)
ладно all right (3)
лампа lamp (1)
лежать лежа- (impf.) be in a lying position, lie (4)
лекарство medicine (6)
лекция (на) lecture (4)
летом in the summer (2)
Ливерпуль Liverpool (4)
лимон lemon (5)
лимузин limousine (1)
литература literature (5)
ложка spoon (2)
Лондон London (2)
Лос-Анжéлес Los Angeles (2)
лучше better (6)
любимый favorite (3)
любить любй- (impf.) кого – что / + inf. love (5)
люди (pl.; sg. человек) people (3)
    Люди как люди. They're just ordinary people. (6)

М

магазин store (1)
магнитофон stereo (5)
Мадрид Madrid (2)
май May (3)
майка t-shirt, sleeveless top (3)
майонéз mayonnaise (5)
макароны (pl.) pasta (6)
Макдоналдс McDonald's (1)
мальчик boy (5)
маленький small (3)

мало little (2)
мама mom (1)
мамуля mom (affectionate) (3)
Манчéстер Manchester (4)
Марсéль Marseilles (4)
март March (3)
масло butter (2)
математик mathematician (1)
математика mathematics (5)
машина car (1)
международный international (6)
мексиканский Mexican (5)
мéнеджер manager (1)
меню (indecl., neut.) menu (6)
Меня зовут ... My name is … (3)
место AB seat (4)
месяц month (6)
метро (indecl.) metro, subway (1)
мечтáть мечтай- (impf.) о чём – о ком dream (6)
милиционéр police officer (4)
милиция police station, police (3)
Минск Minsk (capital of Belarus) (5)
Минуточку! Just a minute! (3)
мир world (3)
много a lot (2)
мода style, fashion (3)
    в моде in style (3)
    не в моде out of style (3)
модный stylish (3)
Можно ...? May I …? (1)
мой, моя, моё, мои my, mine (1)
Молдáвия Moldova (5)
молодой young (3)
молоко milk (1)
молчáть молчá- (impf.) be silent (4)
монитор monitor screen (2)
море sea (1)
мороженое ice cream (5)
Москва Moscow (1)
мост bridge (3)
мочь / смочь (irreg.) + inf. be able (5)
муж AB (nom. pl. мужья) husband (1)
мужчина (m.) man (5)
музéй museum (1)
музыка music (4)
музыкáльный music (4)
мультфильм (мультик) cartoon (6)
мусор trash (2)
мы we (1)
Мэдисон Madison (2)
мясо meat (6)

Н

на[1] (+ *prep.*) on (2)
на[2] (+ *prep.*) in, at (with **на** nouns) (2)
на[3] (+ *acc.*) for (breakfast, dinner, etc.) (6)
наве́рное probably (2)
называ́ться *называ́й-ся* (*impf.*) be called (6)
наоборо́т on the contrary (3)
написа́ть (6) see **писа́ть**
напи́ток drink (6)
наполео́н Napoleon (pastry) (6)
начина́ть *начина́й-* / **нача́ть** *нǎ̆-чн-* **что** / + inf.
  begin (4)
наш, на́ша, на́ше, на́ши our(s) (1)
не (*unstressed*) not (1)
небольшо́й small (4)
Нева́ (на) Neva (St. Petersburg river) (4)
невесёлый not cheerful (3)
невку́сный not tasty (3)
неде́ля week (6)
незнако́м not acquainted (6)
неинтере́сный uninteresting (3)
некраси́вый plain, ugly (3)
не́мец German (male) (3)
неме́цкий German (3)
не́мка German (female) (3)
не мо́жет быть no way (3)
немо́дный unfashionable (3)
не на́до (it is) not necessary (6)
непло́хо not bad (2)
неплохо́й not bad (3)
непро́сто difficult (6)
несерьёзный not serious (3)
несмешно́й not funny (3)
нет no (1)
неэнерги́чный not energetic (3)
ничего́ not bad, all right (3)
но but (3)
Но́вгород Novgorod (city in Russia) (1)
Новосиби́рск Novosibirsk (city in Russia) (1)
но́вость AC (*f.*) news (6)
но́вый new (3)
нож BB knife (1)
ноль BB zero (1)
но́мер AB (*nom. pl.* номера́) number (1)
норма́льно O.K. (3)
нос AB nose (1)
ноя́брь BB November (3)
нра́виться *нра́ви-ся* / **понра́виться кому́**
  like (6)
Нью-Йо́рк New York (1)

О

о, об, обо (+ *prep.*) about (4)
обе́д lunch (2)
обе́дать *обе́дай* / **пообе́дать** have lunch (2)
общежи́тие dormitory (3)
о́бщество society (6)
обы́чно usually (6)
обяза́тельно certainly, definitely (6)
о́вощ AC vegetable (1)
огуре́ц BB cucumber (6)
оде́жда clothing (3)
Оде́сса Odessa (city in Ukraine) (2)
оди́н[1] one (1)
оди́н[2] alone (4)
оди́ннадцать eleven (3)
ой oh, ouch (1)
окно́ BA window (1)
октя́брь BB October (3)
омле́т omelet (6)
он he, it (1)
она́ she, it (1)
оно́ it (1)
они́ they (1)
опа́здывать *опа́здывай-* / **опозда́ть** (*irreg.*) be
  late (2)
о́пера (на) opera (4)
опя́ть again (4)
ора́нжевый orange (3)
организова́ть *организова́-* (*impf. and perf.*) **что**
  organize (6)
о́сенью in the autumn (3)
отве́т answer (6)
отве́тить (6) see **отвеча́ть**
отвеча́ть *отвеча́й-* / **отве́тить** *отве́ти-*
  кому́ answer (2)
о́тдых rest, relaxation (6)
отдыха́ть *отдыха́й-* (*impf.*) rest, vacation (2)
оте́ц BB father (3)
откры́тка postcard (6)
отли́чно excellent (1)
отли́чный excellent (3)
отме́тка grade (A, B, C) (4)
о́тчество patronymic (5)
о́фис office (2)
официа́нт waiter (1)
официа́нтка waitress (1)
о́чень very (1)
о́чень жаль (it's) a shame (3)
О́чень прия́тно. Very nice (to meet you). (1)
оши́бка mistake (3)

П

Па́вловск Pavlovsk (city in Russia) (2)
паке́т plastic bag (1)
па́па dad (1)
Пари́ж Paris (2)
парк park (1)
парте́р orchestra sitting (4)
па́спорт AB (-á) passport (1)
певе́ц BB singer (male) (1)
певи́ца singer (female) (1)
пельме́ни (*pl.*) dumplings (6)
пе́рвый first (4)
перевести́ (6) see переводи́ть
переводи́ть *переводи̌-* / перевести́ *перевёд-* что translate (5)
переда́ча TV show (4)
пёс BB dog (male) (6)
пи́во beer (5)
пингви́н penguin (1)
писа́тель writer (male) (1)
писа́тельница writer (female) (1)
писа́ть *писá-* / написа́ть что write (5)
письмо́ BA letter (1)
пить / вы́пить что drink (6)
пи́цца pizza (1)
плака́т poster (6)
план plan (6)
пла́тье dress (3)
плащ BB raincoat (3)
пле́йер cassette player/ mp3 player (2)
плита́ BA stove (2)
плов pilaf (6)
пло́хо bad (2)
плохо́й bad (3)
по-англи́йски (in) English (2)
пого́да weather (3)
пода́рок gift, present (4)
подру́га female friend (1)
подъе́зд entrance (2)
пое́здка trip (5)
пожа́луйста please, go ahead, that's O.K., you are welcome (1)
позавтракать (3) see за́втракать
позвони́ть (6) see звони́ть
познако́мьтесь get acquainted (3)
по-испа́нски (in) Spanish (2)
пока́ bye (3)
пока́ нет not yet (4)
покупа́ть *покупáй-* / купи́ть *купи̌-* что, кому́ buy (6)
поли́тика politics (4)
по́лка shelf (2)

помидо́р tomato (2)
по́мнить *помни-* (*impf.*) remember (4)
помога́ть *помогáй-* / помо́чь (*irreg.*) кому́ help (6)
по-мо́ему in my opinion (2)
помо́чь (6) see помога́ть
понеде́льник Monday (6)
по-неме́цки (in) German (2)
понима́ть *понимáй-* / поня́ть *по̌йм-* кого – что understand (2)
пообе́дать see обе́дать (6)
поп-му́зыка pop music (4)
популя́рный popular (3)
поро́да breed (6)
по-ру́сски (in) Russian (2)
по́сле (+ *gen.*) after (6)
посмотре́ть (6) see смотре́ть
по телефо́ну on the telephone (6)
поу́жинать (2) see у́жинать
по-францу́зски (in) French (2)
почему́ why (4)
по́чта (на) post office (1)
поэ́т poet (1)
по-япо́нски (in) Japanese (2)
пра́вда true; really (1)
предме́т subject (5)
представля́ть *представляй-* / предста́вить *предстáви-* что imagine (5)
прекра́сно wonderful (6)
прекра́сный wonderful (6)
преподава́тель instructor (male) (1)
преподава́тельница instructor (female) (1)
приве́т hi (3)
пригото́вить (6) see гото́вить
при́нтер printer (2)
приро́да nature (5)
прию́т shelter (6)
прия́тель (*f.* прия́тельница) friend (5)
пробле́ма problem (4)
програ́мма program (4)
программи́ст programmer (1)
продаве́ц BB salesperson (male) (1)
продавщи́ца salesperson (female) (1)
проду́кты (*pl.*) groceries (6)
проси́ть *проси̌-* / попроси́ть кого *inf.* ask, beg (5)
про́сто simply (2)
профессиона́льный professional (4)
профе́ссор AB (-á) professor (2)
психо́лог psychologist (1)
Псков Pskov (city in Russia) (1)
Пу́шкин Pushkin (city in Russia)

пятна́дцать fifteen (3)
пя́тница Friday (6)
пять five (1)
пя́тый fifth (4)

Р

рабо́та¹ (на) work (2)
рабо́та² paper (6)
    курсова́я ~ term paper (6)
рабо́тать *рабо́тай-* (*impf.*) work (2)
рад glad (5)
ра́дио (*indecl.*) radio (2)
раз one (when counting) (1)
райо́н region (4)
ра́ковина sink (2)
ра́ньше previously, used to (2)
расска́з story (6)
ребёнок (*sg.; pl.* де́ти) child (3)
ревнова́ть *ревнова́-* (*impf.*) be jealous (4)
ре́дко seldom (2)
рекомендова́ть *рекомендова́-* (*impf.*)
    recommend (6)
рестора́н restaurant (1)
реша́ть *реша́й-* / **реши́ть** *реши́-* что / *inf.* solve,
    decide (6)
реши́ть (6) see **реша́ть**
Рим Rome (4)
рисова́ние drawing (5)
рисова́ть *рисова́-* (*impf.*) draw (4)
роди́тели (*pl.*) parents (2)
рок rock (music) (4)
    рок гру́ппа rock group (4)
рома́н novel (6)
Росси́я Russia (1)
Росто́в Rostov (city in Russia) (1)
роя́ль (grand) piano (4)
руба́шка flannel or dress shirt (3)
руби́новый ruby (4)
ру́сская Russian (female) (3)
ру́сский¹ Russian (male) (3)
ру́сский² Russian (3)
ру́чка pen (1)
ры́ба fish (6)
рюкза́к BB backpack (1)
рэп rap (music) (4)
ряд BB row (4)

С

саксофо́н saxophone (4)
сала́т lettuce, salad (3)

сало́н salon, (here) pet grooming service (6)
са́мый most (3)
    са́мое гла́вное the main thing (6)
Санкт-Петербу́рг St. Petersburg (1)
Сара́тов Saratov (city in Russia) (2)
Сахали́н Sakhalin (island in the far east of Russia)
    (1)
са́хар sugar (1)
све́жий fresh (4)
сви́тер AB (*nom. pl.* свитера́) sweater (1)
сдава́ть *сдава́й-* / **сдать**¹ (*irreg.*) что rent (5)
сдать (5) see сдава́ть
сде́лать (6) see де́лать
се́вер (на) north (4)
сего́дня today (2)
седьмо́й seventh (4)
сейча́с now (2)
семе́стр semester (3)
семина́р (на) seminar (6)
семна́дцать seventeen (3)
семь seven (1)
семья́ BA family (1)
сентя́брь BB September (3)
серди́ться *серди́-ся* (*impf.*) be angry (5)
серьёзный serious (3)
се́рый grey (3)
сестра́ BB (*gen. pl.* сестёр) sister (1)
    двою́родная сестра́ cousin (female) (5)
сиде́ть *сиде́-* (*impf.*) sit (5)
симпати́чно nice (6)
симпати́чный nice, nice-looking (3)
Сиэ́тл Seattle (4)
Скажи́те, пожа́луйста... Please tell (me)… (2)
ска́нер scanner (2)
ско́лько how many; how much (4)
скри́пка violin (4)
слова́рь BB dictionary (1)
сло́во AB word (1)
слон BB elephant (1)
слу́шать *слу́шай-* (*impf.*) listen (4)
слы́шать *слы́ша-* (*impf.*) hear (5)
смешно́й funny (3)
смея́ться *смея́-ся* (*imp.*) laugh (5)
смотре́ть *смотре̌-* / **посмотре́ть** что watch,
    look at (5)
соба́ка dog (1)
собра́ние (на) meeting (4)
совреме́нный modern, contemporary (3)
сок juice (1)
Со́кол Sokol (subway station in Moscow) (1)
соли́ст soloist, lead singer (4)

соль salt (2)
сосе́д (*pl.* сосе́ди) neighbor (male) (6)
сосе́дка neighbor (female) (2)
сочине́ние essay (6)
спаге́тти spaghetti (6)
спа́льня bedroom (2)
спаси́бо thank you (1)
    Большо́е ~ . Thank you very much. (6)
спекта́кль performance, show (4)
специа́льный special (6)
спорт sport (1)
спорти́вный sports, athletic (6)
    ~ зал gymnasium (6)
спра́шивать *спра́шивай-* / спроси́ть *спросй-*
    кого́, о чём ask (2)
сра́зу at once (5)
среда́ CC Wednesday (6)
стадио́н (на) stadium (1)
ста́рый old (3)
стати́стика statistics (5)
статья́ BB article (4)
стихи́ BB (*pl.*) poems, verses (6)
стол BB table (1)
столи́ца capital (5)
столо́вая (*noun*) dining room (2)
стоя́ть *стоя́-* (*impf.*) stand, be in a standing
    position (4)
страна́ BA country (4)
стра́нный strange (3)
студе́нт university student (male) (1)
студе́нтка university student (female) (1)
стул (*pl.* сту́лья) chair (1)
суббо́та Saturday (6)
сувени́р souvenir (6)
су́мка bag (1)
суп soup (1)
су́ши (*indecl.*) sushi (6)
сча́стлив happy (5)
США USA (3)
сын AB (*pl.* сыновья́) son (1)
сыр AB cheese (1)
съесть (6) see есть
сюрпри́з surprise (3)

T

Таджикиста́н Tajikistan (5)
так so (1)
    Так э́то же ма́ма. Of course – after all, she's
       your mother. (3)
такси́ (*indecl., neut.*) taxi (1)
там there (1)

танцева́ть *танцева́-* (*impf.*) dance (4)
таре́лка plate (2)
Ташке́нт Tashkent (capital of Uzbekistan) (2)
Тбили́си Tbilisi (capital of Georgia) (5)
твой, твоя́, твоё, твои́ your(s) (1)
теа́тр theater (1)
текст text (5)
телеви́зор television set (2)
телесериа́л TV series (6)
телефо́н telephone (1)
телефо́нный telephone (5)
тепе́рь now (5)
террито́рия territory (6)
тётя aunt (1)
тигр tiger (1)
тогда́ then (5)
То́кио Tokyo (2)
Торо́нто Toronto (5)
торт cake (6)
тост toast (6)
тот, та, то, те that (3)
тра́нспорт transportation (4)
тре́тий third (4)
три three (1)
трина́дцать thirteen (3)
тролле́йбус trolley bus (1)
тромбо́н trombone (4)
тру́дно difficult (6)
тру́дный difficult (6)
туале́т[1] restroom (1)
туале́т[2] half bath (2)
Туркмениста́н Turkmenistan (5)
тут here (1)
ту́фли (*pl.*) shoes (3)
ты you (1)
    Дава́йте на «ты». Let's use ты. (2)
тюльпа́н tulip (4)

У

ужа́сно terrible (3)
ужа́сный terrible (5)
уже́ already (3)
у́жин dinner (3)
у́жинать *у́жинай-* / поу́жинать have dinner (2)
Узбекиста́н Uzbekistan (5)
Украи́на Ukraine (5)
у́лица street (1)
у́мный intelligent (6)
университе́т university (1)
университе́тский university (6)
упражне́ние exercise (5)
Ура́л (на) the Ural mountains (1)

успéх success (6)
у́тро morning (6)
   дóброе ~ good morning (3)
у́тром in the morning (2)
у́хо (*pl.* у́ши) ear (1)
учéбник textbook (1)
учи́тель AB (*nom. pl.* учителя́) grade school teacher (male) (1)
учи́тельница grade school teacher (female) (1)
учи́ться *учи́-ся* (*impf.*) to study (at a school, university) (6)

Ф

факс fax (2)
факультéт (на) department (at university) (5)
   актёрский ~ theater dept.
   инженéрный ~ engineering dept.
   истори́ческий ~ history dept.
   киновéдческий ~ film dept.
   математи́ческий ~ mathematics dept.
   физи́ческий ~ physics dept.
   филологи́ческий ~ philology dept.
   хими́ческий ~ chemistry dept.
   экономи́ческий ~ economics dept.
   факультéт би́знеса business dept.
   факультéт полити́ческой нау́ки dept. of political science
   факультéт ру́сского языка́ dept. of Russian language
фами́лия surname (5)
фанта́стика (нау́чная) (*sg. only*) (science) fiction (6)
февра́ль BB February (3)
фи́зик physicist (1)
фи́зика physics (5)
физкульту́ра physical education (5)
Филадéльфия Philadelphia (4)
филиа́л branch office (6)
фильм film (3)
фи́рма firm, company (6)
флéйта flute (4)
фотоальбóм photo album (5)
фотоаппара́т camera (1)
фотóграф photographer (1)
фотографи́ровать *фотографи́рова-* (*impf.*) **когó – что** take a picture of (5)
фотогра́фия photo (2)
Фра́нция France (3)
францу́женка Frenchwoman (3)
францу́з Frenchman (3)

францу́зский French (3)
фрукт fruit (1)
фрукто́вый fruit (5)
футбóл soccer (4)
   америка́нский ~ football (4)
футбóлка sweatshirt, jersey (3)

X

хи́мик chemist (1)
хи́мия chemistry (5)
хлеб bread (1)
холоди́льник refrigerator (2)
холóдный cold (6)
хозя́ин (*pl.* хозя́ева) owner, landlord, host (5)
хозя́йка owner, landlord, host (5)
хорóший good (3)
хорошó good, well (2)
хотéть + *inf.* / **что** (*impf.; irreg.*) want (3)
   Не хóчешь, как хóчешь. Whatever you say. (3)
хризантéма chrysanthemum (4)
худóжник artist (6)
хулига́н hooligan, hoodlum (male) (5)
хулига́нка hooligan, hoodlum (female) (5)

Ц

цвет AB (*nom. pl.* цвета́) color (3)
цветы́ (*pl.*) flowers (4)
целова́ть *целова́-* (*impf.*) kiss (5)
цель goal, purpose (5)
цéлый whole (6)
центр[1] downtown (1)
центр[2] center (3)
цирк circus (3)

Ч

чай AB tea (1)
ча́йник teakettle (2)
ча́сто often (2)
ча́шка cup (2)
чей, чья, чьё, чьи whose (2)
человéк (*sg.; pl.* лю́ди) person (3)
чемода́н suitcase (1)
четвéрг BB Thursday (6)
четвёртый fourth (4)
четы́ре four (1)
четы́рнадцать fourteen (3)
чёрный black (3)
Чика́го Chicago (4)

число BA date, number (6)
читáть читáй- / прочитáть что read (2)
что[1] what (1)
    Ну и что? So what? (6)
    что за (+ acc.) what kind of (4)
    Что ещё? What else? (6)
    Что случи́лось? What happened? (5)
    Что ты! Что вы! What are you talking about?
        What do you mean? (2)
    Что ты молчи́шь? Why are you (so) quiet? (4)
    Что э́то такóе? What's that? (6)
что[2] (in subordinate clause) that (4)

Ш

шампáнское champagne (6)
шарф scarf (3)
Шеремéтьево Sheremetyevo (airport in
    Moscow) (1)
шестнáдцать sixteen (3)
шестóй sixth (4)
шесть six (1)
шкаф AB closet, walk-in closet, wardrobe (2)
шкóла grade school (1)
шкóльник grade school student (male) (1)
шкóльница grade school student (female) (1)
шоколáд chocolate (1)
шóрты (pl. only) shorts (3)
шофёр driver (5)
штат state (2)

Щ

щи (pl. only) cabbage soup (6)

Э

экзáмен exam (3)
эклéр éclair (6)
экологи́ческий ecological (4)
эконóмика economics (5)
экономи́ст economist (1)
энерги́чный energetic (3)
эпизóд episode (6)
этáж BB floor (4)
э́то this (is)/these (are) (1)
э́тот, э́та, э́то, э́ти this, these (3)

Ю

ю́бка skirt (3)
юг (на) south (4)
юри́ст lawyer (1)

Я

я I (1)
язы́к BB language (3)
январь BB January (3)
япóнец Japanese (male) (3)
Япóния Japan (3)
япóнка Japanese (female) (3)
япóнский Japanese (3)

KEY

acc.	accusative		*irreg.*	irregular
adj.	adjective		*m.*	masculine
adv.	adverb		*neut.*	neuter
colloq.	colloquial		*nom.*	nominative
f.	feminine		*perf.*	perfective
gen.	genitive		*pl.*	plural
impf.	imperfective		*prep.*	prepositional
indecl.	indeclinable		*pron.*	pronoun
inf.	infinitive		*sg.*	singular
			v.	verb

A

able: be able мочь/смочь *(irreg.) + inf.*
about о, об, обо *(+ prep.)*
academy акаде́мия
accountant бухга́лтер
acquaintance[1] *(person)* знако́мый *(noun)*
acquaintance[2] знако́мство
actor актёр
actress актри́са
address а́дрес AB *(nom. pl.* адреса́)
advice сове́т
affair де́ло AB
Africa А́фрика
after по́сле *(+gen.)*
after all ведь *(unstressed)*
again опя́ть
airport аэропо́рт
Alaska Аля́ска
algebra а́лгебра
all right ла́дно
alone оди́н
already уже́
always всегда́
America *(USA)* Аме́рика *(США)*
American *(person)* америка́нец (male),
    америка́нка (female)
American *(adj.)* америка́нский
amusement park ride аттракцио́н
and а, и
angry: be angry серди́ться *серди́-ся (impf.)*
animal живо́тное *(noun)*

answer *(noun)* отве́т
answer *(v.)* отвеча́ть *отвеча́й- /*отве́тить
    отве́ти- кому́
anthropologist антропо́лог
apartment кварти́ра
appetizer заку́ска
April апре́ль
Arbat Арба́т (street in Moscow)
architect архите́ктор
area studies странове́дение
Arkhangelsk Арха́нгельск (city in Russia)
armchair кре́сло
Armenia Арме́ния
article статья́ BB
artist худо́жник
    art expert искусствове́д
    the study of art искусствове́дение
Ashkhabad Ашхаба́д (capital of Turkmenistan)
Asia А́зия
ask[1] спра́шивать *спра́шивай-/*спроси́ть *спроси́-*
    кого́, о чём
ask[2] проси́ть *проси́- /* попроси́ть кого́ / *+ inf.*
assignment зада́ча
at в, на *(+ prep.)*
Astana Астана́ (capital of Kazakhstan)
Atlanta Атла́нта
attack ата́ка
attentively внима́тельно
August а́вгуст
aunt тётя
Azerbaijan Азербайджа́н

B

backpack рюкза́к ВВ
bad *(adv.)* пло́хо
    not bad непло́хо, ничего́
bad *(adj.)* плохо́й
    not bad непло́хой
bag су́мка
    plastic bag паке́т
Baikal Байка́л (lake in Russia)
Baku Баку́ (capital of Azerbaijan)
ballerina балери́на
ballet бале́т (на)
Baltimore Балтимо́р
banana бана́н
bank банк
bar бар
bathroom ва́нная *(noun)*;
    half bath туале́т
beautiful: it is beautiful краси́во
beautiful *(adj.)* краси́вый
because потому́ что
bedroom спа́льня
beef Stroganoff бефстро́ганов
beer пи́во
begin[1] начина́ть *начина́й-* /нача́ть *на́чн-* что /
    + *inf.*
begin[2] начина́ться *начина́й-ся*
Belarus Белору́сь
Berlin Берли́н
better лу́чше
bicycle велосипе́д
big большо́й
biologist био́лог
biology биоло́гия
Bishkek Бишке́к (capital of Kyrgyzstan)
black чёрный
blackboard доска́ СС
blue grass (music) блю грас
book кни́га, кни́жка
boring *(adj.)* неинтере́сный, ску́чный
borsch (beet soup) борщ ВВ
Boston Бо́стон
bottle буты́лка
boy ма́льчик
bracelet брасле́т
bread хлеб
break переры́в
breakfast за́втрак
    have breakfast за́втракать *за́втракай-* /
    поза́втракать
breed поро́да
bridge мост

brother брат *(nom. pl.* бра́тья)
brown кори́чневый
building зда́ние, ко́рпус АВ *(nom. pl.* корпуса́),
    дом *(nom. pl.* дома́)
burger котле́та
bus авто́бус
business би́знес
    business trip командиро́вка
businessperson бизнесме́н
busy за́нят, -а́, -о, -ы
but а, но
butter ма́сло
buy покупа́ть *покупа́й-* / купи́ть *купи́-* что,
    кому́
bye пока́

C

cabbage soup щи *(pl.* only)
cafeteria кафете́рий, столо́вая
café кафе́ *(indecl.)*
cake торт
calculator калькуля́тор
calendar календа́рь ВВ
call (on the phone) звони́ть *звони́-* / позвони́ть
    кому́
called: be called называ́ться *называ́й-ся (impf.)*
call in вызыва́ть *вызыва́й-* / вы́звать *вы́з/ва-*
    кого́
camera фотоаппара́т
candy конфе́та
cap ке́пка
    baseball cap бейсбо́льная ке́пка
capital столи́ца
capitalist капитали́ст
Capitol Капито́лий
car маши́на
cartoon мультфи́льм (му́льтик)
cash register ка́сса
cashier касси́р
Caspian Sea Каспи́йское мо́ре
cassette кассе́та
cassette player пле́йер (DVD/MP3/CD)
cat ко́шка *(female)*, кот ВВ *(male)*
Caucasus Кавка́з (на) (mountainous area to the
    south of Russia)
caviar икра́
cello виолонче́ль
center центр
century век
chair стул *(pl.* сту́лья)
champagne шампа́нское

cheap: it is cheap дёшево
cheerful весёлый
    not cheerful невесёлый
cheese сыр AB
chemist хи́мик
chemistry хи́мия
Chicago Чика́го
chicken ку́рица
child ребёнок (*sg.; pl.* де́ти)
Chinese (*adj.*) кита́йский
chocolate шокола́д
chrysanthemum хризанте́ма
church це́рковь (*f.*)
circus цирк
city го́род AB (*nom. pl.* города́)
clarinet кларне́т
class заня́тие (на)
    class notes конспе́кт
classical класси́ческий
    classical music кла́ссика
classics (literature) кла́ссика
classroom аудито́рия
clinic кли́ника
clock часы́ (*pl.* only)
close закрыва́ть *закрыва́й-* / закры́ть *закро́й-* что
closet шкаф AB
clothing оде́жда
club клуб
Coca-Cola ко́ка-ко́ла
coffee ко́фе (*m., indecl.*)
cold: it is cold хо́лодно
cold холо́дный
colleague колле́га (*m. & f.*)
college колле́дж, университе́т
College Park Ко́лледж Парк
color цвет AB (*nom. pl.* цвета́)
comedy коме́дия
comics ко́миксы (*pl.*)
compact disk диск
company компа́ния, фи́рма
complex ко́мплекс
component компоне́нт
composer компози́тор
computer компью́тер
    computer diskette дискета
concert конце́рт (на)
contact конта́кт
contemporary совреме́нный
contrary: on the contrary наоборо́т
cook гото́вить *гото́ви-* / пригото́вить что кому́
country страна́ BA

country (music) ка́нтри
course курс
cousin двою́родная сестра́ (female)
    двою́родный брат (male)
crepe блин BB
Crimea Крым (peninsula on the Black Sea)
cucumber огуре́ц BB
cuisine ку́хня
culture культу́ра
cup ча́шка

D

dacha (cottage) да́ча (на)
dad па́па
dance (*v.*) танцева́ть *танцева́-* (*impf.*)
dance club дискоте́ка (на)
date число́ BA
daughter до́чка
day день BB
    in the afternoon днём
    good afternoon до́брый день
dean дека́н
December дека́брь BB
definitely обяза́тельно
delicious: it is delicious вку́сно
delicious (*adj.*) вку́сный
    not tasty невку́сный
department ка́федра, факульте́т (на)
    business dept. факульте́т би́знеса
    chemistry dept. хими́ческий факульте́т
    dept. of political science факульте́т полити́ческой нау́ки
    dept. of Russian language факульте́т ру́сского языка́
    economics dept. экономи́ческий факульте́т
    engineering dept. инжене́рный факульте́т
    film dept. киноведческий факульте́т
    history dept. истори́ческий факульте́т
    mathematics dept. математи́ческий факульте́т
    philology dept. филологи́ческий факульте́т
    physics dept. физи́ческий факульте́т
    theater dept. актёрский факульте́т
dessert десе́рт
Detroit Детро́йт
dictionary слова́рь BB
different друго́й
difficult: it is difficult непро́сто, тру́дно
difficult (*adj.*) тру́дный
Dinamo Дина́мо (here: stadium in Moscow)
dining room столо́вая (*noun*)

dinner у́жин
    have dinner у́жинать *у́жинай-* / поу́жинать
director дире́ктор AB (*nom. pl.* директора́)
dish блю́до
DJ диджéй
do дéлать *дéлай-* / сдéлать что
doctor врач BB, до́ктор AB (*pl.* доктора́)
dog соба́ка, пёс (male) BB
dormitory общежи́тие
downtown центр
drama дра́ма
draw рисова́ть *рисова́-* (*impf.*)
drawing рисова́ние
dream мечта́ть *мечта́й-* (*impf.*)
    о чём – о ком
dress пла́тье
drink (*noun*) напи́ток
drink (*v.*) пить / вы́пить что
driver шофёр
drum бараба́н
dumplings пельмéни (*pl.*)
Dushanbe Душанбé (capital of Tajikistan)

E

ear у́хо (*pl.* у́ши)
east восто́к (на)
eat есть / съесть (*irreg.*)
eclair эклéр
ecological экологи́ческий
economics эконо́мика
economist экономи́ст
eight во́семь
eighteen восемна́дцать
eighth восьмо́й
elephant слон BB
elevator лифт
eleven оди́ннадцать
emperor импера́тор
energetic энерги́чный
    not energetic неэнерги́чный
engineer инженéр
England А́нглия
English (*adj.*) англи́йский
    in English по-англи́йски
English (*person*) англича́нин (male)
    англича́нка (female)
entrance подъéзд
envelope конвéрт
episode эпизо́д
equipment аппарату́ра
essay сочинéние

Europe Евро́па
evening вéчер AB (*pl.* вечера́)
    in the evening вéчером
    good evening до́брый вéчер
every ка́ждый
everything всё
exam экза́мен
    pass/fail exam зачёт
excellent: it is excellent отли́чно
excellent (*adj.*) отли́чный
excuse (me) извини́(те)
exercise упражнéние
exhibit вы́ставка (на)
expensive: it is expensive до́рого
expensive (*adj.*) дорого́й

F

factory заво́д (на)
fall: in the fall о́сенью
family семья́ BA
fast (*adv.*) бы́стро
father отéц BB
favorite люби́мый
fax факс
February февра́ль BB
fifteen пятна́дцать
fifth пя́тый
film фильм, кино́ (*indecl.*)
    the study of film киновéдение
    film expert киновéд
finish зака́нчивать *зака́нчивай-* / зако́нчить
    зако́нчи- что
first пéрвый
fish ры́ба
five пять
floor эта́ж BB
flowers цветы́ (*pl.*)
flute флéйта
food еда́
    canned food консéрвы
fool дура́к BB
football америка́нский футбо́л
for[1] на (+ *acc.*) (на за́втрак)
for[2] для (+ *gen.*)
foreign зарубéжный
fork ви́лка
four четы́ре
fourteen четы́рнадцать
fourth четвёртый
France Фра́нция
free свобо́ден (*m.*), свобо́дна (*f.*), свобо́дно
    (*neut.*), свобо́дны (*pl.*)

French (*adj.*) францу́зский
   in French по-францу́зски
Frenchman францу́з
Frenchwoman францу́женка
fresh све́жий
Friday пя́тница
fried жа́реный
friend друг (male; *nom. pl.* друзья́), подру́га (female)
friendship дру́жба
fruit (*noun*) фрукт
fruit (*adj.*) фрукто́вый
funny смешно́й
   not funny несмешно́й
future (*noun*) бу́дущее
future (*adj.*) бу́дущий

G

garage гара́ж BB
geography геогра́фия
geologist гео́лог
geometry геоме́трия
Georgetown Джорджта́ун
Georgia Гру́зия
German (*person*) не́мец (male), не́мка (female)
German (*adj.*) неме́цкий
   in German по-неме́цки
Germany Герма́ния
gift пода́рок
girl де́вушка
give дава́ть *дава́й-* / дать (*irreg.*) что, кому́
   Please give (me)… Да́йте, пожа́луйста…
glad рад, -а, -о, - ы
goal цель
good: it is good хорошо́
good (*adj.*) хоро́ший
   Good luck! ни пу́ха ни пера́
goodbye до свида́ния
gorilla гори́лла
grade[1] класс (1st, 2nd, 3rd)
grade[2] отме́тка (**A** – пятёрка, **B** – четвёрка, **C** – тро́йка, **F** – дво́йка)
   grade book зачётная кни́жка
graduate зака́нчивать *зака́нчивай-* / зако́нчить *зако́нчи-* что
grammar грамма́тика
grandfather де́душка (*m.*)
grandmother ба́бушка
great здо́рово
green зелёный
grey се́рый

groceries проду́кты (*pl.*)
group гру́ппа
guest гость AC
guitar гита́ра
guitarist гитари́ст
gymnasium спорти́вный зал

H

hamburger га́мбургер
happy сча́стлив (*m.*), сча́стлива (*f.*), сча́стливо (*neut.*), сча́стливы (*pl.*)
have есть (у меня́ есть)
he он
head голова́ CC
hear слы́шать *слы́ша-* (*impf.*)
hello здра́вствуй(те), алло́ (on the telephone)
help помога́ть *помога́й-* / помо́чь (*irreg.*) кому́
her(s) её
here здесь, тут
here (*demonstrative*) вот
hero геро́й
hi приве́т
his его́
historian исто́рик
history исто́рия
Hollywood Голливу́д
hooligan хулига́н (male), хулига́нка (female)
hospital больни́ца
host хозя́ин (male; *pl.* хозя́ева), хозя́йка (female)
hotel гости́ница
hour час AB
house дом AB (*nom. pl.* дома́)
   at home до́ма
housewife домохозя́йка
how как, како́й
   how many, how much ско́лько
   How are things going? Как дела́?
   How are you? Как живёшь?
   How do you say that in English? Как э́то по-англи́йски?
   How come? Как же так?
   How interesting! Как интере́сно!
   How lovely! Кака́я красота́!
hungry голо́дный
hurry спеши́ть *спеши́-* (*impf.*)
husband муж AB (*nom. pl.* мужья́)

I

I я
ice cream моро́женое

imagine представля́ть *представля́й-* /
  предста́вить *предста́ви-* что
immediately сра́зу
important ва́жный
in[1] в, на (+ *prep.*)
in[2] по (+ *dat.*) (заня́тие по исто́рии)
Indian (*adj.*) инди́йский
institute институ́т
instructor преподава́тель (male),
  преподава́тельница (female)
instrument инструме́нт
intelligent у́мный
interesting: interesting интере́сно
interesting (*adj.*) интере́сный
international междунаро́дный
it он (*m.*), она́ (*f.*), оно́ (*neut.*)
Italian (*adj.*) италья́нский
Izmailovo (region in Moscow) Изма́йлово

J

jacket ку́ртка
January янва́рь
Japan Япо́ния
Japanese (*person*) япо́нец (male),
  япо́нка (female)
Japanese (*adj.*) япо́нский
  in Japanese по-япо́нски
jazz джаз
jealous: be jealous ревнова́ть *ревнова́-* (*impf.*)
jeans джи́нсы (*pl.* only)
journalist журнали́ст (male), журнали́стка
  (female)
juice сок
July ию́ль
June ию́нь
junk ерунда́

K

Kamchatka Камча́тка (peninsula in the far east
  of Russia)
Kazakhstan Казахста́н
key ключ BB
Kiev Ки́ев (capital of Ukraine)
kind до́брый
Kishinev/Chisinau Кишинёв (capital of
  Moldova)
kiss целова́ть *целова́-* (*impf.*)
kitchen ку́хня (на)
knife нож BB
know знать *знай-* (*impf.*) кого́ – что
  Do you happen to know…? Вы не зна́ете …?
    (Ты не зна́ешь…?)

I don't know for sure. Я то́чно не зна́ю.
Korean (*adj.*) коре́йский
Kostroma Кострома́ (city in Russia)
Kremlin Кремль
Kyrgyzstan Киргизста́н

L

laboratory лаборато́рия
lamp ла́мпа
landlord хозя́ин (male; *pl.* хозя́ева), хозя́йка
  (female)
language язы́к BB
late: be late опа́здывать *опа́здывай-* / опозда́ть
  (*irreg.*)
laugh смея́ться *смея́-ся* (*impf.*)
lawyer юри́ст
lecture ле́кция (на)
lemon лимо́н
lemonade лимона́д (carbonated)
letter письмо́ BA
lettuce сала́т
library библиоте́ка
lie, be in a lying position лежа́ть *лежа́-* (*impf.*)
life жизнь (*f.*)
light blue голубо́й
like нра́виться *нра́ви-ся* / понра́виться кому́
limousine лимузи́н
listen слу́шать *слу́шай-* (*impf.*)
literature литерату́ра
little ма́ло
little: a little немно́го
live жить *жи̌в-* (*impf.*)
Liverpool Ливерпу́ль
living room гости́ная (*noun*)
London Ло́ндон
long дли́нный
long: for a long time давно́, до́лго
look at смотре́ть *смотре̌-* / посмотре́ть что
Los Angeles Лос-А́нджелес
love люби́ть *люби̌-* (*impf.*) кого́ – что / *inf.*
luggage бага́ж (*sg.* only)
lunch обе́д
  have lunch обе́дать *обе́дай-* / пообе́дать

M

Madison Мэ́дисон
Madrid Мадри́д
magazine журна́л
man мужчи́на (*m.*)
manager ме́неджер

Manchester Манче́стер
map ка́рта
March март
Marseilles Марсе́ль
mathematician матема́тик
mathematics матема́тика
May май
May I...? Мо́жно... ?
mayonnaise майоне́з
McDonald's Макдо́налдс
mean: (it) means зна́чит
meat мя́со
medicine лека́рство
meeting встре́ча (на), собра́ние (на)
menu меню́ (*indecl., neut.*)
metro метро́ (*indecl.*)
Mexican мексика́нский (*adj.*)
milk молоко́
Minsk Минск (capital of Belarus)
mirror зе́ркало
miss (a class, etc.) пропуска́ть
　　пропуска́й- / пропусти́ть пропусти́- что
mistake оши́бка
modern совреме́нный
Moldova Молда́вия
mom ма́ма, маму́ля (*affectionate*)
Monday понеде́льник
money де́ньги (*pl.* only)
monitor screen монито́р
month ме́сяц
morning у́тро
　　in the morning у́тром
　　good morning до́брое у́тро
Moscow Москва́
most са́мый
movie theater кинотеа́тр
much (a lot) мно́го
museum музе́й
music (*noun*) му́зыка
music (*adj.*) музыка́льный
my, mine мой, моя́, моё, мои́
　　in my opinion по-мо́ему

N

name и́мя (*neut.; gen. sg.* и́мени)
　　My name is... Меня́ зову́т...
　　What's your name? Как вас зову́т?
Napoleon (pastry) наполео́н
nature приро́да
necessary ну́жно
neighbor сосе́д (*pl.* сосе́ди), сосе́дка (female)
Neva Нева́ (на) (St. Petersburg river)

new но́вый
New York Нью-Йо́рк
news но́вость AC (*f.*)
newspaper газе́та
nice: it is nice симпати́чно
nice, nice-looking (*adj.*) симпати́чный
nine де́вять
nineteen девятна́дцать
ninth девя́тый
no нет
　　no way не мо́жет быть
nonsense ерунда́
north се́вер (на)
nose нос AB
not не (*unstressed*)
note запи́ска
novel рома́н
　　detective/mystery novel детекти́в
November ноя́брь BB
Novgorod Но́вгород (city in Russia)
Novosibirsk Новосиби́рск (city in Russia)
now сейча́с, тепе́рь
number но́мер AB (*nom. pl.* номера́)

O

O.K. норма́льно
October октя́брь
Odessa Оде́сса (city in Ukraine)
of course коне́чно
office кабине́т, о́фис
　　branch office филиа́л
often ча́сто
oh ах, ой
old ста́рый
omelet омле́т
on[1] на (+ *prep.*) (location)
on[2] в (+ *acc.*) (with days of the week)
one оди́н
one (when counting) раз
opera о́пера (на)
or и́ли
orange (*noun*) апельси́н
orange[1] (*adj.*) апельси́новый (fruit)
orange[2] (*adj.*) ора́нжевый (color)
orchestra seating парте́р
order зака́зывать зака́зывай- / заказа́ть заказа́-
　　что
organize организова́ть организова́- (*impf. and perf.*) что
original оригина́льный BB
other друго́й
otherwise ина́че

ouch ой
our(s) наш, на́ша, на́ше, на́ши
owner хозя́ин (male; *pl.* хозя́ева),
    хозя́йка (female)

P

pancake блин BB
pants брю́ки (pl. only)
paper[1] рабо́та
    term paper курсова́я рабо́та
paper[2] бума́га
parents роди́тели (*pl.*)
Paris Пари́ж
park парк
pass (an exam) сдать (*irreg.; perf.*)
passport па́спорт AB (-á)
pasta макаро́ны (*pl.*)
patronymic о́тчество
Pavlovsk Па́вловск (city in Russia)
paw ла́па
pen ру́чка
pencil каранда́ш BB
penguin пингви́н
performance спекта́кль
person челове́к (*sg.; pl.* лю́ди)
Philadelphia Филаде́льфия
philharmonics филармо́ния
photo album фотоальбо́м
photocopier ксе́рокс
photo фотогра́фия
photographer фото́граф
physical education физкульту́ра
physicist фи́зик
physics фи́зика
piano (grand) роя́ль
picture карти́на
pilaf плов
pizza пи́цца
plan план
plate таре́лка
play (a musical instrument) игра́ть *игра́й-* (*impf.*)
    на чём
please пожа́луйста
poems BB стихи́ (*pl.*)
poet поэ́т
police мили́ция
police officer милиционе́р
police station мили́ция
politics поли́тика
pop music поп-му́зыка
popular популя́рный

post office по́чта (на)
postcard откры́тка
poster плака́т
potato(es) карто́шка
prepare (for) гото́виться *гото́ви-ся* (*impf.*)
present пода́рок
presentation докла́д
previously ра́ньше
printer при́нтер
probably наве́рное
problem пробле́ма
professional профессиона́льный
professor профе́ссор AB (*nom. pl.* профессора́)
program програ́мма
programmer программи́ст
promise обеща́ть *обеща́й-* (*impf.*)
Pskov Псков (city in Russia)
psychologist психо́лог
Pushkin Пу́шкин (city in Russia)

R

radio ра́дио (*indecl.*)
raincoat плащ BB
rap music рэп
read чита́ть *чита́й-* / прочита́ть что
really пра́вда
receive получа́ть *получа́й-* / получи́ть *получи́-*
    что
recommend рекомендова́ть *рекомендова́-*
    (*impf.*)
red кра́сный
refrigerator холоди́льник
region райо́н
rehearsal репети́ция (на)
relaxation о́тдых
remember по́мнить *по́мни-* (*impf.*)
rent сдава́ть *сдава́й-* / сдать[1] (*irreg.*) что
rest отдыха́ть *отдыха́й-* (*impf.*)
restaurant рестора́н
restroom туале́т
return возвраща́ться *возвраща́й-ся* (*impf.*)
rock (music) рок
    rock group рок гру́ппа
Rome Рим
room ко́мната
Rostov Росто́в (city in Russia)
row ряд BB
ruby руби́новый (adj.)
rug ковёр BB
Russia Росси́я

Russian (*person*) ру́сская (female), ру́сский (male)
Russian (*adj.*) ру́сский
    in Russian по-ру́сски

S

Sakhalin Сахали́н (island in the far east of Russia)
salad сала́т
salami колбаса́ BA
salesperson продаве́ц BB (male), продавщи́ца (female)
salt соль
sandwich бутербро́д
Saratov Сара́тов (city in Russia)
Saturday суббо́та
sausage колбаса́ BA
saxophone саксофо́н
say говори́ть *говори́-* / сказа́ть *сказа̌-* что, кому́, о чём
scanner ска́нер
scarf шарф
school шко́ла
science fiction (нау́чная) фанта́стика (*sg.* only)
script writer сценари́ст
sea мо́ре
seat ме́сто AB
Seattle Сиэ́тл
second второ́й
see ви́деть *ви́де-* / уви́деть кого́ - что
seldom ре́дко
semester семе́стр
seminar семина́р (на)
September сентя́брь BB
serious серьёзный
    not serious несерьёзный
seven семь
seventeen семна́дцать
seventh седьмо́й
shame: it's a shame о́чень жаль
she она́
shelf по́лка
shelter прию́т
Sheremetyevo Шереме́тьево (airport in Moscow)
shirt (flannel, dress) руба́шка
shoes ту́фли (*pl.*)
short коро́ткий
shorts шо́рты (*pl.* only)
show (*noun*) спекта́кль
show (*v.*) пока́зывать *пока́зывай-* / показа́ть *показа̌-* что, кому́

silent: be silent молча́ть *молча̌-* (*impf.*)
simply про́сто
singer певе́ц BB (male), певи́ца (female)
sink ра́ковина
sister сестра́ BB (*gen. pl.* сестёр)
sit сиде́ть *сиде́-* (*impf.*)
sit (down) сади́ться *сади́-ся* (*impf.*)
six шесть
sixteen шестна́дцать
sixth шесто́й
skip (a class, etc.) прогуля́ть *прогуля́й-* (*perf.*)
skirt ю́бка
small ма́ленький, небольшо́й
snack bar буфе́т
sneakers кроссо́вки (*pl.*)
so так
soccer футбо́л
society о́бщество
sofa дива́н
Sokol Со́кол (subway station in Moscow)
soloist соли́ст
solve реша́ть *реша́й-* / реши́ть *реши́-* что
sometimes иногда́
son сын AB (*pl.* сыновья́)
sorry извини́(те)
soup суп
south юг (на)
souvenir сувени́р
spaghetti спаге́тти
Spain Испа́ния
Spaniard испа́нец (male), испа́нка (female)
Spanish испа́нский
    in Spanish по-испа́нски
speak говори́ть *говори́-* о ком – о чём (*impf.*)
special специа́льный
spoon ло́жка
sport спорт
sport(s) спорти́вный (*adj.*)
spring: in the spring весно́й
St. Petersburg Санкт-Петербу́рг
stadium стадио́н (на)
stand, be in a standing position стоя́ть *стоя̌-* (*impf.*)
state (*adj.*) госуда́рственный
state (*noun*) штат
statistics стати́стика
steak бифште́кс
stereo магнитофо́н, сте́рео
still ещё
stipend стипе́ндия
store магази́н
story[1] исто́рия

story[2] расска́з
stove плита́ BA
strange стра́нный
street у́лица
student[1] студе́нт (male), студе́нтка (female)
(university)
student[2] шко́льник (male), шко́льница (female)
(grade school)
student (*adj.*) студе́нческий
student ID студе́нческий биле́т
studio сту́дия
study учи́ться *учи́-ся* (impf.) (at a school,
university)
style мо́да
in style в мо́де
out of style не в мо́де
stylish мо́дный
subject предме́т
subway метро́ (*indecl.*)
success успе́х
suddenly вдруг
sugar са́хар
suit костю́м
suitcase чемода́н
summer: in the summer ле́том
Sunday воскресе́нье
surname фами́лия
surprise сюрпри́з
sushi су́ши (*indecl.*)
sweater сви́тер AB (*nom. pl.* свитера́)
sweatshirt футбо́лка
swimming pool бассе́йн
swindler жу́лик

T

t-shirt ма́йка
table стол
Tajikistan Таджикиста́н
take (an exam) сдава́ть *сдава́й-* что (*impf.*)
take a picture (of) фотографи́ровать
фотографи́рова- (*impf.*) кого́ - что
talented спосо́бный
tall высо́кий
Tashkent Ташке́нт (capital of Uzbekistan)
task зада́ние
taxi такси́ (*indecl., neut.*)
Tbilisi Тбили́си (capital of Georgia)
tea чай AB
teacher (in grade school) учи́тель AB (male;
nom. pl. учителя́), учи́тельница (female)
teakettle ча́йник

telephone (*noun*) телефо́н
on the telephone по телефо́ну
telephone (*adj.*) телефо́нный
telephone call звоно́к BB
television set телеви́зор
tell говори́ть *говори́-* / сказа́ть *сказа̌-* что, кому́,
о чём
Please tell (me) … Скажи́(те), пожа́луйста …
ten де́сять
tenth деся́тый
terrible: it is terrible ужа́сно
terrible (*adj.*) ужа́сный
territory террито́рия
test контро́льная рабо́та
text текст
textbook уче́бник
Thai тайла́ндский
thank you спаси́бо
Thank you very much. Большо́е
спаси́бо.
that (*pron.*) тот, та, то
that (in subordinate clause) что
That's it! Всё!
theater теа́тр
theater critic театрове́д
theater studies театрове́дение
their(s) их
then тогда́
these э́ти
these (are) э́то
there там
(over) there вон
they они́
things ве́щи (*pl.*)
think ду́мать *ду́май-* / поду́мать о ком – о чём
third тре́тий
thirteen трина́дцать
this э́тот, э́та, э́то
this (is) э́то
those те
three три
Thursday четве́рг BB
ticket биле́т
tiger тигр
time вре́мя AB (neut.; gen. sg. вре́мени)
to за (+ *acc.*) (when making a toast)
toast тост
toaster то́стер
today сего́дня
together вме́сте
token жето́н

Tokyo Тóкио
tomato помидóр
tomorrow зáвтра
    until tomorrow до зáвтра
topic тéма
Toronto Торóнто
toy игрýшка
translate переводúть *переводй-* / перевестú
    перевёд- что
translation перевóд
transportation трáнспорт
trash мýсор
trip поéздка
trolley bus троллéйбус
trombone тромбóн
true прáвда
Tuesday втóрник
tulip тюльпáн
Turkmenistan Туркменистáн
TV series телесериáл
TV show передáча
twelve двенáдцать
twenty двáдцать
two два

U

ugly некрасúвый
Ukraine Украúна
uncle дя́дя (*m.*)
understand понимáть *понимáй-* / поня́ть *по̂йм-*
    когó - что
unfashionable немóдный
university (*noun*) университéт
university (*adj.*) университéтский
unpleasant: it is unpleasant неприя́тно
Ural mountains Урáл (на)
USA США
used to рáньше
usually обы́чно
Uzbekistan Узбекистáн

V

vacation (from school) канúкулы (*pl. only*)
vacation (*v.*) отдыхáть *отдыхáй-* (*impf.*)
VCR видеомагнитофóн (*colloq.* вúдик)
vegetable óвощ AC
very óчень
    Very nice (to meet you). Óчень прия́тно.
veterinarian ветеринáр
veterinary ветеринáрный

video вúдео
video camera видеокáмера
viewing room кинозáл
violin скрúпка
visa вúза
vitamin витамúн
Vladimir Владúмир
vodka вóдка
Volga river Вóлга (на)
Volgograd Волгогрáд (city in Russia)
Voronezh Ворóнеж (city in Russia)

W

waiter официáнт
waitress официáнтка
walk (go for a walk) гуля́ть *гуля́й-* (*impf.*)
want хотéть (*impf.; irreg.*) + *inf.* / что
was был, былá, бы́ло
Washington Вашингтóн
watch (*noun*) часы́ (*pl.*)
watch (*v.*) смотрéть *смотре̂-* / посмотрéть что
water водá CA
    mineral water минерáльная водá
we мы
weather погóда
Wednesday средá CC
week недéля
well хорошó
were бы́ли
west зáпад (на)
what что
    what kind of какóй
    So what? Ну и что?
    What are you talking about? Что ты! Что
      вы!
    What else? Что ещё?
    What happened? Что случúлось?
    what kind of что за (+ *acc.*)
    What's that? Что э́то такóе?
when когдá
where где
which какóй
white бéлый
who кто
whole цéлый
whose чей, чья, чьё, чьи
why почемý
wife женá BA
window окнó BA
wine винó BA

winter: in the winter зимо́й
woman же́нщина
   young woman де́вушка
woman's top ко́фта
wonderful (*adv.*) прекра́сно
wonderful (*adj.*) прекра́сный
word сло́во АВ
work (*noun*) рабо́та (на)
work (*v.*) рабо́тать *рабо́тай-* (*impf.*)
world мир
worry волнова́ться *волнова́-ся* (*impf.*)
Wow! Вот э́то да!
write писа́ть *писǎ-* / написа́ть что
writer писа́тель (male), писа́тельница (female)

Y

year (in college) курс (на)
yellow жёлтый

Yerevan Ерева́н (capital of Armenia)
yes да
yesterday вчера́
yet ещё
   not yet пока́ нет
you ты (*sg. & familiar*); вы (*pl. & formal*)
   Let's use ты. Дава́йте на «ты».
young молодо́й
your(s) твой, твоя́, твоё, твои́ (*sg. and familiar*);
   ваш, ва́ша, ва́ше, ва́ши (*pl. & formal*)

Z

zero ноль ВВ
zoo зоопа́рк

Grammatical Index